The World
According to Breslin

The World
According to Breslin

Jimmy Breslin————

ANNOTATED BY Michael J. O'Neill
AND William Brink

Ticknor & Fields NEW YORK 1984

Library of Congress Cataloging in Publication Data

Breslin, Jimmy.
 The world according to Breslin.

 Columns originally appeared in the New York Daily News, 1976–1983.
 I. O'Neill, Michael J., 1922–   . II. Brink, William.
III. Title.
PS3552.R39W6   1984   814′.54   84-8683
ISBN 0-89919-310-2

Printed in the United States of America

S   10   9   8   7   6   5   4   3   2   1

For Kate Cahill

Contents

Foreword

Jimmy Breslin has created many marvelous characters, from Marvin the Torch and Fat Thomas to Un Occhio, mythical boss of all bosses, capo di tutti capi, but his greatest invention is his own public persona, a character he has developed as skillfully as Potemkin constructed his stone village, a cigar-chomping, hard-drinking character designed to make everyone think he's only an ordinary guy, not very smart or sophisticated, just stumbling through life like a plumber from Queens, living in bars, burdened by racetrack losses and unpaid bills, companion of the poor and near-poor, disdainful of great men and great thoughts, of big words and complex ideas.

It would destroy him if his readers were to discover he is as smart as any pontificating pundit in Washington, one of the shrewdest newspapermen around (a jump ahead of his editors so often that it is embarrassing), a sharp observer of human history who can capture crime's threat to New York in a single sentence, "Dies the victim, dies the city," who can quote Camus or Teilhard de Chardin without losing his stool at Kennedy's, who in a short simple story can tell us more about ourselves than tons of traditional reporting, and who can do this with grace, simplicity, humor, and wisdom.

In a column about a young Puerto Rican who was caught stealing a car, Breslin explained New York's crumbling neighborhoods better than a dozen official reports: "At age eleven, he is part of the permanent underclass of 500,000 males in this city between the ages of ten and twenty-five, all black or Hispanic, the majority of whom never will be able to get a job ... At least some of them commit crimes and create the fear that makes the permanent underclass the most powerful cause of change ever to appear on the streets of a major city."

At the same time, Breslin finds hope in the ageless struggle of New York's immigrants for a better place in the American sun. Noting that Chinese students at the Bronx High School of Science were suddenly getting more prizes than middle-class Jews who had dominated the competition, he wrote: "It is obvious that the swinging elbow that runs the life of New York is still at work." Who has ever said it better?

Jimmy Breslin is a short, stocky, rumpled man with scattered hair and thick eyebrows, who could pass in the dark for Jackie Gleason's Ralph Kramden, who in fact still looks like the varsity guard he played at John Adams High School, where, in his zeal for study, he took more than the customary four years to graduate. He lived all but a few days of his life in a middle-class section of Queens, speaking its nondescript dialect in lean, grunted sentences to avoid any suspicion he might harbor long thoughts. He forgot to finish college. He was too busy running copy and writing stories for the old Long Island *Press,* going on later to such other newspapers as the Boston *Globe,* New York *Journal-American,* and the *Herald Tribune.*

He wandered away from newspapers from time to time, to write for the *Saturday Evening Post, Life,* and *New York* magazine, or to produce novels. But he was hooked on news, so he always returned, landing finally at the New York *Daily News,* where he became an instant hit with millions of readers and a constant goad for his editors. He not only stalked breaking stories like a terrorist, looking for his own columns, he also worried constantly about how the rest of the paper could do a better job against the opposition. Around seven every morning, he woke up the city desk with a laconic "So, what's doin'?" fishing for column ideas but also zeroing in, for the editor's benefit, on the one news development that would most interest readers in the next day's paper. And then nearly every midnight, after he had seen the first edition with a bad headline or a poorly played story, he woke an editor at home and shouted, "This is awful! You gotta do somethin'!"

He is Irish to his bone marrow, just as combative as any member of his race, producing an annual list of "People I'm Not Talking To," and conducting numerous feuds with prominent citizens like Bess Myerson and Governor Hugh Carey, whom he dispatched to political oblivion with a series of savage columns about a playboy politician he labeled "Society Carey." He operates on the sound principle that personal quarrels sell numerous newspapers and that, in any case, "the better way is to go through life with the view that no slight, no difference is so small that it cannot be converted into a feud." Including feuds with the editorial page of his employer, the *Daily News.*

With Breslin, it is a matter of professional honor to disagree with the paper's editorials on every possible issue, siding more or less with the IRA on Northern Ireland, for example, and championing the residents of Howard Beach near Kennedy Airport when they fought to prevent landings by the ear-shattering Concorde.

Once, in the Gold Coin bar — we were boycotting Costello's at the time — O'Neill was on his third vodka and tonic and screamed at Breslin, "Why do you have to attack every editorial we ever write? Can't you agree with us just once?" He added, "For the sake of our publisher, if no one else" — not mentioning the angry complaints that kept raining down on him from the eighth-floor command post in the News Building. Well, said Breslin, this was quite out of the question, as it would ruin his reputation completely, and besides, it was in the best interest of both him and the editors to go their separate ways. In this manner, he explained, we were covering all sides of public issues so that the maximum number of readers would be pleased. By this time, O'Neill had had five vodkas while Breslin was still as sober as a church mouse, faking his drinking as usual, ordering spritzers that were so watered down the ice cubes froze them. Consequently, O'Neill suddenly found great logic in what The Great One said and both men agreed to disagree in public for the sake of their readers and tossed down another round for the road.

Breslin's rule about feuds does not apply, however, to ordinary New Yorkers: they are exempt. Like other Irish writers, he feels only compassion for the workingman, the poor, and the downtrodden, a genetic product of centuries of ancestral persecution, perhaps, but reinforced in his case by a childhood that reads like an act from O'Neill's *Long Day's Journey into Night*. His father was a penniless piano player, an alcoholic who ran away from the family when Breslin was only six, disappearing for more than forty years until he died a pauper's death in Miami. Breslin's mother, forced to go to work to support her young son and younger daughter, Deirdre, taught school for a while but later worked for more than thirty years in the city's welfare department. It was a hard life, with too little joy and too little time for the family, so "she used to drink too much," Breslin remembers, developing furious temper tantrums and terrorizing her children while she was suffering from "the tincture," as Brendan Behan, an authority on tinctures, used to put it.

Breslin said of her: "My mother also could use her temper for something useful. As she had been a substitute English teacher at

John Adams High School, she had been thoroughly exposed to that greatest of Queens County usage, *between you and I*. She seethed whenever she heard this. I grew up thinking that to say *between you and I* was an act of treason.

"She also had a hatred for unfairness that was almost as deep as her dislike for *between you and I*. Because of the unfairness creed, she felt most comfortable with the victims of it. Working as a supervisor at Department of Welfare centers, she was mostly with workers who were black, and she reveled in this because she knew that this bothered her own kind. People she worked with came to our house and we went to their houses, although my mother was much happier when they were at our house, because the visits had the added dimension of infuriating others.

"She accepted no compliments and hid anything good she ever did. One day in 1982, I was flying to Los Angeles, and at the trip's end, with people in the aisles to leave the plane, I saw this black woman in a mink coat look at me and begin to push toward me, but as she was too large she was unsuccessful. She tapped a slim white guy dressed in a blazer, who obviously was an assistant. He slid down the aisle to me and said that Graciella Rivera, the opera singer, wanted to talk to me if I had a moment.

"Out in the terminal, I went up to the singer. She said, 'I worked as a clerk in your mother's office. At the Harlem Welfare Center. She is responsible for my career. She encouraged me to keep on with my singing. She made sure that I took the time to study. You should be proud that you had such a mother.'

"Inside, I was saying to myself that I wished it always could have been like this. But then to keep up the front and the family name, I asked the singer, 'How is it going for you?' She said, 'Fine. I am on a concert tour now.' Of course, I then said, touching the mink coat, 'Don't I get something so I can decorate my mother's headstone?' She walked away laughing, and I walked with that hurt and desire to bring back everything and change it. I had never seen nor heard of Graciella Rivera until that day in the aisle in the plane.

"Why did this woman, my mother, thrive on tantrums when she had so much to give?"

As a result of these early experiences or possibly only because it is a common inheritance of the black Irish, Breslin's view of the world is streaked with an indefinable melancholy, mostly about all the people who never seem to get a break — a brooding sense of young lives rotting away amid the splendors of New York, blacks and Hispanics living as neighbors of the rich and powerful but strangers to them, symbols once of the hope Breslin felt when John Kennedy became president but symbols now of his declining faith in the will of the elite or the ability of government to solve the problems of poverty and injustice.

Often, Breslin's anguish over the human waste around him is converted into outrage, an emotion which never erupted more violently than it did during a rail strike in 1983, when commuters went spilling into the subways, complaining about having to mingle with the blue-collar masses they only read about, fearfully expecting every minute to be mugged.

No one can voice the voiceless rage of subway riders better than Breslin. And no reporter — certainly no editor — knows the city's neighborhoods as well as he does, because he is patrolling them all the time, not the way cops do now, in squad cars, but on foot, walking the streets not riding them, because he never learned how to drive, talking to the people, feeling their feelings, fearing their fears, fighting their fights.

For years, his wife Rosemary used to prowl the neighborhoods with him. She was always referred to as "the former Rosemary Dattolico" in Breslin's columns and she was a powerful force in his life, managing the six children, fixing the plumbing, keeping him dressed, and attempting with only minimal success to reduce the administrative chaos in his personal affairs. In this last respect, she was more effective than our editorial management team at the *News*, where Breslin's finances were so muddled he qualified for presidential designation as a national disaster.

In a little ritual symbolizing the problem, his personal handler at the paper, Anne Marie Caggiano, would appear regularly at our desks and slip a green voucher under our noses. We never looked up, never said a word, just signed our names like robots. Another $125 advance on expenses for Breslin. As routine as the next deadline for the bulldog edition. Anne Marie shuttled from one editor to another with her vouchers, to disguise the cumulative drain on the editorial budget, but we compared notes; we knew we were being conned. Still, we signed.

The auditors kept protesting that Breslin was a year behind on his expenses, that we shouldn't give him another nickel until he got his accounts in order. But that was a ridiculous idea; the World Bank

could solve Argentina's economic crisis easier than it could figure
out Breslin's expenses.

Coping with her national disaster, plus six children, was a burden
that Rosemary carried with careless ease and sharpened humor. But
it made her eager to flee the house whenever she could. "She liked
getting away from the kids," is the way Breslin recalls it. "So after
dinner, we'd get someone to take care of them and then we'd go out
to the Bronx or to Brooklyn on stories. To bars, police stations, and
the political clubs. They were fun in those days. When we'd go into
a neighborhood, you could hardly get the story you went for because everybody would start telling you all their troubles. With the
cops or the sewers or the water. You name it. You had to listen to
what was bothering them before you could ask any questions. Finally, late at night, we'd end up at the Copa. Rosemary loved it. It
was fun."

The greatest journalists of our time look at the world from the top
down. They mingle with the movers and shakers. They feel important because they are with powerful people who obviously know
more than anybody else. So they quote presidents and governors
and mayors and police commissioners about what is happening in
society, what is going on in the neighborhoods they don't live in
themselves or have time to visit, and they call this objective reporting. Breslin, on the other hand, looks at the world from the bottom
up, through the experiences of ordinary people who are in the news
or victims of the news or affected by the news. He sees what is happening where it is happening and out of the actions and emotions of
individuals, out of the smells, the sounds, and dialogue of the street,
he produces raw slices of reality which help readers see what they do
not see themselves and understand what they do not understand.
"You get a little picture that reflects the whole," he explains. "You
can get readers interested in the life of one guy, and he can reflect
the whole life around him. And it's a better picture than the politicians give you."

What Breslin does is called the "New Journalism," which he and
Tom Wolfe are credited with inventing in the 1960s when they were
writing for the old New York *Herald Tribune*. This departed from
the third-person-singular reporting of the time by employing the
techniques of the novelist to bring news events alive and kicking
into newspapers, with the writer telling his story in narrative form,

using vivid descriptions and great gobs of dialogue to provide immediacy and realism.

The idea that he and Wolfe started something new makes Breslin shake with laughter. Although he appreciates his own talent and is a celebrity quickly recognized on any New York street corner, he does not brandish his ego the way many less able journalists do. He still chases a story as fast as a cub reporter, and usually works harder. With editors he respects, he is surprisingly cooperative. So it was typical of him to reject any credit for a new journalism which he said must have been developed about the same time as the typewriter.

"I never thought about how to do a column," he said, recalling when he first started writing pieces based on news rather than sports. "It just came naturally, I guess. It had a point of view and it had to spin right out of the news. Everything of moment demands that it be done that day. Even when a few sentences don't work when you get to the deadline, there is an immediacy that makes the column fresh. Like you were covering the eighth race at Belmont. But no one was doing it when I started. That's why everyone thought it was new."

In the early days, he remembers covering the sentencing of the crime boss Tony Provenzano, and treating it "like it was a sports event." "Everybody was excited and they put it on the front page. But all I did was show you didn't have to kill the reader. The story could be entertaining. It was nothing new. Capote had written the book *In Cold Blood* but I was copying Westbrook Pegler. I was copying what he was doing in 1934."

He rattled off the names of John O'Hara, John McNulty, Paul Gallico, and Red Smith, and said they had all used similar techniques. But in the early 1960s, at the *Herald Tribune,* he and Wolfe were an instant success. "We were ahead of everybody in bringing back the past," he said. Hundreds of young writers followed their lead — a few brilliantly, most in only clumsy imitation — and the "New Journalism" movement was firmly established in the nation. It quickly produced a number of offspring, including "personal journalism" and "advocacy journalism." It also kicked off two decades of controversy because it violated the sanctity of such long-held beliefs that only the objectivity of a eunuch and the most impersonal kind of reporting can lead the public to the trough of truth.

Many of journalism's failures — coverage of Joe McCarthy, for example — testify to the tricks that objectivity can play with reality. And yet the clichés linger on in the trade and the prejudices against the New Journalism remain strong. So when we nominated Breslin for a 1982 Pulitzer, we knew it was a futile gesture; the Pulitzer juries convene every year in a spirit of solemn conformity, resolved to reward the conventional act rather than the individual exception. Breslin got the Meyer Berger award once and the Sigma Delta Chi award but not the Pulitzer, which would have been an affront to tradition. And every time there was any kind of ruckus in our profession, we would get calls from suspicious young journalists, without an ounce of Breslin's talent or class, demanding to know why we let him make up characters and commit all kinds of other crimes. Exasperated, we would say that in more than thirty years in the business we had never seen a better reporter, anyone quicker to spot a story and develop the right angle, a harder worker, or a better writer.

Sure, Breslin made up characters, great characters like Un Occhio, who was a spoof on a Sicilian don that was so true to life a lot of readers never caught on and the Arizona State Police wrote for more details so they could put out an APB. He once wrote a satire about the Equal Rights Amendment, making up a story about a lesbian conference at an Illinois college. Breslin aficionados immediately spotted the telltale clues to what he was doing, but others did not and a *New York Post* columnist chimed in with a serious commentary. Another time, someone questioned a powerfully realistic column he wrote about a man who had just learned that his cancer had been temporarily cured. What we knew at the paper was that Breslin was really writing about his own wife and his own relief over a brief remission of her disease. In fact, in all the years we worked with Breslin at the *News,* his reporting generally passed muster. Readers got violent about him. Reporters and editors were constantly sniping. The haughty editors of *The New Yorker,* always offended when city grime rubs off on their white gloves, accused him of "sensationalism" and "irresponsibility" in the famous Son of Sam mass murder case. But there have been few successful challenges to the substantive things he has covered. More important, his nonconformist reporting has brought his readers closer to the truths about their society than much of the conventional journalism which his critics so righteously espouse.

It is Breslin's genius to look into the lives of individuals and, like Dickens in another age, discover in their stories the personal problems, the tensions, the fears, the emotions, the shifting opinions that are the harbingers of social change and future crisis.

Although Breslin's sympathies have been with the blacks and Hispanics, in his view the true successors of the Irish and Italians as New York's immigrant poor, he has also been sensitive to the feelings of the city's white middle class. Before most reporters or editors caught on to what was happening, his columns revealed the emerging revolt of this middle class against the programs of the Great Society, something which produced the first receding wave of the civil rights movement and one of the most significant developments of the last decade.

Early in 1977, for example, when Andrew Young fired a charge of racism against Queens, Breslin instantly took the pulse of the neighborhoods, talking first to a man named Lester, who was taking his family to a beach halfway out on Long Island so they wouldn't have to go swimming in the city with blacks. "I could stay right here in Queens and go down to Rockaway Beach, but who wants that? . . ." Lester said. "By the middle of the afternoon you think you're in East Africa."

Breslin then interviewed a cousin of his who watched "The Rockford Files" on television instead of "Roots" and who complained, "A lot of people voted for this Carter because they thought he could keep these people under control, being he was from Georgia . . . Well, I'll tell that Carter something. Nobody in Queens ever let these people get away with things the way Carter does."

Breslin also has caught the fading self-identity and ambiguous impulses of the American Irish. In one column, he lamented that the Saint Patrick's Day Parade "is about all the Irish have left to indicate where they are from" because they had deserted their poetry and knew little about "death on the crumbling streets of Northern Ireland." At the time of Mayor Daley's death in Chicago, he wrote: "For as they prayed over the body of Richard J. Daley, the immigration of the Irish to this country officially ended . . . Dick Daley, the last boss, took the meaning with him into the ground."

No less than the Irish, the Italians of New York have been captured with brilliant fidelity in Breslin's typewriter. Even with Governor Cuomo's election, no ethnic group in the city considers itself less honored or less appreciated, more deprived of power, than the Italians. And Breslin said everything they felt in a column about an Italian FBI agent named Joseph Pistone who had gone undercover to help convict mobsters in the Bonanno crime family — who testified "for all the people who arise at seven in the morning to go to work for a living and bring to the life of this country the special warmth and gentle humor that goes with their vowels . . ."

The ability to express the innermost feelings of his neighbors, no matter how diverse, constantly surprises his readers, making them say, "Yeah, that's right; that's the way it is," and producing what Aristotle called "the joy of recognition." As a result, Breslin is the champion feature in the *Daily News.* Admired or hated, he regularly leads the reader surveys, topping even such powerhouse columnists as Ann Landers and, in the ultimate testimony to success in America, producing revenue for his employer by selling thousands of newspapers.

How all this is accomplished is a never-ending wonder even to the crisis-hardened editors who regularly handle his column. While we were at the *News* their ulcers would flare in unison every night that Breslin was writing, just after 5:00 P.M. when the last stories of the day were being rushed down to the composing room for the first edition. As usual, the first take of Breslin's copy still had not appeared. Stabs of pain and audible groans would spread rapidly through the editorial ranks, from the city desk to the news desk to the copy desk, finally reaching Brink, the managing editor, who was under heavy pressure to close the edition on time to please the circulation department and the publisher.

"Any sign of Breslin yet?" Brink would cry, as the old four-sided clock over the city desk clacked its way to 5:30 P.M., the final copy deadline. "None," was the invariable reply. For at that same moment, in a far-off corner of the seventh floor, the great man was still mugging his typewriter with his stubby fingers, painfully writing, rewriting, and polishing the first paragraphs of his column, engulfed by coffee-smeared notes and dozens of crumpled false starts, with an anxious copyperson hovering over him, waiting to rush the first take to the news desk. The rest of the staff didn't need this human delivery system because they wrote directly into the computers; Breslin did because he rejected computers as deportable aliens.

Finally, with most of the news desk crew already in the composing room, the first page would arrive with more potholes in it than a South Bronx street, full of changes, cross-outs, and revisions, but with the words somehow tracking. Other takes would come flying in with the breathless copyperson and, somehow, they would all get into the paper, usually the last copy on the edition, later even than last-minute sports results. On a few occasions, when Breslin was outrageously late, Brink simply choked off the flow and his column appeared in the first edition in a decapitated condition. This was always a terrible blow to a perfectionist like Breslin, making him inconsolable but, at the same time, inspiring speedier future performances.

To Breslin, every word, every sentence he writes is what marble was to Michelangelo, something to be sculpted with love and care. Like Yeats, he makes the reader think he writes his columns as easily as he spills drinks in a bar. Yet he fusses endlessly with his ideas. He chews them over with people he meets. He probes for the reactions of editors and accepts their suggestions faster than many less talented reporters, although he regards "somebody else's hand on my work as an attack on my person." He labors furiously to get just the right nuances of expression and the most effective story structure. He shapes the language with affection and is so fanatical about good grammar that he won't even plunge an adverb into the middle of a predicate. This is something he learned from the Sisters of Saint Joseph at the Saint Benedict Joseph Labre grammar school. "The nuns taught us two things," he said, "fear of sex and fear of 'you and I.' "

The end result of the enormous effort Breslin puts into his writing is a style that is very pure, a little like Hemingway's prose, marching along in a natural narrative cadence. Real people, their experiences, and their conversations do most of the work of communication with the reader. But Breslin adds his own special spices — irony, humor, and surprising insight, producing in the process some memorable expressions.

He observed that "gangsters, just like politicians, have yet to find anything that is too small to steal." Because suburban commuters take city services without paying for them, he called them "white welfare." Seeing some familiar-looking soup lines in Paris, he said "it showed that any evil in New York is a communicable disease." A senator stupid enough to vote against a woman justice for the Supreme Court, he said, "is a man asking to have a musical comedy written about him." He wrote that Irish-Americans had lost their ethnic identity because they had taken on "the shopping-center faces" of true Americans. In a piece about Marvin the Torch, he explained that "the place went up like an exception to a test ban treaty." In a sentence that said books about a whole American generation, he wrote that in the case of his mother-in-law, "the Depression arranged all of her life," and explained why she rummaged through grocery stores frantically looking for bargains, lecturing Breslin, "You're cheaper off if you do it my way."

Stories about his mother-in-law, his family, and his personal problems have inspired some of Breslin's finest humor. While his columns about the city are honed with a fine sardonic wit, his tales of personal woe reveal a fuller, more classic kind of humor. They cut to the core of human experience like all great humor, bordering on sadness or tragedy, instantly recognized by every reader as part of the perverse nature we all share. In one gem, Breslin sees a television commercial about a man having a heart attack and suddenly feels all the symptoms, screaming out in the middle of the night, "I'll never take another drink, or smoke another cigar," and concluding by morning that "I had only minutes to go." In another winner, he seized on an announcement that Mayor Koch and City Council President Carol Bellamy, both bachelors, would dearly like to have some children. "When these stories reach my house at night, I read them with the eye of a criminal," Breslin wrote.

Breslin was coping alone and incompetently with family matters because Rosemary had finally died of her cancer in June of 1981. It was the worst thing that ever happened to him, and for months he was in emotional turmoil. In September 1982, however, he was rescued by Ronnie Eldridge, a well-known and politically active New Yorker who was also a widow. Although the *Times* business section missed the story, their marriage was one of the year's most celebrated corporate mergers, bringing together nine children, the Catholic and Jewish religions, several different life-styles, the mutually hostile cultures of Queens and Manhattan's Upper West Side, and two mothers-in-law. It was supposed to be one big, joyous family, a milestone in the ecumenical movement, but it fell a trifle short of these ideals, as the head of household confessed in a column about the refusal of the children to share in each other's celebration of Christmas and Hanukkah.

It was a column full of poignant humor, illuminating a serious contemporary problem with almost cruel realism, doing it in a way every reader could feel personally. The Breslin children were used to the public exposure of their private lives but the Eldridge children were not. They reacted with anger and tears, creating new stresses in the extended family. Breslin sighed. "The trouble was," he said, "the column was true."

In the final analysis, this is what matters most about Breslin's work. That so much of what he says is true. That we discover in his columns so much about ourselves and about our society, that we seem closer to neighbors who are strangers and a little less confused about the world which surrounds and threatens us. It is Breslin's private hope that in future generations, when the words of the politicians and the traditional reporting of his colleagues have been forgotten, people will look back on what he has written and say, yes, this truly was the way it was during his time.

His hope deserves fulfillment.

— Michael J. O'Neill

The World
According to Breslin

1

"Dies the Victim, Dies the City"

It is very nearly an impossibility to imagine Jimmy Breslin existing, living, breathing, writing in any city of the world except New York. That stooped, pudgy figure slouching along State Street in Chicago? Absurd. Along Wilshire Boulevard in Los Angeles? Ridiculous. Washington Street in Indianapolis? Where is that, for God's sake?

No, Jimmy Breslin is as much a part of New York as the Brooklyn Bridge, or the Battery, or the Village, or the boroughs, or any other place or thing you care to name that bears the unmistakable stamp *New York*. And New York is a part of him, too, pounded deep into the marrow of his bones by a thousand and one encounters with its daily life. The rhythms of the great city pulse in his Irish blood, its variegated moods are his moods, its often ugly sights and raucous sounds the stimulus for his reportorial eye.

Save, perhaps, for the late Meyer Berger and the columnist Murray Kempton, no modern writer has ever understood New York like Breslin, and been able to translate that understanding into simple declarative sentences, salted with that special Breslin condiment of hard-nosed realism.

Consider this beginning from one of the first columns Breslin ever wrote for the *News*, in December 1976:

"The cars moaned into the damp morning as they came onto the Williamsburg Bridge, climbing up from an expressway that brought the people from Long Island, where they live, to downtown New York, where they earn their living. The cars had in them only one person, now and then two, never more, as they dipped into Manhattan to choke it with metal. The insolence of invaders."

That last sentence is pure Breslin. For Jimmy is nothing if not protective of his city. He loves it with a passion, and he hates outsiders who demean it, or disparage it, or use it for their own cheap ends. More than anything, Breslin is protective of the *people* of New York. Through his newspaper column he is their sounding board, their spokesman, and their champion.

It is perhaps too much to say that Breslin is the voice of the poor people of New York; after all, he can and does write about the swells, too. But he has a special feeling for the down-on-their-luck, the homeless and the jobless, the black and Hispanic kids hanging around the street corners — all the people who would live and die without ever being noticed if someone like Breslin didn't speak for them.

Says Michael Daley, a young writer on the magazine *New York* who is a protégé and close friend of Breslin's, "He approaches New York as a place populated by decent people, and he writes about how they get hurt and why they get hurt. He really cares about people. That's why his best columns have heart."

A very large part of the reason why Breslin understands New York is that he knows the city with the intimate knowledge of a man who has prowled its byways for most of his life. There was a time when Breslin caromed from saloon to saloon far into the night, but the drink, he has said, was "making a zombie" out of him. He discovered that "you can't write if you have a hangover," and so he stopped the bar-hopping routine and very nearly the drinking.

For many years, Breslin operated out of his beloved Queens, the place where he was born and bred. A creature of almost rotelike habit, he invariably started his workday at the Pastrami King Restaurant on Queens Boulevard, where the counterman, Moishe, went about his chores while Breslin sipped coffee and looked up likely horses for him in the tip sheets. Thus fortified for the day, he headed for the E train to Manhattan or the A train to Brooklyn and the endless search for a column.

Breslin was, is, always will be a hard worker who will trudge up airless tenement stairwells, descend into smoke-blackened ruins, go anywhere he has to for copy. If need be, he will be on the prowl before dawn to get the news while it is still fresh, and before the opposition has rolled out of bed. And somehow, magically, no matter how hard he has to dig for the story, he makes it back to his cubbyhole at the News Building, at Forty-second Street and Second Avenue, in time to bat out his column and make his deadline. Breslin, his hair on end, tie pulled down, flailing away at his typewriter like a drowning man trying to tread water, always makes it. In his drinking days, he would then slip out the back door, walk through the *News*'s garage on Forty-first Street, and seek solace at the quiet, polished bar of Gatti's Italian Restaurant on Fortieth

Street. Sometimes it was another bar, Kennedy's on Second Avenue, perhaps, or the Gold Coin, a Chinese bar and restaurant on the same street. Once, downing Scotches with Breslin at the Gold Coin, Brink asked him why he chose a Chinese bar. "The bartenders don't waste time talking," Breslin answered solemnly, "they just pour."

Breslin's life has since changed drastically. With the death of his first wife, Rosemary, he no longer lives in Queens, and even if he were drinking, his favorite watering hole, Gatti's, has been shuttered and sold.

In 1982, a year and a half after Rosemary's death, he married Ronnie Eldridge, a widow whose husband Lawrence, a psychologist, died in 1970, leaving her with three children to raise. Ronnie Eldridge, who once was in politics on the happy basis of a housewife manipulating government for safer equipment for the local playground, and then went on to become Robert Kennedy's most trusted political operator in the state, but who had never held a paid job in the business, now needed public life for a living. She went into City Hall as a top aide to Mayor John Lindsay, then became a government affairs specialist for the New York–New Jersey Port Authority. She is now the director of the state women's division for Governor Mario Cuomo of New York. The early years of her widowhood were a struggle to make ends meet, but Eldridge's fortunes improved considerably when she led a group that contested the license of station WPIX-TV in New York and ultimately settled out of court for $11 million. She moved with her children into a spectacular apartment on Central Park West in Manhattan. When Eldridge threw her arms open to Breslin, he looked over her shoulder at her apartment and said there was no sense in wasting time out of a quick life by looking for housing. He moved in with three of his six children.

Since that move, Breslin has confessed, "My habits are depressing.

"Each morning the two of us leave for work and Eldridge admonishes as we go, 'Be quiet, don't wake up the kids,' but the bastards sleep on.

"I walk to the *News*. Through the park and to the East Side and then down. I stop at Burt Roberts's apartment [former Bronx District Attorney Burton Roberts] on Fifty-fifth and Lexington and ask the doorman and the garage attendant if he has left yet. They say yes or no. I act suspicious, as if I'm hanging around to shoot the guy.

They don't even look up at me. They just say yes or no and never tell Roberts that anybody was asking for him. He screams that they give him no protection."

Breslin heads first for Clancy's at Fifty-fifth and Third, where he has coffee at the bar with Paddy Reilly, the bartender, who is serving the morning drinkers, a mixture of postal workers getting off their night jobs and advertising people about to start work. The morning hubbub is a fruitful source for what Breslin does best: finding out what interests New Yorkers the most at any given moment.

Breslin moves on to Kennedy's at Fifty-first and Second, where he has another cup of coffee and listens some more. Then maybe Costello's Bar on Forty-fourth Street, a favorite and enduring stopping place of newspapermen in mid-Manhattan, where he has more coffee (Breslin has been known to put away six double espressos at a sitting). All this time he is at the wall phones, checking with the city desk at the *News* as well as other sources and tipsters — anybody at all who might have an idea for a column or word of a developing story. Breslin takes it as almost a personal affront that one of his best places to get information, Licata's Espresso Shop on the corner of Forest and Grove in the Ridgewood section of Queens, was invaded one night by some people who blew away the owner and his brother. The place is now a neighborhood medical center.

If Breslin ever sleeps, not too many people are aware of it. By the same token, Breslin is fat, but not many people have ever seen him eat. "I have," he observed in 1983, "been to lunch on the island of Manhattan thrice in the last eight years." The truth is that Breslin eats, but in places of his choosing with his kind of people. "I do not go into French places," he explains, "because the food is intolerable." What he likes are Italian joints, many of them in the boroughs, where "the customers slap the cook if the food is not exquisite."

Nighttime most often finds him dining at Rao's in East Harlem, which he regards as the prettiest restaurant in the world. Or it may be Dimitri's on Columbus Avenue, Crisci's or Bamonte's in Brooklyn, or Don Peppe's in Queens. Quite as important as the places he goes to are the people he listens to. These include the aforementioned Burt Roberts; Mel Lebetkin, a Queens attorney; Maxine Chevlowe, who is a city marshal; a detective named Bill Clark; Irving Selbst, who is in men's clothing; and lawyer Jerry Weiss. Breslin still treks to the knee of Paul O'Dwyer, the venerable New York liberal, for political advice, and he has a pal in the sandhogs union, Chick Donohue, who guides him on labor matters.

Breslin tries very hard to hide it, but he also associates with celebrities. He is an old friend of Barbra Streisand's, he dines with novelist Norman Mailer, with whom he once ran, disastrously, for public office in the city of New York, and he is close to Governor Mario Cuomo of New York, as well as to the Kennedys. He has been observed sneaking into a bookstore to buy a three-volume collection of Montaigne's essays. And he is softie enough to have a favorite view in his favorite city that no visitor to New York would ever divine. That is the view of the old stone Gate of Heaven Catholic Church from the window of the Café 2000, an espresso place on 101st Avenue in Ozone Park, Queens. There, Breslin often sips coffee and stares at the old women in black slowly climbing the church's high, wide steps.

"It is," he sighs, "a scene out of Europe," somehow reminiscent of the homelands of many of the people he writes about.

Let no one suppose that Breslin sees New York only through one eye; his journalistic lens has many prisms. He has, for example, poked disdainful fun at the hallowed New York Marathon by posing in his column as a participant. His put-down was so tongue in cheek that many readers thought he actually ran the race. (While he is no runner, Breslin is a dedicated swimmer. He swims a minimum thousand yards every night, usually at the Vanderbilt Y on Forty-seventh Street.)

Never one to overlook a chance to sell newspapers, Breslin in the summer of 1983 took up the cause of one Joseph Cruz, an indigent who had been kicked out of a city housing shelter and had set up a makeshift home on a concrete traffic island in the middle of the busy East River Drive. When Cruz was arrested and hauled away, Breslin dramatized his plight by donning shorts and a beach jacket and installing himself on a chaise longue under a gaudy beach umbrella on the same island. The baffled cops let him alone.

This is all fun and games for Breslin, of course, and it *does* sell papers. But Breslin knows full well that the real New York, underneath, is the world of his little, forgotten people — never very pretty and often very, very violent.

The very first column that Breslin wrote for the *News*, on November 14, 1976, was about a senseless street killing. It was a theme he returned to again and again, that violence in the streets, but never to more telling effect than in the summer of 1983, in the aftermath of a free concert in Central Park by the singer Diana Ross that was followed by a chilling, bloody, chain-snatching riot. Breslin found his story in the mouths of the black kids hanging around in the school yard behind the Sumner Housing Project in Brooklyn the next day, the very kids who had started the trouble. He also came away with a philosophy of sorts of his own role in the war in the streets.

"I think I am, as are all Irish, a dreadful snob," Breslin says. "But then I sit in a school yard and listen to the kids talk who caused the riot and I don't know what the reason, but I feel most comfortable there. The park bench is like an easy chair, because it is here that I make my living, that I perform any minor public service by informing others of what goes on here in a place where almost nobody else likes to go. The motive is to try making the one thing that produces just about all the crime of our times — the hopelessness that every young black sees as his future — well enough known so that somebody will think about assisting them."

Breslin's column about that school yard encounter is one of his all-time favorites. And while Breslin is hardly a vain man (he sometimes seems oblivious to his own fame and talent), he has permitted himself a small boast about it. "I think," he says, "I am the only one around who can go to a place like Sumner Housing at noon and deliver such a report by 5:30 P.M." (his deadline). When he finished with that column, Breslin straightened up his tie and walked out into the night and the brilliant lights of New York — his New York — a contented man.

— W.B.

Dies the Victim, Dies the City

They were walking along in the empty gray afternoon, three of them, Allen Burnett, Aaron Freeman, and Billy Mabry, Burnett the eldest at seventeen, walking up Bedford Avenue in Brooklyn and singing out Muhammad Ali rhymes into the chill air. As they reached the corner of Kosciusko Street, it was Allen Burnett's turn to give his Ali rhyme: "AJB is the latest. And he is the greatest."

"Who AJB?" one of them said.

"Allen J. Burnett."

They were laughing at this as they turned the corner onto Kosciusko Street. The three wore coats against the cold. Burnett was in a brown trench coat; Freeman, a three-quarter burgundy leather; and Mabry, a three-quarter beige corduroy with a fox collar. A white paint stain was on the bottom at the back of Mabry's coat. Mabry, walking on the outside, suddenly was shoved forward.

"Keep on walking straight," somebody behind him said.

Billy Mabry turned his head. Behind him was this little guy of maybe eighteen, wearing a red sweater, dark pants, and black gun. Aaron Freeman, walking next to Mabry, says he saw two others besides the gunman. The three boys kept walking, although Mabry thought the guy in the red sweater had a play gun.

"Give me the money."

"I don't have any money," Allen Burnett said.

The guy with the gun shot Allen Burnett in the back of the head. Burnett pitched into the wall of an apartment house and went down on his back, dead.

The gunman stood with Allen Burnett's body at his feet and said that now he wanted coats. Billy Mabry handed back the corduroy with the paint stain. Freeman took off his burgundy leather. The gunman told the two boys to start running. "You don't look back!" Billy Mabry and Aaron Freeman ran up Kosciusko Street, past charred buildings with tin nailed over the windows, expecting to be shot in the back. People came onto the street and the guy in the red sweater waved his gun at them. The people dived into doorways. He stuffed the gun into his belt and ran up Bedford Avenue, ran away with his new coats. Some saw one other young guy with him. Others saw two.

It was another of last week's murders that went almost unnoticed. Allen Burnett was young. People in the city were concentrating all week on the murders of elderly people. Next week you can dwell on murders of the young, and then the killing of the old won't seem as important.

Allen Burnett's murder went into the hands of the Thirteenth Homicide Squad, situated on the second floor of a new police building on Utica Avenue. The outdoor pay phone in front of the precinct house has been ripped out. The luncheonette across the street is empty and fire-blackened. At first, a detective upstairs thought the interest was in a man who had just beaten his twenty-two-month-old child to death with a riding crop. That was unusual. Allen Burnett was just another homicide. Assured that Burnett was the subject, the detective pointed to Harold Ruger, who sat at a desk going through a new manila folder with Burnett's name on it. Ruger is a blue-eyed man with wavy dark-brown hair that is white at the temples. The twenty-four years he has spent on the job have left him with a melancholy face and a soft voice underlined with pleasant sarcasm: "They got two coats. Helluva way to go shopping. Looks like there was three of them. That leaves one guy out there without a coat. I'll look now for somebody who gets taken off for a coat tonight, tomorrow night, the next few days."

In a city that seems virtually ungoverned, Harold Ruger forms the only municipal presence with any relationship to what is happening on the streets where the people live. Politicians attend dinners at hotels with contractors. Bankers discuss interest rates at lunch. Harold Ruger goes into a manila folder on his desk and takes out a picture of Allen Burnett, a young face covered with blood staring from a morgue table. In Allen Burnett's hand there is a piece of the veins of the city of New York.

Dies the victim, dies the city. Nobody flees New York because of accounting malpractice. People run from murder and fire. Those who remain express their fear in words of anger.

"Kill him for nothing, that's life — that's what it is today," his sister Sadie was saying. The large, impressive family had gathered in the neat frame house at 30 Van Buren Street. "He was going into the army in January and they kill him for nothing. That's the leniency of the law. Without capital punishment they do what they want. There's no respect for human life."

Horace Jones, an uncle, said, "The bleeding hearts years ago cut out the electric chair. When the only way to stop all this is by havin' the electric chair."

"We look at mug shots all last night," Sadie said. "None of them was under sixteen. If the boy who shot Allen is under sixteen, there won't be any picture of him. How do you find him if he's under sixteen? Minors should get treated the same as everybody else. Equal treatment."

"Electric chair for anybody who kills, don't talk to me about ages," Horace Jones said.

The dead boy's mother, Lillian Burnett, sat with her head down and her hands folded in her lap.

"Do you think there should be an electric chair?" she was asked.

"I sure do," she said, eyes closed, head nodding. "Won't bring back my son, but I sure do want it. They tied up three old women and killed them. If they had the electric chair I believe they would rob the three women, but I don't believe they'd kill them."

The funeral was held two days later, at the Brown Memorial Baptist Church, on Washington Avenue. A crowd of three hundred of Allen Burnett's family and friends walked two by two into church. Walked erectly, solemnly, with the special dignity of those to whom suffering is a bitter familiarity. Seeing them, workmen in the street shut off pneumatic drills. Inside the church, the light coming through the doorway gleamed on the dark, polished wood of the benches. The casket was brought in by men walking soundlessly on the carpeted floor. The doors were closed, an organ sounded, and the people faced the brutality of a funeral service; a baby cried, a woman rocked and screamed, a boy sobbed, a woman fainted, heads were cradled in arms. The mother screamed through a black veil, "My baby's gone!"

An aunt, Mabel Mabry, walked out of the church with lips trembling and arms hugging her shaking body. "My little nephew's dead," she said loudly. "They find the ones who killed him. I'm tellin' you, they got to kill them too, for my nephew."

The city government, Harold Ruger, just wants to find the killer. Ruger was not at the funeral. "I got stuck in an eighty-floor elevator," he said when he came to work yesterday. "I was going around seeing people. We leave the number, maybe they'll call us. That's how it happens a lot. They call." He nodded toward a younger detective at the next desk. "He had one, an old man killed by a kid. Information came on a phone call, isn't that right, Al?"

"Stabbed eight times, skull fractured," the younger detective said.

Harold Ruger said, "What does it look like you have? Nothing. And he gets a phone call, see what I mean? The answer is out there and it will come." His finger tapped the file he was keeping on the murder of Allen Burnett.

(November 1976)

Fare Beats Must Be Trim

Yesterday morning, at the Rutland Road–Sutter Avenue stop of the IRT No. 2 line in Brooklyn, I attempted to perform a necessary act — getting past the turnstiles without paying. I term it necessary because the only way to preserve and improve a subway system that a working person can afford and ride on safely is civil disobedience.

The problem for me yesterday morning was the absence of exit gates that are usually alongside the turnstiles. At the Rutland Road–Sutter Avenue station, the exit gates have been replaced by thick wire. The turnstiles are used for both entrance and exit.

There are three accepted ways to jump the turnstile. One is to attain running speed and hurdle the gate, left leg straight out, right leg thrown sideways, virtually parallel to the ground. The second is to place both palms on the turnstile, hoist the body up, legs folding under like a duck's, then swinging across. The third way — this for the very young, the very old, or those in abominable physical condition — is to crawl under the turnstile.

Yesterday, when only one man was in front of me on the line at the Rutland Road–Sutter Avenue stop, I dropped to the floor and began crawling. My head bumped into the legs of the man in front of me. He didn't have his token out and was going through his pockets for it. The person behind me, a woman in hospital whites, nearly fell over me.

"What's the matter?" the woman said.

"Nothing."

"Then don't do that. I have to go to work."

The man ahead of me was through the turnstile and the woman in hospital whites brushed past me and went through. As I was about to start crawling, another woman went by me and I saw that the line was both long and impatient and I got up and, in defeat and embarrassment, bought a token for seventy-five cents and paid my way onto the train.

It is the last time I will do it. Starting today, I will use only those subway and el stops that have exit gates. I will walk through them without paying. Of course, there could be arrests from time to time. There could be police to contend with, judges to see.

It was an old train with no air conditioning and all seats gone. I stood at the front window as the train went past a green signal, then another green signal, and then it started down the slope to the subway tunnel that runs under Eastern Parkway. At the tunnel entrance, the train went out of the sunlight and into the darkness and the tracks immediately curved. It was at this spot on Friday that motorman Jesse Cole, thirty-five, ran his train into the back of another one. Cole lost his life, and an essential secret of the city in which we live was exposed.

The subway signal system, the marvel in which all city kids are raised to believe, was installed in this particular stretch of subway line in 1918. In the years since, particularly the last quarter century, through all the famous men and the elections that made them so, nobody thought of the future. Politicians ran and never thought of performing the governmental function of putting in new signals. Subjects like this are too large to fit into a campaign commercial.

Graffiti on the subway cars became an issue in political campaigns, but never the light switches or tracks or subway wheels on which millions depend. And now the public that dozed amiably through all this, taking interest for a day or so in an election once every couple of years, becomes the only force that can save the city's greatest resource and leave it intact for those to follow.

The symbol for the city becomes Jesse Cole, the life crushed out of him in the motorman's cab of a train that was forced to run on tracks that had no signals.

When Jesse Cole died last Friday, it was a holiday and the city streets around the subway tracks were crowded with people, wet in the heat, listening to radios blare. The mayor, Koch, was out in the Hamptons. The governor, Society Carey, was at Shelter Island. The head of the transit system, Ravitch, was on Cape Cod. The president of the City Council, Bellamy, was in Pennsylvania.

In their place was a man named Simpson from the Transit Authority. He came off the tracks and up to the television cameras in a white hard hat and the orange vest worn by trackmen. His gaze was intent. His stance and hand motions, indicating command of all sit)uations, appeared to have been perfected through many hours of looking at himself in the mirror.

"It was human error," Simpson announced. "That, combined with mechanical failure."

Of course, the voice hit "human error" the hardest. Motorman Cole had deliberately gone down the tracks, running out of sunlight and into darkness, knowing there were no signal lights to warn him, because he had wanted to commit suicide.

By saying "human error" while standing at the tracks only a short time after the accident, with nothing having been checked, Simpson was able to place the words "drunk" or "dope addict" in a listener's mind.

Simpson was brought to New York to run the subways from Denver, where there are no subways. Which makes sense. When Denver needs a cowboy, it also looks to New York.

So we had tracks with no signals and an alien from Denver doing the explaining while the politicians were out in the Hamptons, which is much more comfortable for them than Brooklyn for a large number of reasons.

The future, the politician says, is my future. So government is directed at the next election in which the politician is involved. New York now is a city with a most successful loudmouth for mayor and a subway system that suddenly shows how it can kill.

The only answer is to resist. Surely the rise to a seventy-five-cent fare is only the beginning. And surely the subways are in worse condition today than they were last Friday.

The irresponsible method is to allow things to go on as they are, to sit through another election based on men making faces at television cameras. The responsible way to cause change, to force government from New York to Washington to sit nervously and insure the future of this great national resource, the subway system, is to walk through a gate and not pay any fare, starting today.

I had a spot of trouble yesterday because I am built like an overstuffed valise. But I'll find an exit gate today and walk right through, and in the days to come there will be highly accurate reports on others who do the same.

There is instant fame waiting in this city for someone who can lead a fare strike by subway riders, and I sit here waiting for the man to appear and hear my applause.

(*July 1981*)

It Was Merely over Race

The cars moaned into the damp morning as they came onto the Williamsburg Bridge, climbing up from an expressway that brought the people in from Long Island, where they live, to downtown New York, where they earn their living. The cars had in them only one person, now and then two, never more, as they slipped across a bridge suspended over the East River by gray silk and dipped into Manhattan to choke it with metal. The insolence of invaders.

Under the bridge, where the people of New York live in the turmoil and shortages that draw so many amusing remarks from the suburbs, it was a great pleasure to start the holiday season off with a smashing racial fight.

A man came up to me on the street and handed me a pamphlet that was to be distributed later on in the morning. It said:

"Several thousand Hassidic Jews from Williamsburg, joined by Jews from other Jewish communities, demonstrated around City Hall to protest against the city for allowing the Clemente Plaza development in Williamsburg to be tenanted by a majority of Hispanics and blacks."

There is one thing to be said for a racial fight: it does not cloud the faculties with anything delicate. Equally comforting was the thought that somewhere, as you read this pamphlet, a Puerto Rican with a mimeograph machine was getting even.

The dispute is over gloomy red brick buildings that step out of muddy lots across the street from the nearly vacant Brooklyn Navy Yard. The housing development was started about three years ago. There now are 228 units available, with another 304 nearly finished. People have been living for months in decayed housing in the area on the promise of a new apartment. One woman, legally blind, lives alone in an empty building which has a common toilet in the hallway. People walk in from the street to use it. Others live with no electricity. A new place to live, with heat and without rats, is something to treasure.

Williamsburg now is Puerto Rican, black, and white. Most of the whites are Jewish. It is a marvelous example of how the poor are left in the cities to fight among themselves while those with enough money to move to the suburbs watch the fight on the evening news.

Everything started when the city of New York started building the Clemente development, and alongside it a project known as Bedford Gardens. The decision was to allow Clemente to be 75 percent minority and 25 percent American white. Or at least that was the deal, as Puerto Rican groups in the area say they understood it. They were unable to get it in writing. The whites in Bedford Gardens had theirs on paper.

The agility of people to move about the feared word "quota" is remarkable in these affairs. Mention quotas to whites and they scream that it is at least un-American. But when quotas were set in Williamsburg assuring that 75 percent of a housing project would be white, the white people applauded. It was when the Clemente development was given a quota of 75 percent minority that the whites saw ancient fears once more.

The mainly white development was finished first. Then Hassidic — Orthodox — Jewish groups in the area began to say that if the Clemente housing development was to be more than 50 percent nonwhite, the area wouldn't last. Lawyers streamed into court. Eighty Puerto Rican families jumped into the completed Clemente building — named after former Pittsburgh baseball player Roberto Clemente — moved into apartments and, subtly, put a Christmas tree in the window of the lobby.

People running New York did just about nothing during most of the squabble. A politician finds anything to do with racial problems far more frightening than a gun. The most influential political club in this city, the Madison Democratic Club, home of Mayor Beame, Stanley Steingut, speaker of the state assembly, and Arthur Levitt, the state controller, used to be located on a broad avenue known as Eastern Parkway. When blacks moved into the area, the Madison Club packed up and fled. Its members run the business of the city in similar fashion.

And so yesterday morning, under a light rain, one of the sides involved in the housing fight took the matter into the streets around City Hall. Over the bridge they came from Brooklyn, walking and by bus, about fifteen thousand Hassidic Jews.

Black hats packed the barricades around City Hall and chanted, "Save Williamsburg." Over in a section by themselves, the women and children were screaming: "Save our neighborhood."

An old woman, Makra Stein, kerchief wrapped around her head, leaned over the barricade to talk. What appeared to be young girls around her made so much noise she turned around and hit them to make them be quiet. Two of the young girls who giggled the most showed marriage rings.

"Why are we here?" Makra Stein said. "We're here because your family gets married and they don't have where to live."

The Hassidim are of the Satmar group. Once, the group's grand rabbi lived in the town of Satumare in Hungary. At the end of World War II, there were a hundred of them left. They followed the rabbi to New York, to Williamsburg, and the sect grew. They do not allow abortions, birth control, divorce, or extramarital affairs. Their children marry young, at eighteen and nineteen, and have children immediately. All the men wear black hats, from which *peyos* — curls — stick out. The women cover their heads with *shaitels*; the exposure of the hair of a woman is indecent.

There were no Puerto Ricans or blacks at the demonstration yesterday. Lawyers for the Puerto Rican groups say that they want to show the courts that their side is not out on the streets. But the people can be brought out at any time. They had big demonstrations last summer.

The Hassidic people gave one last chant, then were told by their leaders to go home, which they did, quickly and in order.

(December 1976)

On Suburban Riffraff

We have had enough of these cheap looters who ride in here from Connecticut and Westchester each day, grab money they never would earn in the places where they live, and then, without a trace of class, wring their hands over the condition of the city, its transit system, and the people of the city who ride on it.

Usually, this suburban riffraff arrives each business morning at Grand Central Terminal on commuter trains from their lifeless green towns. Because of the rail strike, the commuters now ride buses into the Pelham Bay section of the Bronx, where they get on the No. 6 train for the ride downtown.

These men in their trench coats and attaché cases and the tailored women take up room on a subway line that is normally used by the working people of our city. The suburban people, given the chance, immediately snicker at, or appear in terror of, the working people of the Bronx who get on the train with them.

These whining suburban people have been heard on radio and seen on television news programs. They also inspired what is easily the one lowest story I think I have come upon in my time in this business. It was printed in the commuter paper, *The New York Times* newspaper, yesterday morning. I rarely point a finger at what somebody else does, for this business is tough enough without worrying about the next guy. But the story was used so prominently, and its bad taste was so dramatic, that everybody should know about it.

I herewith quote from the story in order to show that these suburban commuters, who use this city and don't pay for it, and the writer for the *Times* newspaper, who commutes to work from Ridgewood, New Jersey, both regard the people of our city as subhuman. There is, of course, in the story the inevitable police quote about how dangerous the subway train is in the morning. Where there has not been any rush-hour crime worth mentioning since the third rail was invented. As you read the following you will see that it becomes more than merely one newspaper article; it reveals the minds of the people who are the true enemies of the city of New York. The story states:

"The subways are a little frightening to us," said James Reynolds, of Stamford, Connecticut, lurching toward Manhattan on the Lexington Avenue line, flailing about wildly from time to time in an attempt to keep his feet. "The graffiti makes you wonder just who is in charge down here anyway."

... Still, riding the subways was something many of the suburban commuters approached with trepidation — deciphering the psychedelic spaghetti bowl that is a New York subway map, distinguishing between menacing youths and the two boys on the Lexington Avenue line accompanying a sister selling Girl Scout cookies ...

Once aboard, the suburbanites were quick to notice differences between the subways and their trains, where they comfortably drink coffee, read newspapers without having to stab at a moving page for that next word, play cards, and even enjoy cocktails in club cars. Drinking a cup of coffee on a subway car, as one novice suburban subway rider discovered, is a group experience.

As the lights went off, as subway lights are wont to do, Margaret Carmine, another Westchester commuter, gave new meaning to the term "clutch purse," seeming to crush the entire contents to insure no one grabbed it.

Mrs. Carmine said that on Monday evening she had ridden next to two young men smoking marijuana and playing, rather loudly, a radio that she remembered as about the size of her stove. "They weren't hurting anything," she said, "but I was surprised. It's just something I don't see on the train very much."

... Several police officers expressed concern that before too long, thieves might catch on to this movement of jewelry and fur coats each morning and evening traveling through several high-crime areas and begin to take advantage of the situation ...

... When a youth stepped aboard a subway train at East 125th Street in Harlem, he stopped short and glanced at his companion as if, perhaps, they had stepped into the Twilight Zone. To be sure, there were few aboard paying much attention to the subway car advertisements with such headlines as "Check Out the Changes in Food Stamps."

"The best subway ride I ever had," Leland Ott, of Stamford, said with an obvious sense of pleasure and relief. Many of the suburban commuters had viewed being dropped off by buses in the Bronx as tantamount to being let off on Omaha Beach, June 6, 1944. Their fears had been allayed.

They were relieved to see that police were out in force at the Pelham Bay Park station as well as on the trains, and most agreed with Bob Sylvester of Meriden, Connecticut, that "there are enough commuters around to keep things safe."

It must be marvelous to be a black or Hispanic in the Bronx and to get up at seven in the morning to go to work at a minimum-wage job in a factory downtown and you get on the subway and find that people are calling you someone to be afraid of. These suburban commuters and the person who wrote the newspaper article don't know enough about life to realize that someone who is on a crowded train in the morning is a person on his way to honest work; far more honest than the strangers on the train with him, all suburban thieves, stained lawyers, and the bunco artist stock-and-bond dealers. They use the city of New York, without paying for it, and they play all day mostly with OPM — Other People's Money — and then they proclaim that they are making it on their own. There is a term for them: White Welfare.

Shameless people and article to match.

In reaction to it, Steve Dunleavy, metropolitan editor, *New York Post* newspaper, noted yesterday, "I thought I was supposed to know all there is about unfit news. But I never have been associated with anything this low. It takes some fool in a trench coat and jacket and vest to show you what the basement really looks like."

The reaction on my part was to begin planning to take a group of Bronx people on a tour of suburban towns, like Greenwich and Darien, just as residents of those places feel they are touring the Bronx.

I intend to put together, at personal expense and effort, a busload of people and take them for a walking tour of the Darien and Greenwich shopping districts, followed by an inspection of the big estates. Each person on the tour will have a *New York Times* newspaper to deliver to one of the estates.

The date and time for this bus tour will be announced in this space within the next several days. But I can announce today that the fabled Mary Clark of the Bronx will be aboard. In making the date with me yesterday, Mary Clark said, "When we get to Greenwich, I want to visit a notion store."

"Why?"

"Because I got notions."

(March 1983)

How I Shot Down the Concorde All by Myself

At a little before 7:00 P.M. in Manhattan, longshoremen of Local 824 walked along the edge of pier 86, unfastened the hawsers that held the *QE2* to the West Side, and threw them out into the oily water of the slip. High up, ten stories up, seamen of the *QE2* began hauling in the rope. When the last hawser was thrown from the pier, hitting the water with a slap, the great ship, free to move, gave three deep blasts of the whistle. The people standing out on Twelfth Avenue began waving handkerchiefs. From the ship, you could see children looking down at their feet because the sidewalk was vibrating.

Once, it was part of the life of this city, the ocean liners of the world announcing their departure for the sea. Now, with the *QE2* the last big one afloat anywhere on the waters of the world, its deep sound becomes an emotion. On this night, when the tugs pushed the ship into the middle of the river, her twin six-bladed propellers first churning while the tugs slid away, the great ship, on her own, going down to the sea, sent three more proud blasts into the evening air.

I love sounds. Taxicab horns coming through an open window

from the Manhattan street twenty-five stories down. A subway train's pleasant roar as it breaks out of a tunnel and into a lighted station. And the first sound of a jet plane: a whistle in the cold air, calling the eyes to follow a beautiful silver arrow soaring across the sky.

But then, of course, the jet plane's noise changes. It becomes a blare that blankets the ground and grows louder and louder and just when you are certain that now it must stop, now the sound must diminish, the noise only increases and carries to the beginning of pain and beyond.

In a neighborhood of New York such as Howard Beach, which sits on the edge of runways at Kennedy Airport, people grope for a way to explain the noise. How does a bus driver tell of the feeling of irritability that comes over everyone in his house about ten minutes before the landing patterns are changed? Animals uneasy over an impending storm only they can sense.

And now these people in Howard Beach are asked to accept a plane that makes even more noise, the Concorde plane. Howard Beach fears that someday all overseas flights will be Concordes and turn everyone's ears to stone. Because of this I was on this night standing on the boat deck of the *QE2* as she ran with the tide to the sea. Once, it was the only way to go. Now, I sail the Atlantic to the port of Cherbourg, in France, where I intend to confront these French, who build a machine that makes infernal noise and want Howard Beach to suffer in silence. In Howard Beach, people who must go to work for a living say they will blockade entrances to Kennedy Airport rather than allow the Concorde to send its roar through their roofs. In Paris, the president of the country, Valéry Giscard d'Estaing, has made personal remarks about Howard Beach people, thereby causing an international incident. He has entertained American politicians and paid enormous sums of money to American lobbyists who imitate his sneer when Howard Beach is mentioned. I go to Paris to report on the arrogant and thus defend people who work for a living and live in Howard Beach, which is a neighborhood of Queens, from whence I come.

Howard Beach is a narrow, crowded strip of land with bay water on both sides and a subway line, the A train, to Manhattan. A wide street, Cross Bay Boulevard, runs through Howard Beach to the ocean and forms two areas of Howard Beach. In one, the old side, some of the houses are there from the days it was considered a summer resort. Wash blows on lines strung from wooden houses. In the mornings, there is fresh sawdust on the floor of Sal's Butcher Shop and women customers sit on high stools so they can converse with each other while peering over the counter to watch the butcher make up their order. In the early afternoons, the voice of the track announcer over at Aqueduct Race Track sounds on the streets. In the late afternoons, the streets are empty in the painful noise of airport traffic.

On the other side of Cross Bay Boulevard is the new Howard Beach. Blocks of split-level and ranch houses and attached two-family bricks, all built over the last fifteen years, with small lawns in front, some of the lawns with religious statues on them. Incoming planes skim so low over these houses that people standing in the backyards unconsciously duck. As these people have heavy mortgages and no money to run elsewhere, they have organized to fight the Concorde by forming the Spring Park Civic Association and conducting protest meetings at PS 207. Because of this, the Port Authority, which operates Kennedy, has withheld permission for the Concorde to land.

And so Valéry Giscard d'Estaing called Jimmy Carter and said the French would block all American planes from Paris. Giscard kept saying through his nose, "Oward Beach." Next, British Prime Minister James Callaghan, whose country is a partner in the Concorde, flew to Washington to see Carter personally about these dreadful people in Howard Beach. On the next flight came a British cabinet member, Anthony Wedgwood-Benn. When nothing happened, Giscard and Callaghan recruited American political people to help them. American lawyers so far have been paid over a million dollars to represent the Concorde against Howard Beach.

"What do they think we are, imbeciles?" Mrs. Debby McGuire of Ninety-sixth Street said yesterday. "They're not courtroom lawyers. They're fixers. Everybody in Howard Beach has a hearing problem he isn't even aware of yet. Now some big shots put in a fix so the Concorde can come over my house like a cannon and make us move. I know what's going on."

Charles Goodell, one of the big-name lawyers representing the Concorde, was asked about this. Records show Mr. Goodell's law firm has been paid $195,000 by the Concorde people. Goodell is a former United States senator from Jamestown, New York.

"I represent the minister of transport of France; actually I'm the chief counsel," Goodell said.

"Does a French government ministry always pay such high fees to lawyers?" Goodell was asked.

"Well, I've been in court for them on cases," Goodell said. "One is pending. One is fully briefed."

"You once represented the people of Howard Beach as a senator," I said to Goodell. "Don't you feel there is a conflict here?"

"Oh, yes, I represented that area," Goodell said. "And I've been out there at Kennedy Airport many times. It's very noisy. But the issue here is discrimination against one plane."

"Well, were you chosen by France because you're such a good lawyer or because you're a former United States senator with good contacts?" Goodell was asked.

"Oh, I've done a lot of litigation," he said. "I was a litigator before I went to the Senate, you know."

"Did they used to pay you fees as big as this?" he was asked.

"Oh, well. You have to remember, I was in Jamestown," Goodell said.

When she heard this, Mrs. Debbie McGuire of Ninety-sixth Street sniffed. "What do I do, tell you the wrong things?" she said.

I then showed her that the law firm of William Rogers, the former secretary of state in the Nixon administration, received $701,000 from the Concorde.

"Why do you think he got more than Goodell?" I asked Mrs. McGuire.

"Because a secretary of state costs you more," she said. "You won't see either of them in a courtroom. They do all their work out of sight."

This opposition was discussed one afternoon at Lenny's Clam Bar on Cross Bay Boulevard, only yards away from the Kennedy runways. Everybody was eating calamari and scungilli with sauce so hot it caused the mouths to fly open.

"When they try to stick their foot right down your throat, then you got to get up and fight," Ralph Turchio was saying. Ralph Turchio is built like a front end. Once, he was a shoeshine boy; now he has a house that cost him $58,000. What Ralph Turchio would do to defend his $58,000 house is frightening to think about. And now Ralph was saying that noise from the regular jetliners has him crazy, but if they ever let a Concorde fly 200 feet over his house he would be finished. "When that plane flies way up over the ocean, it wakes up the tuna fish," Ralph says.

"When I first moved in here," Turchio was saying, "the plane comes over my house at night and the floodlights come into my room and I could look out and see people in the seats in the plane. I run under the bed. Now what am I supposed to do, let them blow me right out of the house?"

"What do you think of the French argument that they need the Concorde for their economy?" Turchio was asked.

"My money is more important than theirs," he said. "I got an all-electric house. I had to shut down half the house all winter. The kids doubled up. We couldn't afford the electric bills. And I'm supposed to worry about some plane a hundred big shots can ride in? They think we're a bunch of peasants. Hey! We got all the leadership we need to stop them.

"Do you know how I'm living here now? Plane comes in over my house when I'm on the phone, I can't hear a thing. I got to say to the guy, 'Wait a minute.' Now the plane goes by. So I start talking. But now the plane is over the other guy's house. And he has to say to me, 'Wait a minute.' So we wait. Then here comes another plane and we start all over again."

Turchio stood up to leave. "Let's face it," he said, "I never spoke to important people. I got a small business and a house and that's it. But I tell you, the smarter the people I meet on this thing, the dumber they are. They tell me they're going to bank the plane so it won't make noise. Bank it where? On my roof? This house is all I got. The neighborhood is good. You see what's happenin' to the rest of the city. This neighborhood holds up. I got no place else to go. I'm goin' to stay here, and no plane is going to make me move."

When a report of this conversation was printed in my newspaper, read by French consulate people in New York and transmitted to Paris, the reaction from a man as haughty as Giscard d'Estaing was predictable. He went to the NBC cameras in Paris and spoke to reporter Tom Brokaw. "The airport is on the sea and the sea is crowded by fishes, not people," Giscard said with a sneer.

And that morning, in his bedroom in Howard Beach, Ralph Turchio bounced up and down on the edge of his bed.

"What is he, tough?" Ralph shouted.

"Ralph!" his wife, Eleanor, said.

"Ralph nothing!" he said. He made a fist. "Your plane is a dead lox," he yelled to Giscard on television.

"Ralph, you got to go to work," his wife said.

"I'd like to go to work on this guy," Ralph said.

Later that morning, on behalf of Ralph Turchio, I sat in my office on Forty-second Street in Manhattan and called Giscard, whose number in Paris is 261-5100.

First there was a woman who said, "Ooohh."

"I want to speak to President Giscard d'Estaing, he called my people fish," I said to her.

She put me onto a man who said, "Noooooo." I told him the same thing. Then another man came to the phone who gave his name as Monsieur Arnaud.

"I want to speak to Giscard d'Estaing," I said.

"I am speaking to you for him," M. Arnaud said.

"Why did he call us fish?" I said.

"He never said that," M. Arnaud said.

"Yes, he did. I saw it on the television in Ralph Turchio's house this morning."

"That is a distortion. I was there when President Giscard d'Estaing gave his interview to the television. He did not say that."

"I was in Ralph Turchio's bedroom and he said it there."

"But I was directly with President Giscard and he never said that."

"Did he say fish?"

"Yes, but he said that as a joke. That was a joke by the president."

"Joke? Your president has no humor. If he said something, he meant it. And he has all of Howard Beach upset."

"But they cannot be upset. He never said such a thing."

"Do you know what Howard Beach is?"

"Yes, I have heard this name."

"I am glad you know it, because that's the place that's going to put your Concorde plane into a museum. Where is Giscard? I want to tell him this myself."

"He did not say what you say he said."

"What have I got, a drain in my head? Of course he did. Put him on the telephone."

One or two more shouts into the phone and it was over. But it was disturbing. For the last two weeks now, humorless, demanding French and British politicians and technocrats have been all over

New York, seeing politicians and businessmen at expensive lunch-
eons. And every place you go in New York you hear that they are
nearing success, that Americans in power are going to see to it that
people who live around Kennedy Airport are to have no choice but
to suffer under more technology.

It was at this point that the French consulate in New York asked
if they could persuade me to see their president's side. I decided to
go to France and fight them on their own grounds. For in America,
the tactic of the Concorde now was to delay and postpone hearings,
as they understood that time goes on and people get tired, but
money is patient. Perhaps diligent reporting would speed things up
and force politicians to suddenly say, No, the plane won't land and
that is all.

And so I sailed for France on the *QE2*. On the first night out, I sat
in my stateroom and wrote a column about the trip. As I typed, I
read my notes. They were filled with personal insults to Valéry
Giscard d'Estaing. I became so angry that I wrote that I not only
would see Giscard but that I was challenging him to a duel. I
handed my copy to the ship communications officer and relaxed.

A couple of days later, the glasses on the bar were vibrating from
the power of the twin screws, directly underneath, that were driving
the ship at twenty-eight knots along the edge of the ice fields of the
North Atlantic. I stepped outside and looked down. White water
boiled up and spread out into the darkness. I came back inside and
went to bed. The room was creaking from the motion of the ship. A
low, steady, lulling sound.

At Cherbourg, television crews fought with each other for position on the pier.

"You are here to challenge President Giscard d'Estaing to a
duel!" the interpreter for a reporter shouted at me.

"Of course," I said. "He insulted me, and everyone else from
Howard Beach."

The interpreter chattered my answer in French into the micro-
phones.

"How do you dare such a thing as challenge our president?" an
announcer shrieked.

"He insulted me. I shall avenge these insults," I said.

"You would duel our president?"

"And win," I said.

When this was interpreted, the cameramen and soundmen acted

as if they wanted to drop their equipment and assault me. Head high, I walked through this crowd of rabble and took the boat train to Paris.

Where, that night, I sat in my hotel room and watched the evening news on television. The lead story was on my arrival. I was a thug from Howard Beach, the anchorman announced. Then I came on. I thought I was beautiful. Right after me was a series of interviews with politicians who commented on what I just had said. The politicians went crazy. I fell asleep happy.

In the morning, I went to the Assemblée nationale, a stone building made dark by the centuries. It was across a bridge over the Seine. As arranged from New York, a man waited for me in the foyer of the Assemblée, a foyer of white pillars and men speaking in the same low tones as are heard in the backs of storefront political clubhouses back in Queens.

The man clearly found me distasteful. He threw his head in the direction of the doorway and snarled something and left.

"What did he say?" I asked the interpreter. He refused to answer. He led the way through a softly lit room with a desk of polished wood, pushed a door, and stepped into a large barroom which looked onto a garden with gravel paths. The bar had a marble top and a great copper rail. Six bartenders were on duty to serve the politicians, who came off the Assemblée floor to wash the harangue from their throats.

Waiting at the bar was the deputy from Toulouse, where the Concorde aircraft is assembled. He was a short, stocky man in an expensive light-blue pinstripe suit. His name was Alex Raymond and he was agitated.

The interpreter explained my presence and Raymond nodded several times. "Oward Beach. Oui. Oward Beach. Oui."

Four members who were drinking whisky at the end of the bar looked around. You are not an unknown in France, from a railway station bar in Cherbourg to the Assemblée nationale, if you are from anywhere near Howard Beach. Deputy Raymond, who has factories of aircraft workers as constituents, cared only about the Concorde landing in New York. His blue eyes flashed and his hand waved.

"He says it's not noisier than a Boeing," the interpreter said. "He said he knows this because he is in the aerospace section of the Socialist Party."

"Tell him," I said, "that the teachers have to stop when the regular planes pass over the schools in Howard Beach. The Concorde will drive them out of the classrooms."

M. Raymond nodded as he heard this. He spoke. Then the interpreter said, "He said that this is an issue which is not beyond the genius of both countries if they would cooperate to make planes less noisy. But in the meantime, efforts should be directed at not just the French aircraft."

"Tell him the people in Queens say his plane is too noisy for them," I said.

The interpreter said, "He says that the problem really is a rivalry between aircraft companies, between your Boeing and the French company assembling the Concorde."

"Tell him it is a problem of the ear. We don't want to listen to his noise," I said.

The interpreter said, "He says that a friendship binds France and the United States. It is of vital importance to both of us. It is not in the interests of the United States to tarnish the image of Franco-American cooperation."

I said to the interpreter, "Tell him that a study at Queens College shows that the noise of the Concorde makes people impotent."

M. Raymond's eyes widened as he listened to this. His voice barked.

"He says he is most certainly not impotent," the interpreter said.

"Tell him to prove it," I said.

As the interpreter spoke to him again, M. Raymond's mouth opened. The interpreter said to me, "He says not with you."

M. Raymond turned and went to the end of the bar to speak to the other socialists, who drank whisky and glared.

The interpreter said, "It is a problem no one in this chamber can understand. They do not understand why the United States refuses to recognize this step forward that the Concorde represents."

"It isn't the United States stopping the plane, it's Howard Beach," I said, "and everybody's ears hurt. So they're not going to let the plane land. They'll tie up Kennedy Airport on Sundays for a couple of years."

"Here, too, we are très passionnés," the man said.

Deputy Raymond suddenly stepped into the center of the barroom. He held his fists to his chest. Then one hand came out with two fingers raised. Raymond called out something.

The interpreter said, "He said he will show you that he is not impotent from the Concorde going over his head, that you are to get him two Blue Bell Girls from the Lido and he will show you."

Raymond's chin came out defiantly. He turned around and walked out of the barroom and went back to the floor of the Assemblée nationale.

Later that day, an air attaché from the American embassy arrived at my hotel with a serious air about him. He said that Giscard d'Estaing, enraged, would not see me. Giscard had informed the agency that he was too dignified to speak to this person who dared to challenge him to a duel. Giscard d'Estaing then was caught live on French television saying, "This Breslin is uncouth. He opposes the Concorde because he is jealous of the French."

I again attempted to reach the man by phone. He refused to speak to me. Big shot. I then dropped off a note at the Elysée Palace. In the note I told Giscard that to me and to people in Howard Beach, he was a veal chop.

Now I decided to go home by Concorde plane. Perhaps I could start something by that. What, I didn't know. But I booked a flight for the next day. When I got up that morning, I went to Mass at the Cathedral of Notre Dame, where three old women prayed while the priest said Mass in the morning chill. The Mass was in French, which seemed wrong, for the cathedral demanded a particular richness of language, a unifying connection with the past, in order to remind the one kneeling of his insignificance. On the way out, I mentioned this to the priest. It is not my doing, he said. Then in a café across a bridge, the porter handed me a newspaper, *France Soir,* which had a headline about me over the story carrying Giscard's personal attack:

OPPONENT OF CONCORDE MAKES EVEN MORE NOISE

Right away, for some reason, I knew that something would happen that would make me a huge winner on this trip.

On the way to the airport, we went through Goussainville, which sits in the midst of fields where flowers are raised. The road is narrow and lined with Lombardy poplar trees. In the town, the car barely fit between buildings. A young man and woman strolled along, ripping off pieces from a giant French bread. At a crossing, a man in a sweater with a wicker shopping basket on his arm was asked about the plane. He put the shopping basket on a wall and clapped his hands to his ears. Then we headed for Charles de Gaulle

Airport. Coming up the hill to the airport, there was this slim white needle sitting alone out on the tarmac in the pale evening light. In a special, carpeted area of the departure terminal a bartender served somber-eyed, deep-voiced, chuckling businessmen as they waited for the Concorde.

Which took off on time, with a roar inside the cabin, but only the suggestion of the noise exploding in the air outside. The money inside was, as always, well protected. I thought of Frankie Busycorner in Howard Beach, whose backyard, made entirely of marble, is cracking from the noise of regular jet planes.

Somewhere over the Atlantic, more than fifty thousand feet up, with all of us strapped into this flying bullet, the Concorde acted as if it had been punched in the nose. The plane shook. Five, six, seven times. That was it. An air pocket, I figured. Then there was a vibration as the plane suddenly began to slow down. The computer screen showing the air speed began to blink backward and the supersonic numbers descended to old-fashioned figures: five hundred miles an hour instead of fifteen hundred.

Apparently, one of the engines had started to rock off, or the wings started to drop off, who knows what it was. But here was the pilot announcing, "We are going to land first at Halifax, Nova Scotia. It is one hour and thirty-two minutes to Halifax."

Many people groaned in disappointment. But a man in back, who had looked out his small window and seen something happen to one of the engines, like the thing blew up a little, was biting his lip.

The pilot now said, "It is one hour and eighteen minutes to Halifax."

A short time later, he said, "It is one hour to Halifax."

I said to myself, The pilot in the cockpit is praying that we make it.

At Halifax, the plane came in low over snow and onto an airport that was crowded with emergency trucks lining the runway, their roof lights twirling, and behind them, what seemed to be every Boy Scout, policeman, and hospital worker in Nova Scotia. They stood in the winter air, ready for an international tragedy, and the Concorde bumped down and then used all but a few yards of the runway before it could be stopped.

I got off the plane and went to the bar for a beer. Standing there, over the next five hours, I saw television all over America carrying reports of the plane's accident, and shaken Frenchmen saying to the cameras, Oh, but this is the first time anything like this ever has happened. The embarrassment over the accident spread like the noise the plane makes.

And now this feeling I had earlier, that I would win, was overpowering. That punch in the nose the Concorde took up in the sky was going to last a long time. I went to the phone and called Ralph Turchio in Howard Beach.

"You can forget the Concorde," I said.

"You think so?" he said.

"They'll get over today," I said. "They'll keep a plane or two going around, but they'll never sell the fleets of them they were counting on. They'll go broke with the thing. Put that down," I told him. I went back to the bar and felt terrific.

(January 1978)

Pocketbook Politics

Let them all stand in grandeur in the sunlight at the treaty-signing on the White House lawn. Have their eyes sparkle with patriotism and pride when the television cameras move in. Then let them be at their most commanding and gracious and pompous and charming at the big state dinner of roast beef, salmon, and wine.

Let them have it all, for it might not be there for too long and they probably don't even know what's happening to them — Carter and Vance and Brzezinski and Jordan and Powell and the rest of them. They talked of the Middle East yesterday, while around the nation their careers were being spilled into checkout counters like the one Debbie Hassenfratz worked at the Pathmark store near the Whitestone Bridge in Queens.

"Forty-four dollars, would you believe it?" the woman said.

Debbie Hassenfratz made the conveyor belt move and past her went some of the woman's order. Charmin, Quik, tomato sauce, Spam, rice, a dozen eggs.

"I don't get any breaks when I buy, why should you?" Debbie said.

"Oh, it's not your fault," the woman said.

"Whose fault is it?" the woman was asked.

"Carter. Who am I supposed to blame, the girl here?"

Debbie Hassenfratz made the conveyor belt move again and here came lettuce, milk, dishwashing liquid, and two cans of Comet and, right after it, Jimmy Carter sliding by on his way back to a peanut warehouse.

There is no political power outside of a gun available to man that is able to withstand a populace that experiences abnormal pain when it reaches for its money. And in the United States, with the most basic cost of all, food prices, rising at such a rate that both the president and the veteran women shoppers can't keep up with it, then the Middle East treaty day, Carter's greatest moment at the White House, could turn into a last hurrah with a drawl.

When they are broke, people throw out the gods and don't even look. At the end of World War II in England, Winston Churchill still was freezing the world with his "fight them on the beaches" command of language. On the streets of Leeds, the working guys put hands into pockets, came up empty, and decided their hero from now on would be a ten-pound note. Churchill was gone. Carter, who can barely speak, is a candidate to disappear so quickly that we might forget he was ever here. "Look at this, three for three dollars and twenty-one cents," the woman said, holding up a small package of lamb chops. "There's just two of us. Imagine if you had three or four children."

Another woman came to the checkout counter. She took a small order out of the shopping cart and placed it on the conveyor. There was bread, chopped meat, dishwashing liquid, a pie, and a couple of tiny cans of green beans. The woman took out a small brown change purse as Debbie's fingers moved over the cash register. The bill was $22.18.

"For nothing," the woman said. She said her name was Lorenza Crespo.

"Is there anything you didn't buy that you wanted to buy today?" she was asked.

"A lot of things," she said. "I saw steak, but it's too expensive now for me. I live by the check. I'm a senior citizen. If the prices keep going up, I'll be eating nothing."

"Do you blame anybody?" she was asked.

"Only the people in charge."

As Debbie's conveyor belt moved, Cy Vance slipped by, on his way back to the Simpson, Thatcher and Bartlett law offices, where he can reminisce to young clerks about the big days in Cairo.

A man leaving the store bumped into me with a cart that was piled high with bags. "How do you like this, seventy-three dollars," he said. "This doesn't even take care of half the week. My wife has to put thirty dollars more into the house. That's thirty dollars that I know about right now. Who knows, by the end of the week it'll cost you double what it costs you today."

He said his name was Mike Napolitano and that he worked as a clerk on Wall Street. "I didn't hardly buy any meat," he said. "I still got to buy meat, buy cold cuts. Imagine if I did that here today? You know what the bill would look like? Do you blame anybody? Who's got the job, that's who you blame." As he pushed the wagon out the door, sitting atop a dozen eggs peeking out of one of the bags was Ziggy Brzezinski, on his way to the Law Library at Columbia University, where he could look up books for a course he'll teach in a coming semester.

At the rear of the store, Leslie Finkelstein and his wife, Laurie, walked slowly along the meat counter, staring, speculating, but not picking up anything.

"Chicken," his wife said.

"What else can you get?" he said. "The prices are ridiculous. I work as a doorman. I take home a hundred and fifty-seven dollars. When we come out shopping, I bring a pocket calculator. It gives you an idea if you've gone over what you have in your pocket. You won't be embarrassed at the checkout counter."

"Do you ever get out at night?" he was asked.

"Thank God for television, it's all we have," he said.

"We can't go anyplace that costs money," his wife said. "We used to."

"When was that?"

"When we were living with his mother."

"If you take a ride in the car, the gas costs too much," Finkelstein said. "So we walk the dog. That's our night out."

There was a rustling in the shopping cart. Good ol' Ham Jordan was trying to get his legs comfortable for the ride back to the big city, Albany, Georgia.

Anthony Dazzo stood in an aisle with his ten-month-old daughter, Lauren, asleep in his arms. He is a sanitation worker. His wife, Mary Lou, looked at green peppers.

"We have three meats a week," she said. "Chicken, chopped meat, and then fish. Count the fish as a meat."

"We eat a lot of macaroni," Dazzo said. "Then the television broke last night just before the fight was supposed to come on. Now we got to pay for that. Figure what that's going to cost."

"Does it make you mad at anybody?"

"You get mad at everybody. It's a vicious circle. You need somebody to put in wage and price controls. If the government doesn't want to do it, maybe you get one that will."

The store was crowded. This particular Pathmark seems to be known for having prices a little lower than elsewhere. The people in the store walk the aisles with the same look that a factory worker has as he walks down a row of machines. Shopping for food has become one of America's most disheartening occupations. And the entire store was cloaked in the silence kept by losers. The only sounds came at the checkout counters, where now and then a housewife murmured as she saw the total Debbie Hassenfratz or one of the others rang up for an order. Somewhere in those little murmurs is more trouble for Jimmy Carter than can be offset by a thousand toasts at a White House state dinner.

(*March 1979*)

The Dream Killer

In the neighborhoods where people live, the legacy of Robert Moses yesterday was Jean Flannery and Eileen Restilla, who walked with their shopping bags on a hot, empty street in Queens where once there were stores.

"We're tired from the heat, after walking from Forty-first Street and Greenpoint Avenue," Jean Flannery said. She was on Forty-fifth Street, a couple of long blocks up from Greenpoint Avenue. "We've still got blocks to go," she said.

"No stores anyplace around here," Eileen Restilla said.

Where they were standing, there once was neighborhood life: a gas station, a butcher, a delicatessen, a fruit stand, two saloons, a barber, a laundry, two candy stores, and houses. There now was only this service road running alongside a high brick wall, atop which the Brooklyn-Queens Expressway cuts through this neighborhood called Laurel Hill. The expressway's brick wall was designed by the architect who did Attica. The service road was built alongside the brick wall because Robert Moses lived his life making it easier for cars to get in and out of New York City. Cars with what he considered to be the right kind of people in them. From the spot where the two women stood with their shopping bags yesterday, the service road goes down a couple of blocks, curves, and becomes an entrance to the Long Island Expressway as it heads into the Queens Midtown Tunnel.

To build this service road, Moses had 350 families thrown out of their homes in a classic New York neighborhood. The 350 families lived in homes that were built before the Depression. The only changes in the neighborhood had been the decrease of vacant lots because of construction of attached one- and two-family houses, the latest of which were less than five years old when Moses suddenly condemned them in 1967. The people who lived in the houses worked for a living, talked to one another, shopped on the streets, walked the dogs, dropped into the saloons for a beer. They tended small gardens in the front and rear of their houses.

Moses had these people thrown out of the neighborhood so he could make it easier for cars, which usually have only one passenger, to drive in from Long Island and then get back out of the city as quickly as possible, for the city, Moses seemed to fear, was a place packed with undesirables: when Moses built Jones Beach, he had the parkway overpasses built so low that a bus from Harlem loses its roof if it tries to take people to the beach. He was a man whose mind was centered on Old Westbury or Westhampton or places equally as vile.

When Moses threw the 350 families out of Laurel Hill in Queens, he said that housing should be provided for the families. "Preferably cooperative," he said, "where Irish melodies can be played on an accordion in a backyard."

On Forty-sixth Street yesterday, Ann Moriarity, sixty-one, looked through her screen door and tried to remember what had happened to the people who once had lived at the end of her block.

"There was a gas station on the corner, then a house. Wait a minute now, I forget the name. His first name was Bill. Then there was a Crowley and a Rogers across the street."

Somebody else knew the whereabouts of one of David Crowley's daughters, who now lives in North Palm Beach, Florida. Her name is Margaret, and she remembers what happened to her family when Moses had them thrown out of their homes.

"My father was a motorman for the BMT, and he got this letter saying that the house was condemned and from now until he had to leave, he had to pay rent to the Triborough Bridge and Tunnel Authority. The letter said that my father would be paid for the house, but they didn't know how much they would pay him. In the meantime, they wanted the rent from him. He no longer owned his own house. Just like that. One day you own a house, the next day they tell you to pay rent for living in it.

"My father had lived in the house for twenty years. When he wasn't working, he was fixing up the house. He always thought he'd live in the place and talk to the people next door until he died. Then Moses came along and charged him rent, and then my father was given twenty-two five for the house. In the condition that my father had the house, the market price should have been thirty thousand dollars. He had to take what they were giving him. They didn't care about him. They cared about a road."

"Did Moses get your family into this co-op housing he promised?" she was asked.

"What co-op? That was fakery. The people in Laurel Hill who had their houses condemned had to make their own way, and on whatever money they were given. My father went to Jersey. He hated it there. Then he retired and went to Ireland. He never got over losing the house."

Everywhere today, Moses will be referred to as the Master Builder, but in Laurel Hill, in Queens, a place where once there was a neighborhood life and now there are weeds growing alongside a brick wall, Moses clearly was nothing more than a Master Executioner of life in this city.

(July 1981)

His Charm Offended Koch

Among atrocities committed in this city last Friday was the incarceration of Joseph Cruz, fifty-five, for the crime of attempting to live decently while being poor. Mr. Cruz was rounded up on what can only be direct orders of Mayor Koch.

With his personal liberty being crunched under the feet of a half dozen policemen and a crowd of bureaucrats bumping against one another, Mr. Cruz was snatched from his living quarters on a traffic island on the East River Drive and then hurled into a mental ward at Bellevue Hospital, where he undoubtedly was filled with enough lithium to turn him into a door.

Before this outrage, Mr. Cruz had demonstrated that he was one of the few who understood that boredom is Earth's greatest plague, that charm depends upon neither money nor the garments covering the body.

I discovered Mr. Cruz's taste yesterday while walking in the footprints he left in this city, a personal adventure that I will relate in detail, but first we must deal with the most urgent matter: Mr. Cruz's being denied the rights of a country for which he fought.

Two years ago he was thrown out of a single-room-occupancy hotel because his Veterans Administration check had arrived late. Cruz inspected the disgraceful chambers the city runs as shelters for the homeless and decided they were beneath his dignity. He became one of our street people, but a highly imaginative one.

Several months ago, he discovered a marvelous spot under the southbound East River Drive at the Sixty-first Street exit. It is a traffic island, a triangle with a low wall separating the island from the cars rushing northbound on the drive. On the open side of the triangle, cars getting off the drive roll slowly by and turn onto Sixty-first Street.

In this spot, with the roof over his head provided by the southbound lanes of the highway, Cruz set up full housekeeping, with bed, stove, and chair. He washed body and clothes in a Parks Department building that is on the other side of the exit lane. He watched tens of thousands of cars race by him, and his other view was of fewer cars and young trees across the street and the Queensboro Bridge and the towering apartment houses of East Side living, which cannot be as good as Cruz's was, because he sat in the open air.

He sat in the open air, and he was different.

When Cruz's home was discovered by the brilliant Bella English of this newspaper, motorists stopped and handed Mr. Cruz money, beer, and encouragement. In return, they got a wave and a smile, giving the motorists perhaps their only cheer of the day. Sitting in his home, drinking his beer, reading a book, smiling as motorists yelled at him, Mr. Cruz never thought of himself as an aggressor.

Oh, but he was. Mr. Cruz was an embarrassment to Mayor Koch, who runs for governor and whose car went past Mr. Cruz on the way to Gracie Mansion each night. For a week, there were so many calls among so many city agencies that it was apparent the bureaucracy was reflecting nervousness and anger from the mayor's office at City Hall.

"Why are they bothering me now?" Mr. Cruz said. "I've been living on the streets for over two years and nobody cared."

But that was before he became part of an election, Mr. Cruz was warned. For in the city now we have Mayor Koch, voice braying, face muscles so tired that his mugging now comes about an eighth beat off, big-footing about the state in search of coronation but finding that he is in a fight that is quite distasteful because perhaps he could lose it.

On Friday, a psychiatrist arrived with Mr. Cruz's daughter, Evelyn. Mr. Cruz did exactly what any sane man would do.

As the only place where Mr. Cruz could run was out onto the highway, he suddenly gave the bureaucracy all that it needed. Mr. Cruz is a danger to himself and others, the psychiatrist ruled.

Mr. Cruz had been living on the island for months, and there is no record of him ever endangering anything except an official reputation or so. But now the claim could be made that he was a nut who played in heavy traffic. So on Friday, on a day when several murders were committed in the city, on a day when there were so many armed robberies, here were six policemen pulling up to the traffic island to grab Mr. Cruz, dismantle his living quarters, and take him to Bellevue and lithium.

Koch's office said that the mayor felt the action was "appropriate" but that Koch most certainly had not personally ordered the action. Which is another reason why Koch soon will be known everywhere as Cop-out Koch.

Bellevue yesterday said that Mr. Cruz is not allowed to leave the psychiatric ward.

Now on Friday, after Mr. Cruz was placed in Bellevue and his living quarters dismantled, city workers placed twenty yellow barrels, each containing fifty-five gallons of sand, on the traffic island. The drums are the Fitch Inertial Barrier System, made in Canada. They are generally placed around highway traffic islands to soften any accidents. But the drums obviously were placed at Sixty-first Street to prevent anybody from replacing Mr. Cruz as a resident.

This situation lasted until yesterday morning, when I arrived at the traffic island with my friend Desmond Crofton.

"It would make a lovely beach," I said.

I went to Crofton's apartment on Fiftieth Street, changed into smashing beachwear, and returned to my private beach with an umbrella, beach chair, radio, and book. I sat in the sun, digging my toes into the sand, and now and then looked up through the leaves of the young maple trees across the street and followed a tramway car as it slid through the sky on the way back from Roosevelt Island.

I found my beach so thoroughly delightful that I remained for quite some time, and I intended to be there with my book and umbrella, waving at motorists, until Joseph Cruz is freed from Bellevue and returned to his home.

But it never should be forgotten that the temper, whim, and nastiness of the city government, certainly reflecting the desires of one man, Cop-out Koch, resulted in citizen Joseph Cruz's being taken by force of police and thrown into a mental ward on a summer weekend merely because he tried to live decently in New York.

(*August 1982*)

The Body Tingles As I Run

When I held out my dollar, the man in the toll booth for the first time in his career pulled back his hand.

"What's this for?" he said.

"The toll," I said.

"Only cars and trucks allowed on the bridge. You're not allowed to walk across."

Walk, how could the man say such a word to me? Would it ever occur to him to use the word *run*, which was what I was going to do? Run right across the Verrazano Bridge, with Manhattan in the mist to the left and the Atlantic Ocean rolling under a bleak sky to the right. A minute or so earlier, while being driven across the bridge to this toll plaza on the Staten Island side, I was beside myself in the car. What a magnificent, invigorating thing it was going to be, starting my day by running across the bridge and seeing these sights as they should be seen, slowly, a sip at a time, and with the heightened joy provided by a body that now is so healthy that it breaks into a sweat at practically the first stride. And now a member of the bureaucracy was telling me that I could not do this.

"I have to run across the bridge," I said.

"You don't have to do nothing," the toll collector said.

"You don't understand," I said.

He didn't. Yesterday, I was going to run the entire New York Marathon course, from this toll plaza across the bridge to Brooklyn, then along the blue line already on the streets, all through Brooklyn and Queens and Manhattan and the Bronx and on to the finish at Central Park. I had it in my mind yesterday morning that it was important to my mental preparation that I run the exact course. All my life I have believed in a creed taught to me by old men who trained racehorses at the tracks around which I grew up. Horses for courses. I intended yesterday to make the marathon course mine, or as much mine as my legs could make it, so that when I run for keeps on October 21 every yard of the way will be totally familiar to my feet and senses.

"Try the office," the toll collector said.

I walked over to the administration building, which sits on the grass alongside the toll plaza. The entrance door was locked and men walking back and forth in the hallway inside the building only glanced at me and walked on.

The cold sea air made itself felt on my bare legs. I began to move about. All I need now, with a week to go to the marathon, is some ridiculous muscle cramp. Finally, a dark-haired man came to the door and opened it. He introduced himself as Michael Motto. He listened to me, and shook his head.

"I can't let you," he said.

"Why?" I asked.

"Because I can't let you," he said.

"This is crazy," I said. "The New York Marathon is the biggest thing the city maybe ever has had and because of a silly rule you won't let me train properly for it."

"Supposing you're going out there to commit suicide," Motto said.

"I'm not!" I said.

"Well, I don't know that," Motto said. "What do you think, we don't get people go over the side on us? When I came here in 1974, the first thing that happened was the father of a guy I used to know came here and went over the side on us. Splash. Gone. Just like that. It happens here every once in a while. We try to be very careful."

"Well, I'm gonna run across it anyway," I said.

"We'll just have to send a truck out after you," Motto said.

Reluctantly, I went back to the car and was driven over the bridge to Brooklyn. I was outraged at the marathon committee and at the city officials who did not have it set up yesterday for runners to use the Verrazano Bridge. The marathon committee had time to figure out the seven locations where runners will be checked on videotape machines on October 21. And the city was able to get the blue line painted on the streets. But nobody thought to ask the people who make the event, the runners, if there was anything they needed. I got out of the car on the Brooklyn side of the bridge and began running along the blue line up Fourth Avenue. I had the irritation fairly well run out of me by the time I passed the place I call the Lineup, on Eighty-sixth Street, where McHugh's, Dougherty's, and Reda's Corner sit in a row. One false step on the way into Dougherty's and you are now drinking in McHugh's. I took a huge breath, turning my chest into a barrel of fall air, in an unconscious protest against all the years spent, half dazed, wreathed in smoke, taking only the shallowest of breaths, in places such as these.

My body tingled as I got into the run. The stride, the stride, the stride. It is everything. Hold it together. Economy of motion. Pain. Of course there is pain. That is why running is the great discipline. A faint, sharp-pleasant smell of Bigeloil, a solution secret to man, was in my nostrils. I bathed myself in it before running. It is the great solution for the thigh muscles. Once, I watched grooms spend literally hundreds of hours rubbing Bigeloil onto the hind legs of horses like Nashua and Bold Ruler. The grooms would then take the Bigeloil home and apply it to the legs of their own children. They reported remarkably few sprains. A year ago, when I first started working toward this marathon, I went to the stable area at Belmont and bought two cases of Bigeloil. It has been of immeasurable help to my legs. And now, while running in yesterday's brisk air, I began to exult. Where would I be if I had not decided to reclaim my life? I would be in a Legion Hall in Florida, comatose with hangover, waiting for somebody to count the straw vote in the first presidential election test. Carter should win. So what? Carter tried to run six miles and they put White House linen in the intensive care unit. Or I could be in Kentucky. Again sitting down.

Sitting while Kennedy makes his first campaign appearance. Me sitting and watching him tell people what he stands for. He stands for what they all stand for. He stands for the job.

Or, worse, I could have been hanging over a police barricade on Lexington Avenue, hanging there like a record striped bass, and spending hours staring at the building where Fidel Castro is staying. Castro, who looks like his only exercise now comes when he waves an arm to indicate how great he is.

In each case, Florida or Kentucky or Lexington Avenue, I would have written a story about somebody else and then made my way home on dull, flabby legs, through whose veins and arteries blood barely seeps.

But here I was yesterday, pulse throbbing as the blood rushed inside me, my confidence soaring with the realization that of all these people I have spent my life writing about, not one of them was able to change one moment of my life or that of anyone else. How important, then, can they be? How important can it be to tell of them when matched beside the great accomplishment of a marathon runner?

As I ran through Brooklyn and into Queens yesterday, I recited over and over the creed of all those entering the great New York Marathon on October 21:

"The credit belongs to the man who is actually in the arena, whose face is marred by dust and sweat and blood.

"A man who knows the great enthusiasms and the great devotions.

"Who spends himself in a worthy cause.

"Who in the end knows the triumph of high achievement.

"And if he fails, at least fails while daring greatly.

"So that his place shall never be with those cold and timid souls.

"A man who knows neither victory nor defeat."

(October 1979)

He Bites the Helping Hand

As this was the first subway ride in days in which someone's elbow was not in my mouth, I was able to talk to the person alongside me on the train from Queens yesterday morning.

He boarded at Jackson Heights, where people usually rush the doors as if attacking the referee at a soccer match. But rather than assault those in his way, he slid in on the oblique and did harm to none. Nice fellow, I thought.

"What's doing?" I asked him.

"I'm going for a job," he said. He held in his hands a yellow state unemployment booklet. "I signed for three weeks, and they still don't get me a check. It's better to work. The man at the unemployment told me to go to this place." He showed me a slip of paper with an address for Stagelight Cosmetics, 630 Ninth Avenue.

"What kind of a job is it?" I asked him.

"Shipping. The man told me they pay a lot of money, pretty good."

"What's a lot of money?"

"A hundred and ninety dollars."

He took out a pay stub from his last job, at David Goldberg, a swimsuit manufacturer in Long Island City. The stub showed he had earned $150 regular time and $109.48 in overtime.

"I wish I had this money this week," he said.

"What happened to the job?" I asked.

"Got laid off. They closed from May until September. I'm going back there when they open again."

He got off at Thirty-fourth Street, walked over to Ninth Avenue, and started looking for the address, which it turned out was above Forty-second Street. So we walked together up Ninth Avenue. It was only a couple of minutes after 8:00 A.M., so there was no rush.

"By the way, what's your name?" I asked.

"José."

"Where are you from?" I asked.

He gave me an address in Corona. "I was born in Santo Domingo. I came here when I was ten. I'm twenty-three now."

He was a good-looking young man, with close-cropped black hair and a mustache. He wore a red Adidas polo shirt, jeans, and Nike sneakers. Good and neat for a shipping clerk, I thought.

"I hope I get this job," he said. "I got a wife. I don't hang out. I want to work for her. She goes to high school."

"If she doesn't work either, how do the two of you survive without a job?" I asked.

"The last money I got, I got to pay rent. Then I got a thirty-eight-dollar bill for electricity. I hope I get this job. I don't like to work in a place pays a hundred and ten. I don't go for that. Once, I made two hundred and twenty dollars clean. That's a lot of money. That's what I hope this job is like."

"I'll go with you," I said.

"Do you want a job, too?" he asked.

"No, I'll just go with you and see. Maybe I can help out."

It was obvious why I did this. Stagelight Cosmetics is located in one of those film center buildings on Ninth Avenue, and I have been around there maybe a thousand times in my life in this city, doing a voice-over for somebody, or a film spot for somebody else; the last time I was around there, I think it was for the Fresh Air Fund. And I thought I would just walk in with this kid and of course somebody would know me right away and I could say, Here's a nice guy needs a job, why don't you put him on?

Stagelight Cosmetics was on the fourth floor. As José and I walked in, a young blond woman in a striped dress looked up from a curved reception desk.

"Hi!" I said loudly, putting the steam on right away.

"May I help you?" she said.

"My man here needs a job," I said.

"I see," she said.

"Of course, I don't need a job," I said. "I already have a job."

"Well, what he has to do is fill out an application," the receptionist said crisply. "There's nobody here right now from shipping."

"If the boss of the whole place is in, I'd be delighted to say hello," I said.

"Why don't you just be seated next to him?" the receptionist said. How could they hire anyone so unaware, I thought.

"I'll bet the boss would like to see me," I said.

The receptionist handed José an employment application form. "You can put down the person who recommended you on this line here," she said, indicating the back of the form. José nodded.

I turned to José. "Put down Jimmy Breslin as a reference," I said loudly. He shrugged. The receptionist became busy.

"Excuse me, miss . . ." I said. She held up her hand as the phone made a low sound.

"Stagelight Cosmetics," she said. "Hold on a minute." She put the phone on hold. Then she called out to someone in a rear office, "Are you in for Arthur Farmer?"

"No, tell him I didn't arrive yet," a voice called out.

The receptionist relayed this message to Arthur Farmer.

"I'll bet he's in for Jimmy Breslin," I said. She didn't seem to hear me. Dope.

A woman holding a container of coffee strolled out of an office.

"I write myself tons of little notes on Friday so I can remember what I'm doing on Monday," she said to the receptionist.

"That's right," the receptionist said.

I turned to José, who was painfully filling out the application form. He did not fill in the "job desired" or "salary desired" blanks. I don't think English is José's strong game.

"Forget it," I told him. "I know what to do." Of course I did. I would sit down and write a very nice column about this young guy looking for a job and everybody at Stagelight Cosmetics would read it and read it again and, forget about it, José would be working and I could once again assure the only person who counts in my life that I was a hero.

José left the application with the receptionist, and we went across the street for coffee.

"Sometimes life looks tough," I said.

"Like the day the judge get mad at me," José said.

"What judge?"

"The judge in Queens. I don't know his name. He gave me zip-three."

"What for?"

"A robbery. I was only eighteen then. The lawyer says, you going up on appeal. I won the case. I was in Elmira nine months and the guard came to me with the letter and he said you won. That was when there was such a big snowstorm that I had to wait a couple of days before I could get out."

"But you learned your lesson from that, didn't you?" I said.

"Oh, sure I did. I don't get in trouble ever. I want to have babies. I got to have money when I have a little boy, a little girl. Working is the only way to get money."

"What do you want to do with your life?" I asked him.

"Try to be somebody," he said.

The last answer did it. So what if he went to Elmira? A guy like this comes off the streets. What is he going to tell you, that he went to Portsmouth Priory and MIT? I'll take some shot for this kid, I told myself.

I said good-bye, and because I was feeling so good with myself for what I was about to do, I decided to walk for a while. Then, I don't know, for one reason or another as I was passing a phone booth, I ducked in and made a call to David Goldberg, the swimsuit place in Long Island City where José had worked.

"I was just checking," I said. "José was laid off, isn't that right?"

"Oh, yes, he was laid off," the guy at David Goldberg said. "He was laid off after I sat here and looked at him on closed-circuit television as he and the elevator operator were about to take half the place out on me."

"Oh," I said.

I hung up. Stagelight Cosmetics! If it were not for some brilliant office help, José would have had so much Stagelight Cosmetics on Roosevelt Avenue in Queens that people would have been smearing it on their clothes. I then did exactly what I always do on these occasions. I went into a bar and it was only ten o'clock, but that was the end of that day. Maybe tomorrow I will try again.

(*June 1981*)

Editors' note: We originally agreed not to publish the following column because of Jimmy Breslin's reluctance to appear in a newspaper where his fellow reporters and writers were on strike. But the column was distributed to other newspapers, through syndication, and is now in the public domain. It's also terribly good. So we're reprinting it now.

Strike in My Business

The big door rolled up and for a moment the black truck stood motionless in the bright light outside the garage building. The crowd behind the barriers out in the street began to scream, "Scab! Scab!" The mounted policemen turned their horses sideways in case they had to dance them against the crowd.

Then the black truck rolled out of the garage and into the street. "Scab! Scab!" the people yelled again, and bottles broke against the side of the truck, which went across the street, stopped, and then pulled into the loading bay of the newspaper building. The noise of the people shouting mixed with the sound of the truck engine and, through it all, there was this continuous sound, a train never stopping, of the printing presses running inside the newspaper building.

It was, I don't know, you lose track of time, somewhere after 11:00 P.M. Earlier, at 2:00 P.M., the newspaper, the New York *Daily News,* had been hit with a strike by the Newspaper Guild.

union of clerical and editorial workers, with the clerical workers usually the most interested in the union and thus nearly always in charge.

The printers' union did not walk out. The stereotypers, pressmen, and mailers did. Management, however, had been able to get all these production jobs done. So whether the newspaper would reach the public or not all came down to the truck drivers. And now, as the first black truck rolled out of the garage, the answer was that the drivers would cross a picket line. The *Daily News* would get out in the face of a strike.

I write for the *News*. I like the paper. I stood at one end of the block, against the wall of the garage building, and watched as a second truck rolled out. A couple of feet away from me, a guild member held up a fist and began screaming obscenities at the truck. The guild member was about five-feet-eight and weighed maybe a hundred and fifty pounds and did not have a mark on his face — a bent nose or a nick or two about the eyes — to show any experience in handling a truck driver who stops his truck and comes out to see somebody cursing him.

I was surprised to find myself having trouble choosing between the truck and the guild member.

I was raised to believe that the bosses always were lousy and that any human who crossed a picket line deserved anything that happened to him. My favorite line comes from Local 824, International Longshoremen's Association. One February day, as they picketed along the edge of the cold, gray Hudson River, they were asked why it was that no scabs ever appeared at ILA strikes. In unison, the Local 824 members called out the answer: "Splash!"

But now, in the noise in the street behind the newspaper I write for, there was no romantic slogan and no clear feeling. What do I do in the morning? I asked myself. In the morning I was due to turn in a column to the newspaper. I began saying to myself, Why shouldn't I turn in a column? I'm not a member of any guild anymore. I'm a columnist with a contract. I'm not strikebreaking; I'm living up to my obligations, all of this mixed with the old labor sentiments within me. I still could not choose between truck and picket. I edged away from the pickets in the street because I did not want anybody to ask me whether I would write for the paper the next day.

All my life, I thought I had ideals about a thing such as this. I went along coasting for years and now suddenly I was challenged and I found I was at a loss to make a judgment. I was not a kid walking out of a soup factory and throwing a rock through the window and shouting, "Yeah, tell that Dick, that rat boss, to come outside and I got one for him too." That day was so long ago it was an embarrassment to remember it. Now I am a columnist who is over forty-five and I found in one night that I had changed and so had everything about me.

And the next morning I had my agent call up and say that I'd like to go on vacation. Magnificent courage! The management of the paper said, "He wants things both ways. He wants to be a big columnist, outside of any union jurisdiction, and then at the same time he doesn't want to stand up with management people when there is labor trouble."

Which was the most dastardly act of all: telling the truth about me. And it was the start of a day of fluttering and quavering during which I did nothing to distinguish myself, and at the end of which the paper and I agreed that the column would not run in the paper, the *News*, because I had developed such an image of being on the side of the poor against the rich, union against management, that it perhaps could be harmful to the column's image to have it appear in a paper that is being put out during a strike.

My column did not appear in the *News*, then, because of a great principle: I have done so well writing about the working guy that nothing should be done to distort that image.

Which is such a magnificent thing to be able to say about yourself that at the end of the day I felt a compelling need to go to a bar and perhaps never return.

Oh, of course, the decision will cost me money. But it will not cost me everything. And I give it up for self-advertisement, not lifelong belief. I have changed: too many years, too many strikes, I find, have turned me around inside.

I also have decided that I am not alone. All of New York's view of labor has changed. Once, in New York, a charge of strikebreaking was second only to homicide. But yesterday, people had no compunction about picking up the *News* at newsstands. Old prejudices seem to be gone because there is no true social reason to join a union anymore. People no longer scream about the "bosses," for there is never one person, you see, who owns a place.

At the *News* the other night, there were, here and there in open doorways, these thin, young, straight-faced management people in business suits. A shower of bastards, the Irish call them. But these people were not owners; they were only arrogant bureaucrats. And the people out on the street were not "us." The strike leader for the guild was a computer operator and the editorial people spoke of him in such disgust that union solidarity seemed only a matter for the moment.

All of unionism has changed. The head of organized labor in the country is George Meany, who collects a six-figure salary and who spent more time supporting a war that killed the sons of the poor than he did worrying about the poor and the workers of the country. George Meany comes from the South Bronx, where there are no jobs, and he spends his time worrying about Russia.

Most of the unemployed and most of the bottom 20 percent or so of the American working force is black. The highest individual black union man in the country is Frederick O'Neill of Actors Equity, who sits on the executive board of the AFL-CIO. If he has power, nobody else has been told about it.

So there has not been, in organized labor, the traditional pass-along that allowed the Irish and Italians and Jews to rise from the streets to the banks. The old forms stop when they run into the blacks. And so now, when it is the blacks who need the full protection of traditional movements in this country, there is no willingness to give protection. And the movements suddenly change.

The public becomes tired of the growth of both big government and big labor. Therefore, the public cheers a Proposition 13, and today in New York, in the world's great union town, it is acceptable. You can put out a newspaper against a strike and readers will not boycott it. This was something, you always thought, that could happen only in a place like Washington, D.C., a Southern town actually, where *The Washington Post* could break a strike and receive almost no pressure from the working people reading the paper. Now you find it can happen in New York.

(June 1978)

Never Trust People from Chicago

For the past several weeks, I have been edging toward the doorway, jacket on, whistling softly, waiting for an indication that it was time to step out of the newspaper business. As this newspaper, the *Daily News* newspaper, was under the control of hicks from Chicago, a place which raises people who are as stupid as steers, I expected the indication to be subtle: three guys from Chicago carrying a huge padlock, dropping it, someone's toes being broken, the two remaining guys picking the padlock up again and closing the place while the victim with broken toes bellowed.

They had abused a part of the life of New York City. A newspaper belongs to those who now read it in the mornings and trust it to tell them of the life of the city about them, and to those who read it and trusted it in the past and are now gone, and to those who worked on it and are gone and to those who work on it, and to the lights and traffic and noise and excitement of the crowded streets and the subways beneath.

At one time last week, it seemed that the Chicago people had managed something even worse than a padlock. Here came a young builder named Junior with a Big Ego, who let it be known that he was going to buy the newspaper. His civic responsibility in the past consisted of getting tax abatements. The worst political and public-relations riffraff in the city spent days on the telephone congratulating themselves on this happening. The tax abatement builder had as his spokesman a woman named Moonlight or Sunshine or something like that. I know she is on the pad of the New York State Thruway Authority. She is a political subhack who raised money for Society Carey. She received $17,000 a year, a state car, and free gas for driving on the thruway. She was making announcements about the *Daily News* newspaper for Junior with a Big Ego.

Of course, I told myself, I was out of the business. The *Daily News* newspaper was about to enter a phase that would be at least grotesque. And downtown, the *New York Post* newspaper is in the hands of a publisher named Green Card Murdoch, who is a citizen of Australia and often can be found in London, waiting for the chance to fall on his knees in front of the queen and be made a knight or sir or whatever it is that the silly woman gives out to supplicants.

Positively over, I told myself. It wouldn't be the first time I was out of the business, either. In my time, I have written for some of the best and worst newspapers and I have gone through the doorway in many fashions. The first time was by demand.

I had a job at the old *Long Island Press* in Queens, working nights in the sports department. I spent the days standing at a bar and watching the sunlight turn the glass in my hand into gold. No wonder I stopped attending church frequently; I thought that I had found heaven on my own terms in the bar in the daytime. It happened that one summer day I left the bar in the afternoon, drove out to Fire Island, and was caught in a great thunderstorm. I was drenched to the skin. I stripped down to the skin, wrapped myself in a blanket, and arrived at the paper just in time for work. I had the blanket about me, my wet clothes draped on a chair, and I sat at a typewriter and tried to type with one hand, the other clutching the blanket about me. The sports department was located across the hall from the women's department. At night, it was the habit of proud Queens mothers to escort their daughters to the newspaper office in order to deliver an engagement notice and a photo of the ecstatic daughter.

On this night, I was typing away with one hand, the other clutching the blanket, quite groggy from drink taken during the day, when I heard a noise. Here walking into the sports department, by mistake, was a smiling Queens mother and her bride-to-be daughter. A gentleman, I stood up. This caused the blanket to drop from my body. Standing wonderfully naked, I asked mother and daughter, "Can I help you?" The mother gasped, the daughter gave a small shriek, and they were gone. The next morning, I, too, was gone from the newspaper.

I was remembering this, somewhere early Thursday, and I laughed about it and told myself that it was too bad that I couldn't leave the same way this time. I decided to make a fine, self-confident departure from the newspaper.

At which point, Joe Allbriton flew into New York, announced that he was the one who intended to buy the *Daily News* newspaper, and the first thing he said to somebody was that he thought it was going to be a lot of fun to make it with a newspaper of the size and meaning of the *Daily News* newspaper. Of course, he knew the only word to use in connection with this business: If it isn't fun, then nobody belongs in a newspaper office. In one move, the situation at this newspaper went from bizarre to reasonable. I sat in a place on Second Avenue and said, Well, soon you will be back at your trade full-time.

Next thing, there was a call from NBC asking if I could publicize a show that was based on something I wrote a couple of years ago. The show was running on April 25 from 9:00 to 10:30 P.M. The show is called "The Neighborhood" and was originally written for Fred Silverman at ABC. At the time, I thought the producer, David Gerber, had done a poor job of casting. He took an hour-and-a-half show about a street in Brooklyn and used actors from Hollywood, and even worse — one of them told me that he had been acting in Minneapolis, I believe. When the show was finished, Silverman saw it and put it on the shelf. Now, the NBC guy calling me said, the new head of NBC, Grant Tinker, loved the show. "It must be because you're great," he told me.

I felt terrific. Because I knew, by this hour in the fifth bar on Second Avenue, that I was truly great. Then I met someone at the bar who knew television and who told me, "When they made that show, there was a guy in it that nobody knew. Howard Rollins. Now he just got an Oscar nomination for *Ragtime* and so they have to be crazy not to run an hour-and-a-half show with him in it. Who knows, maybe they can get a series out of it as long as they have Rollins."

"Did Rollins ever act in Minneapolis?" I asked.

"I think he did," the guy said.

"Then maybe they're not putting the show on because of me," I said.

"Maybe," the guy said.

Fair enough. I will take victory any way it comes. And with my luck going this way, I know exactly how to take advantage of it. Oh, I understand perfectly how to deal with runs of good luck. First, on Thursday, I knew I had to write something for the *Daily News* newspaper. This is now accomplished. Therefore I am now going to sit down with the great Eddie Kay, the workingman's handicapper, and he is going to pick horses for me that will win. I know I am going to win, win heavily, because I know luck perhaps better than anyone now alive in this city.

I cannot win all this money today, because it is Palm Sunday and the track is closed. Therefore, I shall win all this money tomorrow. As Eddie Kay did not get Monday's entries until last night, and thus was unable to follow proper handicapping procedures in time for me to reveal his winners right here, you must wait until tomorrow morning for his selections. As I do not write in the *Daily News* newspaper this Monday, people who truly need money can call me at 949-2479 and I will tell them the horses that are surely going to win.

I specify that only those in true need of money should call, because I do not want the phone lines to this office tied up by people who are greedy. Need is fine. Please remember, however, that you are calling the offices of a busy newspaper, the *Daily News* newspaper, a paper that will be here for a long time, and the people in the office must be allowed to do their work, which is reporting on the life of the city, just as this newspaper has done so uniquely for so long.

(*April 1982*)

"Por Unas Horas"

One day in April of 1980, Cibella Borges, then a twenty-two-year-old who earned a little over $100 a week as a police department civilian administrative aide, teaching typing at the Police Academy, met a photographer who offered her $150 for posing for pictures that were supposed to give all men the thought of incredible pleasure.

Not quite. Some men who saw her pictures in a magazine had, rather than boiling loins, a cold wind of fear inside. This has caused Cibella, now twenty-five, great trouble.

She sat at the kitchen table of her steaming apartment and waited for her aunt to bring a copy of the magazine. Cibella's mother, Norma, fifty, making coffee, said, *"Por unas horas."*

"She is saying," Cibella said, "that all this is just for a couple of hours. That's all I spent posing for the pictures."

The mother said, "Would it be better if she appeared on the front page of a newspaper shot dead or on the last page of a nudie magazine?"

The daughter, wearing a T-shirt and jeans, went to look out the window for her aunt. *"Por unas horas,"* she said. "And now it does not end."

When she had been asked to pose, back in 1980, Cibella, who had been operated on once for a cyst, had just been informed that she needed another operation and this one probably would end her ability to bear children. "What's the difference, I can't have any kids, so who's going to marry me?" Cibella said. She went to a studio on the West Side, posed for the pictures, put on her clothes, and went home to Orchard Street, where her front door is between two stores, one selling baby clothes and the other men's suits. Clothes hung outside the stores and blew in the wind over Cibella's head as she came home. Her apartment was two floors up.

Nobody ever said Cibella Borges was another Brooke Shields. The child pornography pictures of Brooke Shields were so acceptable to the public that Brooke enrolled at Princeton, where, next fall, gallant young men probably will go charging through the line in hopes of gaining her smile. Cibella Borges of Orchard Street, whose poses had been at least a bit rough, saw neither stardom nor Ivy League schools in her future. She made application to take the police department exam for patrolman.

Her photographer spent many months showing the pictures around town to editors who work in the city's literary underground. Finally, he was able to sell them to a magazine named *Beaver,* which is a publication read with one hand. The *Beaver* editor put the pictures in a file for use sometime. He had no idea of the name of the small Hispanic woman in the pictures.

As months went by, Cibella Borges took the patrolman's exam, passed, attended the Police Academy, and then was sworn in as a police officer late in 1981. At four-foot-eleven and ninety-five pounds, she was the smallest police officer in the department's history. She also spoke Spanish in a city where there are far more Hispanics than there are citizens with Irish names, although the police department is commanded almost entirely by middle-aged Irish Catholics.

Working her job, Cibella, and another officer, stopped a car at Bleecker and Charles, ordered the three occupants out, and found three guns on the front seat. The three previously had committed armed robberies, and for her part in the arrest, Cibella was given a meritorious service medal. She then was transferred to the Nineteenth Precinct on the Upper East Side of Manhattan.

And then on the night of July 27, 1982, nine months after Cibella Borges had started as a police officer, there arrived on the cheaper newsstands in town these stacks of the magazine *Beaver.* A police officer from the Nineteenth Precinct picked up the magazine while going around on his midnight-to-eight tour. There is no record of an arrest being made on a newsstand dealer who forced *Beaver* magazine on the police officer. As the magazine is priced at $2.95, it does not take a cynic to figure out how *Beaver* magazine got from a newsstand to the precinct: the badge beats a grappling hook.

Back at the precinct, the cop went through *Beaver,* whose index listed photo layouts for Sheena, Jackie and Pattie, Corrie, Lisa, and, on page fifty-six, Nina. The cop went through the magazine page by page and, reaching page fifty-six, noticed that not only were the pictures particularly dirty, but the layout starred Police Officer Cibella Borges. The cop took the magazine to his sergeant. The sergeant was aghast. The sergeant gave the magazine to the lieutenant. The lieutenant was shocked. When Cibella was told about the magazine, she went downstairs and found the lieutenant showing the magazine to a whole group of cops. She remembers that as she walked in, the lieutenant shoved the magazine into his desk. Then he took it out as if it were a communicable disease, dropped it on the desk, and allowed her to look.

"This is very serious," he said.

"I posed for these pictures before I came on the force," Cibella said, staring at pictures of her bottom. "I forgot all about them."

Three days later, members of the New York Police Department Internal Affairs Division questioned Cibella. An inspector, captain, and lieutenant, sitting in an office, with *Beaver* magazine in front of them. They hastily shoved it under a pile of papers. They now began to talk to Cibella about pictures taken for the magazine before she even took the test and long before she took the oath as a police officer.

One of the internal affairs men asked Cibella if she ever had thought, while working as a civilian administrative aide in 1980, of the tremendous disgrace she would bring upon the police department by posing for dirty naked pictures. Another wanted to know why she hadn't listed her one-day modeling job in the "previous employment" space on her department application.

The police department should have been proud of the pictures, as they prove that at least one member of the force is in marvelous physical condition; most officers are in such deplorable shape that if called upon to pose for pictures, they would first put on overcoats.

Yet Cibella was in trouble. As an Hispanic, she could not invoke the rules of the Irish-dominated force: the surest way an Irish cop explains away most offenses, and particularly sex offenses, is to claim alcoholism. Misuse of alcohol is acceptable to the Irish; misuse of the body calls for condemnation to a chamber of Hell. If born Irish, Cibella could have walked into the hearing and said, "I drink too much and I don't know what I'm doing. In fact, I'm thirsty right now." Instead, being a dirty Hispanic, she had to admit openly that she had posed for naked pictures. Promoting sins of the flesh!

The most famous defense at a departmental trial was on behalf of a police officer charged with making a Puerto Rican housewife pregnant. The officer's captain appeared as a defense witness at the trial. The captain said it was impossible for the man to make the woman pregnant because the man was a good Irish Roman Catholic with five children at home. If he ever had screwed this Puerto Rican, he would have worn a condom; the officer was too good of a Catholic, the testifying captain insisted, to be unprotected with a Puerto Rican and then go home and sleep with his wife.

One member of the trial board was miserable enough to ask the witness why the officer was in the Puerto Rican woman's apartment to begin with. The captain said, "The man has a drinking problem." The members of the trial board nodded understandingly and the cop was saved.

Cibella Borges, being a dirty Puerto Rican, unable to cry whisky, was dismissed from the force. The police commissioner, who is known as Dead Body McGuire and who has stayed on the payroll longer than any commissioner in memory, who has 9000 murders and 500,000 armed robberies committed while he clings so tightly to his job that the desk squeaks, announced that the pictures were repulsive and he fired Cibella for posing for dirty pictures that were taken nearly a full year before she was sworn in as a cop. These aging Irish Catholics who run the police department are frightened of sex, which is at best the Act of Darkness, and becomes dangerous when it is being committed by some dirty naked Puerto Rican. The Devil in the squad room!

It was at this point that Cibella Borges's mother squalled, "What about the men who are on the police and they take women and they take drugs and they take money?"

There was no answer from the aging Irish. It seemed to me that if we are to have a pure police force, Norma Borges's charges must be confronted. If indeed there was dirty lewd behavior by cops, then the citizens of the city must involve themselves. I volunteered to become an assistant keeper of the morals for the department. For a long time, I had observed police officers ducking in and out of photo-developing shops to pick up sets of photos from private swimming pool parties. And of course I had observed young women out with married police. As an assistant keeper of the morals, I asked every woman who goes out with a married cop to send me the name, shield number, and either the exact location or a description of the place where she meets him. I then would send one copy to the police commissioner, Dead Body McGuire, and the other to the cop's home.

The next mail brought a letter from the Bronx. I immediately wrote in that day's column, "That detective in the Fifty-second in the Bronx who told his girlfriend that he was single and then he got nervous and transferred . . . she knows."

I also read a letter about a summer house at Kennedy Lane, Hampton Bays, where cops and firemen acted like savages with women to whom they were not married. I put that in the paper.

Early, a couple of mornings later, I was having coffee on Third Avenue and was surprised to see a full-page advertisement about me, a direct personal attack on me, in my newspaper, the *Daily News* newspaper. The organization that took the ad, the Patrolmen's Benevolent Association, paid the *News* newspaper, I learned later, exactly $16,240 for the ad.

The writer was guilty of premature semicolons and had the periods outside quotation marks, but the type was nice, the PBA badge at the bottom looked good, and it also was nice to know that the PBA can get mad at something. The problem was, the union was supposed to be representing Borges, who had been paying dues for a year and was a union member in a union city being dismissed for a most minor point. Always, policemen charged with things far more serious, crimes and murders, have a crowd of officers about them in the courthouse and the head of the PBA shouting that the man is innocent. For Cibella Borges, an Hispanic woman who posed for dirty pictures before becoming a police officer, the union did nothing. Instead, they paid over $16,000 for an ad attacking some newspaper writer.

The funny thing about the ad was that, while I could sort of understand it if the head of the union was, like so many of the cops, some fat Irish guy afraid of sex, the guy who is the PBA head now is Italian. They are a people who are supposed to love sex. Still, he refused to help Cibella. The nasty thought arose that the police union did not stand up for a member because in this case she was Hispanic and female.

And Cibella Borges has been suspended from her job, which paid over $400 a week, the most money anybody in her family ever had earned, and she was off the payroll because she posed for dirty pictures before she became a cop.

(*August 1982*)

He Be Robbin'

There were about twenty-five of them playing pitty pat, a card game, on the stone table in the schoolyard behind PS 59 in Brooklyn through the hot afternoon yesterday. They had dimes and quarters on the table. There were no jobs to go to, and it was too early for beer.

"Who went to the Diana Ross concert?" they were asked.

"Me," Chantal Monique Folk, fifteen, said. She held her ten-month-old cousin, Stephen, in her arms.

"Both times," Stephanie Mills, eighteen, said.

"Me!" somebody else shouted.

"We all went!"

"Him!" a girl shrieked, pointing at a young boy, who immediately put an arm over his face.

"How many of you behaved?" they were asked.

"He didn't!" the girl shrieked, pointing again at the young boy, who said nothing.

But an older boy, Jeff White, sixteen, sitting on the card table, said, "Put my address down. Apartment Four D, Eighty-eight Park Avenue." He had on a tan tank top and yellow headband. A dime was stuck in his right ear. "Never mind concerts. They're gone. You better worry about today. They vic you around here."

"Vic?"

"Victim. They make a victim out of you around here," Jeff White said.

The girl pointed at the young boy again and said, "He be a criminal. He be robbin'."

"Did you rob anything at the concert?" the young boy was asked. He looked about ten. He shook his head.

"He be robbin'!" the girl shrieked again.

"Were you in one of the packs?" the boy was asked.

"No packs around here," an older boy said. "Here, you call them crews. We're the SCC. The Sumner Crash Crew. That's from

Sumner Avenue. I smoke White Owl blunts. That's the new thing. The Sumner Crash Crew smokes White Owl blunts. This isn't the whole crew. The rest of them are out scopin'. Looking for vics. You go down the next block, they have the Tompkins Boys. That's after Tompkins Avenue. That's another crew. Everybody went to the concert was in a crew."

"Were you mad at white people?" he was asked.

One of the girls jumped in and yelled, "They're not mad at whites! They're mad at gold. Gold make you jealous. Snatch gold off anybody. Snatch gold off a black lady."

Jeff White said, "Cazzies."

"What's that?"

"Cazal glasses. They got the gold on the sides. You grab them."

"Has anybody got a pair with him so I can see what they look like?" he was asked.

Everybody around the card table laughed. "You need a tool to protect you with Cazals," Jeff White said.

"They cost you a hundred and fifty, maybe two hundred dollars," a girl said.

Thomas Ridges said, "They're glasses without lenses. You go and buy the frames. Then the man puts the gold by the part that goes over your ears. Anyone who can afford them wears them."

"I've never seen them before," he was told.

"Whites don't wear them. Any blacks who can afford them wear them. That was the big thing at the concert. Snatch Cazals. The gold is more important than whites."

Two of them, black and young, probably as strong as you want, were leaning against the schoolyard fence. One of them, in a black baseball cap and blue shirt, said, "I went to the concert. I don't want to tell you if I behaved or not."

The one next to him laughed. He had on a black sweatshirt and a white baseball cap worn backward. He said his name was Terry and that he was nineteen.

"What time did you get to the concert?" Terry was asked.

"Four-thirty."

"Where did you sit?"

"Stay right in front. Where you can see."

"How did you like the concert?"

"She was singing. There was a mob."

A girl named Pat Rivers, twelve, who was on a bicycle, yelled,

"Diana Ross was wonderful! She sang 'Together.' I was going to write her a letter and ask her to be my godmother."

"What happened when she stopped singing?" Terry was asked.

"Youths got going."

"Were they afraid of the police?"

"Youths got going."

A girl said, "They throw firecrackers up. Make believe it's guns going off. Everybody got scared and started to run."

Jeff White hit his fist into his palm. Then he reached out as if to grab something. He pulled his hand back and banged his palm again. "Hit and pull, hit and pull," he said.

Against the fence, Terry pulled his white baseball cap around in glee.

"Did you get going?" he was asked.

A girl in the crowd jumped up and down and pointed at him. "Yes, he did. He did his regular thing."

"What did you take?" Terry was asked.

"Chains."

"What do you do with the chains?" he was asked.

"Sell them."

"Take it to Lenny's," Jeff White called out.

"Listen to him," somebody said. "He droppin' a dime on Lenny."

"I'm dropping a quarter on him right now," Jeff White said.

"What's the difference between dropping a dime and a quarter?" he was asked.

"You drop a dime, that's ghetto talk for telling on somebody. Put a dime in the phone and call up on him. If you say you drop a quarter, that means you got a lot more to tell on him. If you drop a dollar, you may get killed for it."

"How much does Lenny give you for your chains?"

"He gave you fifty dollars," Terry, in the white baseball cap, said.

"Is that good?" he was asked.

"If you start out with nothing and come home with fifty dollars, you can't say that's bad," he said.

The crowd had grown now, and there probably were fifty people around the card table and they all howled at this. "We went to the concert to get paid!" a boy shouted. "They said it was a free concert, but we went there to get paid."

(July 1983)

2

"Not a Social Viewpoint, Merely Addition"

"More bodies! A whole week and nothing but dead bodies!" O'Neill groaned as he scanned the first take of the column. "Dammit, Breslin, you can't wallow around in misery all the time. It'll turn off the readers. Write about something light and funny, like the trouble you're having with your kids, something to take everybody's mind off all the violence."

"Awright, awright!" he grumbled, and knocked out two or three hilarious columns about his wife, the former Rosemary Dattolico, or his mother-in-law, or the kids who left him home alone the night he wanted to show what a good father he was. But then, as inevitably as an incoming tide, he returned to the subject which fascinated him more than anything else: violent crime in the richest city on earth.

. As it happened, the same subject also gripped millions of New Yorkers with fear and outrage, with ceaseless puzzlement over the paradox of a highly civilized community besieged by more muggings and murders than all of Western Europe. Editors, preferring novelty to the commonplace, might suffer lapses of interest, but the public never did. In every opinion poll taken during the 1960s and 1970s, people put crime at the top of their list of concerns, ahead of housing, jobs, or anything else. Breslin's readers shared his preoccupation.

So did the double-domes. They swarmed all over the issue with their studies, their theories, and would-be solutions. But the muggers, not knowing what was expected of them, kept ambushing old women along the Grand Concourse in the Bronx. The experts had never sweated their way up a tenement stairway on a Signal 1085. For all their Ph.D.'s, they teach us less than Breslin, with his high school diploma, who carries us inside the lives of real criminals and real victims and, in this vicarious way, helps us to understand what statistics cannot explain.

Like Dostoevski in *Crime and Punishment,* Breslin looks into the smallest cells of human nature to expose the elemental passions, the cultural tensions, the irrationality, the economic and social pressures that lead to acts of violence. Raskolnikov cried out: "I wanted to have the daring, and I killed her. I only wanted to have the daring, Sonia!" Listen to the echo in a Breslin column about a fatal fight on a basketball court in Brooklyn, as a boy named Kenny Brown tells how his friend Tyrone Hampton was killed because his attackers wanted his red Pumas. "They was brand-new, that's probably why they took them," he explained. Just a boy's thought. Only a small incident, now forgotten, one tiny cell in the city's plasmic sea. But individual cells are the incubators of larger social disorder, harbingers of the crime epidemics, demonstrations, and riots that eventually arouse political leaders and experts from their sleep. New York's future turns up sooner in a Breslin column than in a social tract.

In "the shacks" across from the Bergen Street Station in Brooklyn, when we worked there years ago, reporters covered murders in a mostly sanitary way, getting their tips from "slips" torn off the police teletype and querying detectives for additional details. They seldom rode to the scene, except to cadge or steal a "studio" (photo) of the victim, and their hastily assembled reports were as devoid of graphic detail as a bank statement. Things have improved in recent years, but most reporters still have a hard time matching Breslin when it comes to working a crime story, elbowing his way into blood-spattered rooms, talking to survivors and witnesses, spending hours interviewing neighbors, pursuing questions others didn't think to ask, and developing story angles his colleagues avoid.

When Calvin Klein's daughter Marci was kidnapped in 1978, Breslin immediately rushed to the scene on Park Avenue, between Ninety-sixth and Ninety-seventh streets. But, as usual, he bypassed the cops and the FBI, ignored the unruly mob of fellow reporters and photographers, and began prowling the neighborhood for clues, describing himself "with his collar open and his eyes narrowed as he observed everybody with suspicion." He dragged his resisting body up five flights to the empty apartment of Paule Ransay, a former Klein baby-sitter implicated in the case. Nothing. Then he moved along to the Pioneer Supermarket on Park where the Ransay girl once worked. There, he finally found and interviewed a clerk named Cecil Wiggins, who admitted he knew Christine but was suspiciously closemouthed. Hours later, the FBI finally caught up with Wiggins and charged him with being in on the kidnapping.

Sometimes, Breslin gets so carried away with his sleuthing he becomes a major character in the drama. In one of the biggest crime stories in New York history, the Son of Sam murders, he was so deeply involved he became a storm center, accused of "sensationalism," "irresponsibility," and worse. Admittedly, he dove overboard in one or more of his many columns. The *News* was also guilty of an occasional excess in its news coverage, something that could be explained but not necessarily excused by the enormous competitive pressures. But a lot of the criticism was also hopelessly off the mark and often uninformed.

One example was an intemperate attack by the *New Yorker* magazine. Among other things, it condemned Breslin for publishing a letter he had received in June 1977 from someone who later turned out to be David Berkowitz, the .44-caliber killer who attacked brown-haired women on orders from a mystery man named Sam. "Tell me, Jim, what will you have for July 29?" the letter asked, referring to the first anniversary of a rampage that ultimately killed six people and wounded seven. "You can forget about me if you like because I don't care for publicity. However, you must not forget Donna Lauria [a victim] and you cannot let the people forget her, either. She was a very very sweet girl but Sam's a thirsty lad and he won't let me stop killing until he gets his fill of blood."

The New Yorker suggested that a more responsible journalist would never have printed the letter and given the killer, it assumed, the idea of striking again. What the magazine could have known, if it had done any reporting itself, is that Breslin actually had turned the letter over to the police as soon as he got it. He only put it in his column — and we only agreed to publish it — after the police specifically requested that we do so. As *Newsweek* reported, more accurately than *The New Yorker,* the authorities hoped publication would establish "some communication with the killer that might provide more clues to his identity." In fact, the letter to Breslin eventually played a key role in breaking the case.

Although Breslin was furious with his critics, noting that Shakespeare never shied away from the subject of murder and referring to the *New Yorker* crowd as people who sit in the Algonquin lobby sipping daiquiris "while discussing such as the Herb Society of America," he reveled in the attention he was getting and, especially, in the knowledge that he had beaten his colleagues on major developments in a big story.

But he is less interested in scoops, although very competitive, than in collecting masses of intimate detail to re-create the real world of crime. He does this with compelling effect. A woman climbing her apartment stairs one night was immediately on her guard when a stranger made a casual remark. "Years spent on Bronx staircases," Breslin wrote, "staircases such as this, being assaulted once, told her that when a stranger speaks to you on a staircase at night, he's only doing so in order to ease your fear and make it easier for him to attack." Again, in another column, about an eleven-year-old boy who helped steal a car and then saw cops kill his friend, Breslin reveals in the boy's own words the social anarchy that brews violence, how he had been expelled from school for fighting and couldn't even read.

For the most part, Breslin tells his stories in the dialogue of the streets, the dialogue of Rikers Island prison, where "take him off the count" is the way they say someone should be killed. He lets readers draw their own conclusions. But he has his own gloomy convictions about the reasons for the violence in New York, attributing it mostly to massive poverty, unemployment, poor education, and drugs among the black and Hispanic minorities. The underclass, he says, produces "heartless people" who kill cops for no reason at all. "They'll die young, or go to jail. And there are more of them tomorrow, and more to be with us through all the tomorrows, the way we are going. This is not a social viewpoint, it is merely addition."

As we have seen, a major blowup occurred in the spring of 1983 when Breslin denounced the police department for firing a young officer who had posed nude for a girlie magazine, calling it hypocrisy when male officers were cheating on their wives, photographing "private swimming pool parties," and moonlighting as guards in after-hour bars that were merchandising illicit sex. The Patrolmen's Benevolent Association fired back with a full-page ad in the *News*, accusing "The Old Saloon Philosopher" of "irrational, irresponsible ravings," calling him an "arrogant, immoral sop," and charging he couldn't even pass the physical and intelligence tests to be a cop.

We tried to give the cops a fair shake, supporting Breslin when he was right and admitting when he was wrong. But our relations with the police department were never smooth, far different from an earlier age when the *Daily News* seldom questioned the cops' version of any crime.

In keeping with his populist nature, Breslin strongly opposes the death penalty. "I know of no way to become more popular with a typewriter than to type out angry sentences calling for people to be thrown into the electric chair in retaliation for the death of a policeman," he wrote in one column. "And I know of no greater fakery than to do so. For capital punishment is nothing more than an attempt to fool people into feeling that — at last — something is being done about crime."

He has no romantic notions, however, about the violence he knows so well. Whatever social improvement might promise in the future, he saw crime become more senseless and savage in the 1970s and his views hardened. He killed off some of his own favorite characters, like Marvin the Torch, because there was no longer any room for "Guys and Dolls" in a city where criminals gave heroin to children. He also buried other characters drawn from Attica prison because the convicts he knew were gone, replaced by blacks and Hispanics. "Where once the prison handled many of the individual failures in society, the prisons now suddenly reflected the failure of much of society itself," he observed with despond.

So, over the years, Breslin has changed and his columns have changed. "The notion of lovable hoodlums in today's city," he wrote, "where the business of organized crime consists of drug peddling and virtually nothing else, is not discussable. A writer such as Damon Runyon would be busy on a rewrite desk today. Life is too complicated for the Runyon point of view."

In New York City, in the 1970s and 1980s, Breslin saw the human condition laid bare by violence, stripped of its shielding layers of moral restraint and public convention, and he did not like what he saw. The illusions of his Kennedy years were gone.

— M.J.O.

For a Pair of Red Pumas

They had been up all night and now they sat by a living-room window that was open to the noise and heavy air of a Brooklyn morning.

"Clyde had on red Pumas," Kenny Brown said.

"What did the others have on?" his mother asked.

"Pro Keds."

"Pro Keds won't do," his mother said. "Got to be Pumas or Adidas."

The night had started with Kenny Brown and his friend Tyrone Hampton, seventeen, playing baseball. Tyrone wore the red Pumas he had bought with his first paycheck for being a day-camp counselor for a city summer youth program. He bought the red Pumas at Syl's on Nostrand Avenue and they took $31.39 out of the $69 check.

Hampton and Brown lived on Pacific Street and they played at a park on Atlantic Avenue, a block away. The park has two floodlights on a pole that give just enough light for the basket to be seen. This makes the place popular with young people, who wait until late in the evening for the air to cool and the cement to lose its heat before starting any games.

Somewhere around midnight, there were ten playing on the court, including Hampton and Brown, and one of the players, known only as Brian, got into a shoving match under the basket with Anthony Lee, sixteen.

"The dude smacked Anthony in the face," Kenny Brown remembers. "Anthony said, 'I'm going home, get my stuff.' Just like that."

Kenny Brown and Tyrone Hampton had not been part of the scuffle and they remained on the court after Brian, Anthony Lee and everybody else had gone. Tyrone Hampton, six-feet-one and lean, hoped to make the varsity at George Westinghouse High this year. And at 1:00 A.M. he was still racing to the basket in his red Pumas.

Then Anthony Lee stepped through the hole in the fence and came onto the court. With him was his older brother, Scott Lee, and a third person known as Sha-tik.

Kenny Brown remembers that Anthony Lee said to him, "Where's the dude Brian smacked me?"

"He went home," Brown said.

"I'm taking it out on y'all," Brown remembers Anthony Lee saying.

The Lee brothers and Sha-tik began swinging. Immediately, a gun appeared. Kenny Brown folded his arms over his face and backed away as the punches came at him. Tyrone Hampton fell on the asphalt, by the foul lane. The one with the gun bent over and placed the muzzle against Tyrone's head.

Kenny Brown had backed his way up to the hole in the fence, went through it, and now was out on the sidewalk. He remembers calling in to the three that the Brian they were looking for lived on Pacific Street.

"Come on, we know each other," he called to the Lee brothers. Tyrone Hampton, on the ground, said the same thing to the people standing over him. They took turns smacking Hampton.

One of them saw the red Pumas on Tyrone Hampton's feet. Hands reached down and pulled off the Pumas. The one with the gun pulled the trigger and killed Tyrone Hampton.

The three left the park. One carried the red Pumas.

Police came, and then an ambulance. But Hampton was dead in his stocking feet, his blood covering the asphalt under his head. The morgue wagon was called for, and the body was covered and the basket roped off. The activity drew a crowd.

When the morgue wagon did not arrive, somebody in the crowd went down to a basket at the other end of the court and took a shot. Somebody followed up the shot. Soon they were playing basketball in the night with the body of the dead boy at the other end of the court.

Detective Sebastian Danese had the case. He walked the playground, talking, asking, listening. He got in a car and began driving. He started, he says, "knocking on doorbells." He was looking for someone in a white T-shirt, white checked pants, and white sneakers.

At 3:30 A.M., he had Anthony Lee's brother, Scott Lee, twenty-one, of 1447 Pacific Street, in the car and on his way to being booked for a homicide. Anthony Lee could not be found. The detective also wanted the one known as Sha-tik.

Danese asked Anthony Lee's father, John Lee, to call if Anthony returned.

"Drank me a can of beer, went to sleep, three in the morning the police are at the door," John Lee, the father, recalled later. He has a chest condition and since 1978 has been unable to work steadily.

As the father talked, the phone rang. "Get here, where you at?" the father said. "Never mind why. Get here. They goin' get you wherever you are. What's that you say? Never mind why. I don't know what you did. Scott? Scott downtown in jail for some dumb-ass thing. What? You just get here now."

He hung up. "Wherever he was calling from was a house, ain't no street phone.

"I'm forty-four. Ain't never given my parents no kind of trouble. I'm off a farm in North Carolina. Out of eight boys my father never had to go nowhere for us. No police stations, no courthouse. They was never upset when one of us went out, 'cause we always were goin' someplace good."

He took off his glasses and wiped his face. "I don't know what this is about," he said. "Homicide, they tell me."

In a holding cell in the Central Booking on Gold Street in Brooklyn, Scott Lee, twenty-one, drank an orange soda at dawn and told a cop that he was trying to figure out how to raise bail.

He expected it to be $500 or maybe even $1,000. He said he had to figure this out because he wanted to be released in time to go to his job as a carpet cleaner at noon.

The cop did not tell Scott Lee that there undoubtedly would be no bail on his case. As Lee was big and rangy, the cop thought it better to say nothing and keep the guy calm until court.

And now later, in the morning, still shaken by the murder in the night, Kenny Brown sat with his mother in their apartment, which is a couple of doors up from Tyrone Hampton's building on Pacific Street.

"Why did they take the sneakers?" Mrs. Brown said.

"Just to be taking them," Kenny Brown said.

He thought for a moment. "They was brand-new, that's probably why they took them."

(August 1980)

Five Dollars' Worth of Revenge

She had been to the hospital to visit her father and as she started up to her apartment, the stairs seemed steeper than usual. A man was behind her, but his clothes were neat and she felt no danger.

On the third floor, a girl in bare feet ran past her and headed downstairs.

The man behind said, "I wonder where she's going at this hour."

And Sylvia Lebrón said, "And with no shoes to boot."

She spoke automatically, filling in the second line of the conversation. But years spent on Bronx staircases, staircases such as this, being assaulted once, told her that when a stranger speaks to you on a staircase at night, he's only doing so in order to ease your fear and make it easier for him to attack. Legitimate people save their breath while climbing stairs. Sylvia stopped and let the man pass. She remembers seeing his hand put something back into his pocket. "He was putting away a knife, I know that," she remembers. "He was going to put the knife in my back to take my purse, but when the girl came he stuffed the knife back." The man went up to the next floor. When she heard no door being opened on that floor, she stopped. She was at the landing and now she knew that he was waiting for her and she turned to flee and suddenly he was on her.

She is a large woman, at five feet ten and a hundred and sixty-five pounds, and she remembers screaming and sending all the fear into her feet and kicking him. The man was powerful and said nothing and kept punching her. He yanked the purse from her hands and flew downstairs. Her back was twisted and she couldn't move for a moment. Then, slowly, she rose and went to the window on the landing, which was open.

Downstairs in the courtyard, the guy had stepped out of the entrance door and into a crowd of men and women. He was pointing upstairs. "Man up there ripping a lady off," he yelled.

And now Sylvia Lebrón pointed down at the man and shouted, "That's him! That's him!"

Her voice started an ancient informal system of justice. The crowd jumped on the guy. Later, the one thing everybody agreed about was that he had extraordinary strength. A chubby woman named Martha, who was in the middle of it, said, "He fought all the guys. For what he did to her, we defend the people of the building." A man from the building known as Mr. Quick, who is built like a small car, jumped on the guy. Mr. Quick came flying back with the guy's shirt and jacket in his hands. Mr. Quick fell heavily and hurt himself. Now the guy fought through the hands and arms and began running.

His name was Ricky Grant and he was twenty-four and last year, police said, he was released from jail on a robbery charge. Ricky was fast. Of the seven or so who started after him, only two of them could keep up. With the two chasing him, Grant went up a street called Buchanan and then turned and raced under the elm trees and along the basketball courts of Aqueduct Avenue East. Then he was running across University Avenue, and through the fence and onto the grounds of the Bronx Community College, which is where the two who were chasing caught him. No psychiatrist took the stand in Mr. Grant's behalf.

When the police arrived, the entire crowd that had started the chase was now at the community college. They were looking down at Ricky Grant, who was dying with five knife wounds in him.

One of the two who had done the chasing was standing with an empty sheath strapped to his belt.

"Where's the knife?" a policeman asked.

"I gave it to my friend," he said.

"Where is he?"

The guy with the sheath held out his hands. He didn't know. The police took him in, and sent out word that they wanted the other runner to appear with the knife that was used to kill Ricky Grant. Everybody else went home. The purse Ricky Grant had stolen, with five dollars in it, was missing from the knifing scene. So was the knife used to kill Grant and also the knife Sylvia Lebrón remembers seeing Ricky Grant stuff into his pocket. "This is the Bronx, they take everything," a cop said.

It was 9:30 P.M. Sylvia Lebrón then went to the precinct and she remembers saying that she felt ill.

"You're not as bad off as the guy," a detective said. "He's dead."

Sylvia remembers she started to cry in the police station. "He died for five dollars," she said.

And now yesterday afternoon, she was standing in the hallway outside her apartment. Three guys sat on the steps and listened to her.

"Are the police holding anybody?" she was asked.

She pointed to one of the three sitting on the stairs. He was young and thin and wore a yellow T-shirt. "They speak to him," she said. "He is an innocent bystander. He just happened to be there."

The one in the yellow T-shirt spoke in Spanish, and she rebuked him.

"He is not supposed to talk," she then said in English.

She had dark curly hair and wore tinted glasses.

"When they told me first that he was dead, I became upset, because I thought that maybe he has kids. I'm a mother and I have a beautiful daughter and two grandchildren. Maybe he has a mother, too. This is a human being and because he tried to assault me he's dead."

"Capital punishment," she was told.

"Oh, I'm for it," she said.

"But you had it last night and you don't seem to like it," she was told.

"Of course I don't want it for last night. It does not fit what happened last night. He beat on me for a purse with five dollars. I want capital punishment as a deterrent for murderers. But you can't have it for last night. Not for five dollars."

She thought for a moment. "Where is my bag? Mr. Quick looked under the stairs for me. All we found was my leather cigarette case. So where did my bag go? It had five dollars in it."

As she said five dollars, her face showed that she realized that this was why the purse was gone.

(June 1982)

Rosemary's Mother

The woman I live with, the former Rosemary Dattolico, has a mother who believes that we are not properly using punishment as a deterrent to crime. It is her view that many punishments now on the books are not effective, particularly the firing squad. She opposes the firing squad because it is too quick and doesn't hurt enough.

"They should try things out," the mother says. "Say, you take two or three of these savages up to Central Park and put them in the cage with the leopards."

She suspects everybody and forgives nobody. To her, every chance encounter out in the streets is a chance to be mugged. The other day, shopping in Queens, she saw three teenage boys at a bus stop. She folded her arms and hugged her purse to her midsection. The teenagers stared at her.

"Ma, do you have to do this?" the former Rosemary Dattolico said to her mother. "It's embarrassing."

"Ooohh! They could come jumping out like savages," the mother said.

The former Rosemary Dattolico called to the three boys, "Will one of you young men kindly come over here and steal her purse so she'll be happy?"

The three teenagers stepped out into the safety of the street.

"They should be tortured just once, then they'd leave us alone," the mother said. To her a loose shoelace is a prelude to strangulation.

Then the other day she announced that a relative in the Bronx, a distant cousin, had died. She said he was the victim of a vicious mugging. She gathered up her daughter, the former Rosemary Dattolico, and said they had to attend the fourth cousin's wake in the Bronx.

When the former Rosemary Dattolico and her mother arrived at the wake, there were two Doberman pinschers in black suits who inspected the arriving mourners. The Dobermans smoked cigarettes and kept peering out the front door to watch an unmarked delivery truck that was parked across the street. The Dobermans said they hoped the truck would get hit by a bus and everybody inside the truck would get crushed, along with their movie cameras.

"He must have been a wonderful man for such nice people to be here as ushers," the mother said of the Dobermans.

She stepped into the first of the five rooms that had been opened into one large chapel. "Oh, he must have been a wonderful man," she said. Ahead, in the distance in the front of the chapel, standing at the right side of the closed casket, was a full-sized Thoroughbred racehorse made of brown dyed carnations. On the racehorse was a saddlecloth of white carnations. On the saddlecloth, in red carnations, was the number of the horse, Number One.

A tall, thin man in a florist's jacket stood alongside the racehorse.

There was a commotion at the side entrance to the chapel. Into the front of the room came an old man, small and bald, who wore a tray of diamonds. Behind him were two Doberman pinschers in black suits and pinkie rings. Immediately, the man in the florist's jacket became motionless.

The old man came up and began to inspect the racehorse of flowers.

"Give him a carrot," the old man said.

The florist, overjoyed to be left alive, took a great breath of air and left the room.

"Ma, I think I've been to a few of these things before," the former Rosemary Dattolico said.

"How can you say that about such a lovely man? Young savages killed him in the street. No wonder schoolteachers are so frightened. Teachers have a right to keep a wolf under the desk."

Another man came up and stood in front of the casket. The man took a handkerchief out of the pocket of his black suit and wiped his tears.

The man announced to the rooms of mourners, "You have no idea what a regard I had for this guy."

"Hear that? Oh, what a wonderful man he must have been," the mother said.

"Ma, I think that's the guy who killed him," the former Rosemary Dattolico said.

"How could you say that about this poor man? He's crying so hard."

"Well, exactly how did he get killed?" the former Rosemary Dattolico asked.

The mother got up and went to a group of men standing in the rear. She came back with a satisfied look on her face.

"Just like I told you," the mother said. "The poor soul goes to this little social club, you know, and he was walking out of it and this mugger comes out of a Cadillac and shoots him. For no reason at all. The reason the casket is closed is that the mugger used a machine gun. Oh, what a lovely man this must have been."

(*December 1976*)

At 11, He Dodges Shots

On the morning after the shooting, David Rubio, who is eleven and has large brown eyes in a face that could be covered by a palm, came into the living room in a sweatshirt and jeans, a blanket from his bed wrapped around him, and dropped his eighty-five-pound body onto a couch. He yawned and stretched, his bare feet coming out from under the blanket.

"School today?" he was asked.

"Nope. I don't go to school."

"When was the last time you went?"

"Four weeks ago. They made me go out of school."

"How come?"

"Fight too much."

"What kind of fights?"

"Like this." He jumped off the couch and began dancing and throwing punches. "Pow," he called out. "Pow, ping."

The day before, at one-forty in the afternoon, he was in the backseat of a stolen car that was being driven by his friend, Chino, who was seventeen. David's half brother Juan Rodríguez, fifteen, was in the front passenger's seat. Chino was trying to back the stolen car, a 1980 aqua Firebird with New Jersey plates, into a burned-out grocery store on the corner of Fifty-fourth Street and Sixth Avenue in the Sunset Park section of Brooklyn. Chino was having trouble making the car fit through an opening in the corrugated metal that covered the front of the store. Chino bumped into a Ford Econoline 150 van parked at the curb. The van had plush blue seats, heart-shaped windows, and a tire cover on the back carrying the inscription reading "My Way Too." The Puerto Rican kid in a stolen car dented the creamy white van. The van belonged to a police officer, Richard Agrillo, who was working a side job at a construction site across the street with another police officer, Thomas Fox.

The police officers say they approached the car, one on each side. Agrillo had his .38. Fox, who had not carried a gun to the construction job, had borrowed a .38 from another worker. The police say that the driver, Chino, fired at them and threw the gun out the window. Witnesses on the street dispute this. They say the police did all the firing. A gun was never recovered. Agrillo and Fox, firing at Chino, hit him in the head and killed him. Agrillo was hit in the elbow by a bullet. Upon removal, the bullet was found to be from a .38. Agrillo and Fox, on opposite sides of the car, were firing .38's.

David Rubio, eleven, tumbled out of the car and ran to the roof of an apartment house. When he came down, police took him to the station house, where he was questioned by detectives, bosses of detectives, and an assistant district attorney. David told them that Chino had a gun in the car.

When he was released at 9:00 P.M., he went into the lobby of the police station and did push-ups for the television cameras. At age eleven, he is part of the permanent underclass of 500,000 males in this city between the ages of ten and twenty-five, all black or Hispanic, the majority of whom never will be able to get a job. They have been raised on television and match their lives against it. This appears to influence the behavior of many.

At least some of them commit crimes and create the fear that makes the permanent underclass the most powerful cause of change ever to appear on the streets of a major city. Among those in fear are the police, some of whose members have been shot, and one killed recently, by people as young as fifteen. The number of young blacks and Hispanics killed by a police force that is primarily white, many living in the suburbs, is alarming. But the police are able to instill no fear in children without a future. To them, a cop with a gun is merely a slow opponent.

And now, living this life, and only hours after seeing a friend killed inches away from him, David Rubio, age eleven, danced in the morning in his living room and jabbed at the air with his right hand.

"Pow," he called out with his punches. "Pow, ping."

"You fight southpaw," he was told.

"My friend fights like this," he said. He turned around so that his left hand was out. "Pow, ping."

"You told the police last night that Chino fired a shot?"

He nodded his head yes. "I seen when he went like this," he said. He touched his side. "But I didn't think it was a gun."

His half brother Juan Rodríguez, fifteen, came through the curtains into the living room. Juan was in jeans and bare-chested.

"No, he didn't say it like that to the police last night," Juan said.

"What did you say?" David was asked.

"I say he had a gun. I didn't want my brother to get locked up. They said they going put me in Spofford. I said what ———, I'd rather go to a home than Spofford."

"What kind of a home?"

"Saint John's home in Rockaway."

A woman stood in the entrance to the living room.

"She put me in," David said. The woman nodded.

"Why?" David was asked.

"Because I was too crazy."

"You're telling me now that Chino didn't have a gun?"

He nodded yes.

"But last night you told the police that he had a gun and he fired it?"

"Yes."

"Did you show the police how he fired it?"

He nodded.

"How did you show them?"

David jumped off the couch and put his hands together and held them out, as if firing.

"And Chino didn't do that?"

"No, he had no gun."

"What did you tell them?" his half brother Juan was asked.

"I told them I saw Chino holding out his arm at the cops like this." Juan held his arm straight out and stiff.

"Why did you tell them that?"

"I was scared. My brother already told them a gun. I back up my brother. I was scared. I don't want nobody get locked up."

"Did Chino have a gun?"

"No."

"What was he holding his arm out for?"

"Chino went for the screwdriver."

"Why?"

"Turn off the car, probably." In stealing the car two days before, Chino had punched out the ignition. He then started the car with a screwdriver. On the streets, a screwdriver is known as a "car key."

Another of David's half brothers, Jorge Rodríguez, seventeen, came in with a paper. He studied the paper and talked as he read it. "Wow. Hitting him three times in the head."

"I told you he got it in the head," David said. "The cop he got panicked."

"Want to see the paper?" David was asked.

"I can't read," he said.

"Not at all?"

He shook his head.

"Can you pick out your own name in the paper?"

"Yeah, I can do that." He picked up the paper and saw a picture of himself. He pointed to the name in the caption under it. "That's me," he said.

His half brother Juan said, "What's that headline say? Chino got *slené*?"

"It ain't like that," Jorge Rodríguez said. "It says 'slain.'"

"Chino was a good kid, man," David Rubio said. "Stole a lot of cars. Didn't do no drugs. Just steal. He took nothing but the best. Lincolns, Cadillacs. He didn't do drugs."

"Do you do drugs?" David was asked.

"Joints," David said.

"Many?"

"A couple, just to keep you making jokes and laughing."

"What do you do all day?"

"I get up at about noon, eat breakfast, and go out. When I get my lucky shot, it's good."

"What's a lucky shot?"

"I once stole a Jordache jeans box. Mostly I steal blouses from the avenue and sell them to people. That's why yesterday was such a drag. I just put five dollars of gas in the car before the thing come down."

Juan Rodríguez went into a bedroom and came out with a bloody denim jacket. He held it up.

"That's Chino's blood, man."

He slipped the jacket on. "They was taking me to Spofford and first they took me to Rikers Island to scare me. I seen Chino at Rikers Island. I said to him, 'What's up, Chino?' I wasn't scared of Rikers Island."

He buttoned the bloody jacket.

"Give me a dollar," he said to David.

"What for?" David said.

"Buy Bacardi, man. Something like this, got to get drunk, man."

David Rubio, eleven, took out a dollar and handed it to his half brother Juan, fifteen, who went out to get drunk. David jumped up and threw punches at his other half brother, Jorge Rodríguez.

"Pow," David called out. "Pow, ping."

Then he spun around. "I'm going out to the candy store."

(February 1981)

At 11, His Life Is an Open Book

His dark hair covered his forehead, and his eyes were washed with humor. He went under a desk in his bedroom and brought out some of the books he has been reading: a paperback collection of major American poets, *A Christmas Carol* by Charles Dickens, the novel *April Morning* by Howard Fast, and a coffee-table book, *Colonial Craftsmen,* with drawings and text by Edwin Tunis.

He held the Tunis book. "This is from the library," he said, "for a report I'm doing on iron forging in the time of the Revolution."

"I proofread his reports and I see his mistakes quicker," his sister said.

"The teacher says that if I learn to type, I'll see all my mistakes quicker," he said.

His name is Ruben Blancovitch and he is eleven and he is the most important currency of the city of New York, a Puerto Rican who will make it because he has learned to read in a city grammar school.

Earlier, Ruben was found in a sixth-grade classroom at PS 206, which sits on a desolate street in East Harlem. Ruben was saying to the class, "President Carter does not want his era of being president to include people killed in war. He wants peace and no Vietnam. Almost every president in this century has had to go to war. Carter does not want this."

When he entered PS 206 in the third grade, Ruben read some words in English and others in Spanish. The New York City school system has a reputation for ruining many thousands in this situation. But Ruben is in a school that once had only 17 percent reading at grade level, and he was one of those under the level, and now he and his school are almost in the top third of the city's schools.

After three years in PS 206, Ruben is in a class for the gifted and has been chosen to attend twice-a-week classes to prepare him for attending one of the city's special high schools, or to go away on a scholarship.

The people in charge of PS 206 regard Ruben as a trophy for their business. Barbara Barry, the deputy superintendent of School District 4, mentioned his name immediately and said he was evidence that the teaching of reading was succeeding in the district. "Ruben was taught with a very new method," she was saying. "Work."

The principal of PS 206, Juana Dainis, said that she demands that reading be taught in a systematic way. "The system is work," she said.

Ruben's sixth-grade teacher, Arlene Murphy, said, "We do one hour of reading immediately each morning. Get right at them."

And now, sitting at his desk in his bedroom, Ruben Blancovitch was telling about his reading. "I read slow and get each word. Sometimes it gets faster." He tapped Howard Fast's novel. "When I read this I was very involved. I saw the picture of the whole thing. I could hear the words. When he climbs the wall to get away from the Redcoats, I was the one climbing the wall."

His mother stood in the doorway with her arms folded and her youngest child clutching her skirt. In one hand, the mother held the stick from an ice cream her youngest child had eaten. A few minutes earlier, when the mother had gone to PS 206 to walk Ruben home from school, she also had been holding the ice-cream stick. She does not drop things on the street, and when she got to the eleventh-floor apartment in the gloomy Wagner Houses, she was so concerned with a visitor and his overcoat that she did not take time to get rid of the stick. Her name is Irma; she is thirty-one and she is from Mayagüez, in Puerto Rico. She understands English, but is embarrassed to speak it. Instead, she talks to you in gentle smiles. A couple of months ago, she learned to drive a car so that she could take her son to the special classes for which he was selected.

"Do you watch much television?" Ruben was asked.

"Writing a report for school takes me two hours," Ruben said. "I watch television only when I can. 'Mork and Mindy.' But now it's getting boring. Too realistic. Mork used to be out of this world. I liked it better that way. I like science fiction. I like science. When I get to high school, I am going to take chemistry and biology."

"Do you go out much?" he was asked.

"No, there's always trouble in the projects here. One day I went down with my friend and while we were walking right outside the building here I heard a gunshot. Somebody got killed. So I go out at night with my mother and when she drives to pick up my father from work." The father works in a shoe store in the Bronx.

"Have you ever thought about what you want to be?" he was asked.

"I think of things, but I'm never sure. I know that if I read I will know more and I will like more things."

He opened up the *Colonial Craftsmen* book for his report on work in the Revolution. I took a look at the book. It was put out in 1965 by World Publishing, which is no longer in existence. I don't know the author, Ed Tunis. Looking at the book, I could tell you that it took a good piece of Tunis's life, and I'll bet he made so little money that he would be embarrassed to give the figure.

The only people who command attention by writing books are those who don't do it for major money and whose work often is worthwhile or enchanting for perhaps an instant. You are raised in this writing business to sneer at, or consider mentally afflicted, a man who would sit down and write a book about iron forges in the 1770s simply because there is nothing on a library shelf about this topic and perhaps there should be.

And here, fourteen years after he wrote a book that only a very few cared about, with the publisher gone and the author's name unknown to anybody I ask, Edwin Tunis's book finds its way into the mind of an eleven-year-old Puerto Rican who is in the process of exploding out of the streets and the housing developments of East Harlem. I wish the man, Tunis, who by writing the book fulfilled an obligation to people he never thought of, could have been in the bedroom watching Ruben Blancovitch read his book.

(*January 1980*)

Baby Rock, 13. Charge: Murder

The woman called into the living room, where her son watched daytime television, "Run upstairs and tell your sister to come down here. Your sister knows the boy. She was telling the detectives."

The son ran out of the apartment, and the woman took a seat at the kitchen table of her apartment in the Fort Greene Houses in Brooklyn. "I don't know the boy, no way," she said. "Kids here have so many friends."

The boy she had been asked about was called Baby Rock, who lived two buildings away. Baby Rock is thirteen and he weighs ninety-five pounds and yesterday he was being held in family court for taking part in the murder of a sailor last Monday afternoon.

Baby Rock was with three others, all older, when the sailor was shot in the back, on a street outside the housing project. The sailor, Michael Poulson, twenty-two, was stationed four blocks away, at the Brooklyn Navy Yard, where his ship, the frigate *Koelsch,* was being repaired.

Now the door to the woman's apartment flew open, and her son and three young girls, at the most fourteen, all wearing ski jackets, all home in the middle of a school day, ran into the apartment.

"Who knows Baby Rock?" they were asked.

"We all do," said a girl in a red ski jacket. One of her front teeth was missing. "He's in my school."

"How does he do in school?"

"He don't come to school. He hangs outside of school. Or down on Myrtle Avenue. Ripping off people."

"How does he rip them off?"

"He got a gun."

"Big pistols," said another girl, in a blue jacket. A third girl, in green, giggled.

"They call him Baby Rock because he was all hard," the girl in red said, "but when he rip off people he uses a gun."

"Did you ever see him with a gun?" they were asked.

"Right outside here, on the basketball court," the girl in red said.

The one in blue became excited and said, "He takes out this big gun and he points it and he say, 'Freeze!' He pulled it out on this girl Barbara. He say to Barbara, 'Freeze!' "

"Did you ever see Baby Rock shoot the gun?"

They shook their heads. "People say he did. All I saw him do is say 'Freeze!' "

A man named Tommy Norman entered the kitchen. "Saturday morning a week ago he came here at a quarter to five in the morning," Norman said. "I said to him, 'What you doin' out at this hour?' He pulls his gun out. He says, 'I kill you.' I said to him, 'You better get out of here.' I grabbed a stick and he left. I think I took a chance. A lot of these little kids, they'd just as soon shoot you dead."

"What kind of a gun did he have?"

"I'd say it was a thirty-eight. It had a big barrel."

"It was a long gun," the girl in red said.

"Baby Rock ain't too much bigger than she is," Tommy Norman said, "but he got a gun. So many of these little kids around here have guns."

"Baby Rock keeps his gun in his coat pocket," the girl in blue said.

The girl in the red jacket said, "Baby Rock is hard. Knocked this big boy out with his right hand. On Myrtle Avenue. By the C-Town."

"How big was the other guy?"

"Big. Sixteen years old."

"What was the fight over?"

"Money."

"How much?"

"Two dollars."

"How hard did Baby Rock hit him?"

"The big boy just laid back on the sidewalk and didn't move."

The girl in blue said, "Baby Rock got a bald head."

"Shaved his head at the barbershop as a disguise," the girl in red said.

"What does Baby Rock look like with his head shaved?"

"Looks good."

"Did he have a girlfriend?"

The three schoolgirls laughed. "Everybody here," the girl in red said.

There was no answer at Baby Rock's apartment. Baby Rock and his mother were in family court. Anthony Harris, twenty, who lives two buildings away from Baby Rock and who, police say, was with Baby Rock at the time the sailor was shot in the back, was being held in the Brooklyn House of Detention. The building where Baby Rock lives is across a walkway from the building where Richard Andino, eighteen, lives. On November 29, Andino was arrested in the shooting of a high school teacher on the subway. The street where Baby Rock roamed the most was Myrtle Avenue, which sat yesterday in cold shadows. There were two ten-year-olds standing in a video-game parlor next to a pizza stand, and they turned from their afternoon of pressing buttons and watching dots on a screen and they talked about Baby Rock.

"He be always walking outside, robbing people and all that," one said.

The other said, "He be around, bullying people. He had a big gun."

They walked out of the game parlor and went around to the walk leading into the Fort Greene Houses. They stopped in front of Baby Rock's building and shouted up. Suddenly, a young boy appeared at the window.

"That's Baby Rock's brother," one of the small boys said. The brother, who appeared to be about fifteen, opened the window.

"How did they get your brother?" he was asked.

"They didn't," he called down. "He turned himself in. Went with my mother."

"Do you know what it was over?" the brother was asked.

From the window, Baby Rock's brother called down, "He was away in this youth home and then he came back and he was doing all right. Now, I don't know what happened to him."

Down on the walk, one of the young kids said quietly, "Baby Rock got messed up." The other kid shook his head.

(January 1983)

At 15, a Rough Beast

When they refer to New York as an "aging city," what is really meant is José Rojas, who is fifteen and who had his hands cuffed behind him, and his mother beside him, as he was led to the fingerprint pad in the 112th Precinct Station yesterday afternoon. Rojas was being booked for the murder of a policeman.

The policeman, Robert Walsh, was executed on a barroom floor. Police charged the killing was done by Vincent DiNicolantonio, twenty-four; Carlos Flores, seventeen; Richard Rivera, sixteen; and Rojas.

At the precinct yesterday, James Sullivan, the chief of the city's detectives, said, "The loss of capital punishment was a significant loss to law enforcement. I can't imagine why we're waiting so long for it."

The statement was immensely popular in the room, which was crowded with policemen whose only solace was that they had made arrests in Robert Walsh's murder before he was placed in the earth. Sullivan's words produced a growl of agreement; the desire to get even floods through people.

The call for capital punishment will be heard again today from politicians, who of course will attend the officer's funeral. The politicians will howl to the cameras that we have had enough; that we must have the electric chair as a deterrent and as a way for society to express its outrage.

And then all will disperse and Walsh will be under the ground, his wife a widow, his children fatherless, and the rot that caused his death will live on at the base of the city.

"What did these kids do?" somebody asked in a squad room at the start of the day, when the arrests were announced.

A detective was leaning over and tying his shoelaces. "What was their occupation?" he said. "Stickup men."

There are at this time in this city, at the most conservative count, using records and computers, about 500,000 black and Hispanic males between the ages of ten and twenty-five, the crime years, most of whom will be unemployed for the length of the lives that they live. They are part of a permanent underclass in this city; last year, 125,000 arrests were made of people between the ages of thirteen and eighteen. Too often, the underclass produces people who are heartless. The one who shot Walsh in the bar the other night hit him once in the shoulder, knocking him to the floor, and then simply stood over Walsh and fired a second shot into the temple.

There are more today where the shooter came from. Oh, you can name the street corners and housing developments they hang around. They'll die young or go to jail. And there are more of them tomorrow, and more to be with us through all the tomorrows, the way we are going. This is not a social viewpoint; it is merely addition.

The people who call for the electric chair tell a tormented public that with this one instrument alone, these marvelous sparks, they can handle an opponent as enormous as the meanness that spills from an underclass of 500,000 of crime age. I know of no way to become more popular with a typewriter than to type out angry sentences calling for people to be thrown into the electric chair in retaliation for the death of a policeman. And I know of no greater fakery than to do so. For capital punishment is nothing more than an attempt to fool people into feeling that — at last! — something is being done about crime.

An electrocution would occur only rarely and it would provide the newspapers and television with a great windfall of intimate details — the last sex fantasies of the condemned man. It could not be used enough to deter anybody and, when used, it could produce irreversible error. The history of capital punishment is filled with examples of that. At the same time, the most violent crimes are now being committed by teenagers. When you start putting fifteen-year-olds into the electric chair, you might as well attach wires to everyone else, for now there can be nothing left.

To place someone in the anonymity of a bleak prison and let him vegetate for the rest of his life is a far better punishment than setting up a circus and allowing a Gary Gilmore to fascinate the nation while at the same time soiling our hands with his blood.

Yesterday morning, when they were bringing one of them, Rivera, the one accused of pulling the trigger, out of a police station near his house, he looked intently into the television cameras that were in the process of giving him fame. The detectives with Rivera put him into the backseat of a car and pushed in after him. Rivera leaned forward so he could keep looking into the cameras. As the car pulled away, Rivera twisted around in the backseat and kept looking at the cameras.

He and the ones with him yesterday come out of a world whose existence almost nobody in New York or the nation wants to recognize. In this world of 500,000, for many the fear of being caught for a crime is lessened by the thought that if the crime is good enough, your name will get in the papers and your face will be on television. There are in this underclass young people who get up in the morning and have nothing to do. Their day can consist of going someplace and watching others playing game machines in an arcade or they can go out and commit crime.

The language of their streets is dominated by prison terms. "Take him off the count" is their way of saying that a person should be killed. When a young person is "on the count," it means he is back on the streets. When somebody walks away, the others say, "He booked." This comes from Rikers Island, where, when one guard leaves the control booth, he signs a book. When a young guy stays home at night he says, "I binged it last night." This comes from the "bing," or isolation cell, at Rikers. And the true language of New York no longer is "guys and dolls." Today, the term is male and female, after the detention centers at Rikers.

Somewhere, in so many of these lives, they recognize that there is no future and begin to act that way. Rojas, fifteen, attended Richmond Hill High School. Yesterday, his records showed that in the fourth grade in grammar school his vocabulary and reading comprehension were at seventh-grade level. His attendance was good. He maintained this pace until eighth grade, when his marks suddenly went into the fifties. At Richmond Hill High School, he was given 45s in his last marking period and was showing up so infrequently that one of his teachers yesterday didn't even know what he looked like.

And so, at fifteen, Rojas spent the day in handcuffs and we suffered the loss of a cop.

I'm not telling you about this to explain a charge of murdering a cop. Anyone convicted of this deserves to live with himself in a cell for the rest of his life. All I'm saying is that Rojas comes from a crowd of 500,000, and that the job of protecting ourselves and protecting the life of the next cop might be done best by realizing that we are raising particularly rough beasts in New York. And perhaps it would be healthy to find ways to end this practice. This appears more sensible than listening to somebody who promises to end all panic by pulling a switch on the wall, and who accomplishes nothing — except to fool us for a time.

(*January 1981*)

Desperate Sleep

Wayne Norris and Richard Andino, both eighteen, sat backward on a green wooden bench, their right hands cuffed to a horizontal steam pipe, their faces pressed into the corrugated metal wall above the steam pipe. Around the rest of the room, transit policemen, in undershirts, smoking cigarettes, did the paperwork for their arrests while the two slept with their faces against the corrugated metal.

"They've been up all night," a detective said.

"Doesn't matter," another one said. "Anytime you pick up any of them, in the middle of the afternoon, or you go to the house at five in the morning, the first thing they do, they get in the car, they go to sleep."

The door to the low-ceilinged room was open and the room was pounded by the sound of the subway train pulling into the station downstairs. Behind a desk, somebody typed slowly on an old machine. It was 11:00 A.M. yesterday.

"Still in the operating room?" a sergeant, Michael Hudor, asked.

"Got another forty-five minutes yet, they say," a patrolman, John Morrow, answered.

"Got to be eight hours," Hudor said.

"He went in at two forty-two," Morrow said. "What a nice guy. All he kept doing was apologizing. Apologizing for making a mess. They put in an abdominal drain. The blood shot across from here to the coffee machine. He apologized."

A young woman in a dark blazer, bow tie, and gray skirt walked out of an office. She said she was Patricia Notopoulos and that she was twenty-seven and an assistant district attorney.

"How much do you weigh?" she was asked.

"I'll tell you, I worked at Coney Island," Hudor said. "You weigh a hundred and eight."

"Less," she said.

"Ninety-four, ninety-five?"

"I'd be dead."

"Then you weigh a hundred and three."

"Good!" Notopoulos said.

On the bench, Andino sat up for a moment, arranged himself sideways, and leaned against a wall. With his free hand he tugged on the fur hood of his jacket, bringing it down over his eyes. He yawned and went back to sleep. The other one on the bench, Norris, remained motionless with his face against the metal.

At one-ten yesterday morning, Norris, Andino, and three others were on the subway coming to Brooklyn from Times Square. During the slow ride over the Manhattan Bridge, in a car with approximately thirty other passengers, police charged, one of the five took out an automatic pistol and demanded a sheepskin coat worn by passenger Christopher King, thirty-five, a teacher at Sheepshead Bay High School. King fought. The gun was dropped and then picked up, police say, by the eldest of the five, who was in his mid-twenties, and he shot King in the chest.

The motorman stopped the train outside the first Brooklyn station, DeKalb Avenue, and transit police boarded. Norris and Andino were caught on the train. The gunman, in his mid-twenties, and the others, including a fifteen-year-old, jumped off the train and ran into the blackness of a 1200-foot-long tunnel. Power was turned off for two and a half hours and police fired four shots. At the end, the gunman and one of the others had disappeared, the fifteen-year-old was caught and now, at 11:00 A.M. yesterday, in the transit police's Thirtieth District Station, at the end of the platform of the Hoyt-Schermerhorn station in Brooklyn, the fifteen-year-old was back in a juvenile room and Norris and Andino slept sitting up on the bench.

A large man in a brown leather coat walked in with a camera. A detective walked over to the bench and shook Andino, who sat up. The photographer held up the camera.

"Not enough light," the detective said. He put a hand on Andino's shoulder. "I'm going to walk you inside so he can take your picture for identification."

He opened Andino's handcuff and then directed him toward an office. With the hood off his face, Andino suddenly looked young. He walked stiffly, black leather pants gleaming in the lights in the center of the room.

"What's the matter with his legs?" somebody asked.

"Nothing that I can see. The pants got to cost a hundred and fifty," a detective said. "You got pants cost a hundred and fifty dollars?"

After Andino had his picture taken, the detective brought him back, handcuffed him to the pipe, and then woke up Norris. He opened Norris's handcuff and told him to pull the hood from his head. Norris did this and stood up. It was his eighteenth birthday, and he seemed younger. He wore white sneakers and went in for his picture and then was brought back to the bench, handcuffed again, and left alone.

"They'll go right to sleep again," a detective said. "I don't know what they feel. One time I had another kid shoot a guy in the back at 241st Street at ten o'clock at night. He went downtown to a disco after it."

On the bench, Norris mumbled something. Andino nodded. "I don't go to discos," he said.

"Go to Times Square much?" somebody asked.

"Haven't been there in a month."

"Who's home in your house now?" he was asked.

"My mother."

His mother was in an apartment on the fourth floor of the Fort Greene Houses. Her name was Ida Ortoloza. She said she was forty-nine and was born in Ponce, Puerto Rico. She smoked a cigarette and sipped black coffee and cried.

"What happened?" she said. She looked over the plants hanging in the kitchen window. Her view was of Cumberland Hospital. In another hospital in Brooklyn, one she couldn't see, Long Island College Hospital, Christopher King, thirty-five, a high school teacher, fought for his life. While in the transit police station, they waited to see if the charges against her son would have to be raised to murder.

(November 1982)

Pistone's Cold Smile

He resides on the witness stand, above the evil with which duty once caused him to walk. And his memories of it are expressed in a flat voice and with an economy of words that indicates he is not to lose this precious day by hurling his voice about in thoughtless celebration. His name is Joseph Pistone, and he is an agent of the FBI, but he was, so prominently, over the hours in federal court yesterday, a person in a role of much greater dimensions.

During a trial of five purported organized crime members, all of whom have Italian names, Pistone yesterday was asked, "What did you understand him to mean when he said, 'Got hit'?"

"Killed," Pistone answered.

Only one word, uttered in a tone so understated that it caused the word to move slowly through the ear, immediately forcing the listener to speak to himself: Only animals kill.

Pistone, motionless, looked straight ahead and waited for the next question.

Those with Italian names have been shown as athletes, singers, lovers, and gangsters, but rarely has the Italian been illustrated as a person of dignity, which was what Pistone yesterday commanded the courtroom to understand.

He spent six years as an undercover agent in an organized crime family, the Bonanno outfit of Brooklyn, and it is because of such people, their murders and their nicknames, and their perverse appeal to people who write books and develop movies, that so many of the millions with Italian names have been forced, somewhere, sometime, to endure the smears and smirks and suspicions of those about them.

Joseph Pistone yesterday stood against all of this. As he testified, he spoke for the millions with Italian names who have stayed up through the night to pass an exam, or have walked the streets as policemen, or pulled people out of a fire, or gone out in the night to ease the pain of someone sick; for all the people who arise at seven in the morning to go to work for a living and bring to the life of this country the special warmth and gentle humor that goes with their vowels. They are people who never went to see *The Godfather*. Pistone shames those who have thrilled to the Mafia, for as he speaks in court, he indicates that he regards it as a disease.

A tape yesterday of Pistone, who went under the name "Donnie Brasco," and two people named Santora and Ruggiero spoke eloquently of the life Pistone had lived during his long years of posing as a criminal of ambition:

PISTONE: Think I'll get a haircut today.
SANTORA: You gonna get a haircut now! You going across the street to get it?

PISTONE: Yeah. Why!
SANTORA: Gave Boobie a good haircut the other day.
RUGGIERO: I got the guy.
SANTORA: The girl bought it.
RUGGIERO: The guy don't own it no more.
SANTORA: Sold it to the girl. But he still works there.
PISTONE: She gave Porky a good haircut the other day.
SANTORA: Yeah. He ain't got too much to work with. He's bald, ya know. I mean.
PISTONE: I love Porky. He got that slicked-down look.
SANTORA: Yeah. Everything about. Yeah. I mean. He's effin' ugly to start out with.

As the tape was played, Pistone, tall, his dark hair sparse in front, sat with earphones on and studied a transcript. For nearly all the hours of all the days of the years in which he pretended to be a gangster, he had to sit through deadening conversations such as these. As people become gangsters because they don't want to work, their business consists of walking from one place to another, driving a guy around the corner, driving someone else to buy meat, driving out to inspect a Cadillac in a showroom, then standing in a dreary bar someplace and attempting to pass the time with conversation. As most of these hoodlums can't read or write or speak in a sentence, ten minutes with them can be painfully long. While Pistone had uncommon bravery in the presence of their guns, he had to be terrified of death by boredom.

Now and then, a cold smile appears on Pistone's face as he looks directly at the defendants and then states something of this sort:

"After they shot Big Trin, he [Ruggiero] tried to move him and couldn't. He said he was amazed at how strong Boobie was because Boobie was able to move him."

In the hallway during a recess, one of the defendants was overheard complaining to a friend, "A rat brought him around. When he first come around, he had a rat, Tony Mirra, bringing him around. Then one day these two FBI agents came up to me and said, did I know this Donnie Brasco, and that they were letting me know that he was an FBI agent. I said, 'Thank you for telling me. I don't know the man, but if I ever meet him, then I'll know he's an FBI agent.' What was I going to say to them?"

Then everyone went back to the courtroom, where Pistone resumed his role as a witness who just might go down in the annals of crime and in the annals of prejudice as the American with an Italian name who freed so many from the undercurrents caused by the word "Mafia." At the end of the day, agent Pistone stood up, tall and slender, turned, skipped to a doorway, and trotted through it, leaving the defendants to stare at the vents of his tan jacket.

(*August 1982*)

Small Change

Through the long day in federal court yesterday, FBI agent Joseph Pistone mercilessly exposed one of the city's crime families, the Bonanno organization. Under the name of Donnie Brasco, Pistone had infiltrated this family as a common jewel thief with aspirations of becoming a man of honor. Now yesterday, out in the open, he sat in the witness chair as the man in command, dressed splendidly, his face often showing amusement, but the smile being replaced by the look of an accountant as he recalled days supposedly forgotten with what seemed to be precise detail.

As Pistone spoke, the five defendants in the trial appeared not to like him as a person anymore.

Pistone said that he was in Florida in July of 1979 when one of the defendants, Lefty Ruggiero, just down from Brooklyn, said that everybody should watch the newspapers and be prepared for a big surprise. On July 12, in the backyard of a restaurant on Knickerbocker Avenue in Brooklyn, Carmine Galante, the ferocious boss of the Bonanno gang, was attempting to finish lunch and was shot during the salad. Pistone surely read about it in the next day's papers in Florida. He then was informed that one Rusty Rastelli had taken over as boss of the family.

Readers may become somewhat confused by the fact that the family is called Bonanno on all official documents, but that its leaders of late have been Galante and now Rastelli. This is because the Mafia, copying old Protestant law firms, keeps a famous name no matter how long ago the famous one was shot or garroted. In this case, Bonanno is alive, but apparently meaningless to the family he once owned.

Pistone then told of another conversation in Florida, this time with Dominick ("Sonny Black") Napolitano, who once was a very big shot in the Bonanno family. Sonny Black reported that the crime commission had met and knocked down Funzi Tieri, as boss of New York, because Funzi had screwed things up. Paul Castellano, of Staten Island, then was named the No. 1 man in the city, with Aniello DellaCroce as No. 2 and Joseph Gallo the elder, unrelated to the former Gallos of Brooklyn, as No. 3. Mr. Sonny Black was not in the courtroom yesterday. Mr. Black is an MIA.

In his testimony thus far, Pistone was almost able to match information that ran in daily newspaper stories during those times. However, when Pistone went into some of the business dealings of the Bonanno family, he caused many in the courtroom to look about in wonder as they heard of the low level of fiscal involvement by a Mafia that has become famous, particularly at Paramount Pictures, as an American institution that steals billions.

The prosecutor, Barbara Jones, asked him if he had taken any trips to New York in December of 1980. Pistone said that he had gone from Florida to New York on December 3 after a phone call from Sonny Black, whose headquarters was in Greenpoint, Brooklyn. Pistone recalled yesterday, "He said his bookmaking had been hit hard the week before. He asked me how shylocking was doing. I said, fine. He said to take twenty-five hundred dollars out as a loan to the bookmaking and bring it up to Brooklyn."

To move $2500 to Sonny Black, Pistone flew from Tampa to New York, then was picked up by two people and driven to the Withers Social Club, which was then on the corner of Withers Street and Graham Avenue in Greenpoint. Entering the club, Pistone announced that he had the $2500. Sonny Black said, "Give the money to Boobie," who is John Cesarani, a defendant in this case. As Boobie happened to be standing in the Withers Social Club, Pistone did not have to fly a plane to give him the money. Boobie took the money and then turned around and handed the money to his friend, Boots, who is known as Antonio Tomasulo. He, too, was an official guest in the courtroom yesterday. That afternoon in the Withers Club, Sonny Black explained that Boots was in charge of a numbers operation. No testimony was given as to how much expense Boots went to in order to disperse the $2500 about Greenpoint.

Pistone then returned to Greenpoint on December 17, where Sonny Black spent much of a day worrying about a Christmas party. Then Pistone and Sonny Black went to a restaurant at the corner of Lorimer and Conselyea streets, and over cocktails at the bar, Sonny Black complained that certain people in his crew were not pulling their weight financially and that because of this he was moving out of the Withers Club in order to save $600 monthly rent.

Pistone testified yesterday that Sonny Black then said at the bar that the books were being opened in the Mafia and that he was allowed to make five official new gangsters, and that Boobie would be the first man to be proposed for this honor because he deserved it. However, the four other memberships had to go to sons of prominent gangsters, Sonny Black explained. "Their fathers are friends of mine." There was no testimony to state that Sonny Black or the Mafia family he represented was embarrassed by this nepotism. When the books would open up again, he promised Pistone, then Pistone would be named an official gangster.

After this a tape recording was played of a phone conversation between Pistone and Lefty Ruggiero.

In one place on the tape, Ruggiero spoke in terms that a man of honor always should be using when overheard: "That's right. He told him, he says, 'You can't get satisfaction with Lefty. Now you rat him out, and if Lefty made two hundred thousand dollars . . .' "

Suddenly, Ruggiero's voice on the tape caused mouths to drop open all about the courtroom: "But I was mad at you all day today. I told ya, I called ya early this morning but they shut my phone off the twenty-third. Don't you understand, I called you, right?" And in another spot he was saying: "You know, every week from here on in, every night, fifteen, twenty dollars, according to the crowd. You take responsibility. Ten dollars, fifteen, five, twenty dollars goes in the drawer." And now, in still another spot: "I was all over the neighborhood. Do ya know, do ya, I, I, I come down with six dollars this morning. I borrowed money after Sonny told me. I went all over. I went to Marco's."

And: "In other words, do yourself a favor. You got everything going for you. I'm behind you a hundred percent money-wise and everything. And that's it. So Tony's gotta understand one thing, he's got to put money aside. In other words, what does he rate taking around three hundred dollars a week. He takes down two hundred and fifty a week, or two and a quarter, gotta put it aside, we gotta come out there. Now suppose I wanna come out there, you guys this here coming week . . . The hotel is thirty dollars a night. He's gotta lay this out."

These words were accepted in the courtroom with a certain amount of anguish. For if these figures Lefty Ruggiero used were correct, if it was actually ten dollars that he, a man of honor, dared mention, then by his words alone yesterday, Lefty Ruggiero was threatening a great part of American culture, the Mafia movie. How could we ever believe Marlon Brando again if we knew that he stayed in a thirty-dollar-a-night hotel room, practically a flophouse, and that what he was actually mumbling about was twenty dollars that somebody owed him?

At first, some people dispelled this threat to our culture by assuming that the mention of tens and twenties by Lefty Ruggiero was simply gangster code for tens of thousands. But then Ruggiero's voice was heard saying: "Oh, no, no, no, that's the truth. I'm sending my son out next week . . . He takes care, carries his own weight . . . He'll do wonders for you . . . You can travel with him around. He's a good kid."

By this act of moving his son into a job, something with which nearly everybody in the room could identify, the sums of money Ruggiero spoke about suddenly became real. Yes, Lefty Ruggiero, on trial as a major gangster for racketeering and murder, was a man who worried about stealing twenties. In relating this to the court, Pistone showed that gangsters, just like politicians, have yet to find anything that is too small to steal. In his own words yesterday, Mr. Lefty Ruggiero placed himself in the basement, rubbing shoulders with such as Mr. Richard Allen, who as a White House adviser to President Reagan took two watches from the Japanese.

It will be interesting, as this case goes on, to see if Pistone, who was involved with handing about small sums of money from shylocking and gambling, talks of any large amounts of money. For all large scores are made in narcotics, which is the main business of the Mafia.

(August 1982)

The Enemies of the People

In the morning yesterday, there was knocking on the door of Ann Quiller, who lives in public housing on Graham Avenue in Brooklyn.

"Miss," a boy's voice called out.

"What do you want?" Ann Quiller called through the door.

"I'm sick, miss."

"Go to a doctor. I'm not a doctor."

"Just a drink of water, miss, I'm sick."

"Go home for your drink of water," Ann Quiller said.

She was unnerved. She had her coat on to go out, and now she had to wait alone in her apartment until she was sure that the young person outside was not waiting for her in the hallway. The boy's voice had sounded very young, but that sound is another measure that is dangerous to use when you live amidst the disarray of Brooklyn in 1981. Two months ago, the woman at the end of the hall opened the door for an eight-year-old, who then pushed his way into the apartment and attacked her, and ran off only when the woman was able to scream. The woman immediately moved.

Ann Quiller, at sixty-four and living alone, has no place to run. So she sat on a kitchen chair yesterday until she felt comfortable with the idea of going out.

The hallway was clear, but she walked with her head turning rapidly. Only when she got outside, and saw her friend Diana sitting on the bench, did she feel relaxed.

"You answer the door, you never know who knocks your brains out," Ann Quiller said to her friend. Ann sat down and pulled her raincoat about her in the chill afternoon.

"The kids today, I get so mad at them," her friend Diana said. "They just push in doors on old ladies like us." Diana wore a red scarf and a heavy wool coat. Her hands twisted nervously around house keys.

Ann Quiller was born in Jeffersonville, Georgia. She has been a widow for sixteen years. Her friend Diana Petrovich is seventy-three and was born in a village in the woods in Yugoslavia. She came here when she was eighteen, sold flowers in the street to survive, got married and had five children, and then, like Ann Quiller, became a widow sixteen years ago. Diana lives alone one floor above Ann Quiller. The two of them sat on the bench in front of their building yesterday and looked about them with eyes kept as open as a gate in order to recognize any hand holding the spike that could end them.

One of the places, Ann Quiller said, that she watches the most for enemies is the television.

"Since the first time he came on, whenever I hear Reagan's voice on television, no matter where I am in the house, I go sit right down and listen. I knew that he was going to hurt me. It takes all this time for everybody else to say it. They say it on television now. I knew right away, a whole year ago. He is for the rich, and I am going to be hurt."

Diana nodded. In the places where their enemies thrive, in the halls of government, young men with marvelously combed hair, such as David Stockman, rush about apologizing for revelations that fiscal responsibility in the Reagan administration actually means social work among the rich. On a cold day in Williamsburg, two women whose lives have been spent without money regarded the present stories as simply stale news of their adversary's behavior.

"They worry about hairdos in Washington, and we got to worry about food," Ann Quiller said.

Her friend Diana said, "My Social Security is two hundred and sixty-six a month. I get seventy dollars SSI. I have to stretch it. Thank God last month I had three dollars left."

"I had a dollar last month," Ann said.

"This month is rough," Diana said. "Maybe I won't have three dollars left. I'm not a woman to go buy things. If I need something, I spend a dollar, two dollars, for something I need. But that's all. I get ten dollars in food stamps. If they take away anything, a dollar in food stamps, a dollar in Social Security, I can't make it."

"I get two hundred and sixty-eight Social Security and thirteen dollars SSI," Ann Quiller said. "I get ten dollars in food stamps just like her. What I cook on Sunday, I cook beef with a bone and some vegetables with it that has to last till Thursday."

"I have a special diet," Diana said. "I can't have salt. A loaf of bread costs me a dollar five. If they cut a dollar from me, then I only have a nickel for the bread."

"When I worked in school lunchrooms," Ann Quiller said, "the kids were so hungry one morning that I went to pick up a case of milk and threw out my back. I couldn't work anymore. So this beautiful lady at Social Security showed me how to live on a budget. She told me what all to buy, and when I had to buy it. On account of her, I made it. Now my two daughters call me up from Chicago and say, "Mommie, how you doing?" I say, 'Oh, fine.' I don't tell them. I'm living right to the dollar."

"We'll starve, that's all," Diana said. "If my daughter had a room, I'd go live with her. But she don't. I don't want to be nobody's burden. If they do something to us and I can't make it here, I'm going to kill myself. What am I going to do?"

"I knew all along they were going to do something to us," Ann Quiller said. "I watched it on television."

"I kill myself. That's the truth," Diana Petrovich said.

(November 1981)

The Dispute Was over a Dispute

While at the bar last Sunday, I looked up at television, which at the moment was carrying the Yankee Stadium ceremony for Bobby Murcer, the old outfielder who now announces the games on television. Here was Murcer accepting gifts. Suddenly, he was handed what I thought was the most imaginative present ever given in the modern Bronx: a twelve-gauge shotgun.

The weapon was presented by the American Repeating Arms Company. When it was handed to Murcer, he stood with the shotgun in the air. Stood at home plate in Yankee Stadium in the South Bronx with a spanking new shotgun.

I thought it was a magnificent sight, as it was the first full shotgun anybody has seen in the Bronx in years.

The style on Westchester Avenue calls for the barrel to be sawed off so the shotgun can be worn comfortably under a coat when you walk into a neighborhood store.

My friend Panama, who also watched the show, said, "I don't see so much wrong with it. Everybody in the Bronx has a shotgun. Besides, a shotgun can't hurt you as long as it doesn't hit you."

Panama decided this one afternoon when he became involved in a dispute at a construction site on 138th Street, a short walk from Yankee Stadium.

In an attempt to end the dispute, somebody produced a shotgun. Panama departed. He returned well after the police had both arrived and left. "There is nothing to be afraid of as long as you're not here," he said that day.

During the ceremony at Yankee Stadium, in the knowledge that shotguns in the Bronx tend to get discharged, Panama and I were waiting for a sudden explosion that would disperse the crowds in the stands. Which is what happened in the Bronx over the last couple of days.

Friday night, José Contrera found himself out on the sidewalk with a man who is unknown at this time. The gunman shot Contrera once in the stomach and took off. Contrera was dead when they got him to Bronx Lebanon Hospital.

Although the police work was not finished yesterday, they knew what type of gun was used on Contrera. Rest assured that the picture of Murcer with the shotgun applies: The word shotgun is a collective in the Bronx.

On the next night, at eleven, George Ellis, forty-two, was shot once in the chest at 2111 Southern Boulevard, and he was dead by the time they got him to Jacobi Hospital.

And then there was Gary Walker, twenty, who got into a dispute with someone at 800 Hunts Point Avenue. This time, all the people did not remove themselves from the area.

There were witnesses, and they said that Walker got into a dispute with a young man. A young man of about seventeen. The seventeen-year-old pulled a gun and shot Walker in the throat. Walker died at Jacobi Hospital.

"What was the dispute about?" one of the detectives in the Forty-first Precinct was asked yesterday.

"The dispute was over a dispute," he said.

The presentation of a shotgun in Yankee Stadium shows how one part of the country, with its American fame and bright lights illuminating the sky, sees and knows nothing of the country of the South Bronx, which sits in the darkness just beyond the reach of the stadium lights.

At a day for Murcer, a shotgun was a symbol of males walking through the hunting fields of Georgia or Oklahoma. A shotgun in the country of the South Bronx, only a block or two away, is what is used on a bodega owner who is slow coming up with the money.

The gift, which was meant to show respect for a popular name in American athletics, will not win any awards for setting good examples. The picture of a man at home plate with a shotgun was at least jarring if you watched it on television in the real Bronx.

Detective Sergeant Frank Bruno of the Forty-fourth Precinct, which covers Yankee Stadium, thought about it yesterday. He then issued this statement: "I think the last thing that the people of the Bronx need is a new shotgun."

Bruno's precinct won the New York City championship for homicides for 1981, with seventy-six. Last year, the amount dropped and only fifty-six or so persons were shot to death in a place where the light glows in the summer night sky over the famous baseball field.

Up the hill from the stadium yesterday, Ed McCarthy, who works in Bronx District Attorney Mario Merola's office, said that when he saw Murcer with the gun on television he was afraid that Murcer was going to throw it into the stands as a prize for the faithful.

Which is not such an insane thought, for the Bronx remains as the only place in America where one of these "death wish" movies became a part of daily living.

This occurred only last month in a bodega on West 133rd St. A man in a blue jumpsuit came in and pulled a gun on the owner, José Landa. A customer in the store pulled a gun and the holdup man panicked and ran. The holdup man was headed for a ten-speed bike.

The customer in the store regarded the matter as personal. He fired six shots, at least a couple of which went into the holdup man's back and killed him.

The customer put his gun away and left. Nobody knows who he was and he's never been seen again.

Yesterday, nobody could find the name of the dead holdup man. There is too much crime in the Bronx for people to look up such useless information.

And the picture of Murcer holding the shotgun goes alongside all the famous ones taken in that ball park. Ruth hugging a dying Gehrig, Stengel mugging, Mantle swinging. Now Murcer with a shotgun.

His picture tells more than any ever taken in that ball park. For it shows that in America there are two separate countries, and in the Borough of the Bronx they are within mere yards of each other.

(August 1983)

Where Angels Tread

From the start, there really was no way for him to lose. Curtis Sliwa had an idea called the Guardian Angels, which was one more idea than anyone else has had in the city in years, and it put together the two most important matters in the lives of the people of New York: crime and the subways. We will work as volunteers at the job that we pay government to do and government fails to do, Sliwa announced.

Of course, government fought him. Frightened by a new idea, and also obviously terrified by the fact that Sliwa's organization consisted of young Hispanics and blacks, the city government tried to get in the way of hope. The mayor sneered and the police steamed. We suffer the worst crime in the history of the city, and those who cannot protect us were busy trying to prevent anybody else from trying.

A Guardian Angel would be arrested. The cops would charge, Sliwa would deny. He carried the fight brilliantly, and for a long time I had him winning every round. Then one night in a desolate transit police station under the tangle of el tracks in East New York, there were eleven Guardian Angels on an iron chain, being taken off to night court, and the smiles of city officials were everywhere. Now, they kept saying, we have them.

And now the other night, Sliwa decided that the fight had gone long enough, that he knew exactly what to do to end it. He had been jabbing at this bald man who substitutes comedy for government, and now Sliwa would hook off the jab and go home with the trophy.

Sliwa took 450 Guardian Angels and put them on the sidewalk outside Gracie Mansion. Each had a candle that was given to him by a supporter in Parkchester. They stood in silence with their candles. Blacks and Hispanics are expected to be unruly in their demonstrations. The Guardian Angels stood in silence.

"I know that Koch is totally uncomfortable with the idea of a black or a Hispanic," Sliwa says. "I was going to confront him with four hundred and fifty of them, but not with everybody screaming in some auditorium where he could walk out. I was going to make Koch go to sleep at night with four hundred and fifty blacks and Hispanics right under his bedroom window. When his car drove past us into his driveway that night, he was slumped down. We could see his head, but not his mouth."

A couple of days later, the city sanctioned the Guardian Angels as an "independent, autonomous citizens group" that patrols the subways and streets. Yesterday, this most remarkable winner, Sliwa, twenty-six, sat in the apartment on University Avenue in the Bronx that serves as his home and headquarters. It is a four-room apartment with holes in the walls and long benches and a few old chairs that obviously were retrieved from sidewalks or empty lots. A large dog sprawled under a bench. Sliwa looked in the refrigerator. There was a half can of beans, a can of corn, a stick of margarine, and a large bottle of soda. He took out the soda and walked into one of the rooms and sat down.

"You'll get a lot more people joining now," he was told.

"It's not a question of more," he said. "It's the sense of calmness among the parents of these kids that helps us the most. Now they know that their sons and daughters are in a program that isn't an outcast. Their kids are not members of some radical organization. Their kids are in the Guardian Angels, and the city recognizes the organization. Now we can magnify the fact that Hispanics and blacks are not just good for going out and mugging people and getting sent to Rikers Island. The Guardian Angels are good. The kids in the Angels are positive and good. This is the first time that the blacks and Hispanics have done anything in this city. These kids have won the right to be proud of themselves."

One of the Angels, Miguel Quiñones, seventeen, came into the room wearing gray sweatpants and dark-blue basketball shorts outside the sweatpants.

"That's his outfit for the week," Sliwa said. "On Sunday, he'll put on black sweats and red trunks over them and clean white socks and his best sneakers."

"Cooling out," Quiñones said.

"Sometimes you see them take out a bottle of polish and start shining the sneakers while they're walking," Sliwa said.

"Got to look good," Quiñones said.

Knowing dress and music are as important to Sliwa's success as his considerable ability to just about demolish any opponent who wants to take him on in public.

"This is just the beginning," Sliwa was saying.

"Being a Guardian Angel on the subways is glamorous. What I want to get into now is unglamorous work. Escorting senior citizens. You don't see anybody old on the streets up here. They are locked in their houses day and night. Why can't we have volunteers take them to the stores, or out for walks? Look at the subway stations. The city has all these technical high schools. Why can't the students rewire the subway stations or repair the tiles as part of their school work?"

He stopped to answer a couple of phone calls. When he walked back into the room, his dark eyes were intense and he started talking immediately. "Do you notice all the kids on the subway platforms with cameras? They're taking pictures of their graffiti work. They stand there and wait for a train they sprayed to come into the station. I know kids have big scrapbooks of pictures of subway trains they worked over. If you took these kids and had them repair a subway station, do you think they'd ever let anybody tear their work down? What they need is a challenge. The only way the city can get anything done is for the people to do it themselves. You can't work through the political process. That failed us. We just have to do the work ourselves."

Sliwa thumbed through a newspaper and glanced at the story of the agreement beween the Angels and the city. Part of the agreement calls for the Angels to wear official identification badges issued by the police department.

"The badges make the *New York Times* crowd feel good," Sliwa said. "The people on the subways in Brooklyn never needed to see a badge. They were always happy enough just to see us get on the train."

(*May 1981*)

Meyer Didn't Know How to Behave

He was a man who loved Israel, but not enough to behave in it.

There was this time a few years back when Meyer Lansky, living in Florida, decided that a prosecutor's questions could best be answered with movement, and Meyer left the United States, went to Israel, and asked for asylum. Which he received for a while, and Meyer could be found in the Dan Restaurant, Ben Yehuda Street, in Tel Aviv. He ordered the food for those who sat with him, and if somebody ever tried to order on his own, Meyer would frown. The

waiter would inform the guest that the whole restaurant wou[l]
happier if people ate exactly what Meyer Lansky ordered.

When the Israeli government announced one day that they were
sending Lansky back to Florida, the rumor was that the United
States was holding up an order of Phantom jets until Israel shipped
Lansky back. But then one day I was at the bar of a place called
Fink's in Jerusalem and I asked the guy from the Israeli government
about this and he said, "Please, we sent him away because he
doesn't believe in laws. He was causing trouble with taxicab fleets
and nightclubs and women. Prostitutes. We don't need him."

He lived under the name of Meyer Lansky on Collins Avenue in
Miami and he died yesterday. His true name was Maier Suchowl-
jansky and he was born on July 4, 1901, in Russia, and he came
through Ellis Island on April 4, 1911.

He lived on Avenue A and knew a kid named Salvatore Lucania,
who was called Lucky. On April 24, 1918, Lansky was arrested for
the first time, for a felonious assault, on Ludlow Street. The matter
was discharged. On November 18, 1918, he was convicted of disor-
derly conduct and paid a two-dollar fine in Manhattan court. On
March 7, 1928, he was arrested for homicide, but this, too, was
thrown out and he was able to become a citizen later that year. On
January 6, 1929, he had a narcotics arrest; heroin is at the bottom of
every known criminal career. He was twenty-seven by now and
known for violence.

In those years, people who became famous criminals went from
cold-water flats on the East Side to Sing Sing and then to Central
Park West. Lansky did not like cold water and didn't like prisons.
He stayed out of jail in New York and went to Florida, Cuba, Las
Vegas, and Israel. He was in jail only once in his career, for three
months in the Saratoga, New York, city jail. That was in 1952. His
legend is that he was the genius of the underworld, the man who ran
everything with his brains. But this, of course, was a fable: Lansky
was the boss because he probably was the most vicious.

I don't know where Barney Baker is now, but when he was
around he always was considered the finest witness, allowed to remain alive, of Meyer Lansky's temper.

It happened when Baker, who had boxed as a heavyweight, decided to stop fighting and start eating. He grew to 385 pounds and
became a registered gorilla. He went to work as a muscleman for a

gambling place in Hollywood, Florida, called the Colonial that was owned by Lansky, Frank Costello, Joe Adonis, and Benjamin ("Bugsy") Siegel, with Lansky at all times in charge.

On his first day at work, Baker was told to go over to Lansky's motel and wake him up. The other hoodlums lived in hotel suites and slept until it was time to make the first race, but Lansky, living alone in a cheap hotel, wanted to be on his feet early, for he counted the money, haggled with purveyors and liquor salesmen, and booked the acts for the gambling club. He did very well at this, mainly because salesmen were afraid of him. On his first morning, Baker took a key from the motel room clerk, went to Lansky's room, and opened the door. He walked over to wake up Meyer, who appeared to be quite asleep, except for a right hand which went under the pillow and brought out what Baker said was the one largest gun he ever had seen.

When Lansky focused his eyes and saw who was in the room, he put the gun back under the pillow. A picture of it, however, remained pasted on the front wall of Barney Baker's brain.

There then came a late night and Baker, hanging around the bar, had a few drinks and began arguing with a customer who had just walked out of the gambling casino. The customer appeared drunk and he also got on Barney's nerves, and Barney took him out with a left hook. The customer wandered out of the place with his hands holding his jaw, which appeared to be at least broken.

When Lansky arrived at the club the next day, the porter said to him, "What a shot Barney hit a guy with last night."

At a table, having morning coffee, Barney Baker glowed. You bet it was a good shot, Barney reminded himself.

"What guy did he hit?" Lansky asked the porter.

"This guy Al. You know him. The guy who's always here."

"Al from the hotel?"

"That's the one, Mr. Lansky."

"The guy is the best player we ever had in this place," Lansky said. His voice turned into a high, dangerous whine. "Did you hit that man?" he yelled to Baker.

When Baker didn't answer, Lansky started for him. A small man, perhaps one third of Baker's size, and with eyes made in a freezer. Inside Barney Baker's head, the gun pasted on his brain wall began to pulsate. Barney was up from the table and going backward. This little Jew coming at him was berserk. You touched my money, you big slob. Baker kept moving around the tables and Lansky kept chasing him. Once, Lansky stopped and pounded his hands against his pockets in anger. He had left that gun of his in the office. Lansky made one quick pass into the kitchen, coming back out with a meat cleaver, but Baker was gone now. Out on the street in a dead run.

If Lansky had any redeeming qualities, they probably can be found in his three children, one of whom went to West Point and did well and can be best left alone here. And then there was one night, years ago, when Meyer worked his way into a charity party run by somebody named Mrs. Vivienne Wooley-Hart Akston on Park Avenue. And he busted everybody out with crooked dice. There was a major investigation, instead of the proper action, which should have been to award Meyer a medal.

Otherwise, if he leaves anything, it is the memory of his eyes.

There was a day when Sid Zion, writing his book, *Read All About It,* sat with Lansky and said to him, "Tell the truth, didn't you give the okay to get Ben Siegel hit?"

Lansky had been smiling, and now his face became straight. The eyes became small ice ponds.

"He was the best friend I ever had," Lansky said. "His grandchildren are coming to visit with me. Why don't you stay here a few days and see for yourself? How could I get a guy killed if I have his grandchildren coming to visit me?" Lansky's eyes kept staring.

"That was when I knew that he had Siegel killed," Zion said.

(January 1983)

3

"A Dream Character in Dancing Pumps"

They had liked each other for years. From the earliest days when Hugh Carey was first pushing himself up through the Brooklyn Democratic Club and Breslin was still writing for the old New York *Herald Tribune.* They used to close the bar at Snooky's in Park Slope or at the Pierpont House near Borough Hall, where Carey liked to treat the patrons to his Irish tenor. And later, when Carey looked around and found Breslin, with a book to publicize, running in the same Democratic primary for City Council president, they spent a lot of nights in P. J. Clarke's, the Irish saloon on Third Avenue in Manhattan, where the bar always looked like a midtown traffic jam.

The friendship, not chummy close but palpable, continued after Carey was elected governor of New York in 1974. Like the Kennedys, he was a loophole in the Breslin law that says politicians should be beaten every morning to keep them honest and attentive to the people's will. Jimmy Carter was attacked for his Southern Baptist ways, his neglect of blacks and the poor, and his bias against New York. "I never believed a word he said, and therefore did not feel he was lying." Richard Nixon was "a perfectly horrible president, the worst of all time." Mayor Koch came under repeated fire. "You can never say that Koch is uneven or that he gives false hopes," Breslin observed once. "The man does absolutely nothing all the time."

With the Kennedys, however, it was different. Breslin never was able to camouflage his enthusiasm for John Kennedy when he covered his brief presidency. He viewed the assassination — which inspired some of his most memorable reporting — as a terrible loss for liberal ideals. And afterward, when only the memory of a hero remained, Edward M. Kennedy became the new promise of a better future, and this showed in Breslin's columns, particularly in the peroration he wrote when the senator lost to Carter in the 1980 Democratic primaries: "He lost his election, but never his breeding. He never whined and anger was an alien. And now he simply would do what he was supposed to do: continue in style. Perhaps we best get used to him. He might be around for a long time."

Breslin's hopes for Carey were never so great, nor his opinion so high, but the old tie kept tugging at his columns all through the governor's first term and into the second. Although he continued to sound off about things he didn't like, Breslin did not really attack Carey personally. When we needled him about this uncharacteristic behavior, he would just grin with sheepish guilt. "Yeah, yeah, you're right," he would say. "I gotta do somethin'. It's hurtin' my reputation."

Not much happened though until the fall of 1980, when, quite suddenly, the long personal relationship collapsed — with a crash that eventually drove the governor out of office and ended his long political career. There were two immediate causes: Carey committed the political blunder of trying to evict a dentist from land next to his summer home on Shelter Island, and he broke with a lifelong friend and supporter, Dr. Kevin M. Cahill.

The eviction attempt, with its image of a little guy being shoved around by a powerful political leader, was more than Breslin could resist. "I have to go with the people," Breslin shouted defiantly, as he buried his old pal in an avalanche of tough columns about the "imperial governor" spiked with a great deal of original reporting — "even the state troopers were feeding me tips." After the appearance of these columns and news stories enthusiastically generated by the city staff, Carey retreated in disorder and the dentist kept his property.

At about the same time, the Cahill episode further soured the Breslin-Carey relationship. Cahill had been Carey's family doctor for years, his chief adviser on health policy, and probably the most influential member of his inner circle in Albany. But the two friends finally split over internal issues, generated mainly by Cahill's enemies; Cahill resigned his multiple state appointments. Breslin was outraged. Although it was not generally known, he was very close to Cahill, who had cared for his dying wife. He heaped all the blame for the breakup on Carey and his aides.

Other misgivings about the governor's character and behavior, which had been building for months in Breslin's conscience, came to a boil and a whole series of brutally critical columns began jumping out of his old Underwood typewriter. The timing was perfect. During the first years of Carey's administration — particularly during New York City's fiscal crisis in 1975 — Carey had established himself as a highly intelligent, strong, and effective governor. But as the years passed, he became increasingly bored with governance, and by the middle of his second term, his administration was drifting badly. The governor himself supplied much of the incriminating evidence by showing up constantly at New York's classier watering spots — he was a standard item at Elaine's and "21" — and attending all the best parties from Park Avenue to the Hamptons. His regular date at the time was the rich, beautiful Anne Ford Uzielli, who kept refusing his offers of marriage but who attracted paparazzi like an Onassis and therefore guaranteed that his inattention to business would be well publicized.

These facts, plus a number of odd related incidents, ascribed by some to love, kept the city's cognoscenti in a buzz. From bankers to political leaders, Carey's misadventures were the subject of constant private gossip. Some of this spilled over into the newspapers but in a mostly unfocused way that did not fully reflect the concerns about the governor that were growing ominously among the city's leaders. Breslin remedied this by packaging the problem in a single devastating phrase — a phrase that insiders privately cheered and millions of New York voters quickly adopted: "Society Carey." The nickname stuck like a tattoo and exposed the governor to the kind of ceaseless ridicule few politicians can withstand.

"Society Carey likes to ride planes," Breslin observed cheerily, launching a running attack on the governor's life-style. "Helicopters, too. Many times he rides in them with a girlfriend. Society Carey sits in the planes and helicopters and looks at the clouds, which often match those inside his head, and talks to his girlfriend."

To show the relevance of this to the ordinary taxpayer, Breslin produced records showing that numerous trips were highly unofficial. He also dug up impressive statistics about the costs being borne by the public — twenty-one pilots at thirty thousand dollars a year, for example — because "Society Carey wants proper air cover in case of war with Vermont."

Breslin knew he had a winning horse in Carey and rode him like Eddie Arcaro, getting a steady stream of tips from cops, bartenders, and even from celebrities like Charlotte Ford. This was highly popular with the customers of the *Daily News* but posed some serious editorial problems. The governor was such an inviting target that he became a cottage industry. Our reporters were constantly breaking stories about new Carey antics or indiscretions, like taking freebie junkets to Greece and Japan. His whirligigging with Anne Uzielli and later Evangeline Gouletas popped up all the time on our People Page. Other *News* columnists, like Beth Fallon, were accusing him of such crimes as being disloyal to his friends. And our editorials, which had been supportive, became more critical.

Taken singly, the stories and comments were generally fair. Although Carey was incensed, he had provoked most of the criticism himself. What worried us editorially was that the collective mass of unfavorable copy, however accurate, might be interpreted as a *News* vendetta. We had worked hard to build a reputation for fairness and did not want this jeopardized. But doing this in Carey's case was difficult, particularly for O'Neill, who had a close working relationship with the governor — too close, some thought — and therefore was especially reluctant to tamper with the patterns of coverage.

Early on, when concerns about Carey's behavior were still confined mainly to insiders, O'Neill asked the city desk to develop a series of investigative reports that would reveal everything taking place behind the scenes. By the time the project was finished some weeks later, however, the *News* was literally awash with Breslin attacks and other negative comment. To publish the articles at that time, we felt, would simply support the charge that we were "out to get" Carey, so we ordered the series postponed. Some reporters and subeditors were upset and, predictably, accused O'Neill of suppressing the facts to protect a friend, a charge that was only reduced to a misdemeanor some weeks later when we felt the timing was better and finally published the series.

Editorial balance or no balance, the legend of "Society Carey" gathered momentum like a tsunami wave until finally, in 1982, the governor stood amid the ruins of his public reputation and announced he would not run for reelection. After two decades of elective office, he would return to the private practice of law. He had become convinced that he could not prevail against the drumbeat of "Society Carey" ridicule, which he mainly attributed to his onetime friend Jimmy Breslin.

A few years earlier, Bill Brink's classic headline in the *News*, "Ford to City: Drop Dead," was cited as a major reason for Gerald Ford's defeat in a presidential election. Now, some people accused

Breslin and the *News* of again driving a political leader from office. This disturbed us because we insisted Carey had shot himself out of the sky. Breslin was not disturbed; his conscience did not register a single seismic squiggle. He broke down and wept for quite another reason: it destroyed him to think he would not have the governor to kick around anymore.

"Once every many years, nay, once every many decades," he mourned, "one will come along like this, a dream character in dancing pumps, splashing champagne all over his head, a mind made of sky, doing so many things at once that you simply don't know where to begin when telling of them. Suddenly he was gone. Forevermore, I would have to attempt to write a newspaper column without Society Carey as a running character."

Quel dommage!

—M.J.O.

Society Carey

There arrived in this office yesterday, and thus prominently, this message that came whizzing through the communications satellite and joined the flood of worldwide news:

> CABLES
> H (CAREY) DRYDENS 08200: ELEVEN-PERSON CAREY GROUP ARRIVED
> HERE HONGKONG SATURDAY EVENING FROM TOKYO. DUE LUNAR
> NEW YEAR'S HOLIDAYS NIGHTCLUBS ETC CLOSED UNTIL TODAY.
> CAREY STAYING AMERICAN INTERNATIONAL UNDERWRITERS' GUEST
> HOUSE AND MOST OTHERS AT MANDARIN HOTEL. (ABOUT DLRS 80
> MINIMUM.) PLANNED MEETINGS TODAY LEAVE TUESDAY ABOUT
> NOON. TOKYO ANSWER SEPARATELY. RGDS. ANDERSON-HKG UPI.

Beautiful. We in New York are privileged to have the most marvelous representation by the government for which we pay. Let these other states have governors who slobber around state fairs and supermarket openings. Look at Connecticut. The governor who just died, Ella Grasso, was a dear woman, but she sold the state plane and helicopter and drove around in a Citation. Our governor in New York is different. Our governor is Society Carey. For the last several days, Society Carey and a party of ten, paid for by tax funds out of the money you work for each week, have been sweeping across the Orient.

The object of the trip is to let Society Carey see the Orient, which he never has, and to let the Orient see Society Carey, which it never has. In that way, a whole new part of the world will know that we in New York have a governor, which we have, and his name is Society Carey.

There are many thousands living without heat in Brooklyn who say that they never knew they had a governor until newspapers ran pictures of Society Carey looking out of a helicopter in Japan. But these people living in the cold in Brooklyn are not Society Carey's kind of people, and you can be sure that he will keep the same distance from them that he always has, and that is quite a lot of distance. Tokyo is not that far.

We in New York could be proud of the first picture of Society Carey, the one showing him in a helicopter, because that let all of Tokyo know how our governor lives in New York. Society Carey has a great big million-dollar helicopter that he rides all over New York while we take subways, if you can get on them, and he also has two planes, one of which is so big it can barely fit on a runway, and he uses it every night to go back to Albany from Manhattan and it costs only $750 a night to do this.

The Society Carey party in the Orient includes three advance men. An advance man is a traveling doorman. He sees to it that the right luggage is in each hotel room and that cars are available and helicopters ready on the pad, and that, always, doors are held open for Society Carey. The luggage is much more important than you think. As someone from the governor's office in New York was pointing out yesterday, this trip to the Orient involves dramatic climatic changes. The trip started in Albany, where the temperature drops to the low teens, and went through Hawaii, in the high seventies, to Tokyo, which was in the forties, and on to Hong Kong, which is in the sixties. But this is weather in the winter and is highly unreliable.

Why, here one morning you could have Society Carey arising in Hawaii and the temperature could be in the high seventies. Moreover, if Society Carey ever put on a heavy Albany suit and went out into the street, he most certainly would boil like a cabbage. By noon in Honolulu, Society Carey would keel over. Yet on the other hand, if Society Carey ventured out in his truly tropical suit, his tea planter's white, he might be out and about the whole town and have the temperature suddenly plummet many degrees. Here would be Society Carey in the middle of Honolulu, being attacked by chilblains.

So here is what the three advance men have been doing each day on Society Carey's trip through the Orient:

One advance man stands outside the hotel each morning for a half hour in order to fully acclimate himself to the temperature. Then the first advance man makes a policy decision as to the weight of the suit Society Carey will wear. This outside advance man waves his arm, in coded signal, to a second advance man, stationed inside the hotel lobby. The second advance men grabs a phone and calls up to the third advance man, who is positioned in Society Carey's suite. Upon getting the message, the third advance man pounces upon Society Carey's wardrobe and pulls out the proper suit for Society Carey to wear on this day.

Sometimes this system, which worked beautifully at hotels, had to be modified to fit a change in Society Carey's living quarters. As the UPI cable from Hong Kong indicates, Carey in Hong Kong stayed in the American International Underwriters' guest house. American International Underwriters appears to have some connection to the insurance industry. By staying there, Society Carey placed great hardship on his advance men. They had practiced long hours for hotel duty, but this method of climate control at the American International Underwriters guest house could be done by only two advance men. And the two advance men were able to do the job, and apparently quite well. The trip has gone so smoothly for Society Carey, wearing all his suits in all the different weather, that he has not even taken a Dristan.

Society Carey's party in the Orient also includes two New York State policemen. This causes some people in New York City to say that since there have been 9851 murders in the city in Carey's time as governor, then perhaps any loose cops should be used on Nostrand Avenue instead of Honolulu. Other people say that if Society Carey's trip to Hawaii, Japan, and Hong Kong is so dangerous that he cannot make it without great protection, then perhaps he shouldn't go at all.

You must disagree with those who say such things. It is now official American policy to face up to terrorism wherever it may be. If there is terrorism on Waikiki Beach, or at the American International Underwriters in Hong Kong, then it should be fought vigorously. We in New York State have sent Society Carey and two state troopers to make sure that this national policy is carried out.

These same people squawking about the cost of sending secretaries, advance men, and two state troopers around the Orient — round-trip plane fare is $1600, and that is only the start — are the same ones who made the most noise the other day when Society Carey, before leaving for Hawaii and the Orient, put in an expense voucher of $6400 that was to be paid to Dr. Philip D'Arrigo. He is the dentist whose house on Shelter Island was seized by the state because it blocked the view of the water from Society Carey's family house. They had to give the house back to the dentist. This switching back and forth caused the dentist to run up bills of $6400. As the problem was part of the governor's personal life, he sat down and, of course, asked the taxpayers to pay the $6400. This is why Society Carey has such great style; he has 14 million people paying for him.

Officially, Society Carey has announced that his trip, his eleven-man sweep of the Far East, has nothing to do with sightseeing. In Japan, Society Carey announced that the great Okuma Machinery works would expand its business and set up a huge production plant on Flatlands Avenue, Brooklyn. The Okuma plant would sit alongside the great new international headquarters of the Mitsubishi Corporation, which will move here on March 3. These announcements of great industries coming here are similar to those made when Society Carey took his last overseas trip, to Germany. Society Carey then announced that the main Krupp plant in Dusseldorf would move to Flushing Avenue, Maspeth, on February 16.

Society Carey's tour of the Orient does make a fool of at least some of his critics. Society Carey has maintained that the state cannot run without the services of his assistant, Robert Morgado. To prove this, Society took Morgado with him all over the Orient and he and Morgado even stopped at Morgado's home in Hawaii. And the state ran just as it always did, which proves how important both Society Carey and Morgado are to us.

Also out of this great, quite costly trip, I personally learned a lesson. Some time back, I noted that Society Carey was unique in government: he had invented the eleven-hour workweek. A person I respect and cherish called me on this. He said I had my figures wrong and should be embarrassed. I can now report to this man that, yes, he was right and I was wrong. By careful addition, I have determined that since January 1 of this year, Society Carey has worked an average of nine and a half hours each week. As this is not the eleven-hour week I said he worked, I stand corrected. Beautiful.

(February 1981)

Society Carey Betrays Us

There was an old judge in Manhattan named Hymie Bushel, whose proudest statement was that he never had sent a prostitute to jail. And on the day that Bushel announced he was retiring, a few guys got together in an office behind the bench and it was late in the afternoon and drink was taken and stories were being told.

Out in the courtroom, an old prostitute walked in, looked around the empty room, and called to the court officer, "Is it true that Judge Bushel is retiring?"

"Yes, he is."

"Then you tell him that I'm getting out, too."

And now the other morning, here I was sitting around the *Daily News* newspaper office and I was handed a slip of wire copy which said that Governor Hugh Carey had just announced that he was not going to run again. No, I said to myself, even he wouldn't pull a thing like this on me. I looked at the wire copy again. It still said that Carey wasn't running.

Then from deep inside me, in the place from which warnings and wails arise, there came this angry shout:

"You just lost Society Carey!"

Once every many years, nay, once every many decades, one will come along like this, a dream character in dancing pumps, splashing champagne all over his head, a mind made of sky, doing so many things at once that you simply don't know where to begin when telling of them. Suddenly, he was gone. Forevermore, I would have to attempt to write a newspaper column without Society Carey as a running character.

I sat at my desk and shook my head. No way to make it without him.

And then, like the old streetwalker in Hymie Bushel's courtroom, I turned and looked for the door.

To make the day even drearier, Society Carey went out like a wimp. He mouthed phrases somebody wrote for him: "Throughout my public life, I've done the very best I could. Let the people decide if that was good enough. The people have been generous with their trust." Or, "And I want to emphasize that I am not relinquishing a commitment which has been the center of my public life."

Awful. One of the most marvelous things about Society Carey is that he is a petty man and I want my petty people to act that way right to the end. Society Carey had an obligation to stand up and tell people the truth, to blame everybody else for the things he did wrong, then to glare at the people in front of him and yell out, "Mongrels!" After which, he should have raced to the airport, closed his eyes and felt his way inside a vehicle, and then waited until he had his head way up in the clouds before finding out whether he was flying in one of the wonderful helicopters or one of the wonderful planes that the people of the state pay for.

In making a pompous exit, Society Carey succeeded in polluting all of politics. The moment he finished mouthing his nonsense, it immediately was picked up by the people who will run for his job. Mario Cuomo called him a champ. He and Carey always called each other so many names that I don't know which one to tell you of first. Carol Bellamy announced that Carey was a great man. Carol Bellamy called Carey even more names that Cuomo did. Bob Abrams said Society Carey was a wonderful man. Abrams has been backbiting Carey for so long that his teeth hurt. If Society Carey had stood up and done it properly, had called everybody curs and mongrels, like he really wanted to, then all of the other candidates would have been obliged to call him names right back, and the public then would have had a sight most rare: politicians actually being honest.

In his farewell speech Friday, Society Carey seemed to forget he was alive, and he talked about public service as if it were a reality. What Society Carey knows about public service is this:

For the summers of 1979 and 1980, at his personal family house on Shelter Island, Society Carey charged the working people of the state $28,597 for "seasonal housekeepers and aides." All day long in Society Carey's summer house, there were good, strong-armed Long Island cleaning women rubbing away at the mirrors. As one cleaning woman left a mirror another cleaning woman approached it, in order for the mirrors to be so absolutely spotless that Society Carey could check the true color of his hair at any moment of the day.

Once, a long time ago in this country, there were people like Jefferson, who returned from public office to find his family home in shambles from years of neglect and who immediately said that the repairs were his responsibility, and not the taxpayers', for he had gone to Washington to serve government, not to use it.

Society Carey, however, appears to get most of his philosophy from *Women's Wear Daily*. He decided that he not only wanted to work like a king — still, today, Society Carey has yet to put in an eleven-hour week as governor — but he wanted to live like one. Which he did. In the end, this regal living, and the aloofness required of monarchs, did him in. The last time he ran for governor, he had about a hundred people who raised $3.5 million for him. The moment he got elected he decided that never again would he speak to such common trash. But recently, with his term getting along, he decided that he just might give one or two of his old friends a call. He did. He found that nobody really wanted to talk to him anymore.

Several people began to say that Carey was uncomfortable with the idea of trying to run again with no money and without even a hundred people who would answer his phone calls.

I knew all of this was happening. But somehow, I simply counted on Society Carey being around forever. Which was a natural feeling, for when one is blessed with something as truly great as Society Carey for a character, he cannot envision ever being without it. I mean, here is Society Carey last spring, honeymooning in Greece, and announcing that it was perfectly all right for the Greek government to be paying for his trip. "After all, I am entitled to see the homeland of my bride once," he said. And then a bartender on the island of Corfu looked up, saw Carey, and said, "I see Society Carey is here again." And then a bartender on Mykonos turned and smiled and said, "Society Carey. It is good to see him again." On each of the two previous trips Carey had made to Greece somebody else had paid bills.

Now he is gone, and where is there, in this pack of earnest people plugging for his job, someone who can fill the space of a Society Carey? Therefore, if there were any tears on Friday, they were here, in the eyes of this old streetwalker, who sat at a desk and found that Society Carey had just taken away the typewriter.

But he will remain forever in mind. Here he is, here is Society

Carey at the bar, with a bottle of New York State wine in front of him, passed around for all to see. And then, when it came time for the bartender to fill Society Carey's glass, he ducked down and poured from a bottle of French wine, looked around, and then slipped the glass to Society Carey.

"New York State wine!" Society Carey called out.

(January 1982)

His Sport Was Cockfighting

At the end, he was alone in his house with a parrot that never learned how to swear, no matter how many times the words were used. He was in the same house in which he had lived for more than fifty years, a wooden house with no number or name on the front door — the old Irish show you nothing — and he had no job or title and he had been sick for years and groped when he had to put more than a few words together, and he ran everything around him. With Dan O'Connell, the last and oldest Democratic city boss, only the mortician could pry the power out of his hand.

Dan O'Connell was ninety-one when he died yesterday in Albany. He was of Daley and Curley and Hague, around before them and after them, and he ran the city of Albany his own way, no matter who was president or who was across the street in the governor's office or, much more important, who was the new special prosecutor. And yesterday, when he went, O'Connell took with him a fondness for methods that are not allowed in American politics anymore because they are not considered nice.

Uncle Dan, as he was called, always liked his voting booths to be accessible. And each Election Day, when things were the way they were supposed to be, the firemen of Engine 9, on Second Avenue in Albany, had to roll their trucks out into the street while the board of elections people brought in the booths. The booths were arranged about the brass fire pole. Up above, in the circular opening in the ceiling, was one of O'Connell's organization. The man peered down at the voting machines. Each time a citizen stepped into the booth, O'Connell's man cleared his throat. A tiger's growl is less threatening. The citizen in the booth either did the right thing, vote for Uncle Dan's ticket, or the citizen's name went on a list. If he had any relatives on a municipal payroll — and everyone in Albany always had somebody on a payroll — a process known as getting even would take place.

O'Connell was famous for having a large group of people such as Solly Saul who were ready to come out of the woodwork and go to work in a tough election.

One Election Day, when special investigators trailed Solly around, they decided to make the arrest on the occasion of Solly's twentieth visit to a voting booth.

"I'm doing my duty as a citizen," Solly roared as he was lugged out.

In court, he entered a plea of guilty. "I throw myself on the mercy of the court," he announced.

The court in this case was a judge known as Double-or-Nothing Gallup, who knew the full meaning of Albany justice: it is unfair for a judge to lose his job. Solly Saul walked out of the court.

O'Connell was a growling man who considered his style of politics, him being the boss, as being far more sensible than any of this openness that is now practiced. He regarded the 1970 New York statewide election as the best evidence of this. The Democrats, after much arguing, came up with a ticket headed by Arthur Goldberg for governor; Basil Paterson, a black, for lieutenant governor; and Jewish candidates for the remaining statewide offices.

"That's the most unbalanced ticket I ever heard of," O'Connell announced. "How the hell can I support it?"

John Burns, then the state chairman, and candidate Basil Paterson went to Albany, the O'Connells' house, to soothe the old man. O'Connell sat on his back porch and glared at them.

"Dan, I'd like to point out one thing," Burns said. "Basil here is a Catholic."

"In that sense," O'Connell snarled, "he's the only white man on the damn ticket."

His enemy was Thomas E. Dewey. When Dewey ran for governor of New York, O'Connell ordered civil-defense blackouts of all radios in the Albany area at the times when Dewey had speeches scheduled. As governor, Dewey appointed a special prosecutor — to get O'Connell. Uncle Dan always had brewery interests, he was connected with the Albany Baseball Pool, and everybody in his immediate circle always cheered when there was heavy snow — and thus major snow-removal work for private companies.

O'Connell sneered at the investigation. He decided that all the telephones were tapped, and he began talking abusively into all phones. Soon everybody in the Albany city government was using this language. He knew there were cameras on him, and whenever he came out of the Elks Club, he paused, tipped his hat, and waved at a camera he knew to be hidden across the street. He then had his district attorney open a sweeping investigation of the state legislature, whose members immediately wailed to Dewey.

O'Connell always said, "There are three kinds of people can never be elected president: a Roman Catholic, a Jew, and Thomas E. Dewey." When John F. Kennedy was elected in 1960, O'Connell said, "I'm still right on two of them. And one of them I'll be right on forever. Ask that — Dewey."

His power came from the streets around him, from the saloons and the municipal workers. Insecure about himself, he favored Wasps as mayors of Albany. He could run the town from his living room. He had Albany organized and financed: committeemen always had money to send flowers to a wake. Because of this, he could say to Paul O'Dwyer, running in a primary for United States senator, "I'll see that you carry it up here. So don't waste your time campaigning. You'll win by fifteen thousand votes whether you come up here or not." O'Dwyer won by a few votes over the fifteen thousand.

O'Connell died believing that cockfighting was the greatest sport in the world, because it is the only one that you can't fix, and that Harry S Truman was the greatest leader in the history of the world. This was not because Truman saw to it that O'Connell received patronage. It was for something more important: Truman beat Dewey. Dan O'Connell never had any qualms about revenge in any form.

"My father was a committeeman for him," a woman named McManus was saying in Albany yesterday, "and on the day after election he would have crews go around and paint yellow no-parking signs on the curbs in front of any stores that didn't vote right."

(March 1977)

A Big Guy Arrives

It seemed to be about nothing. For Mario Cuomo, the wait was done at the kitchen table of his house in Holliswood, in Queens, and he sat through the afternoon in a shirt that was hanging out and un-buttoned and dungaree pants, the floppy kind that come off the shelf of a hardware store. Those raised alongside the railroad tracks in Jamaica don't understand much about who designers are, much less designer jeans.

Long ago, the charm went out of the business of waiting for election results. Once, men sat in crowded halls with people cheering or cursing the results when they were put up on a board in front of a room. The computer has replaced all of it; the sounds and smells and pacing belong to when men instead of machines counted. And at two-thirty yesterday afternoon, while housewives in his neighborhood were beginning to think of children getting out of school, the blue wall phone rang in Cuomo's kitchen and he answered it. He took out a large loose-leaf book, a diary he has kept for a long time, and he began writing in it as he spoke on the phone.

The caller was somebody from a television network, where interviews of people leaving the polls were placed into a computer.

"Two hundred interviews," Cuomo said, repeating what he was being told. "Cuomo forty-nine. Koch forty-nine. And this is weighted to New York? Thank you."

He hung up, wrote more, then looked up. "I have to win," he said. "They have New York City, the suburbs, and Erie County and Koch is only up seven points in those areas. The way we have it, he can be up fifteen in those places and we win statewide."

It was only a short time later that Jimmy Carter was on the phone. "I hope," Cuomo said.

Cuomo's mother called him at four-thirty. "Whatever it is, Ma, it's *buòno*," he said. "*Spero che non vi disturbo.*"

At four-forty-five, the phone rang again, and he flipped open the big diary and began writing and repeating what he was hearing. Somebody at the network was on the other end.

"Even," Cuomo said, "with this sample not properly reflecting upstate, where presumably I will do well."

He hung up. He said, "Can you imagine tying Koch in the city and suburbs?"

The next call said there was a sample of six hundred and it showed Cuomo with a fifty-to-forty-eight lead, and the poll still not reflecting the upstate vote.

"My prediction is starting to look pretty good," he said. The night before, after the last television appearance of the campaign, he sat in a place called the Racing Club on East Sixty-seventh Street and somebody at the table asked him how he thought it would go now that it was all over, and he said, "I expect to win by three to five points."

Always, the candidate thinks he can win and uses hope and conjecture to support it. Cuomo is different. From the start, from a night in March when he sat down to figure out how he would run against Ed Koch, he thought that the idea of Koch leaving his job as mayor to try for governor would cost Koch at least 10 percent of his natural vote. That night, Cuomo said the idea came to him to tell people that they could keep Koch as mayor and let him finish the job he promised to do, and also have Cuomo, the lieutenant governor, become governor.

The people with him that night disagreed. You are too soft on Koch, they argued. Attack him. Cuomo shook his head. "I'm not going to say that Koch has done a good job. I am going to say that he has not finished the job he said he would do."

The campaign went on that way and in the last few days, when the Koch people found out what was happening to them, they put Koch on television in a commercial that perhaps did more damage to a candidate than anything seen in recent years. Koch pleaded with voters to let him go to Albany, and as he did so he underlined everything that Cuomo had been doing since March.

And at the table the night before the election, when Cuomo spoke quietly of how he thought he would win, nobody smiled and eyes looked away in embarrassment.

And yesterday afternoon, as people still voted, Cuomo sat at the kitchen table and began going through an envelope filled with papers, all of them lists having to do with political moves to make for the general election: a meeting with the governor, phone calls to the three newspapers that had been against him, a note to get entertainers.

And at nine o'clock, they called from Manhattan and told him to come into the hotel, and he called to his son, "Christopher, get brown polish for your shoes," as he went in to get dressed. Then he rode from Queens with his wife, Matilda, and the son. The other four children already were at the hotel.

He sat in the front and listened to music on the radio. He was a guy from Queens, who comes out of places like the Beaver Gym and Jamaica Arena and Saint Monica's Hall, and he was, as he drove through the streets of Queens, a guy from a neighborhood who had just made the rest of the nation shake. For that was no local election Mario Cuomo won in New York last night; that was a national earthquake. With every politician in the state against him, and most of the newspapers, and with a philosophy that draws smirks from those who always seem to win elections these days, Mario Cuomo had upset a big political name, a candidate who was supposed to win by as much as he pleased.

And here was Cuomo, of Queens, who spoke of Ronald Reagan as a threat to everything the country stood for, who said that being mean was a disease, who spoke of the old and the blacks, riding up to a hotel in Manhattan. By the time he stepped out of the car and went up to the seventeenth-floor suite, he was a national figure. If all Democrats are old, he is new.

He stepped out of the crowd around a television set and combed his hair in front of the bathroom mirror. There was a loud cheer in the room.

"What's that?" he said.

"You just won," somebody said.

He nodded. "Do you know that once we beat the Baisley Park Civics with only four players?" he said.

(*September 1982*)

We Give You "First Today"

He gave himself the name, and it is such a great name that he shall be known forevermore as "First Today Moynihan."

Now I will tell you how he gave himself the name. He was at the bar of Charley O's Restaurant in Rockefeller Center one Saint Patrick's Day morn, at the bar for the party he was throwing in honor of himself; Moynihan's family crest reads, "After me, you come first!" He stood at the bar and held up the glass and crowed to the ceiling and the sky above it.

"First today!"

And down it went. The drink did not survive. The name sure did.

First Today Moynihan is the second greatest name I have ever known, the first being Society Carey. And, frankly, I was finished in this business when Society Carey retired. Now along comes First Today Moynihan to save whatever career I have.

Recently, First Today, who is one of these senators we have from New York, announced that he wouldn't march in the Saint Patrick's Day Parade because a man named Flannery, who is sympathetic to the IRA in Northern Ireland, is grand marshal.

To be factual, nobody cared about the man Flannery being grand marshal, and beyond that a lot of people didn't even care about the parade until First Today Moynihan announced, right in the morning, that he would have nothing to do with such a parade.

Now, so many people are planning to attend the parade on March 17 that Grand Marshal Flannery, eighty-one himself, finds that his major duty is to insure the presence of enough emergency medical equipment along the line of march to take care of hordes who haven't walked a full block in twenty years.

For a moment, everybody thought that this left First Today in an unfamiliar position. Here was a parade and he could not be in it, waving marvelously to the crowd — Oh, I'm so grand! — his Irish hat pulled down over his face. Usually, First Today can save himself, because he has at least four positions on any subject on the crust of the old earth. This time, he had announced that he would not march and there was no place for him to issue his usual second statement saying that he would march.

So he had his hat and his wave and no place to take them. Or so it seemed until it was learned yesterday through news channels most acceptable that First Today Moynihan will not deprive himself. He will be seen in front of a crowd.

There he was, we have learned, prancing through Balboa Park in San Diego yesterday, practicing his gait for the great show on Saturday when the queen of England arrives with her prince husband for the start of her California tour.

It was bright and warm and First Today's head was broiling inside that Irish hat of his, sweltering and sweating away, and if he ever keeps this up until Saturday he will have boiled the whole head down to some kind of size.

"Why are the animals in the zoo growling so much?" we learned that First Today asked the zookeeper.

"We are not feeding the animals so that they'll be hungry and animated, pacing around a lot, when the prince arrives," the zookeeper said. "If we feed them, all they'll do is flop in the sun and snore. We want action for the prince. Hungry animals provide it."

And First Today Moynihan exulted, "Good show!"

He walked on through Balboa Park, did First Today Moynihan yesterday, getting those legs out, footfall loud and sure, arms moving, one in the air waving, the other swinging, the great head boiling away under the hat, walking just as he will on Saturday when the queen and prince arrive. Now First Today came to a man who was lugging a giant cooler.

"What have you got?" First Today asked.

"This is Malvern Spring water for the queen," the man said. "They sent it over here from Worcestershire, in England. The queen never goes anywhere in the world without this water."

First Today trumpeted, "Good mixer!"

He walked on, in his great jacket from Taylor and Solash, London. Oh, of course, London. First Today Moynihan dresses and does his best to speak as if born and raised in one of the flats on Eaton Square, Belgravia, London, SW1.

He is a great scholar on England. Remembered forever is the day he lectured, at a time when people in New York were discussing housing for the South Bronx. Once, a long time ago in England, he said, there were people in row houses who complained about being crowded together. So the government built houses with space around them, and everybody caught pneumonia.

"So much for new housing!" First Today Moynihan announced.

At the time, I believe, he was living in the large, free apartment of the United Nations ambassador in the Waldorf Towers, and before that he had an ambassador's house in India, and before that one of those Harvard professor's places in Cambridge. So of course he could tell people in the South Bronx all they ever wanted to know about housing.

This is one of the reasons why First Today is considered so brilliant.

It also explains why nobody in New York yesterday was surprised at these reports of First Today Moynihan being in San Diego, getting the legs in shape so on Saturday he could walk and wave in front of the crowds gathered to see the queen of England.

(*February 1983*)

The Best Night Club in Plains

As a person who lives in a city of this country, the first time I remember becoming apprehensive about James Earl Carter, Jr., and his Georgia piney-woods boys was on a Saturday afternoon in Plains, in Georgia, in July of 1976. The sky turned the color of metal and rain fell. I was standing under the shedrow on the main street, looking up and down for a place to step in. There was none. There was a Carter campaign office and a Carter antique store. I walked to the end of the shedrow and looked out. Here, just down the side street, maybe fifty yards down, was a small building with a sign on it saying "Night Club." I knew that this was my splinter of life. I stepped out into the rain and headed for it.

The "Night Club" was a place with a broken jukebox and rain dripping through a cracked skylight and forming puddles on the floor. Four or five black people sat at a small bar and drank bottled beer out of paper cups. I stayed there for an hour or so. The only people to come in and out were black. When the rain stopped coming through the skylight, I picked up my change and left.

Up at the corner, fifty yards up, in front of the shedrow, Jody Powell sat in a pickup truck. He had one hand on the wheel and a bottle of beer in the other.

"Want to stop over at Billy's and get a beer?" he said.

I said, no, I had just finished all the beer I cared for at the moment.

Powell seemed surprised. "Where?" he said.

"Right down there," I said.

Powell looked down the street, down the fifty or so yards from the world of the Carters, and his eyebrows went up as he saw the sight: "Night Club."

"I didn't even know the place was there," Powell said.

And now, on Tuesday, when President James Earl Carter, Jr., comes to New York City, we can expect the same attitude from him and his people. New York is the place of the South Bronx and Bushwick and Central Harlem. President Carter, therefore, has plans to appear at the United Nations and then sit in a hotel suite and receive heads of the UN delegations. Harlem might as well erect a sign saying "Night Club." Carter neither knows nor cares that the place is there. After all, the man must prepare for his trip around the world, the trip to make people forget Bert Lance, the trip to such places as Caracas and Brussels, of which we all know how important they are to us right now.

Meanwhile, we live in New York. We are America's national city, the idea and cultural center of Western man. And, still, our tax money goes to Washington and then is sent out to Arizona and California and foreign countries and we are left, at nightfall, with the young unemployed taking to the streets in sneakers and bringing true oppression to the poor neighborhoods. The people of Harlem and Bushwick are locked into their musty rooms at night as if they were jailed. And outside, as police make their rounds, there always can be found, sprawled grotesquely on the street, somebody like Victor Pagan, who was twenty and was shot in the head and left for dead last night in front of 1340 Nelson Avenue in the Bronx.

When Carter ran for president, he made many promises to people in big cities such as New York. He would help with welfare, he would do all he could to correct the way the money of the cities was being used for everything but the slums of the cities. When Carter talked, I kept seeing a sign saying "Night Club." I never believed a word he said, and therefore did not feel he was lying. This is something that other people should begin to consider at this time.

Senator Pat Moynihan, for one. He screamed this week that Carter personally made phone calls to defeat a welfare proposal that would help New York. Moynihan acted as if he had been betrayed. I don't know why Moynihan even bothered to raise his voice. He knows a better way to do things. He can write one of those articles of his.

Moynihan is a rather poor writer, his sentences drag across the page at textbook speed, but he knows how to make these ponderous lines cause great impact on his personal career.

In 1970, Moynihan wrote a rather long-winded article about how the Catholics lost out to the Jews in New York politics. "The Jews ousted the Catholics," he wrote. "They did this in direct toe-to-toe encounters in a hundred areas of the city's life . . ." The article was terrific. The Jews loved reading about how they outclassed the Catholics, and if you were a Catholic and you read the article, you had to ask: "If they're killing us, then what are we going to fight them with?" The answer was obvious: Moynihan.

Then a couple of years ago, he sat down and wrote a tortuous article for the magazine *Commentary*. The theme of the article was that the United States should stop cowering in the face of attacks by Third World nations at the United Nations. We should stand up to these two-bit black dictators, Moynihan said.

When they read it in Washington, it was clear that there was only one person who could do this: Moynihan. President Ford named him to the UN, where he immediately began his campaign to run for the Senate.

It now appears that the time has come for Moynihan to take that typewriter of his, the one with the slow velocity but the big knockdown power, and write an article about the need in the Democratic party for somebody to begin gathering up people for a 1980 primary campaign designed to make James Earl Carter, Jr., the one-term president he deserves to be. Who would the candidate be? When you read the article, you will get the answer: Moynihan.

There is no personal love here for Moynihan. He is so pompous that he ought to be a doorman for Buckingham Palace. His ambition always has shown very little difficulty in overpowering ethics and taste. He was a Kennedy man. When Nixon offered him a job, he dived through the window to get it. He was in the White House at a time when the Nixon people were committing the high crime of attempted fascism. When he left the administration, Moynihan declared that Nixon was a "decent man."

But once this is said, you still are left with D. P. Moynihan, senator, a man who knows about Harlem, who knows about welfare, who seems to know more than anyone else about the way federal aid formulas leave the great cities of the nation almost defenseless against the times in which we must live.

I could care less about Moynihan personally. But the people who live in the cities of this country might be concerned about getting Carter into political trouble immediately, setting the tone, spreading the impression that he could be a one-term president. If there is movement, I have a notion that Carter and his piney-woods boys will become defensive and obvious and help the matter along.

(October 1977)

Always, the Judge Keeps His Left Up

WASHINGTON — He was brought up not to quit. He came out of the back room of a grocery store and he set pins and punched out guys in bowling alleys and when he couldn't find a job as a lawyer he fought with his fists for money, and if the fight was scheduled for ten rounds, then he was there in the tenth, with the left hand out. His name is John Joseph Sirica, and yesterday in Washington he was all we had left.

The rest of them had decided that it was proper to make the past meaningless; it was proper to have Richard Nixon seated at a state dinner in the White House. And, by every implication, it was proper to begin rewriting history: Richard Nixon the innocent victim. He was caught attempting to destroy the Constitution, and now we are asked to smile.

There were in Washington yesterday people who are supposed to be entrusted with the honor and dignity of the country and with all that this means for the generations to come, and yet the load of them, from president to House Speaker to cabinet officer, had less shame yesterday than a Brooklyn district leader. Richard Nixon, who sold out his oath and his country, who committed the high crime of invading freedom of citizens, who scuttled away and evaded an accounting, was back in the tailored warmth of official life. And no one raised a voice because everybody was too busy making sure he was getting in to the same dinner. Apparently, the price in Washington now is a meal with a politician from China, in this case Teng Hsiao-ping.

John Sirica, who never learned how to go back, would have none of this.

In the morning, he was in his chambers on the second floor of the federal courthouse here. He was making some instant coffee at a table that was under a framed letter written to him by James McCord. A paragraph of the letter says, "Others involved in the Watergate operation were not identified during the trial when they could have been by those testifying." Another paragraph says, "There was political pressure applied to the defendants to plead guilty and remain silent."

"This letter will go down as having more to do with Watergate than any other," Sirica was saying. "You'll notice the date, that's March 19, 1973. That was my birthday."

"What about the White House dinner tonight?" he was asked.

"I'll be going home tonight," he said.

"Did they invite you?"

"No."

"They invited Nixon," we said.

"That has to do with the Chinese," Sirica said. "He did a good job on foreign policy. I'm not going to criticize the White House today, but it's what it'll be in the future that bothers me. The trouble is, twenty-five years from now he'll have people saying that the politicians and the press ran him out of office and people will believe it. That isn't what ran Nixon out of office. He was going to be impeached and he was facing indictment.

"The other morning on the television I saw this English novelist and he was saying that Watergate was all built up into a big to-do about nothing. How can people forget? These men went around paying witnesses not to talk. They had tremendous amounts of money. You call that obstruction of justice. It's bribery. Well, that's what it is."

On the wall behind him was a picture of his wedding day. The best man was Jack Dempsey. I remembered that when Watergate first started, and a judge named Sirica had the case, Jack Dempsey sat at his old restaurant on Broadway and said to me, "I don't know about that big case down there, but I can tell you that the little judge is going to make them all give up."

Sirica, drinking his coffee, asked, "You much interested in the fights anymore?"

"I saw a guy on television fighting in Detroit, his name is Hearns," I said. "He's a six-one welterweight. If they ever match him with Roberto Duran, I'm going to go to that one."

"A six-one welterweight," Sirica said. "Reminds me of a fella I fought in Miami, Tommy Thompson. He was six feet. Little bit over. I was only five-six. I looked like a boy compared to him. Jack Britton, you remember him, the old welterweight champ, told me, 'He won't hit you in the backside.' I box him, duck, jab, let him come lunging off-balance. Britton was right. He didn't hit me in the backside."

He went over to a table and sat down. He had the jacket to his book. The title is *To Set the Record Straight*. Sirica said it was going to come out in April. The publisher, W. W. Norton, has as the cover of its spring catalogue of books to be published a picture of Sirica in robes. There is no type, not even the name of the publisher. The picture speaks for itself. The hope is that the book is bound well, and that librarians keep an eye on its condition, because this is one that should be read for the next two centuries.

It was about noon, and he decided to go to lunch. At seventy-five, Sirica is a senior judge in the Federal District Court here. He doesn't take on much criminal work anymore, and yesterday he had motions on his desk in a civil matter. He wore a navy blue blazer, subdued plaid pants, a white shirt, and blue striped tie. His hair and eyebrows are still dark, and the blue-gray eyes seem gentle enough, but experience reminds one that there can be this little flick in the eyes and then you are under a full glare.

He drove his car to lunch at a lawyers' club downtown. "You balance things out, Watergate was a plus," he said. "When they see a Mitchell and Haldeman and those fellas going to jail, somebody in jail can say, well, they put the big guys in, too. But then of course they can point out Nixon and, well, it's too bad they can. Equal justice. Kleindienst, too. Got slapped on the wrist. Got probation."

The record shows that when he got away with it, Kleindienst was the first in Watergate to resurrect himself. He is the only former attorney general of the United States who was guilty of a crime and has his portrait hanging, alongside such as Robert Kennedy, on a wall in the Justice Department.

To get to lunch, Sirica had to drive past the South Lawn of the White House. Inside the fence, the driveway was lined with the cars of people who were setting up the place for the big state dinner.

The program called for Richard Nixon to be allowed in the door, and then to be brought into a predinner reception in the Yellow Room for the most important of the guests, a select handful, Carter the president and the Chinese leaders and a few others and that's all. After which, Nixon was to be brought out and seated at a big state dinner.

And all the time they really should have had him in a courtroom, standing in front of John Sirica, who does not quit.

(January 30, 1979)

Kennedy's Campaign Steps

Edward Kennedy was leaning against the wall, reading his speech over, while Nate Allen, a detective, stood with his arms folded and watched the people who came around.

A Manhattan lawyer, Tim Hanan, peered out at the stage of Avery Fisher Hall, which had been set up for the graduation of the Mount Sinai School of Medicine.

"Where will he be sitting?" Hanan said. "He's going to have to leave at about three-twenty-five and we don't want to disturb anybody as he's leaving."

"We have him in a seat right in front," a man from the medical school said.

"Could you show me the seat, I'd like to see it for myself," Hanan said.

The man from the school pointed to the seat where Senator Kennedy would sit. Hanan and Allen, the detective, nodded.

"And you'll be at this entrance?" Hanan said to Allen.

"Right here," Allen said.

"Who watches the entrance on the other side of the stage?" someone asked.

"We have people there," a uniformed police sergeant said.

Kennedy, reading his speech, heard none of this. Then the music started out in the hall and Kennedy, in cap and gown, walked onto the stage with the school president and the auditorium was afire with blinking strobe lights as the crowd pursued the great American occupation of trying to preserve all of life on three-by-three glossy paper.

The head of the school, Thomas Chalmers, introduced Kennedy: "This is the sixth straight commencement for which the senior class has requested Senator Kennedy as the guest speaker. We're happy that he finally was able to fit it into his busy schedule."

Most of the people in the hall smiled or nudged each other. Kennedy fit the school into his schedule by having Mount Sinai change the graduation date. He wanted to fit the graduation into a day in which he could make two other appearances in New York. He wanted to be at our commencement, everybody in the hall was saying, because this year Kennedy is starting to run for president.

It does not go away for Edward Kennedy. In 1976, when Jimmy

Carter won, Kennedy thought he had eight years before he would have to weigh danger against desire and start around the nation. But here, less than three years later, the subject is up again. How many times do you pass it up? And so Kennedy stood on the stage at Lincoln Center in New York, and meanwhile in Iowa there are people already working on placing Kennedy's name in the party caucuses for convention delegates. That occurs in January: Kennedy does not have to declare in Iowa; the election law gives the people the right to run a candidate whether the candidate declares or not.

In New Hampshire, a politically substantial group plans a write-in for Kennedy in the state primary. The New Hampshire people point to 1964, when Henry Cabot Lodge won over Rockefeller and Goldwater on a write-in. "How hard is it to teach people how to write the name 'Kennedy'?" one of the Manchester, New Hampshire, Kennedy people was saying on the phone yesterday.

By now, Kennedy's position in all this would seem to be simple: If he does not take himself out of it, then he is in it. And with Jimmy Carter finding out daily that "the Bible tells me so," is an answer to nothing, it suddenly seems almost impossible for Kennedy to take himself out of it at this point.

So here, in Lincoln Center, Kennedy was making his third speech of the day in New York. It was about the future of medicine and was not designed to produce screams from an audience. Kennedy read the speech without making much eye contact with the audience. Which was surprising; I thought he had the business down so well that he could deliver a speech without making it appear as if he were reading it.

On the first page, he spoke about the maldistribution of medical talent around the country. I thumbed through the graduation book and went down the list of graduates. Kennedy was on the mark. Mount Sinai School of Medicine is part of the City University of New York. This means we pay taxes for the medical students. Of the 119 graduates, 46 of them were listed as going for medical residencies outside of the city, to places such as Harbor General Medical, Los Angeles; Baylor College affiliated hospitals, Houston; University of Texas Southwest affiliated hospitals, Dallas; Vancouver General Hospital. The anger rose as I read the program. Why bother to be a doctor if you start your career by cheating the place that educated you?

Kennedy's voice brought back my attention. It is about as powerful a public-speaking voice as there is in the English language. The voice alone is a reason why all polls show that people prefer Kennedy to Carter. A speech is a medium to lead. To Carter, a speech appears to be a boring, disagreeable task to be carried out with a smile of glucose at the end.

When Kennedy finished his talk there was loud applause. Nobody stood or cheered, but the clapping was continuous and became louder after Kennedy sat down, and he had to get up again and as he stood you looked past him, to the policemen in the entrances on both sides of the stage, and now, in the noise and the blinking camera lights, things came back to you. There was Malcolm Perry, the doctor, walking out of Parkland Memorial Hospital, Dallas, the jacket over his arm, the first lines of his life showing in his face. The patient, John Kennedy, was in a coffin in the plane on the way to Washington. And in downtown Dallas, in a packed hallway in police headquarters, a door opened and two detectives in cowboy hats pushed out. Handcuffed to them was a guy with a sallow face and wearing a plaid sports shirt. The detectives pushed through the crowd to take the guy, Lee Harvey Oswald, to the men's room, they said. Somebody in the crowd in the hallway said, "They'll get this guy killed." He was wrong. This was only Friday night and they didn't get Oswald killed until Sunday morning.

And then there was the hotel kitchen in Los Angeles and Jesse Unruh was up on a steam table, stamping his foot down on the hand of Sirhan Sirhan, trying to make Sirhan drop the gun, and on the floor, with one eye closed and the other seeing nothing, Bobby Kennedy was dying.

Now here in Lincoln Center there was another one of them on the stage, with people cheering, and you could feel the trouble. On July 18, it will be the tenth anniversary of the night Mary Jo Kopechne and Ted Kennedy went off a bridge at a place called Chappaquiddick. Wherever Kennedy goes in a presidential campaign he will be asked what really happened on that night, and the people are entitled to an answer. The issue may not be overwhelming, it probably could not stop Kennedy from winning an election for president, but at the same time it most certainly is not out of the public mind.

The issue becomes dangerous in that it gives someone out there a moral justification for reviving the incident of the death of Mary Jo Kopechne. When you mention Kennedy running in a campaign you just think automatically of danger. The most blameless and innocuous man to be president in our generation, Gerald Ford, had two assassination attempts on him. For an Edward Kennedy, whose name stirs emotions, the risk is daily.

When Kennedy finished his speech to the medical school, he slipped off the stage and went out to his car with Nate Allen walking alongside him. The car started off into the traffic on Broadway. Kennedy sat in the backseat. I don't know what he has on his mind, if even he knows where he stands at this point, and it all could change in a week and he could take himself out and therefore he would not be in, but no matter what he does, as his car pulled away, all I could hear, over the sounds of the traffic on Broadway, was Jesse Unruh's foot stamping down on Sirhan Sirhan's gun hand, which was on the steam table.

(June 1979)

The One-Night Comeback

There was one night, after the New Hampshire primary, when Edward Kennedy sat in his house in McLean, Virginia, with Steve Smith, his brother-in-law, and people from his campaign and they were talking about getting out of the race for the presidency.

"I'm going in Massachusetts," Kennedy said.

They nodded.

"I have to do that," he said.

They nodded.

Then Kennedy said, "Listen, I'm tired. It's not hard to consider stopping this. I'm not having any fun. It's easy to consider it. But let's forget about it. I didn't get into this to get out of it. You want power because it's an opportunity. We don't quit."

He did not. He took Massachusetts and went on to Illinois, to one of the worst beatings a major political candidate ever has taken, a vote that was delivered with insults. He came to New York, where he had no chance.

And now it was last night, a soft spring night in Manhattan, and people walked the street outside and smiled, and Edward Kennedy stood in a room with his family, with children and sisters and wife and friends and everybody seemed young.

"Give me," Steve Smith was saying, "one guy who waded through more personal abuse than this guy. First, you had a suit there and no guy in it. Then the baby brother. He wasn't a Jack or Bobby. Then the mess. No character. Whoever took more than this guy? And here he is."

His brother-in-law Edward Kennedy was standing outside in the hall, talking quietly, smiling a little, seeming, as the results came in, to become more imposing with each phone call.

"It's a complete blowout," somebody called out. "He's winning twenty-three out of twenty-four downstate congressional districts."

"You'll have to continue by popular demand," somebody said.

"I wasn't going to stop no matter what happened this evening," Kennedy said.

He had been saying this all day. In the morning, when he could not vote for himself, Kennedy took the 10:00 A.M. shuttle to Washington. He sat in a front seat with the briefcase on his lap, papers spread on it, his pen tapping the stories that said he would end Jimmy Carter.

"Here you are," he said, "a short-term investment brings seventeen and a half percent yield. The fellows with money will ride this right through. They won't feel it. But what about the people who don't have ten thousand dollars?"

"Do you think that's starting to register with people?" he was asked.

"It's Carter's demise," he said.

"What do you do if you lose tonight?"

"Keep going, Carter's through. These things are starting to catch up with him. I could see it in New York. Ten days ago. They started listening when you talked about the economy. The look told you that. People were interested. There was an interaction with people. The campaign started to sing."

He had no chance in New York, of course. All you had to do was read a paper or watch television to know that. The polls showed that he was doing surprisingly well to be only twenty points or so behind Jimmy Carter. The ear listening to him tried to catch the dead tones of a candidate talking away the last hours of his endeavor.

But Kennedy's voice was firm and his hands moved as he talked. "Well, the economy is why it doesn't matter what happens to me tonight. Fifty-three, fifty-four percent, or whatever numbers Jody Powell or somebody says, it doesn't matter to me. I'm staying in because Carter is through. I felt it in Berlin, New Hampshire. Workers after the shift were in this back room and the minute I looked at them I could see a change. I spoke to them about gun control. Then the economy. I saw it right there. I couldn't get it across. There was no dialogue. Carter wouldn't permit it. But it's there. I've seen it. He's finished."

He was asked about a couple of theories people have had about him. That he didn't want to win. And that he was going through these beatings as a penance.

"That's all chatter," he said. He waved his hand. "I don't listen to that. I'm going out now and I'm going to do it. We can't out-Republican the Republicans. That's all we've been doing. Turning back on all important social goals. We're going to keep our traditional commitments and values."

He began talking about a Carter commercial that said a man running for president brings two things with him, his record and his personal character. "He also brings twenty percent inflation," Kennedy said. He said it with a smile. The idea of bitterness doesn't seem to occur to him.

When he mentioned Vice President Mondale, he said he was disappointed. "He should have said something about all this. Cutting back, giving up on our values. I guess, well, that's the job and that's one reason why I'd never take a job like that."

When Mondale's remark about Kennedy's patriotism was mentioned, Kennedy stood up and laughed. "I could've said a lot worse about me than that."

When the plane landed, he ducked into a car waiting on the runway and went to his house in McLean for the day.

Somewhere around 3:00 P.M., Steve Smith called him from New York and said that early polls of people who had voted showed that New York looked good. At 7:00 P.M. Kennedy boarded a shuttle back to New York. It was different this time. In the morning there had been nobody, only one aide, Rich Burke, and a couple of agents. Now the plane was crowded with reporters and camera people. And from the front three seats of the plane, where Kennedy sat with Rich Burke and his campaign manager, Paul Kirk, there came the first laughter of the night.

They were talking about a Boston politician named Sonny McDonough, who was in the hospital and was keeping a cross, decorated with diamonds, in the hospital vault because, Sonny said, he didn't want a priest to snap it up.

When the plane landed, there was a motorcade waiting on the

runway. When the cars moved off the runway and into the airport, you saw it for the first time in the campaign of this Kennedy. People stopped to look.

And now he was at Steve Smith's house in Manhattan, in a dark-blue suit, holding a cigar, waiting until it was time to go to a hotel and speak to the television cameras.

"It's an old thing," Steve Smith was saying, "but every time you start talking, you come right back to it: We can do better."

"Shall we go?" Kennedy said.

He walked upstairs to get his wife and then they went out to the car for the ride to the hotel. He had taken everything they had to give to him, laughter and innuendo, plus judgments and street insults. He lost his elections, but never his breeding. He never whined and anger was an alien. And now he simply would do what he was supposed to do: continue in style. Perhaps we best get used to him. He might be around for a long time.

(March 1980)

He's Worried about Rose Kennedy

Until I saw something with my own eyes yesterday in New York, I always felt that many of the stories I read about Richard Nixon's personal quirks were preposterous, the unavoidable result of writers having no access to a subject and at the same time having much blank paper to fill.

An illustration of this was his supposed craze over the subject of the Kennedys. Whenever I'd read a story dealing with this, I'd make a face and turn the page. Nixon is a perfectly horrible president, the worst of all time, I reasoned, but he still is the president, the winner. He can't be as insecure as they try to make him.

I began to waver during long nights of reading through Nixon's Watergate transcripts. The burglary was done in an effort to get something on Larry O'Brien of the Democratic National Committee, who had been John Kennedy's campaign manager in 1960. "Look out for him, he's tough," Nixon kept telling his people in the 1968 campaign, an election in which O'Brien controlled, at the most, one vote.

On the day that Nixon left the White House in disgrace, on August 9, 1974, he was in tears as he told the White House staff: "Nobody will ever write a book about my mother ... Yes, she will have no book written about her. But she was a saint."

I remember shaking my head and saying, "He just blew everything and he's worried about Rose Kennedy. Maybe he really has a problem."

It was a passing thought and I certainly could not be sure.

But I was yesterday, when Richard Nixon's five-car motorcade came out of La Guardia Airport and cut through Astoria, in Queens, and then went on to the most stirring view probably in the world. All of Manhattan climbs from the banks of the East River and spreads itself in front of you, right and left. Then the bridge plunges into the midst of these buildings. Nixon, who has spent almost the last four years staring at palm trees, crossed the bridge and his limousine went into the side streets and headed uptown, to the Hotel Carlyle on Madison Avenue. The Carlyle. Jack Kennedy always stayed at the Carlyle.

The sign for the Café Carlyle yesterday said that Bobby Short was appearing. Bobby Short is a major part of the elegance of New York. He is the sophisticate, playing café tunes for terribly beautiful people. The Kennedy kind of people. And here, coming into the Carlyle yesterday, was Richard M. Nixon, who plays "Melancholy Baby."

Yesterday, on his first trip to New York since losing his job, he went directly to the hotel where Kennedy stayed. Nixon might have a problem with truth, but the man certainly finds great comfort with eeriness.

An obvious reason for his visit yesterday was to see his daughter Tricia at her apartment on First Avenue and Eighty-fourth Street. All afternoon, a Secret Service station wagon blocked the driveway in front of the building and the lobby was filled with agents and with New York detectives in their best suits.

It takes a lot of people — five cars full — to protect a former president of this country. In Russia, which is a society of barbarians, they let the man out of the side door of the Kremlin and he gets home by himself. Once a year or so, somebody would see a Khrushchev walking along a street alone. Here, we need machine guns.

(*April 1978*)

The Last Rites, the Old Wrongs

WASHINGTON — They brought out Rockefeller and Kissinger and Ford, and now in the dimness of the entranceway on the Senate side of the Rotunda, here it was: the furtive look to the right, the eyes darting. Shoes flapping on the marble floor as he began walking. Richard Nixon came into the light and the steady chunk-chunk-chunk of the still cameras. The people in the crowd shifted to look at him.

He had been invited and of course, once that happened, he had to come, to fly here from California for the funeral of Hubert Humphrey, and as Richard Nixon walked across the marble floor of the Capitol of the United States, the wasting fires rose again. The man, you thought, is now down to robbing somebody of the honor of his own funeral.

Now, Isaac Stern stood up. The polished violin gleamed in the light. The bow moved. Not a grand motion. The bow just moved. Stern's hand seemed to be still, and the bow moved; the economy of motion that always accompanies greatness. The sound rose to the Rotunda. A high, clear sound. The joy of flight, that rose to the top of the great dome, where the noon sunlight poked through winter-frosted windows.

Isaac Stern played Bach for his friend Hubert Humphrey, who was in a casket with a flag over it. He played Bach with a wounded face and melancholy eyes and everything in this hushed chamber became different. The scoundrels became tiny and all dislike irrelevant. I never looked at Nixon's now-gray face again. It seemed like nobody else did, either. For Isaac Stern drew all attention to the life of Hubert Humphrey, a man who cried when he told of a three-year-old child of migrant Mexican farm workers drowning in an irrigation ditch because there was nobody to watch him while the parents worked in the fields.

The rest of the service was splendid. Carter, the president, got to a point where the occasion called for him to speak of Humphrey's greatness, and Carter, who gives no indication of doubt in his omnipotence, came at this on the oblique and said that Humphrey "may well have blessed our country more than any of us." Which is Carter's idea of clever English and it is terrible, but the singing that followed overcame this and at the end of the ceremony, after they lifted the casket up and carried it away, the crowd was trembling and felt purified. One traditional act was needed to complete the day.

Down the marble stairs, at the office of Jim Malloy, the door-keeper of the House of Representatives, mourners were stopped by the vile sight of coffee cups set out on a table.

Mario Biaggi frowned. Hugh Carey stared. Fred Rooney of Pennsylvania shrugged. A clergyman came in and sniffed. I do not know his denomination, but his emotion was correct. I poked my friend Thomas Ludlow Ashley of Ohio. "Why don't we go for a little air?" I said. I was absolutely right. How can you attend a funeral and not sit down at the end of it and discuss the man's life in a civilized setting?

And a few minutes later, Lud Ashley was in the lounge of the Carlton Hotel and he recalled, "In 1968, we had Humphrey at the Lucas County Recreation Center in Toledo and there was a big crowd, about seven thousand people, and I had him on at a quarter past two in the afternoon. Just before he went on, I said to him, 'Hubert, I have to be out of here in forty-five minutes to catch a plane in Detroit.' The plane was at quarter of four and it takes you about forty-five minutes to drive to the Detroit airport from Toledo. That's in a fast car. So I'm figuring, Hubert will do about twenty-five minutes, I'll slap him on the back and run for the car.

"Well, he got going. I'm sitting right next to him. He is going and going and I'm starting to writhe. I've heard it all so much. Spare me, please. He didn't even give a hint of stopping.

"I reached up and grabbed his sleeve and gave it a little tug. Come on, let's get out of here, Hubert. With this, Humphrey wheels and points at me and shouts to the crowd, 'And your congressman, Lud Ashley, was right with me in that great fight!' Then he went on to tell in great detail this great fight. The next time I went to the coattail, I gave it a real pull. I was actually giving him the hook. Here's Hubert, waving his arm at me. 'And Lud Ashley was in the middle of that fight.' And he started to tell them all about that fight. I couldn't duck out. He was talking about me and I sat there. He finished in forty-five minutes and I had to struggle through the crowd to get the car. I got to the airport in Detroit in time to see the plane rolling nice and smooth away from the gate."

Somebody else said, "His doctor, Berman, said that the other day he went to Humphrey and said, 'Well, they've just taken a poll of the best United States senator in the last twenty-five years and who do you think won?' And Humphrey, who could hardly talk, whispered to him, 'Who?' And Berman said, 'You did.' Now Humphrey's voice got a little more to it. 'And who second?" he asked the doctor. Berman said to him, 'Lyndon Johnson.' Berman said that Humphrey's head came right up. He said, 'Lyndon isn't going to like that.' "

Somebody else began to talk about a time in the 1972 California primary when Humphrey started to talk at a school for the deaf and they had a priest sitting below him who translated the speech into sign language. At the end of the first half hour, the priest's hands were becoming a trifle slow. At the end of the next twenty minutes, the priest had his hands down near his lap. At the end of the speech, which went over an hour, the priest was like an exhausted fighter, hands hanging at his sides. Up above him, Humphrey was waving to the crowd, few of whom knew what he had said, wishing he could start all over again.

Now everybody laughed and the stories continued, and as I sat with Isaac Stern's violin still in my ears I began to think about the pawnshop I happened to go into on H Street, down from the Capitol, after I walked past Humphrey's casket on Saturday afternoon.

As you went into the pawnshop, the front of it was crowded with men who stood and watched a movie on a television set. It was a Sidney Poitier movie, one of them said. Most of the pawnshop was taken up by television sets. This is the big item that poor people in Washington hock. The owner gives them thirty or thirty-five dollars for the set. And then when something is on that they want to see, like a Sidney Poitier movie, they go down to the pawnshop and the man lets them turn on a set or two and stand in the store and watch.

I asked them if they were going to go over and see Humphrey's body. They didn't know the body was in the Capitol. News moves slowly through poor neighborhoods. One of them was uncertain of Humphrey's position. Titles elude them. But all knew who Humphrey was. "He was a friend to the people," one man said. The others nodded.

The final honor is not to need robes or planes or titles or bowing in order to live in people's minds.

(January 1978)

The Right Stuff

I have seen two political performances on television in recent years that so clearly burned the opposition to the ground that it took no particular instinct to recognize this.

The first was when Ronald Reagan, as candidate, talked affably about Russia and nuclear arms. Rather than seem threatening, he was so utterly reasonable that you knew the election was over weeks before the vote. Carter can go home, I said to myself as I watched Reagan; if they are not afraid of this guy, then they vote for him.

The second performance involved John Glenn yesterday. This came when I watched the spaceship take off on television. For the first time, the camera plane above Cape Canaveral was in the correct place and the air had been scrubbed so clear by wind or moisture or both that it sparkled from the grass on the ground to the clouds at the door to space. And so here on television was a shot of the rocket with spaceship on it rising toward you through a brilliant sky and with the land underneath.

It gives John Glenn the Democratic nomination, I said to myself. Again, I consider this as glancing at the obvious and will take no particular credit when it happens, as it most certainly will.

The connection between yesterday's thrilling television and the Glenn candidacy is fundamental.

Glenn the politician, in the heart of his campaign for the nomination, will have an entire movie of these space shots, with Glenn the astronaut as the movie's hero, all over the country. The movie, *The Right Stuff*, will be promoted with so many television commercials that it will perform most of the campaigning for Glenn. The title, taken from Tom Wolfe's book, is so unique that even now it is a part of advertising language. Glenn's part will be played by an actor in the movie, but the public will consider Glenn as a movie star in the middle of his campaign. There is no way for him to lose. He will be a live celebrity standing alongside a table of dead fish.

The fact that the leading Democrat as of now, Walter Mondale, appears to stand for nothing except want of job, if he even has that in him, makes it all the easier.

Not that a stronger candidate than Mondale could stand in the way of the movie and the one big scene that probably will do it all for Glenn. In the scene, taken from the book and from space history,

Glenn — in a space capsule at Cape Canaveral — hears that his wife, Annie, at home in Houston, is being pushed to allow Lyndon Johnson into her house. Johnson is accompanied by many television cameras. Annie Glenn, who stuttered and was too embarrassed to go on television, is called on the phone by Glenn. He sweats in his spacesuit. He says on the big screen, "You tell them I said no! I don't want Johnson or any of the rest of them to put so much as one toe inside our house." That cheer you hear in the movie house is the nomination at the Democratic convention.

"The scene is an Academy Award thing, or somewhere around that," Irwin Winkler, one of the producers, was saying at dinner the other night. "As we're cutting the movie, we get more and more good scenes with Glenn. I guess we forgot how many good days this guy had in those years." The amusing thing is that Glenn tried to block the movie from being made, which is something that he now has forgotten and only four people or so ever will remember.

I had these reasonable thoughts yesterday in unreasonable surroundings. I was standing and watching television in the restaurant on Second Avenue owned by my friend Larry, who was in the service with John Glenn.

With only a few moments left before the spaceship rocketed off, Larry gave a noisy yawn. "How can this be boring?" somebody asked.

"I didn't sleep last night," Larry said. He didn't. Last Saturday night, he went to bed in the belief that it was going to rain in Philadelphia, where two professional football teams named the Washington Generals and Philadelphia Stars were to play. Before putting the lights out, he called the bookmaker and bet $3500 on Washington and seven points. His theory was that the rain would hold the score down and give him a great chance with his seven points. He needed a victory desperately, for he has been notified that his restaurant stoves are going to be repossessed for nonpayment.

He woke up Sunday to find the game in Philadelphia was being played in sunlight. The Philadelphia team won by thirty-four to three. On Sunday night, Larry went to bed and thought about his stoves being repossessed. Because of this, he had difficulty sleeping. Now yesterday, he was yawning at a fantastic television sight.

"This is good for your man Glenn," he was told.

"Is that going to save my stoves?" Larry asked.

"Maybe. Where were you stationed with him, anyway?"

"In Maryland. I was at the Patuxent Naval Air Station in 1956. I was a seaman deuce in the office. Glenn was in the same office. I used to hand him memos. Memos come out a million a day. He tested guns and cannons on the planes. He liked that."

"What did you used to talk to him about?"

"What did we have in common? I only cared about going to the racetrack at Laurel or Bowie. All he wanted to do was go out and shoot the cannons on planes. I didn't think he was very smart. But neither was I."

"Did you like him?"

"He was all right. I read about him since then. He fell in the bathtub and everything."

"Maybe he can get you out," I said.

"How?"

"Find somebody who will take a bet on him to win the Democratic nomination in 1984. Get some good odds. I don't think most people believe he can win right now. But don't worry about it. He will. Go naked on the proposition."

"He doesn't get it until 1984," Larry said. "That means that if I have to bet now, I wait over a whole year to collect my money."

"It's better than losing the money overnight the way you've been doing," he was told.

"You make it a sure thing?" he said.

"I'm giving you the right stuff," I told him. I was.

(*April 1983*)

Bella Was Old Hat

At noon on Tuesday, Vincent F. Albano, Jr., the Manhattan Republican leader, watched some absentee ballots being counted in Peter Cooper Village on the East Side. There were twenty-eight votes for Bill Green and eight votes for Bella Abzug in the special election for Congress. Albano mumbled something.

"What's that?" a guy with him said.

"I said, I got something going for me," Albano said.

He was on the streets working in elections when he was twelve years old, Vince Albano was, and now, fifty-five years later, he only had to look at a few numbers.

At night, twenty minutes after the polls closed, Albano sat in his office at the Roosevelt Hotel, the radio on, phones ringing. On the radio, the newscaster was conceding the election to Bella Abzug. With 12 percent of the vote in, he said, Bella was so far ahead that we could be expecting her victory statement quite soon.

On the telephone, one of Albano's captains, Joy Tannenbaum, was calling in the arithmetic from the 63rd Election District of the 65th Assembly District.

"Green two sixteen, Abzug ninety-three," she said.

"I love you," Vince said.

"It's terrific, isn't it?" Joy Tannenbaum said.

"I love you," Vince said.

Albano hung up the phone. "We pulled it out," he told everybody in the room.

An hour or so later, the broadcasters started to catch up with his figures.

And, in the morning, the national newscasts were saying that a Republican won a congressional seat in New York and that to do it he had to upset Bella Abzug. The Republican win was spoken of as perhaps the start of a swing around the country. Which could be good for Albano, who has a candidate for governor. But the more important part of the story was that Abzug, by losing, seemed to reveal the weakness of the women's movement.

As Gloria Steinem said after the count, "We no longer can depend on the electoral system. The street is the only place for our movement."

The mathematics seems to support her. In the medieval year of 1962, there were eighteen women in the House of Representatives and two women in the Senate. Now, after the tumult of the late sixties, after the awakening, the raising, and pushing, there are eighteen women in the House and one senator, Muriel Humphrey, who is there on a maneuver we once thought was reserved only for backward Southerners; the wife taking the husband's seat. This tawdriness is nearly enough to force you to recall Hubert Humphrey's cheerleading during the Vietnam war.

"The figures in state legislatures are discouraging too," Gloria Steinem was saying. "Eighty percent of the women elected are from the opposition party, which means that nobody thought they had a chance to win. If an election seems winnable, the man is the candidate. The average age of a woman in the state legislature is much higher than that of a man. The legislature is a woman's ultimate reward for years of civic work, while the male politician normally starts out on his career in this job."

The Equal Rights Amendment, which has been thrown out of many state houses as if it were a disease carrier, appears as more evidence. Yesterday, an intern named Barbara Smith at the National Women's Political Caucus said gloomily, while compiling statistics, "Much of the language used by people against the ERA is the same as was used against women's suffrage. What do we hear? 'Vulgarizing the image of women. Robbing women of their inherent privileges.' These are right out of textbooks about women's suffrage. Nothing ever changes."

So on Tuesday night, when its greatest figure, Bella Abzug, went down to an astonishing upset, the women's movement seemed, to many inside it, to be floundering desperately. Male prejudice has triumphed as surely and as easily as it did when the Iroquois were in charge.

Perhaps not. For Bella Abzug's loss also could be seen as an example that being a woman is not enough to win a national office.

Last week when she could have been on the streets of the district campaigning, Bella Abzug went to Washington and dropped into the office of House Speaker Tip O'Neill. She discussed committee assignments she might be able to get. Bella was uncertain of exactly which committee she wanted to be on, so O'Neill caused the postponement of a meeting of the House Steering Committee, which assigns committee jobs. The Steering Committee was to have met today. Bella did not think she would have her mind made up by this point.

While she was in O'Neill's office, Bella also brought up the number of table reservations she would need in the House dining room for people attending her swearing-in.

Then she came back to Manhattan and she lost.

There might have been reasons other than overconfidence for Bella's defeat. There has come to be a tired quality to Bella's pushiness; even her hats seem boring. Perhaps the real trouble is that she has been in an election or so too many.

Therefore, her loss could have nothing to do with the strength of the women's movement. For on election day, the same day the great woman figure lost, the New York State Court of Appeals, conservative and sluggish, held that a divorced woman can live with another man and still collect alimony from her ex-husband. This is about the largest crack so far in the thick wall of double standards behind which all men live. The climate is being set for women to begin living the same lives, including cheating, that men do.

A political election is much less of an indicator than it is supposed to be. Abzug loses. But talk to your daughter: the past is over. The reason the women's movement has trouble making its expected indent on politics is that the movement is too new, the people in it too young. Politics is, like croquet, a sport for the old. The males who dominate it are either white-haired or bald. The bellies protrude, the eyes weaken, the faces grow flush from even a flight of stairs. A touch of emphysema is the badge of a great political pro.

The women's movement, then, will begin to make it big in politics only when its leaders are a lot of old ladies who have been on ballots for about a half century.

The case of James Earl Carter, Jr., seems to be a contradiction. It is not. Carter is a smart technician who spotted a flaw in the Democrats' system of nominating a president and he took advantage of it and won. Won resoundingly. Terrific. Good for Jimmy. And then he went to Washington with all his bright people around him, his new faces in town, and they all strode briskly past the old heads of Washington politics. And the old heads looked up and gave a little nod. They had seen it all before. And then one day Carter's best friend, his great new face in Washington, Bert Lance, came into the Oval Office wailing. A bear trap hung from Lance's ankle.

White House rudeness turned to apology, independence into reliance. And Carter, the brilliant technician of primary elections, turns out to be an aimless guy whose latest decision, selling planes to the Arabs and Israelis so they both can be a bit more certain that they are able to kill each other, is a classic.

The Abzug election, then, has nothing to do with either the end or the slowing of the women's movement. It has to do only with the slowest part of life, politics. Nobody suggests that slowness is a sign of health: inability to change is the reason for all the trouble in the country. If a system of old men will not make room for women except over decades, then how long must we wait until blacks get an even chance?

So that election in Manhattan on Tuesday was less significant than women yesterday were saying it was. The movement will make it in politics. Only when it does, the women will be gray-headed and able to tell stories from a lot of years back. Certainly, it's lousy. It has to be. It's politics.

(*February 1978*)

The Last Boss Goes into the Ground

CHICAGO — The mourning did not stop. At night the priest insisted we follow him from the street, into the rectory, and through a passageway that brought us out onto the altar of the Nativity of Our Lord Catholic Church.

Here, in the lights, was the body of Mayor Richard J. Daley. His people, crimson from the freezing air, filed past. The priest led us off the altar and into a front pew on the side of the church. Right away the family complained. One of Daley's sons came over and spoke softly to the priest. They wanted us out. "I told you," I whispered to the priest. At the end, in their trouble, the family had no room for strangers inspecting grief.

We got up and went out into the night. Heaters had been placed along the street to warm the people on line. There was a good contingent from the plumbers' union. The boys had arrived by bus and had waited for some time on line, but now they looked with disdain on the orange flames licking from the tops of the heaters. The plumbers needed something warmer. A group of them broke from the line and went down the block to Dan Sheehan's, a saloon on the corner behind the church.

The plumbers sat at a table surrounded by stacks of beer cases. On the wall was a color poster for the Super Bowl football game. The plumbers did not bother to take off their quilted zipper jackets while they drank whisky and beer chasers. It was late in the evening and none of them had eaten and they kept roaring over to the bartender that they wanted more whisky. One of the plumbers, a man with a gray crew cut who had hands big enough to connect sewer pipe, got mad at a guy in a blue ski jacket across the table from him. The guy in the ski jacket was slouched in the chair. When he stood up, he was much bigger than he was supposed to be. The two plumbers went into each other like billy goats. The sound of one of them slamming against a refrigerator brought the owner, Dan Sheehan, out from behind the bar. Sheehan, out of Boilermakers Union No. 1, knew exactly what to do.

He hit them with power, a strong hand on each chest, and also with sharpest reasoning.

"The language!" Sheehan said. "I got a priest from Ireland at the bar. How can you do this on a night like this?"

Yesterday morning, with the wake over and the funeral about to begin, the people of Chicago were gone and the ones called dignitaries came out of their limousines and up the steps of the church. Jimmy Carter, with the stinging breeze lifting his razor-cut hair. Nelson Rockefeller, showing the stains of age. George McGovern, unnoticed, and Edward Kennedy.

For as they prayed over the body of Richard J. Daley, the immigration of the Irish to this country officially ended. The Irish came here out of the famines and the death boats, out of the denial and ridicule, out of the stockyards and the trades unions, out of the political clubs and the city halls of the big cities of the nation, and yesterday, Dick Daley, the last boss, took the meaning with him into the ground. The word *Irish* now means grandchildren and great-grandchildren, and as it goes beyond this, as it does with each year, the meaning of the word fades and the people are American and nothing else.

Organ music came into the clear air from the loudspeakers hooked up on the street. At the first sound of it, women standing at the storm doors of their bungalows disappeared inside to watch television. We went into the McKeon Funeral Home on a corner across the street from the church. Upstairs, in the family apartment, a woman held out coffee for anybody walking in. When we realized which McKeon family lived in this house, the day grew disturbing.

The mother, Margaret McKeon, a widow, runs the funeral home. In 1967, her son Joseph T. McKeon was killed in Vietnam. When the body came back to the neighborhood, back to Bridgeport, one of the neighbors, Richard J. Daley, was shaken. The war that he said all loyal Americans should support became a question to him. And in 1968, during the California primary, Robert Kennedy sat in a convertible going along a freeway and he said that he thought he had it, he thought he would be the Democratic nominee for president, because Daley of Chicago was going to support him. Daley of Chicago wanted the war ended.

"He had this awful funeral, a boy from his own ward was killed," Bobby Kennedy was saying. "So now he wants it over." He thumped his fist on his knee. "Daley," Bobby Kennedy said, "Daley is the ball game."

The next night, Kennedy was shot. At the Democratic Convention in Chicago, Richard J. Daley forgot everything while he took on the college students. The moment had passed, the combination was gone, and the war went on. More than twenty thousand of our young were yet to die.

"The mayor put up a playground around the corner," a woman was saying. "He named it the Lieutenant Joseph McKeon, Jr., Play Lot. Isn't that nice?"

Across the street the Mass was ending, and everybody went outside. The women were back at the storm doors again and the priests stood on the steps, arms folded against the cold, while the casket was brought out. Then the dignitaries were out and into the limousines. As the line of black cars began moving, the police and firemen on duty stopped saluting and ran for warmth.

"This way," an officer named Bernard Brice said. The radio attached to his black leather jacket made a scratching sound. Brice led us down the street to Sheehan's. The bar was crowded with cops and firemen from the neighborhood, who were assigned to the funeral at the request of the Daley family.

There was a tapping sound in the room, as if somebody were using a hammer. The bartender named Hughes was walking along and placing an empty shot glass in front of each cop and fireman. When he reached the end of the bar he picked up a bottle and began going the other way, filling each shot glass.

Brice lives at 3537 South Lowe. The mayor's house is at 3536 South Lowe. "My grandmother's from Kerry. The mayor's family is from Waterford. We've got quite a few Irish around here."

A lieutenant of police, Bob Reilly, came in for a drink. "This is the end of the trail," he said. "This affair today was Celtic. Last time you're going to see it. Forget about the Irish. They went to Notre Dame. They all came out different. Now they're all out in the suburbs wanting to be Wasps. It's not that good either, you know. I'm with the mayor. The mayor says, 'You don't move out of a great city.' "

Outside, the streets were empty in the weak afternoon sun. To drive out of Bridgeport, you go up the mayor's street, South Lowe, past his brick bungalow, with an American flag and a Christmas wreath at the door, then turn right on Thirty-fifth Street, and you pass S. Wallace, S. Parnell, S. Normal, streets known to everyone in Chicago. Then you pass Comiskey Park and suddenly here it is: the twelve-lane Dan Ryan Expressway, with commuter rail tracks in the middle, and on the other side of the expressway, cut off by something smarter and more effective than a wall, are the gloomy apartment houses where the blacks live. Newspapers blew along streets lined with boarded-up stores.

This was the Chicago nobody mentions when they tell of how well Dick Daley can make a city work. And it was a neighborhood for people whom the Irish and Daley seem most reluctant to help.

Turning to go back to the expressway, there was a dead German shepherd in the middle of the street. The driver tried to go around the dog, but could not. It was a big dog and the car bounced as it went over the body.

(December 1976)

4

"You Give Them Food and They Die"

It is Jimmy Breslin's proudest boast that one of the most successful and enduring of his newspaper column "characters," a grasping, impecunious counselor-at-law named Klein the Lawyer, first saw the light of print in the pages of *The New York Times,* a dignified, no-nonsense journal that Breslin figures might very well have declined the honor if it had known what was happening.

As Breslin tells it, this journalistic coup d'état occurred some years back when he was chewing on book royalties and announcing he never would lower himself to newspaper work again. The *Times* was planning a special section of Super Bowl coverage, and invited Breslin, who had once been a sportswriter himself, to send in a piece of fan reaction to the big football game. Breslin chose to write about a group of guys watching the game on a television screen in a Manhattan bar, the central figure of this little tableau being a person he identified as Klein the Lawyer. And that's the way the *Times* ran it.

"Right there in the headline," Breslin chortles now, "Klein the Lawyer."

The significance of all this could well be lost on someone who does not know that over the years Breslin, in between bouts of straight reporting, has peopled his column with a variety of rather implausible characters engaged in equally implausible pursuits. In addition to the aforementioned Klein the Lawyer, there are Marvin the Torch, a moderately successful arsonist, Eddie Kay and Fat Thomas, two hopeful gamblers, and perhaps the most plausible of the implausible, Un Occhio ("One Eye" in Italian), whom Breslin elevated to boss of bosses of the underworld when Carmine Galante, a real boss, was gunned down by some unsavory persons in a Brooklyn restaurant in 1977.

Breslin insists, always has insisted, that his characters are based upon real people, and that the adventures befalling them, by and large anyway, really happened. Klein the Lawyer, for example, is based upon a real, honest-to-God attorney who has offices in Kew Gardens, Queens (and whose name, of course, is not Klein). But if this long-suffering unfortunate has any misgivings about being cast as a womanizing shyster plodding through his second wife (or perhaps his third, Breslin does not make it quite clear), he has steadfastly kept them to himself.

These Breslin characters perform so outlandishly that Breslin finds no need to spend time verifying each detail of their activities. He uses as a guide in these matters the immortal Colonel John R. Stingo, whose biography, *The Honest Rainmaker*, was the only writing of A. J. Liebling that Breslin felt was not smothered by dumplings. In the book, Stingo proudly told Liebling that he had worked a newspaper editing desk on the day the liner *Morro Castle* was afire in the Atlantic. Handling wire service copy, Stingo would pencil in, "as blood-maddened sharks circled the scene." Stingo did so because he said he felt the sharks belonged on the scene.

Although Eddie Kay still flourishes as a fixture of the character columns, Fat Thomas is practically defunct. The reason: he used to weigh 475 pounds, but, says Breslin with a curl of his lip, he has slimmed down so much that he no longer is a credit to his name.

Why, you may well ask, has Breslin chosen to pepper his newspaper column with these zanies when his real shtick is the straightforward, tell-it-like-it-is report from the streets of New York? Good question, and one for which Breslin has a ready answer.

"It's for fun," he says flatly. "I'm trying for conscious humor, because you can't get much of that in a newspaper except through something like these character columns."

Therein, however, lies a problem. In his earlier days, Breslin leaned heavily in his character columns on the sort of raffish humor that could be drawn from such underworld caricatures as Marvin the Torch, a rather engaging arsonist-for-hire whose specialty was torching failing businesses so the owners could collect the insurance, and who took a quiet pride in a job well done.

But not long after he began writing a column for the New York *Daily News* in late 1976, Breslin visited a social club in the Bronx where twenty-five people died in a fire set by an arsonist. That disturbing experience, plus the rampant rise over the years of drug traffic, rape, and other heinous crimes, convinced Breslin that he must change the underlying philosophy of his character columns. By 1983 he was telling his readers:

"How, in a city being torched by the entire block . . . could you have a great laugh about somebody setting fire to an unprofitable business?" Breslin wrote only one Marvin the Torch column for the *News,* in 1981, and that was to report that Marvin had gone to pasture in Tucson, Arizona. But even as he was disappearing into the Western sunset, Marvin (so Breslin recounted) could not resist torching an ailing Tucson restaurant for a fee of $2500. "It'll be a grease fire," Marvin confided to a crony with a touch of his old professional skill. "Three ladles of bacon fat and twenty-five gallons of gasoline."

The evils of modern crime also have cast a pall on Un Occhio, a wrinkled old man of seventy-three with a fondness for feeding his underworld enemies poison ("You give them food and they die"), although much of the humor in the Un Occhio columns was derived from the evils that hoodlums visit on each other rather than on the public.

To Breslin aficionados, Un Occhio has been one of the more fascinating of Jimmy's columnar characters. With a sort of deadpan verisimilitude, Breslin endowed Un Occhio with so many humdrum, everyday trappings of reality that the casual reader could begin to believe that old One Eye really existed. He had a birth date (November 26, 1905), a place of birth (Lercara Friddi in Sicily, where Lucky Luciano also was born), a growing-up place (East Tenth Street in Manhattan), a present home (off Pleasant Avenue in East Harlem). And so on and on.

Small wonder that the Arizona State Police wrote Breslin. Small wonder that the FBI and the Organized Crime Task Force in New York spent more than a month poking around East Harlem looking for Un Occhio.

At least one hoodlum, Phil ("The Squint") Lombardo, then residing in Florida, was so convinced that Breslin had him in mind when he was writing about Un Occhio that, one morning when he woke up and found a police car at his door, he wailed: "What has Breslin got against me?" Or anyway, that's the way Jimmy tells the story.

All this has left it pretty much up to Klein the Lawyer and Eddie Kay to carry the load. And of the two, perhaps Kay, a simple soul, comes closest to the Everyman who is the bread and butter of Breslin's writing.

Eddie Kay's main problem is that he is a born loser. Or refining it a little more, his main problem is that he is near-sighted, very nearly a fatal flaw in a compulsive gambler. Kay once dropped a bundle in a stud poker game because he thought he saw an ace when he peeked at his hole card. It was the four of diamonds.

But our boy Kay can be resourceful. Driven to a frenzy by his continuing losses, Kay in one notable column seized a religious statue from his dresser top and locked it in a closet. Then he scrawled a ransom note, touching a match to it and holding it out an open window so the smoke would rise to the heavens. The note said: "Dear Lord, I have Saint Francis of Assisi locked in a dark closet. Let me win my bet on the fourth race today at Aqueduct Race Track, Rockaway Blvd., Ozone Park, Earth."

Kay might very well have brought off this daring, reckless measure, clearly the work of a desperate man, if he had not been betrayed once again by his eyesight. Reading the *Racing Form,* Kay thought it said that the horse he picked in the fourth race had won only the week before against formidable opposition, hence could be expected to do well against the crumb-bums entered in the fourth at Aqueduct. Alas, what the *Racing Form* really said was the nag hadn't run a race in a whole year. The creature staggered down the track, Breslin reported, "as if he were in leg irons."

So what happened to Saint Francis of Assisi, you ask? Well, all this occurred on a Tuesday, and Kay wrote another ransom note giving the Lord until Friday to deliver.

As it turned out, the Lord never did a blessed thing, but Breslin, Eddie Kay's earthly creator, did. Breslin decided to try his own hand at picking a horse that Kay could win with, and such is the generosity of his large Irish heart that he invited his readers to phone in and learn the name of his choice. Many did, and the wonder of it all is that the horse actually won, paying, as Breslin remembers it now, ten or twelve dollars.

But then Breslin did what everybody does who can't handle success: he went too far. Breslin announced that the following week he would pick another sure-fire winner and anyone calling in bright and early Monday morning could learn the name. Such was Breslin's spreading fame as a handicapper by now that five thousand calls poured in, swamping trunk lines in the neighborhood of the News Building at Forty-second Street and Second Avenue.

Naturally, the horse ran dead last. Eddie Kay, meet Jimmy Breslin.

— W.B.

Un Occhio: Boss of Bosses

There is no glamour on the streets. Last night, as the rest of the nation sat in living rooms and thrilled to *The Godfather* on television, the real members of organized crime wriggled under the cold hand of a new ruler, a seventy-three-year-old man who is mentioned only in whispers as "Un Occhio," or "One Eye." He suffered the loss of a left eye from flying glass after throwing a bomb into an East Side bakery in 1934.

"Un Occhio" came out of retirement to take over the criminal empire from Carmine ("Lilo") Galante, who had the underworld in disarray. Galante, suffering from acute ego, was in the newspapers and television so much that he became a "must" target for federal authorities. A couple of weeks ago, Galante was thrown back into jail for parole violation. Suddenly, One Eye, a much-feared man, reappeared on the streets of East Harlem and Lower Manhattan and it became known that he was the boss of all bosses.

He spends nearly all of his time behind the counter of a dim, narrow candy store on Pleasant Avenue in East Harlem. A prospective customer walking into the candy store finds copies of the *News World*, the Reverend Moon's paper, out on the counter. Perhaps a dozen packs of cigarettes are in dusty wooden racks behind the counter. Over them are four boxes of anisette-flavored cigars. As there is no candy, One Eye does not appear really to be in the candy business.

Asked for a soft drink, One Eye went to the fountain and filled the paper cup with soda water. He presented this to the customer.

"There is no Coke in this drink," One Eye was told.

He shrugged. "Tomorrow when you come back there will be Coke in the drink," he said.

The hard glare in his one eye, the right eye, asked you to leave.

It is rumored that in the rear of the store there is a large oven into which Un Occhio has people thrown.

Last night, as the deposed Galante watched *The Godfather* on television in a dayroom in the Metropolitan Correctional Center, Un Occhio watched it in a marble palace, a triplex which has been built inside a tenement with a crumbling front and a graffiti-marked green metal door on a block off Pleasant Avenue in East Harlem. He lives in the triplex with his wife, Neenel, who is seen only at funerals of men who have had particularly violent deaths. The walls and floor of the triplex are of Norwegian rose marble but mainly onyx. Un Occhio and his wife pad about in stockinged feet because the sound of a heel striking the marble is too loud, and it also gives the listener the impression that someone is coming to kill him.

Un Occhio, who for years was the hidden boss of organized crime, using men such as Vito Genovese as publicity-catching fronts, retired about seven years ago. When the latest new boss, Galante, made such a mess of things, including a demand that the word Mafia be used again, Un Occhio was asked by the International Crime Commission to resume command of all crime in New York, and thus the nation. The meeting, in Hollywood, Florida, began a day late because of weather conditions at the Catania Airport. Also, Meyer Lansky had acute indigestion.

In 1931, One Eye bribed Herbert Hoover, but he has been able to escape publicity over his lifetime to the extent that there are no printed stories about him that anybody can locate. This week, One Eye told all his new subjects, "When I say hello to you, then you say hello to me. If you recognize me before this, then I will feed your tongue and both your eyes to my dog."

Early in his life, growing up on East Tenth Street in Manhattan, One Eye still remembers the day his close friend, Charley ("Lucky") Luciano, received his first press notice, a three-paragraph story about an old assault, which ran in the old *New York American*. Luciano danced on the street corner. One Eye hid in a cellar. "Anyone who ever gets to know me will want me to die," he reasoned.

One Eye is wrinkled man who stands only five-feet-six and weighs, at most, a hundred and thirty pounds. He was born on November 26, 1905, in the same town as Luciano — Lercara Friddi in Sicily. He arrived in New York in 1911. He has bitten men to death, but he has no criminal record in this country. He did amass an extensive record in Sicily.

He is partial to poison. "You give them food and they die," he says fondly. Organized crime members in New York, who always expect a change in command to produce a certain number of funerals, now are terrified that One Eye might invite them to a banquet.

On the streets, it is known that One Eye has such a low opinion of the condition of his organization that a thorough housecleaning is mandatory. His opinion comes as a result of the tremendous number of new members brought in under Galante. Once, they were known as "made" people. Today, they are referred to as "nice fellas" or guys who have been "straightened out." At one time, a man had to commit a legitimate number of murders before being allowed in. But Galante became so careless and greedy that he conferred memberships on people who promised him extra cuts of anything they made as full-fledged gangsters. And in some cases, Galante took bribes to allow the man in.

In one such case, constantly referred to by One Eye, the mother of an inept salesman paid fifty thousand dollars to get her son into organized crime. She got the idea from legitimate people, who pay the same amount to be named a judge. Galante took the money and officially declared the salesman a fearsome killer. The mother was proud. She also went into her clothes closet and spruced up what was there, in case the son found the future a little rough. Better a black dress than a miserable failure as a son, she told herself.

The salesman, now that he was a gangster, went out and got himself his first gun. He got up in the morning and went out and did what gangsters do all day, which is nothing. At night he went on parade with his new girl, who is nearly seventeen. When the salesman came home at 4:00 A.M., he was stiff from whisky. He did not want to put the loaded gun under his mattress because he was afraid it would go off. He went into the bathroom and decided to empty it in style. He filled the bathtub and aimed the gun at the water, as he had seen ballistics people do on television. He pulled the trigger. The bullet richocheted off the hard enamel and hit his shoulder. His mother had to come and take him to a doctor, who charged her almost as much for the bullet as Galante did for the membership.

The other day, the salesman, his arm in a sling, was walking down Elizabeth Street in Manhattan when One Eye arrived for an inspection tour. One Eye said to an associate, "Go over and ask him if he likes a nice sea bass dinner next week."

Then *all* of Elizabeth Street shivered as the new Boss of all Bosses walked along, teeth grinding like a timberwolf.

(November 1977)

Un Occhio's Portrait with a Singer

In the summer of 1977, Un Occhio, or One Eye, the leader of all organized crime in New York, and thus the nation, arrived at the Westchester Premier Theatre for a concert by Frank Sinatra. Federal agents and New York City police in the audience were surprised to see Un Occhio, who rarely makes an appearance in public.

With Un Occhio was a slim young man named Polo the Artist. Polo jiggled while he stood and wriggled when he sat. Polo was in that half-place where fear and hunger mix and a man is forced to decide whether a meal is worth risking his life. Polo carried with him a large artist's pad. His pockets were full of charcoal. Polo was going to make a charcoal drawing of Frank Sinatra and Un Occhio after the concert.

A year before, Don Carlo Gambino had gone to the Westchester Premier Theatre and had his picture taken with Sinatra. Un Occhio had disdain for this. Pizza stands have pictures of people with singers. Un Occhio would have an oil portrait of himself and Frank Sinatra. Polo the Artist, his hunger greater than his sense of self-preservation, had agreed to do the portrait.

Polo the Artist had wanted to bring a camera and take a couple of pictures of Sinatra and Un Occhio and use the pictures as he did his portrait. Un Occhio became angry when he heard of this. "No camera," Un Occhio snarled. What was this artist speaking to him of cameras? The police use a camera. Old has-beens like Gambino use cameras. Did not this artist know that he, the artist, was allowed to be in such important company only because Gambino had used a camera and that Un Occhio always must be better than Gambino?

Anger rays came from Un Occhio's body. When Polo the Artist felt them, he said, "I am going to smash every camera I see in this place tonight."

When Sinatra came out to sing, Polo opened his pad and began to chalk in some of Sinatra. Suddenly, Polo's hand was on fire. He had to bite his lip in order to prevent himself from crying out.

Un Occhio, who wears as a ring a metal cutter that newsboys use to open wired-up newspaper bundles, had brought his ring hand down on Polo the Artist's hand. The wire cutter had taken a bite out of the hand.

"No picture without Un Occhio!" the old man warned.

At the end of the show, Polo was taken backstage and thrown into a jammed hallway. By peering around the shoving mob, he could see Sinatra, who was standing in the doorway to his dressing room. Suddenly, Un Occhio was alongside Sinatra. Un Occhio's wrinkled face attempted to smile, but the man has done this so little in his life that it goes against the lines of his face and makes him appear cockeyed. But the ceaseless glare from Un Occhio's good eye, the right eye, caused Polo's knees to buckle. He never had seen such true evil in his life.

With all the shoving and noise distracting him, Polo tried desperately to capture Sinatra and Un Occhio together and his charcoal worked furiously. But then, when he raised his head, he saw that it was over. And there was Un Occhio saying to him, "Now we go home."

It is known that Un Occhio took Polo into the living room and pointed up to the great cathedral ceiling, three floors up.

"Make a mural," Un Occhio told Polo.

Un Occhio then produced for Polo a copy of a portrait of Enrico Caruso. He wanted the mural to have Caruso and Sinatra, as lesser persons of course, and Un Occhio in the middle, with a glow spreading from his entire body, not just from the top of the head, as they do with the saints in church.

The next day groups of workmen went in and out of Un Occhio's house. They were erecting a scaffold for Polo the Artist to work on. Polo the Artist climbed up the scaffolding and began the job of sanding down the marble ceiling to give it some tooth. Then Polo the Artist put on the first of four coats of prime. When he was finished, he decided to climb down and relax while the paint dried.

Polo the Artist was halfway down when he heard the growl. It was Un Occhio's dog. Un Occhio tells people the dog is a husky, but it really is a timber wolf. Polo the Artist stared at the wolf. Two slanty eyes looked back. Polo decided to test the wolf. He came down and put one foot toward the floor.

Soundlessly, the wolf came into the air. Polo the Artist was not quick enough pulling the foot up. The wolf caught the heel. His fang went right through the Cuban heel and gave the bottom of Polo the Artist's foot a slight tickle.

A few minutes later, Un Occhio came into the room. He patted the wolf. "Hey!" he called up to Polo the Artist. Then he tossed Polo a bottle of iodine. With the wolf standing guard, Polo the Artist stayed on the scaffolding for two days until the ceiling was primed with four coats and was ready to take the great masterpiece of Un Occhio, Sinatra, and Caruso.

To do the painting, Polo worked off the Caruso print and his meager charcoal of Sinatra. But to capture Un Occhio's face, which looks like an old time bomb, Polo the Artist needed a sitting by Un Occhio.

He explained to Un Occhio that he could not work well unless he had the most even light, north light, and in Un Occhio's house this was present only in the early morning. At quarter past seven the next morning, Un Occhio appeared on the living-room balcony dressed in the suit he wore to Tommy Brown's funeral.

"You paint," Un Occhio said.

Polo the Artist began to work. After ten minutes, Un Occhio's voice ruptured Polo's concentration. "You stop painting," Un Occhio said. Un Occhio began to scratch his thigh.

Everybody agrees that it went like this for the next two years. Polo the Artist tried to paint and Un Occhio would be digging at himself like a monkey. Some say that Polo the Artist was allowed to come off the scaffolding at night. Others insist that Polo lived on the boards for the entire time, and that the wolf was taken out of the room and Polo allowed to come down only for washups and, on two occasions, to combat influenza.

At the end, Polo climbed down and Un Occhio came in and stood alongside him and they both stared up at this great masterpiece on the ceiling. Polo the Artist had a bottle of wine. As he swallowed it, he became giddy. I have duplicated Saint Peter's, he told himself.

Un Occhio loved it at first glance. Here on the left was a subdued Caruso, looking respectfully at Un Occhio, who was in the middle and looked like an angry deity. And on the right was a filmy Sinatra. Un Occhio's eye snapped back to Sinatra. Frank Sinatra was looking straight ahead. He was not gazing respectfully at Un Occhio!

Un Occhio snarled. Did Polo see him as somebody like Gambino, who appears in a picture with Sinatra and does not even have Sinatra looking at him? Polo the Artist, his brain paralyzed by wine, disagreed. He did more than disagree, apparently. Some people say that Polo exploded.

Authorities differ on what happened after that. A woman on Pleasant Avenue says she heard a noise in the middle of the night coming from Un Occhio's candy store. The noise reminded her of an oven door slamming. Then a man who was out walking his dog on the East River Drive says that on the same night he saw three men throw what seemed to be a large object, the size of a body, into the water. Authorities think the stories could be conflicting. Their theory is that if Polo the Artist was burned up in Un Occhio's oven, how could there be so much of him left to throw into the river?

After all, detectives agreed, ashes usually can be put in a small urn.

Authorities do agree, however, that Polo the Artist is not anymore.

The other day, Un Occhio was followed downtown, where he was met by three burly men who kissed Un Occhio on the hand and then led him upstairs to a loft that is rented by a young artist.

(December 1978)

For the Love of a Thief

Her name is Joan and her nationality is thief. She is dark-haired, exciting, and thoroughly believable.

When she told an old lady in Central Park that she had just found all this money on the walk, the old lady immediately said, "Did you? What are you going to do with it?"

"I'm going to give the money back and get a big reward," Joan said.

"Isn't that wonderful," the old lady said.

"Do you want to get some of the big reward with me?" Joan asked.

Of course the old lady wanted some of the reward. And of course before the week was over, Joan had taken the old lady for $10,000 and the old lady, wailing, was in a police station identifying a picture of Joan.

The old lady, Klein the Lawyer decided, was a greedy old thief herself, one too ignorant to figure out any decent larceny on her own, and therefore her attempt to join in Joan's reward plan brought her exactly what she deserved. Klein the Lawyer formed his opinion when he was called in by Joan's friends to be Joan's lawyer. However, if Klein the Lawyer announced that the old lady was a greedy thief, he would be admitting that his client, Joan, had been doing something wrong too.

Bail was set at $4500. As none of Joan's people came forward with any money — thieves are always broke, which is why they steal — Joan was sent to Rikers Island. Leaving the court, Klein the Lawyer muttered, "If she can't make bail, how can she do something more important, pay me?"

At 6:00 A.M. the next day, he left his bedroom without making a sound. Recently, his woman friend, or second or third wife, or whatever the legal standing is this time, Rosalie, moved into Klein's apartment. When she moved in, she brought her dog with her. The next week, an aunt arrived. Now Klein the Lawyer tiptoed past Rosalie, past the aunt's door, and stepped over the sleeping dog. He did not do this because he is so considerate. He did this because he has decided that he is irritated with Rosalie, hates her aunt, and wants the dog killed.

As he was closing the door, Rosalie's sleepy voice called out, "Now it's all right with the party?"

"Do what you want," Klein said. He neither knew nor cared what she was talking about. His mind was on business. By eight-thirty, he was at the women's jail at Rikers Island to talk to his client, Joan, about money. She came into the room in a drab smock and sad face. A beautiful sad face. She took Klein's hand and looked into his eyes and said, "Thank you for coming to save me."

Klein the Lawyer has fallen in love in many places. At the bar watching the Super Bowl; in a dry-cleaning store; in the elevator of his apartment house. This was the first time he ever had fallen in love in a jailhouse.

Joan handed him a bankbook with withdrawal slips made out. "Go to the bank and get all this money and take out your fee and then put up my bail and tonight we will be together someplace," Joan said.

Klein the Lawyer never looked at the bankbook. His eyes remained on Joan.

Later, at a bank in the Bronx, a teller smirked at Joan's bankbook. "She's got eighteen dollars in the account," the teller said.

This woman is trying to make a fool of me, Klein told himself. She doesn't know what she is up against this time.

He drove back to jail, waited an hour for his client to be produced, and had a growl in his throat when she walked in. Joan walked over to Klein and brushed her lips against his.

"I'm sorry I failed and didn't get the money," Klein said.

"Somebody must have forged my name at the bank," Joan said. "Go to my uncle's house tonight. He'll put up all the money we need."

Some hours later, the uncle stood in his doorway and said, "I don't even want to hear her name."

"Her name is Beautiful Joan," Klein the Lawyer said.

At Rikers Island the next day, Joan told Klein the Lawyer, "If you can get me out of here, we'll be together forever."

Klein brought forth all of his instinct and training to solve the matter. All of his life, Klein had seen true love separated by prison bars and he felt it terribly sad, but now that it was his love that was being denied by prison bars, he felt the true agony of such a situation.

And he went to court, in a smashing new suit and with long hours of preparation behind him. He confronted the old lady. Klein looked down at his notes. The detective, hired for considerable money out of Klein's pocket, had done a beautiful job of looking into the background of this greedy old lady.

"How long did you have the money that you say you lost?" Klein asked.

"My husband left it to me," she said, in her best old-lady weak voice.

"I understand your husband was in the banking business," Klein said.

"The trucking business," she said.

"Is a term that your husband always used to use, 'six for five,' part of the trucking business or the banking business?" Klein asked.

The greedy old lady said, "I don't think I lost ten thousand dollars. Maybe it was only a thousand."

No Roman conqueror ever strode through public halls as did Klein the Lawyer as he took Beautiful Joan out of the courthouse and to her freedom in the early evening. She kissed him on the steps. She said she was going home to change and that she would expect Klein at 8:30 P.M. She kissed him again. Klein's heart soared. What did it matter that he wasn't being paid? He was in love. He headed for his apartment. His effort had left him wringing wet and he wanted to change clothes.

When he stepped into his apartment he thought he was getting on a subway train. There in the living room was Rosalie, her aunt, her mother and father, her dog, and nearly everybody whom Klein the Lawyer ever had known on Queens Boulevard.

"What's this?" Klein said.

"The housewarming party for our apartment together," Rosalie said. "I told you about it twenty times." She guided him toward the kitchen. "You're in charge of making the drinks."

Later that night, Klein the Lawyer, an island of silence in a loud room, stood at the picture window of his living room and stared down at the lights of Queens Boulevard. After a while, bars appeared in the window.

"I get her out of jail and I wind up in jail myself," Klein the Lawyer said. He stood at the window and drank until it didn't matter where he was.

(May 1980)

Klein Always Tries

He had a fine night. Klein the Lawyer stood at the bar of his new hangout, the United Nations Plaza Hotel. He goes there because his home bar on Queens Boulevard suffered a fire. So now, instead of talking with a bail bondsman and bartender on Queens Boulevard, Klein the Lawyer was discussing international matters at great length with the representatives from Senegal and Nigeria, who came to the bar from the UN building across the street.

"It's time I went into government," Klein the Lawyer told them. "I, too, should do the right thing and serve the public."

Under Klein's elbow was a newspaper with these great stories of New York public servants robbing City Hall of everything but the light bulbs. One departing servant, a deputy mayor named Zuccotti, is said to have developed a permanent stoop from carrying all the money. As he read about Zuccotti in the newspaper earlier in the night, Klein the Lawyer's chest began to thump. Zuccotti was a well-connected lawyer. Perhaps Klein the Lawyer could follow in his footsteps.

He thought he had a way. A major city politician had sent Klein a criminal case involving the politician's cousin. If Klein did well with the case, perhaps the politician would get Klein a job. All I want is the same chance to lift up things that Zuccotti had, Klein the Lawyer told himself. At the bar, he saluted his future with another drink.

The next morning, however, was rough. When Klein the Lawyer, hung over, called in from court, his secretary, Ronnie, told him that, once more, the people who sent him the law-book supplements were pestering for payment. "If you don't send money, they'll come in and take the books back," the secretary said. "You'll wind up using *Huckleberry Finn* for a research book."

"Stall them," Klein said.

"What about American Express?" she asked.

"Stall!" Klein said.

"And the phone company?" she said.

"Stall! Stall!" Klein the Lawyer shouted.

"I'm not a football team; I'm a secretary," she said.

Klein the Lawyer went upstairs to the district attorney's office for a final conference on the case sent to him by the politician. The client was named Roth. Roth had been trapped in a woman's bedroom by the woman's husband. Roth yanked an old baby carriage out of a storage closet and hit the husband over the head with it. The suggestion was made that Roth tried to kill the husband. It was made by the team of doctors who worked long hours to revive the husband.

Klein the Lawyer wanted the case dropped to a simple assault, a misdemeanor. The assistant DA maintained that a felony had been committed.

"You take a simple lovers' spat and turn it into the Battle of Stalingrad," Klein the Lawyer said.

"The victim was in the hospital for four months," the assistant DA said.

"I don't recall society stopping because of his absence; he's such a great man," Klein the Lawyer said.

He got nowhere. The trial was set to start the next day. Klein went downstairs and called his client and told him to be at the office at 6:00 P.M. to prepare for the case. Roth arrived on time, and Klein worked with him until midnight. As he sent Roth home, Klein told him to be in court at 9:00 A.M., and under no circumstances to bring Mrs. Roth along.

"I don't like to bring this up," Klein said. "But we do have a balance of seven hundred and fifty dollars. I wish you would bring it to court with you. I'm only human. When my lights get turned off, I can't see any better than the next guy."

At court the next morning, Klein walked past the pay phones in the lobby. He was not going through the torture of speaking to his secretary until he had the $750 from Roth in his pocket. Then he could snarl at his secretary over the phone.

He sat in the courtroom and waited for his client. After a few minutes, he heard Roth walking up to him. Klein turned around to see Roth and, on Roth's arm, a woman who was large enough to work in a violent ward.

"This is my wife," Roth said. He placed his wife in the second row. Then Roth sat down alongside Klein.

"If you'll give me the balance, the seven hundred and fifty dollars . . ." Klein said.

"Oh, I couldn't bring that," Roth said brightly. "The notice was too short for me."

Klein the Lawyer said, "If the judge decides to give you eighteen months, how much notice do you think you'll need?"

Klein looked down at his hands. He brings his wife and leaves the money home, Klein thought. I oughta let the wife defend him. Then something stirred inside Klein. In the world of Klein the Lawyer, the measure of what you are is determined by how hard you fight for a client when the client has no money. Klein slapped both hands onto the defense table and glared across at the assistant DA. I outfoxed your kind in grammar school, why shouldn't I do it here? Klein the Lawyer said to himself.

He threw himself into the case. His defense was that Roth and the woman had been in love for years. Therefore, the husband was the intruder and Roth had hit him in self-defense. He put Roth on the stand and asked him for how many years he and the woman had been maintaining a relationship. The answer was supposed to be ten years. Klein now heard a growl behind him. He turned to see Roth's wife baring her teeth at Roth. On the witness stand, Roth began to stutter. He did not answer. He kept looking past Klein and at Mrs. Roth. Klein called a temporary halt. He sat Roth next to him at the defense table. On a pad, Klein wrote: "Dinner Menu, Attica State Prison — one bologna sandwich, one cup lukewarm coffee, one apple. Lock-in time for the night, 5:45 P.M."

He pushed this note in front of the client. Roth turned gray. He went back to the stand, closed his eyes so he wouldn't look at his wife, and said, "Ten years."

Klein the Lawyer immediately launched into such displays as "his and her" toothbrushes the couple had. As Klein did this, he felt his shoulder blades tingling. This was because Mrs. Roth was looking at him with a death stare. But Klein did not stop. Driving brilliant wedges into the assistant district attorney's case, he took it all. The jury was out only forty-five minutes before coming in with an acquittal.

Klein the Lawyer said he would meet the Roths out in the hallway. Then he sat at the defense table alone and allowed pride to wash over him. I stood up and fought, he told himself. I never squawked. What a beautiful business this is, he told himself. It allows you to display your nobility.

Outside in the hallway, he came up to Mr. and Mrs. Roth. He had a sobering glance at the pay phones on the wall, which reminded him of his secretary in the office. "We have one bit of business still hanging," Klein said to the Roths. "Whenever you can see your way clear, there's the matter of seven hundred and fifty dollars."

"We'll never pay," Roth said.

"We give you nothing," his wife snarled.

"What do you mean?" Klein said, his voice rising.

Roth exploded. "After the way you embarrassed my wife in front of all those people by making me talk about that other woman, I'll never pay you or speak to you again. You ruined my life and I'm gonna tell that to a lot of people."

By this, Roth obviously meant the big politician who had sent the case to Klein. Klein dropped his briefcase on the floor. "I'm about to become a defendant, right here," he said. He spread his feet. Klein's look was so fierce that even such a dangerous person as Mrs. Roth backed away.

Then Klein walked out of the courthouse. It was late afternoon. He was in deep trouble everywhere. He stared across the street at the charred remains of the Part One Bar, his old hangout. Then he ran out, got into his car, and drove to Manhattan. When he got to the bar of his new hangout, he found it loaded with his new international friends, including the people from Senegal and Nigeria, who were sitting there with several women. Klein ordered big drinks so they would crash into his empty head and make him dizzy right away. This is his favorite feeling. Quickly, he was able to think of what was important. The politician probably never would have gotten him a job anyway. Strange thieves are rarely welcomed at City Hall.

After many drinks, at 11:00 P.M., the people from Senegal and Nigeria were gone, with all the women except one, the one Klein the Lawyer was at the bar with. He was telling her that he was thinking of becoming a big international lawyer and representing countries, and perhaps continents.

"This is the best day I've ever had in my life," he said, swallowing some more of a drink and squeezing the girl around the waist.

(*January 1978*)

The Chinese Verdict

From the start, Klein the Lawyer felt it was going to take another power, the hand of the unseen, a Christmas ghost to get him through the case. On the day he went to court to begin the case, back in the first week of December, all the signs were bad for Klein.

At lunch on his first day, a new waitress came up. She looked exactly like Klein's wife. Klein is not with his wife at this time. He is with a woman named Rosalie, who also looks exactly like Klein's wife. The waitress, Klein thought, would make a great new girlfriend for him. She would remind him of both his wife and his girlfriend.

"You must be very unhappy at home," Klein the Lawyer said to the waitress.

"Who isn't?" she said.

"Call me up at the office," Klein the Lawyer said. He handed the girl his business card with a twenty-dollar bill folded around it. The waitress put the bill into her pocket and handed the card back to Klein.

"Going to order now?" she asked, pad and pencil out.

Walking back to the courthouse, Klein looked up at the sky. "Whoever you are, I need help."

Usually, when he has a particularly rough case, Klein has ways of handling it. You will hear him, as he walks about, humming this little private tune: "It is far better/ To know the judge/ Than it is/ To know the law."

Klein the Lawyer then goes to every Bar Association dinner for the next month. Sooner or later, the judge handling his case will be there. Around a barroom, judges think they should be treated like cops. While pouring whisky into the judge, Klein the Lawyer seeks to carve out any edge for himself.

"Justice is truly human," Klein the Lawyer says.

But when he started this particular case, defending a client named Richard, in a case of commercial fraud, Klein the Lawyer sensed he needed more than a drinking companion up on the bench.

"What happened here?" Klein asked the client.

"What happened?" Richard sneered. "Who the hell else do you know smart enough to pull off a thing like this?"

"You'd better not say that again as long as you live," Klein the Lawyer said.

Actually, he was pleased. "All my clients are guilty," he says. "I never want the burden of an innocent client."

The case against his client Richard began on December 1. Klein the Lawyer estimated that it would take two and a half weeks. That would get him to December 17, which was too early for what he had in mind.

"My client is a Christian," he said. "All he hurt were some suckers, and they're entitled to be harmed at all times. Therefore, I think, my client deserves a nice Christmas verdict. I'll have this jury settling this case on Christmas Eve."

He liked the jury foreman, who was Chinese. Klein figured that the guy, new to the community, would conform more than anybody else. A guy like this, Klein felt, would not only have the spirit of Christmas, but also be able to handle the actuality of Christmas.

Klein the Lawyer sat in the Part One Bar on Queens Boulevard across the street from the courthouse, and began to make little notes to himself.

"I am getting my summation ready right now," he said. "Do you know all the words to 'God Rest Ye, Merry Gentlemen'? Christmas is going to get me out."

"You'll be through a whole week before Christmas," somebody said.

"Watch me," Klein the Lawyer said.

On the first day in court, he asked for frequent private conversations with the judge. Richard, the client, noticed that whenever Klein would hold up proceedings the Chinese man would squirm uncomfortably. He mentioned this to Klein.

"Don't worry about it," Klein said. "Those people can wait twenty years for a bus."

In the middle of the first week, Klein the Lawyer got up early in the morning, took the thermometer out of the medicine cabinet, and walked into the kitchen with it. He put the thermometer in the oven. He took it out when it said a hundred and four. He called the judge and said, "I have the thermometer right here in my hand and it says a hundred and four. It must be swine flu."

"Don't come around here with it," the judge said. "We'll take a day off."

In court the next morning, Richard said to Klein, "The Chinese guy went nuts yesterday morning, when they told him to go home."

"Forget about it," Klein said. "You worry about getting me the rest of the money for this case."

The next week, Klein began talking with one hand clamped to his cheek. "Infected root canal," he mumbled to the judge. When the judge told Klein to go to the dentist, there was a loud squeak in the jury box, caused by the Chinese man jumping up and down on his chair.

With a few other delaying tactics thrown in, Klein brought the case into last week, the week of Christmas. On Wednesday, when the jurors were told the case now was theirs, the Chinese man began pushing the jurors toward the room.

"What timing!" Klein said in the hallway. "There is no way a jury can convict at a time like this. It feels like Christmas, even inside the courtroom, doesn't it?"

The jury came back at midnight. The first thing Klein saw was that the Chinese man had his coat over his arm. Asked for the verdict, he dropped the coat, called out the word, "Guilty," twice, then grabbed his coat and headed for the door.

Klein the Lawyer sat in the wreckage. A court attendant said to him, "Am I glad this is over. I never heard so much moaning."

"What do you mean?" Klein the Lawyer asked.

"The Chinese guy," the court attendant said. "All you could hear him saying was, 'I'm getting killed. I'm getting killed.' He owns some kind of novelty shop that sells Christmas decorations."

All day yesterday, Klein the Lawyer sat at the bar, staring out at the emptiness of Queens Boulevard. By mid-afternoon he was lifeless. "Christmas verdicts," he snarled, "are a myth to lure Jewish lawyers to trial."

(*December 1976*)

Klein Lives

The one most scurrilous charge in my time in my business came during a call from *Newsweek,* which is a magazine where imbeciles sit in cubicles and say they see the world.

The man first asked about Janet Cooke. She worked on a newspaper in Washington, made up a story about an eight-year-old drug addict and won a Pulitzer Prize. Why she had to make up the story is beyond me. Walk the city streets and you get anything you want; in Brooklyn the other day there was a seven-year-old who took part in a felony homicide. Besides, I saw nothing wrong with her getting the prize because Pulitzer used to fake even the weather reports in his papers.

And then came this underhanded question: "We've been reading your stories about Klein the Lawyer and some of us were wondering whether he was real or not."

I was stunned. I don't mind people being new in this business, but a question like this went beyond inexperience and into stupidity. The last person who doubted the existence of the people I write about was Abe Rosenthal, the editor of *The New York Times* newspaper, who, of a night some years ago, came to the old Pep McGuire's on Queens Boulevard for a personal inspection. When Rosenthal arrived, somebody was cleaning a machine gun in the office. At the bar was the late Norton W. Peppis III, whose Con Edison payment had just bounced off the rim in the final moments of a game at Boston. Also there was Jimmy Burke, Fat Thomas, and a blonde as tall as an apartment house, perhaps the tallest stewardess in Lufthansa airline history. In Rosenthal's presence at the bar that evening a historic conversation took place. It is remembered clearly by everyone who was there and it is repeated here, and thus prominently:

JIMMY BURKE: What airline did you say you work for?
BIG BLONDE: Lufthansa.
JIMMY BURKE: Gee, that's a very good airline.

Now, years later, Mr. Burke is in Danbury Prison because federal prosecutors think he robbed $8 million from Lufthansa. Fat Thomas is still around, although you'd never know it from me; I am not speaking to him for this entire year, and even as I type this out, I am sorry that I am putting his name in the *Daily News* newspaper.

Rosenthal, I'm told, is still around. And he knows. So now, along comes some guy from a cubicle at *Newsweek,* and he wants to know if another of the Queens Boulevard people, Klein the Lawyer, actually exists.

On the day that this question was asked, on the day that Klein the Lawyer's presence on earth was being questioned, here he was sitting in a courtroom, and in great turmoil.

At the defense table next to Klein the Lawyer was a man of ill repute. An extortion trial was going on, and not well; every time the prosecutor spoke, the ears of jurors seemed to prick forward, like those of a Thoroughbred horse. Whenever Klein spoke, the jurors' eyelids slowly lowered.

Nor had the client paid Klein. The client kept saying, "Concentrate on the case. The case is the important thing, not the money."

Klein, however, was under great pressure. For weeks, he had been promising Rosalie that he would take her to Florida on a Thursday-to-Monday weekend. Rosalie is Klein's second or third wife, nobody is quite sure; public figures seem not to tell the truth about matrimony. But one thing was certain: Rosalie was on Queens Boulevard getting clothes out of the dry cleaner for the trip to Florida and Klein was in the courtroom without the money for the trip.

He had one chance. A father had been calling him for weeks about his daughter, who was in danger of being indicted in federal court for her part in a large fraud operation. The father wanted Klein to take over the moment the indictment came down. The father said he understood that it would be an expensive federal case and that he was prepared to pay an immediate retainer.

At the luncheon break of the extortion trial, Klein called his office. He was told that the young woman's father had been calling all morning about the federal case. A band struck up. Klein the Lawyer kept saying "Florida" as he dialed the father.

"I can't tell you how happy I am," the father said. "My daughter agreed to turn over some people to the prosecutor and now he isn't going to indict her. So we won't have to bother you."

"Wonderful!" Klein said. "I'm so busy I truly didn't know how I was going to fit you in. Now, I won't have to go through all the trouble to juggle my schedule to make room for you."

Klein felt like he had diphtheria. In the courtroom, his client stared at him. "Something the matter?"

"Yes, I thought that maybe I could break even today," Klein said.

"I told you. Forget about the money and concentrate on the case," the client said.

Later, after being pummeled by life through another long day, Klein the Lawyer, hopes dashed, had to call Rosalie and tell her that the Florida trip was off. Then he sat at the bar on Queens Boulevard and listened as I told him about the question from the magazine.

He thought for a while. Then he brightened. "Could you get them to put in print that I don't exist?" Klein the Lawyer said. "I'll sue them in Queens."

(April 1981)

What Are You Going to Eat? Nothing.

Eddie Kay turned up the edge of his hole card. Beautiful, he said to himself. Ace of diamonds. He already had an ace showing. There were no pairs and no higher card out on the table.

"Twenty," Eddie Kay said.

The guy next to him, a luncheonette owner, put out forty.

Luncheonette, Eddie Kay said to himself. Ha! Go for your coffee urns. Eddie Kay covered and raised it another twenty. Silently, the luncheonette owner pushed out another forty. Eddie Kay's insides squealed. Here you go for your stockpots, you moron. Eddie Kay covered and raised the guy still another twenty.

"I'll see you," the luncheonette owner said.

Oh, an imbecile! The best the guy could have — the best — was a pair of tens. Eddie Kay turned over the hole card. "Aces!"

Eddie Kay leaned back in the chair, raised his arms, looked up at the ceiling, and began to stretch. After sixteen hours at the table, he finally was wearing these bums down. Class, Eddie Kay told himself. Class is the father of luck.

"You better look at your pair of aces again," the luncheonette owner said. "One of them is a four."

Eddie Kay grabbed the hole card and held it at arm's length. He cannot read anything that is less than a full yard from his face. And here it was, blurry and wavering: a four of diamonds.

When he woke up in the morning, Eddie Kay leaned out the window and put a match to the ransom note he had written, sending the message up to the heavens in a thin stream of smoke.

The ransom note said, "Dear Lord, I have Saint Francis of Assisi locked in a dark closet. Let me win my bet on the fourth race today at Aqueduct Race Track, Rockaway Blvd., Ozone Park, Earth."

The religious statue had belonged to Eddie Kay's mother. He usually kept it on the top of his dresser. Now and then Eddie would ask the statue for a favor, hit a number, catch a winner, draw a few good cards; and if the statue failed to deliver, Eddie would threaten it: "You ought to get a good choking." This time, when Eddie Kay came home from the card game, he went into a full kidnapping. He put Saint Francis of Assisi into the closet and locked the door. There Saint Francis would stay, a hostage in darkness, until the powers above paid the ransom, a winner.

"You can come out when I got money," Eddie Kay said.

Eddie Kay lives alone and he likes it because he does not have to deal with other people who are always so nice. But, for the big holidays, he likes people over. Family, old friends. He had invited eight so far, and at the moment he did not have enough cash to entertain a party of two. So he sat at the kitchen table and stared down at the past-performance charts, which were spread out on the floor so he could see them.

The numbers in the form told him that a horse he liked in the fourth race had won his last outing against stronger opposition than he seemed to be in with today. Eddie Kay gathered his papers, went downstairs to his car, a great car, a car that survived the Kasserine Pass, and drove to the track.

The horse in the fourth race ran as if he were in leg irons. Seeing Eddie Kay suffer, a young horseplayer, a college student with thick glasses, said to Eddie, "How could you take that horse? It's his first time out in a year."

"He ran last week," Eddie Kay said.

"Last week last year, you mean," the kid said. "Look." He held the form chart up to Eddie Kay's face. Eddie saw only gray fog, but he would not admit this to the kid.

When he got home, the first thing he did was free Saint Francis of Assisi. "This isn't your fault," Eddie Kay told Saint Francis. Then Eddie Kay sat in the gloom of his empty apartment. "I got eight people coming for Thanksgiving Day and I can't take care of myself," he mumbled. He looked into the kitchen. "You better have some Swiss cheese left for me tonight," he yelled at the kitchen.

The next day, Eddie Kay left his work at the Four Ones Car Service, Fresh Pond Road, Ridgewood, and went to Delancey Street in Manhattan, where there is a shop with a big outdoor sign saying that glasses are ten dollars. For ten dollars the man who owns the store holds a black cloth over your face and asks you how the new glasses are. For fifty-nine dollars Eddie Kay received a pair of gold-rimmed glasses that are so big and heavy they threaten to cave in the bridge of his nose.

"New world!" Eddie Kay said, holding the charts against his nose. The figures for a horse called Ruby River soared right off the page. "Hot horse," Eddie Kay announced to himself. "A holiday special."

On Tuesday, in the seventh race, Eddie Kay bet everything but his new glasses on Ruby River, ten to one. "Eight for dinner Thursday seems small," Eddie Kay said as he walked out to watch his sure winner. "Maybe I better ask Jimmy Flynn and his wife and kids. We'll have a real old-fashioned day."

Outside, a raw breeze had the small crowd standing with hands deep in pockets. On the track, taking their horses to the post, the South American jockeys were singing to the flat sky. The sounds of their voices mixed with the squeal of the sea gulls swooping over them. On horse No. 3, Ruby River, jockey Jacinto Vasquez bounced lightly as his horse galloped slowly toward the starting gate.

"Do you know the first thing you do to make stuffing for a turkey?" Eddie Kay said to people around him.

"What?"

"Get a turkey."

He became silent as the horses got into the gate. The sound of metal slamming carried through the cold air, and the horses lunged out. Ruby River took the lead, as Eddie Kay's figures said he would. In the backstretch, a horse called In Mischief took the lead. "He'll fade," Eddie Kay proclaimed. They raced around the turn and came to the quarter pole, where Ruby River appeared to get shot. In Mischief ran on. Olive-drab blood circulated through Eddie Kay's face.

Yesterday afternoon, a woman on Eddie Kay's block looked at him holding his burning piece of paper out the window.

"Where are you goin' tomorrow?" she said.

"Nowhere."

"What are you goin' to have?"

"Nothing."

Eddie Kay followed the wisps of smoke, his latest kidnapping note, as it carried its message to the sky. The note said that if Eddie Kay didn't get a winner by Friday nobody would ever see Saint Francis alive again.

(November 1976)

Fat Thomas Broils Them

After breakfast yesterday morning, Fat Thomas watched the snow whirling out of a mournful sky and decided that he had to take action immediately. "Winter is for poor people," he said. He was broke for so many winters that the condition appeared permanent.

Then last fall, Fat Thomas suddenly shook the Eastern Seaboard with professional football betting that was so precise that many people felt he was part of a coup. He immediately brushed off poverty as if it were lint and became the sort of spender of which songs are written.

Now, in his living room yesterday morning, he reached for some grass. He had spent most of the night drinking whisky; he clutches bad habits as if he has found treasure. "Only God behaves," he says. He is terrible at rolling grass: the joint yesterday morning came out the size of a clothespin. As he lives with his Aunt Sis, who would explode if she found him with grass, he had a can of hairspray at his side to battle the smell of grass.

Some housewives, however, are not appalled by his clothespins. Because of his appearances on the daytime soap opera "Ryan's Hope," Fat Thomas is recognized by many of the housewives in his home area, Fresh Pond Road in Ridgewood, in Queens. And on several mornings, Fat Thomas passed a few of his large joints around to the women, who giggled, took their first passes at grass, and then strolled into Key Food babbling.

Yesterday morning, Fat Thomas smoked his grass and, after many phone calls, announced that he was going to winter in Florida. "I'll be back here for the summer," he said. He had arranged for his friend, trainer A. Fink, to reserve a suite of rooms near the Florida Downs Race Track. Fat Thomas then went upstairs to pack for the 11:00 A.M. flight to Tampa.

He went out into the snow in a light sports jacket and flowered shirt open at the neck. "Rich guys don't feel the cold," he said. "Rich guys can walk around a blizzard in a T-shirt and they don't feel anything. If you're broke, you got on an overcoat, a jacket, and three sweaters and you're still shivering."

In the cab somebody asked him about the Super Bowl. Fat Thomas scowled. He feels the game is too tough to bet. Past that, he has no interest in it. He dislikes Dallas for personal reasons: he once saw Coach Tom Landry on television speaking at a Billy Graham crusade. Similarly, he has disdain for Denver quarterback Craig Morton, whom Fat Thomas once heard earnestly discussing religion. "God does not catch passes!" Fat Thomas yelled at the television with great self-righteousness.

During the past season, however, when Fat Thomas won two major bets on the Patriots on consecutive Sundays, he stood at the bar and said, "I love New England so much I wrote Steve Grogan's mother for his baby picture." Steve Grogan is the New England quarterback. "Here, you want to see Steve Grogan's baby picture?" Fat Thomas then showed everybody a holy picture. People turned away, calling it blasphemy. Fat Thomas held the picture over his head. "Steve Grogan's baby picture!" he shouted.

It all started last July when, in the course of his travels, Fat Thomas met a guy who worked in a gas station in Brooklyn. "I shouldn't even be here," the guy said. "I picked one pro football game every Sunday last year and I won twelve out of fourteen."

"You'll never have luck like that again," Fat Thomas told him.

"Oh, no, it's not luck," the gas station guy said. "I'm a genius."

"He's tellin' the truth," a mechanic said. "I followed him the whole season. I was always cleaned out with cards and I never had enough to bet."

Fat Thomas began to cultivate the gas station guy. "I got a genius who'll straighten me out forever," he said.

The question that should have been asked here was, of course, if the gas station man was such a genius, then why wasn't he rich from his own selections? But if you were to ask Fat Thomas this, you would be displaying your stupidity. For this is the same as asking why newspaper racing handicappers have to make deadlines every day. And why stock market and financial columnists write at least five times a week.

Besides, the rule always is: When confronted with genius, never inquire as to the man's personal habits.

And so at noon on September 20, on the first day of the season, the phone rang in Fat Thomas's house and the gas station guy came on the phone and called out, "It's Houston. Beat the bookmakers!"

Fat Thomas went out into the streets with borrowed money. He bet $2000, returned home, and went to bed for the afternoon. He would, as in the manner of a presidential candidate, take returns upon awakening. His Aunt Sis sat downstairs in the living room, hands clutching the arms of the chair. Soon, the arms relaxed. On television, Bethea, the Houston end, pulled passes from the sky and destroyed the Jets, twenty to zip.

Fat Thomas won nine games in a row. All over the East people were talking about the streak of the "man from Queens," as bookmakers called him. At night, Fat Thomas had champagne parties. This was to help conserve his money.

And now, in New York, there were scenes from another era. Fat Thomas at Nickles with a dinner party of six. Fat Thomas at Storyville with a party of ten, drinking champagne and whistling loudly at David Chefsky's band. And then, in the late hours, at Jimmy Ryan's and Sweet Basil's downtown. One night he had so many people with him that two of the people rode in the trunk of the car. They could have hailed cabs, but they were so afraid they might lose Fat Thomas that they dived into the trunk. One week, he called in for the game, and then called in his bets, from a Dutch liner cruising the Caribbean.

A friend in real estate, Charles U. Daly, called him on the phone late one night and begged Mr. Thomas to put his money into something that would keep him from being broke again.

"Is real estate as much fun as hookers?" Fat Thomas said.

On the tenth Sunday, Fat Thomas bet the New York Giants against the Cleveland Browns. "The guy has to be a genius to pick the Giants," Fat Thomas said. "What a guy this is." For some reason he decided to stay up and watch the game. Bobby Hammond of the Giants scored on a screen pass. As he went into the end zone, the referees were jumping up and down. Somebody from the Giants named Hicks had committed a foul, clipping, twenty yards away from the play. The Giants collapsed. At 4:00 P.M., a television set came out of a second-floor window in Fat Thomas's house.

In the playoff game between Oakland and Baltimore, Mr. Thomas had Baltimore and three and a half. The game went into sudden death. The first team to score would win the game.

Oakland had the ball, second down on the Baltimore ten, and obviously was getting ready to kick an easy field goal. Stabler, the quarterback, handed the ball to the fullback, who would dive into the line. Stabler took the ball back, turned, and threw it into the back of the end zone. Casper, an end, grabbed it. Fat Thomas was watching the game in the living room, his own television set being indisposed. His Aunt Sis had to come in and assist him up the stairs. This time he went to bed for real.

Illusions survive catastrophes quite well. On the street, Fat Thomas appeared lame after settling up the Oakland game. But yesterday, boarding his plane for the winter, he said, "What a year. The guy is a genius."

"Where is he if I want to see him?" I asked him.

"He's at the gas station every day but Sunday."

Fat Thomas then boarded the plane for his winter in Florida, which might last as long as two weeks, seeing what Casper, the end, did to him with that catch. But this is something, of course, that you do not bring up at a time like yesterday, when a man left triumphantly for a time in the sun.

(January 1978)

Guest Appearance: Marvin the Torch

Some time back, the owner of an apartment building in the Bronx paid a call on a person named Marvin the Torch and said to him, "Make my building go away."

"I'm just about out of that line," Marvin the Torch said.

"I got to get rid of this building," the landlord said. "I got the insurance in beautiful shape."

"It'll cost you fifteen thousand dollars," Marvin said.

"You're crazy," the landlord said. "My janitor said he'd do it for two hundred and fifty."

Marvin the Torch handed the apartment house owner a book of matches. "Tell the janitor to close the cover before striking."

Marvin went home. He was a man who specialized in taking a losing business establishment and turning it into a parking lot. All around him in the city, there were people burning down entire blocks and getting expense money, or even doing it for nothing. "I'm a professional, not some kid pyromaniac," Marvin said. He and his wife packed up and moved to Arizona. He became the first retired professional arsonist in the Sun Belt.

"You heard of Tucson?" he told his friends. "Well, I'm not even living there. I'm living in a place between Tucson and Mexico. They got swimming pools and golf carts. I bought into a messenger service. They used to use smoke signals around here. Now they use my messenger service. I don't want to know from nothing about the other business anymore."

He meant what he said, as he always does, but man is not always in control of his own destiny. One morning, under a cloudless sky, Marvin sat by his pool and read the local newspaper. On page three was a two-column headline stating, "Police Term Fire Suspicious." Marvin read the story. There had been a fire in a restaurant someplace on Camelback Road and the firemen arrived in time to save the building. It was discovered that the fire had started in five different places, which did some harm to the theory of coincidence. In the next paragraph, Marvin read where the prosecutor reported that the restaurant owner had been losing money and taking out new insurance.

"Amateurs," Marvin said, dropping the paper.

It was about a month later when he sat in the living room and watched the late news. The show started with footage of a fine restaurant fire. To Marvin's disappointment, the footage then showed firemen everywhere and a chief announcing triumphantly that most of the restaurant had been saved. The camera now went on the restaurant owner, who appeared to be fighting back tears.

Marvin shook his head and went to bed. Let me worry about my messenger service, he told himself.

But then one day Marvin unfolded the local paper to find a headline saying, "DA Probes Condo Fire." The story said a developer of a failed condominium was being asked questions about the fire in his building. Firemen putting out the blaze had found an empty gas can in the ruins. The proper word for this is evidence.

That day, Marvin the Torch went out and, instead of watching over his messenger business, he went to a few bars. When he heard people talking about golf, he left. The next day, he was in a place where a man was explaining that there were three factions in the state prison, whites, blacks, and Indians. I'm getting closer, Marvin said to himself. Finally, he found a bar in Tucson where he heard one customer say, "The old man loses his appeal." The bartender said, "He didn't do nothing wrong down here. Why didn't they leave him alone? Anything he did, he did up in Brooklyn, not here."

Marvin the Torch knew two things out of this conversation. One, they were talking about a man named Joe Bonanno and, two, this bar was the place to be.

While Marvin was in the place one afternoon, there arrived the owner of a restaurant that did not serve good food; the owner was so tied up with a new girl that he didn't have time to taste his own soup.

"I owe everywhere," the guy said. "It looks like I'm going under."

"Why don't you close up the right way?" Marvin the Torch said.

"How's that?"

"Return the place to nature and let the insurance company pay."

"I can't do a thing like that," the owner said.

"I can," Marvin said.

The guy had $2500 front money and insurance papers in excellent order. Marvin said that the balance could be paid when the insurance check arrived. Marvin then called Astoria, in Queens, and asked his old partner, Benjamin, who also plays with matches, if he cared to spend a few days in the sun. "There'll be a ticket at the airport," Marvin said.

When Benjamin arrived, Marvin the Torch picked him up at the airport. On the way to the house, Marvin stopped and bought a plastic garbage can. The next evening, he and Benjamin stopped at a gas station and had the garbage bucket filled with twenty-five gallons. They went back to Marvin's house and watched a game show on television. After the restaurant closed that night, Marvin and Benjamin drove out to the darkened place, lugged the plastic garbage can into the kitchen, and set it down alongside the stove.

"It'll be a grease fire," Marvin said. "Three ladles of bacon fat and twenty-five gallons of gasoline."

They attached a fuse to the garbage can, lit it, dashed out of the place, and got into the car. They were just out on the highway, speeding under a magnificent desert night sky, Benjamin on his knees in the backseat, looking out the window, Marvin driving with his eyes riveted on the rearview mirror, when the restaurant went. It went as if it were an exception to a test ban treaty. Benjamin jumped up and down in the backseat. Marvin's eyes rolled.

"An Apache Indian job," Marvin said proudly. This meant that by the time the firemen arrived, all that would be left would be the chimney and a few charred timbers. The plastic garbage can, of course, melted the moment the fuse ignited the gasoline. The only evidence on the scene was of catastrophe.

"You can't do this in New York anymore," Benjamin said.

"I didn't even think I'd be doing it down here," Marvin said.

"Maybe I ought to come down here," Benjamin said.

"It looks like it," Marvin said. "These people down here don't know what they're doing." As they raced on through the desert night, Marvin took a last look at what was once a restaurant and now was scenery most thrilling, fire in the sky, and he knew and Benjamin knew — and all of the Southwest soon will know — that Sun Belt businessmen now have a professional to turn to when they go bad.

(March 1981)

5

"Only Shopping Center Faces"

British diplomats spill their tea and crush their crumpets at the mere mention of Breslin's name. It comes like an oath to their ears, grating and offensive. They regard him as a sinister force, constantly fomenting trouble, stirring up American-Irish emotions against England and undermining U.S. political support for their position in Northern Ireland.

Her Majesty's representatives in New York repeatedly made it clear, in the polite understatement required by the Foreign Office, that they regarded the entire *Daily News* as boorishly anti-British. To them, the editorials seemed biased, despite their moderate tone, and, worse, the editors were forever sending reporters off to Northern Ireland to provide graphic accounts of English brutality and injustice. But it was Breslin who provoked the most official ire, requiring spokesmen at the British Information Service to complain frequently to the editors, mostly by telephone or in office visits, but also, during more cordial interludes, at pleasant diplomatic lunches to which we gracefully submitted in the national interest.

In our professional zeal to represent all points of view — we could not be influenced by lunches, of course — we occasionally allowed the fading empire to air its grievances on our op-ed pages as, for example, in 1979 when Breslin wrote a column about secret gun-running to Protestant terrorists. "I have read with a sense of shock and incredulity the Jimmy Breslin article of last Thursday," wrote the minister of state for Northern Ireland, the Honorable Michael Allison, MP. Warming up to his subject, he then plunged ahead with a rebuttal that included such unfriendly phrases as: "Mr. Breslin's theme ... is contrary to all fact —" "Equally is the implication that —" and "Contrary to Mr. Breslin's assertion —"

These official exchanges were quite genteel, however, compared to our relations with the nationalistic British press. Fleet Street is always flapping its wings over real or imagined misdeeds by the United States but it gets positively apoplectic on the Irish issue, charging, among other things, that American newspapers have unfairly pictured Britain as the chief villain in the Northern troubles. The *News* was often singled out for attack, most notably in a long diatribe published in the spring of 1981 by the London *Daily Mail,* which no doubt was having circulation problems at the time.

Although we were rigorously objective in our news reports, there was a slight problem: we had three Irish columnists — Michael Daly and Pete Hamill as well as Breslin — who were free to express their own opinions and never seemed to be able to write anything nice about the English, especially when they were writing from the scarred Falls Road section of Belfast. Breslin, of course, was the most menacing member of the trio because of the huge following he had among Irish-Americans in the New York area and the political damage he could therefore do to British policy in the United States.

For similar reasons but to a lesser degree, of course, he was also unpopular with the Irish Republic. Dublin felt, with merit, that Breslin did nothing whatever to encourage American support for its conciliatory, nonviolent approach to the Northern problem. One typical piece of evidence was a column in which he wrote that Dublin, London, and Washington were all conspiring together to keep Northern Ireland as "a small, wet corner" of the British Isles. Comments like this naturally rattled the Belleek in the Irish consulate in New York and, because O'Neill was regarded as a sympathizer, the consul general or his aides were frequently on the phone to him to do something. With chagrin, O'Neill had to concede that inasmuch as we couldn't get Breslin even to subscribe to our very reasonable editorials, it was idiotic to think we could persuade him to follow the Dublin line.

All this international turbulence did not sadden our hero. Au contraire. The idea that he was making diplomats shake with rage gave him fits of ecstasy. Causing trouble is the greatest pleasure he finds in life — loading his bloodstream with large overdoses of adrenaline — and when entire nations are involved he nearly goes berserk with joy. So every time we reported the latest foreign protest, he would bounce with delight, laughing out loud, shouting "Wonderful!" and immediately bubbling with new ideas about how he could keep the controversy going.

Breslin is more a son of Queens than of the old country, more at home in the tunnels of the Flushing subway line than in the pubs of Dublin, but he is Irish to the core. Not a professional Irishman singing "Danny Boy" off key and short on lyrics, but a writer with a strong emotional attachment to his heritage, a great affection for Irish culture and literature, and, most of all perhaps, a feeling of guilt because the American Irish have forgotten so much of their inheritance and have failed to fight as hard for their persecuted brethren in Northern Ireland as the Jews have fought for Israel.

More than any other Americans, New Yorkers wear their ethnic differences like a badge. They automatically identify everyone by the cultural warrens they come from — Italian or Jew, Irish or Wasp, black or Hispanic, Chinese or Korean. They keep close watch on the distribution of economic and political power, worrying forever about one group gaining an advantage over another as new waves of immigrants roll in against the earlier tides. As Daniel P. Moynihan and Nathan Glazer observed long ago, the city's celebrated melting pot doesn't do much melting.

Yet it has had an effect. There are great variations in the intensity of ethnic feelings in New York, ranging from the powerful convictions of the Jews to the disappearing self-identity of the Wasps — and the waning cultural consciousness of the Irish, which Breslin laments again and again in his columns. When a Boston newspaper called Joseph P. Kennedy an Irishman, he exploded: "I was born here. My children were born here. What the hell do I have to do to be called an American?" The answer, of course, was to wait a couple of generations. "In New York, as the old Irish die and their descendants take on the shopping center faces and mannerisms of true Americans," Breslin explains, "the Saint Patrick's Day celebration has grown longer, and fewer people know what it's about."

It is an embarrassment to him that Irish voters haven't forced Washington to denounce the English, whom he calls "the foulest race on the face of the earth," and to drive them out of Northern Ireland. It is even greater embarrassment that the most militant supporters of Ireland's cause are not Irish-Americans at all but Italian politicians, like Representative Mario Biaggi of the Bronx, who don't know a de Valera from an Ian Paisley but who do know how to rustle Irish votes in Queens and Nassau. The Italians have marched in Saint Patrick's Day parades and led the sword rattling because Irish-American leaders have taken the political risk of denouncing the violence which so many of their constituents privately endorse. In a historic policy statement in 1977, the four leading

Irish-American politicians — Speaker of the House Thomas P. O'Neill, Jr., Senators Moynihan and Edward M. Kennedy, and Governor Hugh Carey — called for urgent negotiations to end the strife in Northern Ireland but strongly condemned the gun-slinging policies of the IRA.

Breslin is no bomb-thrower himself: he both knows and likes the moderate leader of Belfast's Catholics, John Hume, who opposes the IRA. But he is personally much closer to his good friend Bernadette Devlin McAliskey, "this small woman with a thrilling voice," as he describes her, who has been a champion of force to end opposition and who was herself nearly killed by assassins in 1981.

So Devlin's views generally prevailed over Hume's, putting Breslin in happy collision with three governments, with the four horsemen of American-Irish politics, and also, as usual, with the editorial position of his newspaper. Without ever exactly delivering any guns to the IRA, he left the impression that while the politicians and editors cowered in the shadows, he stood undaunted on the ramparts in the fight against British tyranny. This made him a champion with most of the *News*'s Irish readers while the editors became the goats, attacked in the letters columns, criticized even by some of their own reporters, and, most ominously, threatened by tough IRA supporters who are numerously present in the production department of the newspaper.

All of which filled Breslin's black-Irish heart with satisfaction and made his heart pound with excitement.

— M.J.O.

The Backgrounds Are Distant

The first thing I saw as I came out of the subway was the big sign in the saloon window, which said: "Saint Patrick's Day Party Tonight — Free Corned Beef and Cabbage."

I looked in and said to the bartender, Michael Glynn, "Aren't you a bit early?"

"Just to get the motor running," he said.

"But you're still a full week ahead of time," I said.

"And they'll stay for the week," Michael said.

In New York, as the old Irish die and their descendants take on the shopping center faces and mannerisms of true Americans, the Saint Patrick's Day celebration has grown longer, and fewer people know what it's about.

This is at once the work of the weather and the saloonkeepers. On Friday in Manhattan at 5:40 P.M. a young woman in a striped dress trotted out of an office building on Third Avenue, and began waving for a cab. She had been in too much of a hurry leaving her office to pause and throw on her coat. She held the coat over one arm and waved for the cab with the other, her young slim body stretching to see a taxi in the traffic. She stood facing a sky that had great swatches of pink spread across the gray.

The air becomes soft, the snow melts, the darkness arrives slowly. The greatest strength of the city, our four seasons, begins to exert itself. Soon we will have spring. The change raises the level of activity and quickens the thought. In the places where there is one season, the people sit in the sun and the mind turns to grapefruit. Here in New York on one day we have snow and bitter darkness, and then you look up and here is a young woman standing in the soft dusk with a coat over her arm. Of course it is time to celebrate.

The Irish saloonkeepers have seized on this and used the holiday falling at this time, Saint Patrick's Day, as the basis for a week of as many parties as the customers can handle. In many cases, the Irish saloonkeepers are the last of the line: Born on the other side, in full possession of the great immigrant drive, they wave shamrocks and corned beef at the multitudes who are Irish in name. It is the season for a party and they cause people to feel guilty if they do not celebrate an ancestry most don't know much about.

Strings of corned beef stick in the teeth, and the cabbage is like water. Put the plate aside and do what the season calls for: have a drink.

Apparently, this is the only thing the Irish have left. Their day, their parade, and the parties in pubs which led up to it. All week we can look for Koch the Mayor, who perceives these people to be his executioners, to come up with a cute remark about how much the Irish drink.

The parade on Friday is about all the Irish have left to indicate where they are from. They have pretty much deserted poetry and the novel and the spoken word. You have to put a gun to their backs to get any amount of Irish to support a play. In the great American communications form, television — a form made for storytellers — the American Irish, born of a race of storytellers, have Carroll O'Connor and virtually no one else on the air.

Their idea of creativity is a corporation, and their idea of rebellion was to vote for Richard Nixon.

The parade on Friday, starting fashionably, with an Irish governor, soon thins, and the heart of it — people marching under the banners of the counties from which they come — has dwindled to small groups. A noonday sun will line the sidewalks with one of these incredible crowds of which only New York is capable. But it all will be about something that no longer exists.

What is alive, and Irish, is a subject few with Irish names either know or care very much about: death on the crumbling streets of Northern Ireland.

In New York on Friday night, the mayor of Cork in the Republic of Ireland assured an audience that everything in his country was booming. Please, he kept implying, do not mention the place in the North. We have nothing to do with it, and if you have anything to do with it, you will only make matters worse. Leave the North alone.

His speech was about the same as American politicians with Irish names always make. There is never a thought of political pressure. The politicians don't care enough to do anything more than speak.

After hearing the mayor of Cork, I went home and put in a call to a friend in Belfast. I have known him for some time, since 1970, when I lived in the city researching a novel. He spoke over the phone in a tired, almost bored tone.

"What's it like?" he said. "We used to talk about outrages, you know. We've gone well past that. Now we're dealing with a suicidal element. You read about the bombing at the hotel, the LaMon House. Twelve were killed. Protestants. That was about the same as the bombing at McGurk's Bar a couple of years ago. What were there, fifteen Catholics killed? You can almost expect this sort of thing.

"But the suicidal element is in this one matter we had here, the man driving his child to school. The man was a lovely, hard-working man. Somebody said he was a member of the UDA, the Protestant organization, but it didn't look like it to me. Well, here he was taking the wee one to school and the bomb in the car blew them both up. A week later, your old school bus develops trouble, with a dozen or more children. Protestants, you know. The driver stops and looks at it, you know, and here's dynamite falling out of the motor. Now that's suicidal.

"Just when you're at your lowest, then the other side performs on schedule. The other day there's a man named Trainer, a Catholic, coming from his job on Portadown, and two fellows pull up to him on a motorcycle and one of them has a machine gun. They kill him. The man's seventeen-year-old brother was assassinated a few months back. Two years ago, his mother was assassinated. That's a fine family under the ground.

"Oh. I forgot this. Just the other day here, the Queens University students had what they call a 'rag day.' They go around town dressed as cowboys and Indians and the like, you know. So now here's two people dressed as Arabs sneaking out of the crowd of students. They lift up the Arab veils and shoot a soldier and a woman security guard. But why bother talking about it? Nobody does anything, and the killing goes on. Tell me about something else. What's doing where you are?"

I told him about the big parade the Irish are having on Fifth Avenue on Saint Patrick's Day.

(March 1978)

A Bride's Disdain

BELFAST — For several minutes the bride inspected herself in the small mirror on the parlor wall. The chauffeur waiting in the doorway said that they were late, that they had to leave now, and the bride turned her face so that she could inspect the right cheek more thoroughly. She is of a street, Sugarfield Street, where people have chauffeurs twice in their times, at marriage and at death, and therefore a chauffeur's impatience is answered with inattention.

The bride frowned as she considered her right cheek, which had three blemishes. The veil failed to obscure, the thick makeup didn't cover. Still the blemishes showed.

"It's a shame, actually," she said.

"You look beautiful," her father said.

"It's a shame," she said.

"How old are you?" she was asked.

"Nineteen. Say I'm twenty."

"And you're getting married on the day the pope visited Ireland."

In the mirror, her eyes became disdainful. "The pope." She said it in a flat voice.

"Did you watch any of it on television?" she was asked.

"I did, yes. Saw him getting off the plane."

"What do you think?" she was asked.

"I think he's a nice wee mon."

"And that's all?"

"He means nothing to me. He means nothing to the children I'm going to have."

Her father, hair wet and combed straight back, a white carnation on his severe brown suit, said, "We shouldn't have wasted the electricity on him."

"It's time we're off," the chauffeur said again.

Kim Gilbert touched her veil. She cocked her head one way, then another. Perhaps a change in angle, a change in light, would disguise the blemishes.

In the street outside, a street of miniature brick row houses, women huddled inside folded arms and children leaning against their mother's skirts waited to see the bride. This is the section known as Shankill Road, and in 1969 the men from these row houses rushed down the little street and into the adjacent Catholic neighborhood to start the killing that still endures. On walls everywhere in the Shankill yesterday there were signs saying, "No Pope Here." They were not new signs to signify the pope's visit to Dublin yesterday. These slogans have been on walls for years. And their words have lived in the Protestants' minds in Northern Ireland for centuries. No moving pageantry, no magnificent political expression by a pope, even a pope as gifted as this one, can place a warm hand on the winter emotion of the Protestants of Northern Ireland: he and his are not theirs and they are not his.

"The pope?" one of the women outside the bride's house repeated. She turned to call after her little boy, who had run into the street after a soft-drink truck. "Stay ye here!" she called to the boy. The woman went after him, slapped him on the head, and dragged him back. With her free hand, she pointed to a woman who was in the doorway alongside the bride's house. "She'll tell ye all ye want to know about your wonderful pope."

The woman she indicated, an old woman with gray hair and long tooth showing, said her name was Mrs. Curran. She pulled open her front door. On the wall inside was a large poster of King William III, William of Orange, the conqueror of the Catholics in 1690. To the Northern Irish mind, this date is more recent than the 1976 election is to an American. "There's my pope," Mrs. Curran said, touching the poster.

"What about the pope that's down in Dublin today?" she was asked.

"Don't know a word he says, I need an interpreter."

Another woman said, "Wouldn't waste the electricity to watch him."

"Why should she? Doesn't mean anything to us," another woman said.

"Nothing."

"Waste the electricity."

Now the bride came on to the sidewalk and all the women threw confetti and called out, "All the best!" And the bride got into her chauffeured car and drove away, and I went for a walk along the narrow streets, which were filled with the smell of coal smoke. Many blocks of these row houses, so familiar in pictures of Northern Ireland, were deserted and the windows bricked up. The violence has caused the authorities to rearrange the area, spreading people out in council houses in other parts of Belfast. Parts of the Shankill look like a damp South Bronx. But the "peace lane" must remain. It is a high corrugated iron fence, topped with barbed wire, that separates the Shankill from the Catholics on the other side of the fence.

Nothing, of course, stops the gunmen. On Thursday night, two of them came to the door of the apartment of Peter Heathwood, who lives in a Catholic area. The wife answered the door, saw the guns, and ran back toward her husband. Their three children were in the living room. The code in Northern Ireland appears to call for nearly all shooting to be done in the presence of the wife and children, in order to insure that the event will remain in family memory. The husband, Heathwood, braced up and slammed the door shut. The gunmen fired through the door, hitting him twice. Heathwood's father, sixty-four, hearing the shots, came running up to the apartment house. At the entrance he dropped dead of a heart attack. The son survived. Yesterday, nobody knew if the son could be out of the hospital for the father's funeral.

Heathwood was listed as a Catholic. In the Shankill district yesterday, people were more interested in talking about an attempted ambush on Friday night of two prison guards. And the funeral last Saturday of the assistant governor of the Crumlin Road jail. The shots on each occasion were said to have been fired by the Catholics of the IRA provisionals. And now, yesterday in Belfast, walking away from the "peace lane" and up Conway Street, here was Elizabeth Smith, a blue kerchief on her head, on her hands and knees scrubbing the tiled entranceway to her tiny house.

"I'll bet you have the pope on television inside," she was told.

"Don't believe so," she said. "I'm bloody sure he's not. I'll put my feet through the television if I see him on."

"Why does he bother you?" she was asked.

"I never had any trouble with Catholics in my life and I don't intend to bother with them," she said. "They did enough to me. I have an ailment from them. I took a diabetes in 1969. It came from the shock they gave me."

"What shocked you?" she was asked.

"When I looked out and saw all the houses up in flames." She stood up. "Dirty pack, that's what they are."

Andy Tyrie, the head of the Ulster Defense Association, was found in an office one flight up over the Shankill Road. He sat with a man named Harry Chicken. The street below was alive with traffic and shoppers, although entire blocks of small businesses and corner saloons are burnt out or bricked up. Tyrie says there are fifteen thousand in his organization, but he can summon more with a raised eyebrow. In 1974, he put fifty thousand men into the streets and shut down all of Northern Ireland. Two years ago, his organization announced that it was through with violence. Tyrie maintained that Protestant shooting now is being done by a much smaller, outlaw group, the Ulster Volunteer Force.

"I think the pope is a smart man, and he showed it," Andy said. "Why?"

"Because he didn't come to Northern Ireland."

Tyrie is a stocky man with a mustache who has been head of the UDA since 1972, which is at least a couple of lifetimes in his business. "Go down and look for yourself on television," he said. "A million people pray with the pope. Is this the united Ireland you want us to be in? People see this thing today and you wonder why they get nervous. We don't want any more sectarian strife. But we don't want to live under this, either.

"The politicians and the ministers will be making all the statements. We don't bother with them anymore. They used to lead us around by the nose. They did the talking, we had to go and do the fighting. The minute that started, the ministers would run away.

"Altogether, on both sides, there are fourteen hundred men in prison. You know how many politicians are in jail? None of the bastards. They start it and then we're supposed to be the ones to go to jail. Those days are over."

Harry Chicken said, "I'll tell you one thing people in America can watch out for. Kennedy is going to announce for president the minute the pope gets there and gives him the word. The pope'll get to America and he'll forgive Kennedy for the woman in the water and for everything else, and then he'll tell him to run for president. You watch. Kennedy will walk right out and announce he's running. He'll get all his support from the pope."

Downstairs was the Royal Bar and it was in startling condition. Packed, smoky, and with the pope on television. Which did not mean the death of sectarianism. It means only that television is the most powerful drug known to the world. Dialed morphine. For not one head in the crowded room was lifted from a pint to look at the pope on television. "I don't know why it's on, it's out of habit, I just turn the set on Saturday mornings at eight and leave it on all day," Stanley Rossborough, the owner, said.

From the television I heard Frank Patterson singing the Mass in Dublin. He is a friend of Kevin Cahill, the doctor, and out of respect I wanted to watch Patterson, but this would have made mine the only head in the Royal Bar raised to watch the Catholics on television. I did not exactly deny my faith, no cock crows for Breslin, but I did become busy talking to a redheaded guy about a horse he fancied, Running Rocket in the two-fifteen at Redcar, in England, and, in the middle of Patterson singing a hymn and the pope praying, I walked out the back door of the Royal with the redheaded guy and went down to McLean's bookmaking shop and bet a couple of pounds on the horse. Later, I could hear the great phrases of the pope's second sermon, "Call murder by no other name," but he was in Ireland and the Royal Bar is in Northern Ireland and even great words did not travel that distance yesterday. No one listens. Later, when the pope was off television and I could look up, a sports announcer said that Running Rocket finished second at Redcar. The bar groaned. The horse had been a hot tip.

(*September 1979*)

The Rev. Ian Paisley: Selling Death from the Pulpit

BELFAST — The Reverend Ian K. Paisley strode to the pulpit of the Martyrs Memorial Free Presbyterian Church, Ravenhill Road, to start the Sunday service at eleven-thirty yesterday morning. Before speaking, Paisley led his congregation through a wonderful old hymn that his mortal enemies, the Catholics, should steal: "At the Cross! At the Cross! Where I First Saw the Light . . ." Paisley's large frame bucked as he hurled the notes about the building.

He then set down his hymn book and, face flushed, hands jabbing, bellowed:

"Thank God we're not subject to pope and popery! Thank God we're not on our knees at some Mass!"

His congregation of women in velvet turbans and men in dull ties stirred.

"Hallelujah!"

"Amen!"

"Yes! Yes!"

"Rid snookishness, carelessness, and laziness from the soul. The congregation now will read, not mumble, from Isaiah. '. . . And I will wait upon the Lord . . .' " In Paisley's Northern accent, "wait" becomes "wayet."

He interrupted to welcome a visitor from the Republic of Ireland. "This man said he prefers to worship here this morning rather than in Ireland, where the pope is, and of course we agree. At the seven P.M. service today my sermon will be, 'Why our controversy with Rome must continue.' We also will continue going forward to battle for souls. Evangelism! Last week, the contractor who built the church for us in Ballymena got gloriously saved. I read in the *Irish Times* that the collections for the Mass for the pope reminded them of the collection at Reverend Paisley's Martyrs Church. Heh. Heh."

There were, in all of Northern Ireland, a couple of Protestant ministers who suggested that the pope should be tolerated during his visit, particularly since the man wasn't even coming to the six counties of Northern Ireland.

"Traitors!" Paisley went on. "I'm glad I dissent, I'm glad I stand opposed to the pope. There is no weakening on our stand for Christ. The pope is anti-Christ. He said: 'I as pope am not an enemy. You need feel no fear.' Those ignorant people don't know Rome. They have fallen for the massive propaganda. The BBC is an agency of the Jesuits. If Rome had her way today they'd still put Protestants to the fire. Don't go to sleep. When the pope speaks peace, beware. We'll sing hymn number four-one-seven now."

Throughout Northern Ireland, many people are heard to say that Paisley is of the past, that he is not representative of today's Protestant attitudes. British commentators on television made a point of saying that Paisley sounded the only objection to the pope's visit. Which is about the same talk heard from Catholics here who, until yesterday anyway, always deplored the IRA while gladly hiding a gunman in the house at night. For yesterday, the Reverend Ian Paisley, standing with a gray brick wall behind him and facing a crowded Scandinavian-modern, double-decked church, spoke with the true voice of Northern Ireland's Protestants. His thunder is their belief: When Paisley runs for political office he receives about the vote of any other two winners combined throughout the country. His exaggerations are buffoonery to a visitor and reality to his people. The rain and brooding clouds of his land keep thriving on ancient rot.

"I reject and repudiate that the pope is infallible," Paisley now said. "The pope is not infallible. He is an impostor and a blasphemer and a liar. I'm sick of mollycoddles and lollipops who don't stand up to him. We even hear Protestants calling the pope 'Holy Father.' He's not Papa to me. I must ask myself: Would I be prepared to stand up if it means burning? My answer is, I'd stand up and die at the stake rather than take the wafer."

The "wafer" referred to the Catholic Communion. Paisley immediately went into an attack on the Catholic theory of transubstantiation: The bread and wine being transformed during the Mass into the body and blood of Christ. A Catholic today, upon taking Communion, is not quite nibbling on Christ's toes. As I understand it, he is a person taking the responsibility to be present through transition at the Last Supper and to accept the terrible blend of life: The body betrays and we all die. It's a fair enough way to treat life, if you choose, but to Paisley it is a burning stake awaiting the next Protestant victim. The fundamentalist Northern Irish Protestant thinking, as reflected by Paisley yesterday, is that no man who worships in this form, who would go to the wafer on a Sunday, should be given equal opportunities for things like a job. It is insane thinking, of course, and it also is an accomplice to killing.

On Saturday afternoon, in the Royal Bar on the Protestant Shankill Road, Tommy Lyttle, a bookmaker, tie pulled down, smoking cigarettes, assured me, "Paisley is a complete bigot and that's all he is." Lyttle had just registered his discomfort at the idea of millions of Catholics deciding to rule him. As he is an officer of the Ulster Defense Association, which has killed some Catholics in its time, his estimate of Paisley seemed amusing. But, while thinking of this in Paisley's church yesterday morning, there was an absence of mirth. I was listening to a man sell death from a pulpit at a time when at the least a phrase of love might have softened a treacherous way. The scrubbed, proper people of Paisley's congregation yesterday do not tumble into the street and call for the death of Catholics. Their prejudice, however, is pervasive, a handful of pain that over the many years seems at ease only when helping to dig fresh graves.

To the south yesterday, the pope again called for the end of murder by Catholic gunmen in the North. He created disgust with the IRA style of fighting oppression with a combination of nationalism, religion, and thuggery. "Love is never defeated," the pope said, referring to the struggle to overcome the prejudice faced by Catholics in the North. The wisdom is undeniable; the opponent ferocious.

After the service yesterday, Paisley went into a small office, where he was asked if he really thought the pope was as great a menace as outlined from the pulpit. The faint hope was that Paisley would smile a politician's smile and say, Well, I was just out there talking to my people. Instead, his eyes cold, he said, "The pope coming here was bad. He failed to condemn those who give comfort and succor to the IRA. He failed to pay any tribute to our security forces. The pope could stop the violence if he wanted to. He could excommunicate the IRA. I think it's very bad that he's here."

Outside, a woman in a green wool dress and green velvet turban said, "Well, did he save your soul?"

"Mine's too black for that," I said.

"No, only the pope's can't can be saved," she said. "He's a blasphemer. He could end the violence."

"How?"

"The pope could make the priests tell the police what they hear in confession. The IRA kills somebody, then they go to confession and tell the priest and he tells them that they are forgiven and then they go out and kill somebody else and then they go right back to a priest."

"You believe that?" she was asked.

"Yes, I do. Didn't you just hear Reverend Paisley say the same thing inside?"

(*October 1979*)

Oh, We Hate Murder, Too

BELFAST — The door opened and a woman in a brown coat, a cigarette stuck in a corner of her mouth, stood in the light and glared at the visitors.

"You can go in," she said, stepping out of the way. Inside, in the IRA Club, a band on a platform exploded with a song. A crowd of two hundred young people, probably more, young males mainly, with cigarettes stuck behind their ears and pints in their hands, sat at long unsteady tables and sang out:

". . . Where are the boys who stood with me when history was made; the Boys of the Old Brigade!"

Alfie, the manager, stood at the bar, a bar that had six bartenders whirling from bottle to bottle, and shouted through the music, "It's a Provo internment song, you know. It's very popular here, you know."

At the table nearest us were two girls with large sad eyes. The pints in front of them were as big as their faces. High school seniors, maybe, I thought. The five boys with them were perhaps a year older. They all sang, but you could hear the voices of the two girls over the boys' when it came time to shout out, "The Boys of the Old Brigade!"

This particular club was on a dark, littered street off the Falls Road in a cramped, mean Catholic slum. There are many of these IRA clubs in Belfast. They were crowded with young people on Sunday night. The day had belonged to the pope of Rome, who cried for peace to hundreds of thousands in Ireland. The night was for the young of Belfast, whose songs were of prison and death.

"The pope?" one of the girls said when she stopped singing. "The pope didn't say anything bad about the IRA."

"The pope was dead on," Alfie, the manager, said.

"Did he do any good?" Alfie was asked.

"Great job. He gave it to all the politicians for allowing the injustice."

"What about when he talked about violence? He said, 'Call murder by no other name.' "

Alfie said, "Well, we're all against murder." He turned and motioned to a table. "Here, you talk to him."

A thin, sandy-haired fellow of about thirty walked up. "You say murder, well, you didn't hear exactly what the pope said," the sandy-haired guy said. "The pope pointed out that this is not a sectarian war, thus identifying it as a war of liberation. We are against murder. Murder is the taking of a life for personal revenge or satisfaction. But you can't call a war of liberation murder. That would make all of World War Two a murder. We're fighting the British. So you can't call that murder."

"So what the man said really meant nothing to you?" he was asked.

"Oh, of course it did," he said. "Everyone was moved by his sincerity. Everyone should be examining their conscience to bring about a just and lasting peace."

Earlier, in the lane in the morning, I had gone to see an old woman I've known for years. Her row house, known as a home for snipers, was decorated with a gold-and-white paper flag and a poster of the pope.

"I went to see the pope, yes I did, and it brought tears to men's eyes, just the sight of him," she said. "We went down by bus to Drogheda to see him. There was somebody from almost every house on this block on the bus with us. Down to Drogheda."

"Did you all hear him speak about the violence?" I asked.

"Oh, we did. I'm positive sure it will do a lot of good. The IRA says they'll have an announcement Tuesday about laying down their arms. They should lay their arms down, too. The minute they get justice they should stop the shooting.

"Your man Pat Crowsan had two sons killed around here, you know. One son was cut up in pieces, you know. They butchered him. The other one was on the bus, and they stopped the bus and came on and shot him in the brain. Oh, I wish the sun would come out. We had two winters this year, not an hour of summer. But it was a beautiful day for His Holiness. I tell you, to see the tears in men's eyes. Oh, he'll bring us peace when we get justice."

Around the corner from her house was an honor roll of those from the area who have died in the violence of the last ten years. Wreaths covered with plastic were at the base of the monument. At the top an inscription read, "It is not those who inflict the most but those who endure the most shall win." The sign listed twenty-two IRA members and sixty-eight civilians, twelve of them women.

Two young women stood in the doorway across the street. They smoked cigarettes and kept pushing their children back into the dark box of a living room. "Why would fighting the British soldiers stop?" one of them asked. She threw her head toward the honor roll. "You just can't forget the people who died," she said. Her child tried to sneak past her and out into the rain. She hit the child and shoved him back. "Don't want ye to catch cold," she said.

And now, at night, amidst the noise and smoke and sad young faces at the IRA Club, the band played "Sean South" and the entire room was singing. Singing in their youth about dying in their youth.

The IRA guy in the brown sweater shouted to me, "Sean South died on December 31, 1957, in a raid on a police barracks. You see how long this has gone on. Don't you think that after seven hundred years Ireland should control her own destiny?"

"And that's dead on," Alfie the manager said.

They live in a place where the past constantly destroys today.

Sitting along the wall, elbows on the table, was a white-haired man with a square red face. He was the oldest person in the room. He was dressed in a dark suit with a sweater underneath and a collar and a tie that were as tight as a garrote. Opposite him were two large women who wore coats and drank whisky and sweated in the smoky, airless club.

"We saw the pope at Drogheda, dead on, he was," the man said. He said his name was Billy Brady. He had a midsection shaped like a flour sack.

One of the women said, "They call him right when they say 'His Holiness.' Oh, the face on the man."

"He said it right," Billy Brady said. "The pope put it out there for the whole world to know. Did you hear him? He said the British are the cause of all this. Oops. Oh. Oh! Alfie, you can't do that."

Alfie was covering the bar with plywood boards to close it for the night. Billy attempted to burst out of his seat, but his flour-sack midsection hit the table edge and he couldn't make it; and Alfie covered the bar while Billy moaned and the women with him laughed and the young people in the club sat at their rickety tables and kept singing songs about prison and dying young in the streets.

(*October 1979*)

Neither God nor Devil Would Take Her

Her name is Bernadette Devlin McAliskey, and she does not quit. On January 16, an assassination team in Northern Ireland shot eight bullets that made fourteen holes in her body. "I think I was run over by a sewing machine," she said. Her husband, Michael, had thirteen holes in him. He was released, and she came out of the hospital on February 27. Yesterday, dragging around a leg in a cast, she was out at political meetings. "Neither God nor the Devil would take me in, so here I still am," she told people.

She is thirty-three now, and has a husband and three children. That is very old, and the encumbrances perhaps too many, for a ghetto hero. But she returns to the shacks and alleys and bleak housing estates of Northern Ireland, this small woman with a clear, thrilling voice. Yesterday, there was support for a man on a hunger strike in prison. Then there were preparations for a by-election for a British Parliament seat that her supporters now feel can be won. "It is my kind of fight," she said over the phone yesterday. "Dirty."

She called in the morning, with a child screeching in the background, from a house where she has been staying in the town of Coalisland.

"We stay with friends because the children won't go home," she said.

"They were in a room of their own when it happened. Three men came into the house. If they had arrived slightly earlier, it would have been dark. That didn't suit them. If they had arrived slightly later, we would have been out of bed. That didn't suit them either. They came at eight in the morning. The kids were in bed in their room. Michael and I were still in bed in our room. The little one, Fenton, was in with us. He's two. I'd brought him in with us earlier.

"We heard noises at the back door. Somebody was trying to break in. Michael got up and went to the door to stop them. They broke the door down. Michael started to run to the front door to lead them out of the house. But they shot him in the kitchen. A bullet stuck in his skull and didn't go through. We make heads like that over here.

"I was standing in the bedroom. I wanted to do something but I couldn't think of what. I was afraid to lift the baby out of bed because I knew they'd blow up both of us. While I was standing there, the man came in and shot me in the back. I fell over on my back. I never saw who it was. He kept firing at me. I pretended I was dead. He had one last shot left and he leaned over and shot me in the leg. He went away.

"I thought Michael was dead in the kitchen. I gave a mental runaround to see where I was shot that could cause death. Then I could concentrate on that part of me. I found I was having trouble breathing. So I put my mind on breathing so I could stay alive for the children.

"I crawled over to the bed and pulled the kid down with me. I got the blanket off the bed and covered the two of us. I heard talking outside. I thought they were back to shoot us again. A British soldier shouted into the house and I heard Michael answer. I knew Michael was alive. He told the soldier to ring for an ambulance. The soldier said the phone was out of order. Michael told him to use his radio. The soldier said that was out of order, too. The soldier wanted to know what Michael wanted done with the kids. The soldier wanted the name and address of somebody he could take the kids to. The soldiers were from a paratroop unit. The paratroopers were right there when the gunmen went into our house. Their job was to catch the gunmen on the way out. The paratroopers did just that. Both the gunmen and we were set up.

"I called out from the bedroom, 'Get a helicopter or we won't make it.' The paratrooper went outside the house and stood there. For the next thirty to thirty-five minutes the paratroopers stood outside the house and never came in. No first aid whatsoever. Once, Michael yelled out, 'Are you going to stand out there until we bleed to death?' Michael had been hit in an artery. Finally, another group of soldiers came in and gave us first aid. They took us to the hospital in Belfast. I'm still not sure myself what happened after that. I know I had one operation and then I had to be taken back for another one. Every time I see the doctors I forget to ask them what the second operation was for. My lung, I guess. I know there were two bullets almost touching the heart. If you have to be treated for gunshot wounds, there's no place better than Belfast."

Her conscience bothers her, she said, over the number of people who became alarmed during her second night in the hospital, when there was great fear that she would not pull through.

"All the people who dislike me came out and issued statements about my courage and character and said that if, perhaps, I was misguided now and then, I still had spent my life fighting against oppression and that was a wonderful thing to do. I even had uncles and aunts who haven't spoken to me in years standing around and saying how wonderful I was. All these people were acting on assurances that I wouldn't make it through the night. And then for me to do dirt on everybody and not die at all! Here they're praising me through the night on the promise of a funeral and the next morning I'm sitting up reading the newspapers."

During her stay in the hospital, she recalled yesterday, her chief adviser was a man named Tommy, who is one of Belfast's leading experts at using the welfare system.

Bernadette recalled the first morning that her head was clear and Tommy stepped into her room.

"How do you feel?" he asked.

"Great to be alive," Bernadette said.

"How did you sleep last night?"

"Never better," she said.

"Don't say things like that," Tommy said. "You never know when it'll be told back on you."

"What do you mean?"

"They'll use it against you at the compensation hearing," Tommy said.

Yesterday Bernadette laughed over the phone. The last time I heard her laugh was during the American presidential primaries and she was at the bar of the St. Moritz Hotel with Ricky Zucker and Mel Lebetkin, who had driven her to Manhattan from the airport. Bernadette went upstairs to a cocktail party to see Edward Kennedy, but the Secret Service agents wouldn't let her in because her name wasn't on their list. "Security," the agents told her.

(March 1981)

An Allowable Suicide

Professional fasting used to be limited to forty days and the idea was to charge admission and not die. Bobby Sands, fasting in prison in Belfast, clearly is changing these rules. When he went to sleep last night, he was finishing his fifty-eighth day of starving. His intention is to go one day too many.

Most people think that the great starving was done by Gandhi of India. This is another example of reputation outgrowing performance: Gandhi went only twenty-one days and mixed fruit juice with his water. The Irish champion, Terence McSwiney, went for seventy-four days in 1921. He did it one day too many. But his death caused people to overlook the fact that he, too, had been given fruit juice in his water for a time.

None of this for Bobby Sands. He will accept no nourishment and heads for death, and the violence to follow probably will take many with him.

Oh, Sands must go on with his starving, for there are great principles involved. He wants the right not to do prison work in Belfast, the right not to wear prison clothing, and the right to free association with other prisoners — unlocked doors — during those hours when present rules call for him to be locked in because he refuses to work.

The British, under Mrs. Thatcher, proclaim that they will not yield to such demands, that to do so would amount to giving political status to the IRA and turning the prisons over to an illegal organization. We will not, Mrs. Thatcher announces, assign control of the prisons to the prisoners. They would still be prisoners for years, yes, but this is not the issue. The issue, she says, is that the prison administration and the warders are in charge of the prisons.

Therefore, Sands, over the right to wear his own underpants rather than prison issue, starves toward death.

In New York yesterday, an old friend, a priest from Belfast here on a rest, was talking about the last time he had said Mass for Bobby Sands in prison. It was a month ago, and he mentioned quietly to Sands that his organization, the Irish Republican Army, had announced after the last hunger strike, the one that ended without death, that it had won.

"They're saying that outside?" Sands said.

"Yes," the priest said.

"I'm not saying it inside," Sands said. "And we're the ones that are doing it."

The priest said no more. In his church in Northern Ireland there had been a debate among religious people as to whether Sands is committing suicide, and thus a mortal sin, by starving himself to death. The same religious leaders who are clear that abortion is a sin and that killing yourself by rope or gun is a sin make no proclamation on Bobby Sands's starvation.

Similarly, the British government will not interfere. If Sands were to hang himself, the warders would race to cut him down and breathe life back into him. But they will do nothing to prevent him from starving to death.

"No force-feeding here," the administrators say proudly, although force-feeding would consist only of a needle in the vein attached to a bottle or so of something called TPN. But British wisdom in the face of an irrational act calls for the clinging to small rules.

Church and state, then, have set a rather poor precedent, for someday surely the public again will lose interest in fasting and Irish prisoners then can be counted on to accelerate their protests and begin biting off their own fingers and then entire hands, and there is no official policy, religious or temporal, to cover that either.

And so Sands starves on today, his act uncontested by those around him.

As long as it must be done, then, the purity of Sands's act, and the record of it that will be handed down through the generations to follow, should be protected. That Sands took not a morsel, not a flake of crust, that he had no fruit juices in his water, that he went to death clean, must be verified.

In the old days of professional fasting, they had observers — local butchers, I've read — who stood in front of the case and watched the faster's every move to make sure that he did not cheat and swallow some hidden chunk of food. As there is no dishonor to match that of a man who cheats while starving, the butchers chosen were those with the sharpest eyes and noses that went off like an alarm system at the whiff of food.

The professional fasters demanded this caliber of observer, for they sat in their hunger and knew that many people were spreading rumors that they were being dishonest and eating. The thought of this upset the fasters so much that after a time they began to suspect the butchers of being incompetent and they demanded even better watchers.

As certification of Sands's act is so important, the ruling British should place an expert on food in front of Sands and have the expert follow each move, each twitch, to its completion, in order to be able to testify later that Bobby Sands died of perfect starvation.

It is obvious that there is no one better qualified in the British Empire for this job than Mrs. Thatcher, who was raised in her father's grocery store. By upbringing, and sheer nose, she can tell at a sniff if Bobby Sands has as much as a mushroom stem within fifteen yards of him.

As it would upset prison discipline to have Mrs. Thatcher sit in one of the H-block cells to watch Sands, perhaps Sands could be moved outdoors, into a circus cage, and Mrs. Thatcher could sit in an official car and rivet her eyes and nose on Sands and do her job quite properly, and without the embarrassment of being inside a men's prison.

She is a woman born to smell milk in the mouth of an unworthy, and she has the eyes of Captain Bligh. She is admired everywhere because when she takes her stand, she does not change it because if she changed, why, then, it would mean that she had changed. And this she would never do. Therefore she is best suited to watch Bobby Sands sit and starve himself to death.

After which she must rush to her office in order to supervise the suppression of the riots that will be everywhere on the wet, dirty streets of Northern Ireland.

(April 1981)

Marching to Sorrento

Probably the one subject I know better than anyone on earth is the history of Irish-Italian warfare in New York. It began at the turn of the century, when the Irish construction workers tried to get two dollars a day. As the Irish produce more traitors than any race on earth — Liam O'Flaherty, who wrote *The Informer,* always said, "It really wasn't a novel; to create Gypo Nolan all I had to do was look to my left and right and take my pick" — it was a contractor named Crimmins who brought over two boatloads of men from Sicily who were contracted to work at a dollar a day.

It never stopped from then on. The Irish tried to shut the Italians out of the building trades, and they lost and could lose more as they go on. The Irish tried to keep the Italians off the docks, and now the Irish are left with empty piers on the West Side and whatever work is left in the city is in Brooklyn, and controlled by Italians. In the police department, the Irish tried to hold it all, and today all the big jobs are still held by Irish, but Italians are the largest group in the department. I don't have to tell you how long that one has to go.

In politics, the Irish — who came here with English as their language — felt they were doing tremendously while competing against people who spoke another language. Invincibility was lost when three Jews on the East Side learned to put a sentence together. The Irish were then left with the Italians still under them. Italians who could be mimicked and maneuvered. A couple of years ago, the Irish made a strong comeback, with Hugh Carey as governor and Patrick Moynihan as senator in a state where the major voting bloc is Italian.

Then, on the Republican side, Alfonse D'Amato became senator. Then Mario Cuomo was governor. Suddenly, the Irish were left with Patrick Moynihan, senator, and a strong breeze coming through the window at night sends him rolling over in bed.

And today on Fifth Avenue, during the Saint Patrick's Day Parade, there will be an official dismembering of the Irish as political powers — secular and, if the cardinal and his Irish underlings do not watch out, in religious politics, too.

It is all because of Michael J. Flannery, now in his eighty-second year. A year ago, an attempt was made to shift the Saint Patrick's Day Parade to a Sunday. At that moment, many people with Irish names suddenly realized that the only thing they had to connect them to their past was being taken from them. The parade was put back to March 17. The parade committee, which had stayed away from politics in the past, named as honorary grand marshal Bobby Sands, who had starved to death during a hunger strike in a British prison.

It was inevitable that someone like Michael Flannery would wind up as grand marshal of this year's parade. A short while before the vote was to be taken, Flannery was in the midst of another election. He had been indicted for trying to buy a cannon from the FBI and send it to the IRA in Northern Ireland. Flannery called his cannon "the big animal." Flannery's defense was that he had been led by federal agents to believe that he was working with the CIA on the purchase. The jury took a vote and Flannery won. There was no question that he would be the choice of the parade committee.

It meant nothing. Nearly all the people who watch the parade and most of the marchers in the parade know very little about the IRA and even what the trouble is in Northern Ireland. Whether Flannery was grand marshal or not, the parade would have the same meaning: a traditional, colorful walk up Fifth Avenue, in honor of being Irish.

And then everybody went insane. The government of Ireland withdrew its endorsement of the parade. Carey, out of office, dying for publicity, jumped in and said he would not march. Moynihan said the same thing. And Cardinal Cooke pulled out his schools. The Pentagon, because of Moynihan, said it was not allowing West Point or any army bands to appear.

The Italians were happy to fill in. At a Saint Patrick's Day Parade in New Jersey, with Flannery as grand marshal, Governor Kean did not appear. Nor did former Governor Brendan Byrne. But Representative Peter Rodino, whose family comes from San Valentino, near Naples, did march. So did Representative James Florio.

In New York today, Governor Cuomo marches. His roots are outside Naples. Alongside him will be Major General Vito Castellano of the National Guard.

"Maybe the Pentagon is against the march. Vito is a general whose checks are signed in Albany. If Cuomo marches, Vito marches," somebody in Albany explained.

Marching with them will be D'Amato, Lieutenant Governor Al DelBello, and Representatives Mario Biaggi and Geraldine Zaccaro-Ferraro and on down the line.

Flannery means nothing to them. For they seem sensible enough to know that anyone who marches in a parade is there for the parade and not the politics of the grand marshal. The political statement is made by some fool who stays away seeking publicity. "I marched in a Columbus Day Parade where Frank Sinatra was the grand marshal," one of the Italian politicians was saying yesterday. "What's a Flannery compared to a Sinatra?"

The Catholic schools of the New York Archdiocese are not being allowed to march. However, the bishop of Brooklyn, Francis Mugavero, will allow his schools to march. He also will allow the Irish to applaud him for this.

So today, in the sun and the music and the crowds, if you notice the Italians walking with a little more assurance in an Irish parade, understand that it is for a good reason. They are winning, perhaps forever, too, and they are doing it right in front of you on Fifth Avenue.

"The Italians are top dog this year," old Mike Flannery said to Paul O'Dwyer last night.

(March 1983)

6

"The Steam Was Evil"

Jimmy Breslin is a curious mixture of bravado and something close to foot-scraping deference when confronting his editors. Breslin never makes an appointment, nor is he announced by a watchdogging secretary. He simply lurches into the unsuspecting editor's office like a baby bulldozer, head lowered, eyes barely raised from beneath his heavy brows, mumbling a kind of shorthand that takes long familiarity with to understand. "Nice paper," he growls, by which he really means that in his opinion, that day's edition of the *News* may well be one of the worst ever committed to newsprint and ink. "That Koch," he says, wagging his head without further elaboration at the latest civic outrage of the mayor of New York.

Breslin slumps into a chair, and if he is smoking a cigar, which is usually, sends large, lazy puffs ceilingward, as if lost in deep thought. Very often ashes will fall from this cigar upon the Breslin tie or shirt, which he brushes off with an absentminded wave of his hand. People tend to think that because Breslin always looks rumpled, he wears indifferent raiment. Nothing could be further from the truth: his clothes, selected for him by his wife, are expensive, well-tailored, and even modish. It's only that five minutes after Breslin puts them on, they *look* like they have been slept in.

The pleasantries over, Breslin is ready to get down to the purpose of his visit, a task he approaches from the approximate direction of the upper deck in left field.

"That thing down in Atlanta," he said to Brink a few years ago, "that's not something for me, is it?" — this in a deferential tone suggesting that an editor's opinion about anything is something close to God-given.

"I think it could be," Brink replied. "That kind of thing is right down your alley."

"Is it really that big?"

"Of course it is. Anytime you have twenty young blacks killed, it's a big story."

"Yeah, but everybody else is writing all over it. What's there left to say?"

"Aw, c'mon," Brink scoffed. "You can always find your own angle."

"Well, maybe . . ." (head shaking, fingers running through the shaggy hair) ". . . Naw! What am I, crazy or something? That's not for me . . ." (long, long pause) ". . . or do you really think so?"

There you have it, what Breslin has been after all along, a choice out-of-town assignment. The truth is that while Breslin is the quintessential New York writer, he likes to hit the road a few times a year to flex his editorial muscles on a big story breaking somewhere else in the world.

And how was our hero as a "foreign" correspondent? In the opinion of his editors he did not always bat a thousand, although it is entirely possible and even highly likely that Breslin might dispute that judgment. Standard operating procedure for Breslin when he approaches almost any story is to leave the central facts to the spot news reporters and dig for his own angle — very often the impact the story is having on the little people, the guy who has no power on earth to influence what is happening but is going to get socked with the consequences, whatever they may be. Thus in March of 1979, when former President Jimmy Carter made a dramatic trip to Jerusalem and Cairo to try to win a peace accord from Menachem Begin and Anwar Sadat, Breslin, writing from Israel, chose to tell the story from the viewpoint of refugee Palestinians in a village on the West Bank. In Egypt, Breslin recorded the views of a simple peasant, living in a one-room hovel with his chickens, goats, and a water buffalo, who had turned out with a few others along a lonely railroad embankment to watch the train bearing Carter and Sadat pass by. Not quite the sweep of history there, one might say, but the pieces seemed to work reasonably well.

In covering the death of Pope John Paul from Italy in 1978, Jimmy got off one piece calling attention to the arrogance of the cardinals who guided the destiny of the Catholic Church and their lofty attitude of disdain toward women. Standard Breslin stuff. But when he viewed the pope's body at Castel Gandolfo, what impressed Breslin most was the perceptible deterioration of the pope's visage in the summer heat (it was August), and around this he wove a scholarly dissertation on the sad state of the embalming art in Italy, complete with quotes from Italian undertakers in the crowd.

Not only did this column seem to miss the grandeur of the moment but it was in the poorest possible taste. Brink killed it out of hand, the only Breslin column the *News* ever refused to run. Breslin then wrote a column about a woman in from the farms with her children and grandchildren, who kept shouting her name, "Mama Virginia." The column was met with tremendous enthusiasm inside the *News*. That night, however, the pressmen started a long strike, and the column never saw the light of a subway car.

Breslin quite regularly will deal with distant major stories without leaving New York. Writing about the Falkland Islands war gave him a chance to heap abuse on the people he loathes and despises, the English. But, typically, his best column told of the plight of a simple Irish fisherman whose nets were caught in the screw of a British submarine speeding to the war.

Breslin wrote several scathing columns attacking the Reagan administration for failing to pursue the rape and murder of U.S. Catholic nuns in El Salvador, as well as several penetrating pieces dealing with the Iranian hostage crisis and its aftermath.

The truth is that Breslin's best out-of-town work seems to come when its basic subject matter is close to his common-man franchise, and never did he demonstrate this to better effect than when he journeyed to Three Mile Island in Pennsylvania during the nuclear leak scare of spring 1979.

Long afterward, a group of New York University journalism students with probably not enough talent among them to carry Jimmy Breslin's notebook wrote a critique of Three Mile Island coverage by the press in which, among other things, they took Breslin (and the New York *Daily News* generally) to task for alleged sensationalism.

There also was criticism of Breslin for stating that steam from the cooling towers was laced with radiation when, apparently, it was not. In fact, the official version now, years later, is that little radiation was released at Three Mile Island. Also, first reports from those running the power plant said that there was a hydrogen bubble in a cable running to the water pumps. Much later, it was announced that any such bubble was in the steel case around the reactor and was no threat. Journalism students working on the federal grant had their paper turned into a federal report, in which Breslin was blasted. "The reactor was a fraud and I got taken in by it," Breslin said. "I was waiting to see a big blowup and now they say the thing can't blow up and kill everybody. I don't know why people are always afraid of a nuclear blast."

The federal report was due as President Carter's rather desperate reelection effort was being put together. News of the journalism students' report reached Breslin on the same day that he was visited in Costello's by three campaign people from the White House who wanted to socialize for an hour before returning to Washington.

"That ———— report of yours," Breslin growled. "Doesn't anybody know when you're trying to write about being a human?"

"I'll be back in Washington by four o'clock and the report will be burned by five," one of the Carter people said. At this moment, a Breslin sour at an administration that had to run in a New York primary was more important than a government report of college students.

Breslin's hand waved, much as a pope calms a crowd from his balcony.

"I censor nothing," he said. "Put down that I have personal class."

The report appeared. But all of this really missed the point. What Breslin did, in a few short sentences, was sum up that lump-in-the-throat feeling that a great many people get when they face the unknown, such as the nuclear menace at Three Mile Island. That, it can be argued, Breslin did better than any other journalist at the scene. Quite clearly, the real reason for this is that Breslin himself is Everyman, and what happens to him, what he senses and feels about a story, is what most of us would sense and feel if we were there and could put it into words. Equally clearly, Breslin's common-man touch begins to weaken the farther he strays from his home turf, the more alien are the people and the culture he is writing about. Or to put it another way, you can take Jimmy Breslin out of New York, but you can't always take New York out of Breslin.

—W.B.

Public Bitches

MIDDLETOWN, PA. — At first yesterday, I wasn't all that afraid. At six-thirty of a gloomy morning, I was standing at the gate to the Three Mile Island nuclear plant and watching steam drift out of the tops of the four cooling towers and run down the sides like candle wax.

The steam was evil, laced with radiation, and I was standing just across a narrow bridge from the towers, but, as I say, I wasn't terrified; I didn't even become ill.

A breeze carried the steam out toward my side of the river, and I walked backward quickly, turning an ankle on railroad tracks, but then the breeze shifted and I walked right back to the plant gate. The workers going on the seven-to-three shift were laughing and pushing each other.

One of them clapped his hands on the white hard hat of the man in front of him. Everybody laughed. The foaming towers provided a nice backdrop. A short distance up the road, in a parking lot at the edge of farmland, another crowd of workers drank coffee, and one of them, Ed Davies, calmed me so much that I could breathe with my mouth closed.

"Trouble with the energy business is the public," he said. "Public bitches no matter what you do. I been in this business thirty-one years. Worked at the Crawford station up the river here, and we was the first to burn pulverized coal. Public bitched about the coal smoke, so we put out the coal and put in oil, and then you should have heard them squawking when they had to pay for that. So then, they put in nuclear power to please the public. And now you see what the public is doing: bitching to beat the band."

"I think some people might be afraid of radiation," I said to Davies.

"No, they just like to bitch," he said. "They don't know the first thing about radiation. The whole thing's over nothing anyway. I was in there the morning it happened. It was nothing. The alarm went off and we just went to the auditorium like we're supposed to, so they could count us and make sure nobody's missing, and then we sat there and some of the guys started playing cards. You call that dangerous?"

I guess not. And then, standing with Davies, drinking coffee, I put the situation together as I have learned it since my arrival here. I didn't have a nerve in me as I went over everything, because on Friday night the nuclear people from Washington formally announced that they were putting their best computers to work on the whole problem.

Here is how things stand as the power plant people explain it: They must keep the nuclear reactor from getting too hot, because if that happens, if this uranium fuel rolling around like dropped quarters at a subway change booth goes up to, say, fifteen thousand degrees, which it can do real quick, then the cement in the reactor will melt and the dirt underneath the reactor building will disintegrate and the reactor core will drop into the ground until it hits the water table, which isn't so far down, what with the Susquehanna River right here. And then all that heat hitting all that water could cause a truly sensational "event."

They say it isn't easy to keep the reactor cool because something is growing inside a large cable that runs from the water pumps that cool the reactor to the reactor itself. They call the thing in the cable a bubble, although nobody has seen it and can say with absolute certainty that it is indeed a bubble. This is because if anybody tries to look at the bubble, he will get his eyes burned out.

Gas keeps the pressure on the bubble and stops it from growing. This is good because if the bubble grows and cuts off the cooling system, then the reactor will, as I pointed out earlier, get too hot to handle and hit that water real good. However, the gas pressure also has a bad feature, as far as the reactor is concerned. The gas pressure irritates the hydrogen that seems to be in the bubble and as things now stand, if the hydrogen gets the least bit more of a tickle it will blow up. This is known as a hydrogen explosion. It might be something to see.

"It's just a whole big bunch of nothing," Ed Davies said. Then he told me about his son-in-law, Joe Hipple, who works in the hottest areas around the damaged reactor. Hipple's job is called Health Physics, and it requires him to enter areas before other workers so the safety can be determined. I went over to Hipple's attached two-story brick house on Oak Lane Drive and banged on the door and woke him up.

When Hipple reported for work last Wednesday morning, he put on coveralls, a rubber suit, a hood, rubber boots and gloves, and an oxygen pack. He carried a Telector, a radiation-measuring instrument that poked sixteen feet ahead of him as he moved down a cement corridor in the building, checking the small cubicles off the corridor. Hipple was at a part of the corridor that always gives a zero reading and suddenly he had 15 rems on his dial. A millirem, the figure doctors use to measure the radiation normally received by humans, is one thousandth of a rem. The fifteen-rem reading disturbed Joe Hipple. He poked his radiation finder into a cubicle. The reading was a hundred rems. Hipple went backward, bumping into the electrician following him, and he jerked his thumb for both of them to get out of the place.

Yesterday morning, sitting on his couch in his paneled living room, Hipple said, "People don't really understand nuclear power. It's not dangerous. You've just got to learn to respect it."

"You like the job?" he was asked.

"Sure do," he said. "I get just about ten dollars an hour. Where else around here can I get a job like that? If it's not the power plant, then it has to be from the government. There's no other place."

By now, the middle of the morning, I was feeling real good. I was relaxing in a comfortable chair and talking to a pleasant, obliging guy. I smirked as I thought of all the frightened news people who moved out of their hotels in Harrisburg and went to places twenty and twenty-five miles away. The younger ones were particularly intent on running away. A twenty-four-year-old woman from a Florida paper said to me, "If I ever do have kids, I sure don't want any with three arms."

As I was thinking about this, I happened to glance into Joe Hipple's dining room. A playpen was in a corner and alongside it was a rack of clean, carefully ironed dresses belonging to a little girl.

"Where's the wife and kid, out shopping?" I asked.

"No, I sent them away to the mountains," he said.

"Oh," I said.

When he held the door open for me to go outside, my breath stopped and my legs would not move. Finally, I shut my eyes and ran out into the street.

At the American Legion hall, I threw myself against the bar, the sweat pouring off me, and watched a big press conference. It was being conducted by Metropolitan Edison, the terrific people who own the nuclear reactor that any minute is going to go belly whopping into the water table. A great guy named John G. Herbein was at the podium. He is the company's vice-president for generation. When the reactor goes POP! as I'm sure it will, Herbein's title will be the truest that a man ever carried.

"There has been a concern over the buildup of hydrogen," Herbein said. "We stopped venting gas because of this. The hydrogen buildup was at one point seven percent. The explosive region is four to six percent. We don't seem to have a problem over getting into the area of achieving a hydrogen explosion. Is there a chance for a potential hydrogen explosion? I think it's exceptionally minimal."

That meant for sure there was going to be a hydrogen explosion.

Herbein now said proudly, "I personally think the crisis is over."

The next press conference was in a gymnasium and it was conducted by Harold Denton, who is director of the Office of Nuclear Reactor Regulation for the Nuclear Regulatory Commission. Denton is supposed to be here to check on the Metropolitan Edison Co., which has trouble handling both reactors and truth. But Denton likes nukes so much that he talks about the reactor as if it were an ice-cream cone.

Denton announced, "We're having some people listen to the interior of the reactor. They tell me that it's not making much noise, so that means that there's no large parts rattling around in there. The trouble is, if you don't hear much, then you don't know what's going on."

He was asked, "Have you ever heard of a bubble in a reactor before?"

Denton began to cry. "We've not had a situation like this that previously existed until today."

It was great nuke language, but it was the first statement that I've heard about the damaged reactor that I believed: They never saw a thing like this before. That does it, I told myself. Bingo! What a steambath they'll have in this town when the reactor gets its feet into the water.

I walked out of the press conference and went around the corner to the Naples pizzeria on the town's main street. I ordered a slice of pizza and a Coke. When the man handed me the slice of pizza, I slapped it against my chest. The tomato sauce splattered all over the front of the shirt. Then I went to a phone booth and called New York to tell them that I was coming home. "I don't have a shirt," I said. As I stood in the phone booth, my knees began to shake. I figured the reactor, only three miles away, was going into its act at this very moment.

(April 1979)

No Backsliding Today

MIDDLETOWN, PA. — When the few people still living here yesterday heard that Jimmy Carter was coming to pay a sick call on the nuclear reactor, they started the day with the first particles of security that have been available to them since last Wednesday.

The citizens figured, as I did, that Denton, the Nuclear Regulatory Commission man in charge of curing the reactor, would not bring Carter to Middletown and get him blown up in a nuclear holocaust yesterday, because that would cost Denton his job.

Nevertheless, at the 10:00 A.M. Mass at the Church of the Seven Sorrows, a general absolution was given on orders of the bishop. The absolution was not taken lightly by the church, which was less than half full. The people who were there were the ones who could not run, who were too old or too afraid of losing a job or too broke to go up to the corner, much less to Ohio.

Usually, this particular Sunday service is packed to the walls. So those in the pews had been thinking about things such as life and death, and watching neighbors drive away with packed bags, pretty steadily for the past few days. The Mass, therefore, developed an intensity that was far from ordinary.

I was in the back of the church, staring out the open doors and wondering where I would go for breakfast, when I had a thought about the giant reactor three miles away melting down into the earth and hitting the water table under Three Mile Island and causing me to die in the world's biggest steam bath ever. When I thought of this, I turned my head and became quite attentive to the Mass.

After church I walked along streets where my footsteps were the only sounds. I went down the main street, Union Street, to look for Frances Russ, who runs the Blue Room Bar. She and her friend Peggy Folsom — "just like in the prison" — say that they never would leave Middletown, even if there was going to be an explosion that noon, and that they wanted to sit in the bar and drink whisky with me on the day the reactor blew up.

"You never know what can happen to us in the last ten minutes," Frances promised me. But when I got to the bar yesterday, it was closed because of the Sunday law and Frances was next door in her house. There was no way to get a drink. They ought to bomb this town, I said to myself.

Up at the newsstand, Mary Loranzo, who was taking cash, was saying that she was the only one now living in her neighborhood, and it had been an upsetting experience for her on Saturday night.

"The landlady went away and turned the heat off before she left," Mary said. "Then last night the only other people left in the house — you see I live in this apartment house right down the block. Well, the only other people in the house knocked on the door and said, 'We've come to say good-bye!' Don't say things like that to me, I said. So I yelled over to Mrs. Hauser across the street. I yelled, 'Hey, you stayin'?' Mrs. Hauser said, 'Yeah.' I said, 'At least I'll have somebody to yell over to.' "

"Why don't you go too?" I asked Mary.

"I got this job here," she said. "I work as a typist during the week, and I'm not so sure where I stand with that, so I'm not leaving during the week and I've had this Sunday job for a long time and I don't want to lose it. Start at five-thirty and go till one in the afternoon every Sunday. I get fifteen dollars for it. I can't afford to let it go."

"If you get blown up, that's the world's toughest fifteen dollars," I told her.

"Oh, I have another reason," she said. "I made my three children stay in Harrisburg. I figure that if I stay here, I'm only five minutes from the site, and if anything is going to happen, the people here will be told first. So I can jump right on the phone and give my children the first flash. I can give them a few extra seconds' head start. I can tell them to get out on that highway and start driving.

"They can be out on the road before the big traffic jam. I'll tell them, 'Get going. I'll see you in Ohio if I get there.' "

She shook a head of recently champagned hair and laughed. "You do for your children. What's the difference? You know that our lives are over anyway," she said.

"Mine isn't," I said.

"You know it is," she said. "Who are you fooling?"

"If I don't get blown up here, I'm going home and have twins," I told her.

I went across the street and walked up one flight to the clubrooms of the Middletown Elks 1092. A group of shrieking women sat around a large round table in the room adjoining the barroom.

One of them yelled out, "A reporter asked her if she was pregnant!" She pointed to a woman clearly in her sixties.

"What's your name?" I asked her.

"Vivian Gingrich. Put down, 'subject to pregnancy.' "

The women at the table all shrieked.

Somebody opened the door leading out to a fire escape and the women went out and looked down at the fire engine and the police and agents who were milling in front of a gray community building where Jimmy Carter was to appear.

"Do you feel better that he came here?" I asked one of them.

"Doesn't matter to me who comes, who goes," she said. "I know I'm staying. I live here."

When Carter arrived, the crowd was behind ropes on the opposite side of the street. It was surprising to see this many people — there might have been a thousand — in one place in Middletown or anyplace else in the area. Most of Middletown must be gone by now and people who know say that almost a third of Harrisburg must be gone. And if the engineers at the Three Mile nuclear plant make a mistake this week, all of Middletown, Harrisburg, and Pennsylvania could be gone.

Carter made a statement that was suspicious because of its shortness. He did everything but officially announce that the area was going to be evacuated when the engineers finally take a deep breath and begin to fiddle with that bubble and the hydrogen involved with it inside the reactor.

When there is a call for an evacuation, Carter said, it will not indicate greater danger; it will merely mean that changes are being made in the reactor. They will give that bubble a little prick, and maybe ask the hydrogen to move over.

Carter did not remain for any questions about this, the most obvious one being the one that apparently he and anyone else involved cannot answer:

Do the people working on the reactor, who by now represent the total nuclear wisdom available to the nation, know how they are going to bring the reactor back to normal without losing a chunk of the northeast United States?

(April 1979)

Sweating in Line

CASTEL GANDOLFO, ITALY — At the head of the line, clusters of police began to fuss about the crowd, and then at themselves. There were policemen in blue shirts, known as the Polizia Municipale, and they smoked cigarettes and were very jealous of another group of policemen, who wore khaki and white belts and were called Carabinieri. There was a third group of policemen, dressed in white shirts and identified only as plain policemen, and they appeared furious over the presence of the other two groups of policemen.

The line of people to view the dead pope was five and six wide and it started far down a hill, in an alley under an arch, and the people sweated their way to the top, with nuns holding rosary beads and fathers clutching children. It was a crowd of cameras and T-shirts and blue jeans, the same kind of a crowd that you see at the White House on a summer day or, to keep it in religion, hopping around on the steps of the Sacré-Coeur in Paris. But now, at the head of the line, the crowd spread a bit and the Carabinieri decided that they wanted to compress the crowd. A half dozen of them walked up to the crowd and stuck out their hands and began to push people as if they were pianos. The crowd swayed and shuffled and grumbled.

Otherwise, it was a fine day for Castel Gandolfo. The police would not let the tourist buses use either of the two paths up the steep hill to the pope's residence. So, the many thousands either got on line in the alley under the arch and shuffled up to the policemen or they went the other way, walking up a steep cobblestone street that sat in wet heat at the bottom and was swept by a mountain wind at the top.

Walking up this street, the crowd had to pass shops that had been waiting for them for many weeks. This pope had been an inactive pope, an ill pope, and the big crowds of tourists had been missing from Castel Gandolfo. Yesterday, with the pope dead in his sand-colored castle, the tourists were everywhere and the townspeople were delighted. People pass, the institution goes on.

In a doorway, leather handbags were on racks. In the Bar dello Sport, old men drank beer and young men played a pinball machine. At the top of the hill, in the center of a wonderful square, children leaned into a large fountain and caught water in their mouths. The square was lined with stunted trees and souvenir shops and a bar that sold whisky and ice-cream cones. At one end of the square a street ran up a wall that overlooks Lake Albano, white-capped and a thousand feet down. At the opposite end of the square was the house where the pope lay dead.

In front of the Bar dello Sport, I spoke to a group of Italian college students, who were catching the sun. One of them, who gave his name as Marcello Giovanelli, said that he wouldn't criticize the pope. "My family takes bread from the Vatican," he said. "My father works for them." I walked to the opposite end of the square and talked to a priest from Newcastle, in England, the Reverend James Burke. He wore a straw hat and a rumpled black suit and drank a bottle of lemon soda. "I had the chance to be at this pope's last audience," the Reverend Burke said. "That was last Wednesday. He was doing quite poorly then. He told us he wanted men to seek the depth of truth. He smiled once at the beginning, but then he couldn't manage it anymore."

While standing on line, I read in the *Rome Daily American* that Pope Paul VI had heard his last Mass on Sunday. He was in bed. I could not prevent myself from recalling an uncle in my family, a New York City detective, who, for bodyguarding Giovanni Cardinal Pacelli (later Pope Pius XII) at the World's Fair, received a framed prayer of blessing signed personally by the pope. My uncle hung it in his room and on Sundays, when I'd be getting dressed for mandatory 9:00 A.M. Mass with my grammar school, my uncle would roll over in bed and point to the blessing on the wall and say that it meant that he didn't have to go to church for the rest of his life. Nor did he. I saw him inside a church only once, on the occasion of his burial.

Now, suddenly, the line started to move. The police stepped back and the moving line took you through an old high doorway and into a large cobblestone courtyard. All the windows of the great sand-coated house were shuttered. From the top floor, awnings were strung out, so that they put a roof on the courtyard, like a circus tent. A car bearing a cardinal rolled into the courtyard. It was a surprise to see one of them in the Rome area this soon. Yesterday, with the pope dead, there were only fifteen cardinals around. The rest of them were spread in private vacation castles throughout Europe.

The line in the courtyard moved. You walked along, speaking to a woman from Long Island, a Mrs. Eceiza, and at the top of the staircase the line halted and became silent while the wind outside howled and caused the shutters to rattle.

The line moved again and you took a step, another step, and looked up and had the nonchalance sucked out of you.

The room is known as the Sala dei Swizzera. It is a palace room, with a gleaming, intimidating marble floor and walls lined with art. At the far end, there was a great candle burning and in its light were four motionless Swiss Guards, wearing black peaked Renaissance helmets and carrying halberds, axlike weapons. And the pope of Rome lay on his back in his robes. Lay on a slanted board with his chin gray and his eyes closed and the high white hat, the miter, on his head. At his left side was the silver papal staff, the symbol of his role as a leader of 550 million Catholics. More than two thousand years of continuing authority lay on this board. Men grow in size and their theories change and their governments differ. They slay and they mediate, they oppress and they liberate, believe in God and don't, usurp and aid. None of it really matters to the Church of Rome. It goes on. A walk through this room yesterday, a walk that became solemn, told you of this.

This was, yesterday, merely the first display of the pomp of the Church of Rome. The week will move on, and the body will be moved to Saint Peter's and the crowds will grow into the hundreds of thousands. Against this power and history, even the questions of cynics will require enormous effort to ask.

(August 1978)

A Giggle at the Old Cardinals

ROME — In the evening at the Vatican, Mercedes cars carrying cardinals were waved through the gates at the start of the first meeting since their pope had died. They had much business, the Vatican said, but it actually was the first gathering of the executive board, the nominating board, of a political organization. Anybody in the Catholic Church over the rank of monsignor usually can be considered a professional politician.

Within a month, these cardinals, 115 aging males, will lock themselves in a narrow chapel, from time to time stare in prayer at Michelangelo's ceiling, and then return to the business of grabbing arms and counting votes and naming a pope. A male pope named by male cardinals. With even the attendants, hovering outside the locked doors, being male. Because the old men who run the Catholic Church, even with such graphic evidence of man's frailness in front of them yesterday, still regard themselves as so vastly superior to women that it is sinful to allow a woman to be ordained.

The cardinals are going about the naming of a new pope with an arrogance from the ages. There shall be no change in Rome to reflect what is surely one of the two significant movements of our time, that of women rising.

On the way home from the Vatican, passing through a shabby neighborhood, the car had to stop for a nun, who carried garbage from a doorway that was only a step back from the street and the rushing traffic. We stopped and walked back to her. She smiled pleasantly and leaned in the doorway of her residence, the convent of a grammar school, and nodded rapidly as the question of women was brought up.

"There will be no women as priests," she said.

"Do you think that is right?" she was asked.

"No. Some women are ready to become priests. Some are not. But you will see that there will be many deacons, men, doing the work priests once did. No women will become priests."

"Why?"

"That is a matter of women becoming equal to men," she said.

"When will that be?"

"In this church, I think never."

"Even with what is going on in the rest of the world?" she was asked.

"The rest of the world?" she said. "America is not the rest of the world. In the rest of the world, women are regarded as they are here. They are not equal to men."

She gave her name as Sister Felicita Suore. A question about her age or background was dismissed with a glare.

"What do you feel," she was asked, "is the church's reasoning for this?"

"I think they got this way because Jesus Christ was a man," she said. A slight smile softened her serious face. "I read today in the Communist Party newspaper that they will find it very difficult to find a new pope because none of them are qualified to be pope."

"Do they let you read the Communist newspaper?" she was asked.

"Certainly, we have complete freedom. What you learn when you read depends upon your maturity, how you decide whether what you read is true or not."

"Is the Communist Party newspaper correct in what it states?" she was asked.

She waved a hand to dismiss us and stepped back into her school, to Scuola Pontifica, a world where women are officially inferior. She giggled as she shut the door.

(August 1978)

The Cuban Baseball Fan

HAVANA — Campos's street-cleaning cart has crooked wheels and when both yellow drums are filled with trash the weight causes the wheels of the cart to wobble and threaten to fall off, and Campos finds he must stop and give his cart a rest.

One of the rest stops was under the portico of a building that is on one of the streets of Old Havana, a good place for Campos on this day because he was protected from the morning rain and at the same time nobody was about who would look at him and see that he was standing there, dry and in important conversation, while the cart was out in the street.

"Rogelio García is the greatest pitcher in Cuba," Campos said.

"What hand does he throw with?" Campos was asked.

Campos pumped his right arm up and down and pulled his body back and came forward like a baseball pitcher. "García!" he shouted. He wiggled his hand and his hips to show how Rogelio García can make a baseball curve. Campos's eyelids drooped and his mouth, which always shows amusement, became an oversized smile. When the interpreter and I laughed, Campos was even more delighted.

Campos is sixty now. His jowly face is a sun ray. The nose of a great nobleman presides over a thin mustache. Campos is proudest of his thick hair that is almost entirely black; he keeps his frayed cap tilted so that curls of his hair, only the very tips of which are gray, can be seen by the people on the streets he sweeps.

Campos earns about six dollars a day for seven hours of street sweeping. He works twenty-six days each month. Now, Campos stuck his head out from under the portico, squinted as he felt rain, pulled his head back in, lit a cigarette, folded his arms, and smoked the cigarette without taking it from his mouth.

"What did you do in the revolution?" Campos was asked.

He shook his head. "Working people are not political," he said. "I was not part of the politics and I did not fight in the mountains. I am a working person, I do my job every day, and then I go home to my house and have my dinner and at night I watch the baseball."

"You own a television?" he was asked.

"I saved for one whole year to buy a television so I could watch the baseball game," he said. "The television costs six hundred and fifty dollars."

When his cigarette was finished, Campos leaned out from under the portico, felt only a few drops of rain this time, and decided to push his cart through the streets again. He went up a narrow street that was covered with banners proclaiming the twentieth anniversary of the Cuban revolution. Campos halted his cart in front of a building that was cloaked with banners and posters of Lenin and Che Guevara. He faced the posters.

"Agustín Marqueti!" Campos called out. He swung an imaginary bat and waved his arm at a spot far over the posters of Che and Lenin. "Marqueti! Boom! He is the greatest hitter in Cuba. I have eight children and I try to raise one of my sons to be a baseball pitcher."

Campos pushed his cart around the corner, passed an office of the Committee for the Defense of the Revolution, and at the end of the block he was at the opposite end of the same portico he had just left. He stopped to give his cart another rest. He folded his arms and inspected the air.

The streets that Campos sweeps each day are narrow and many of them seem useless to sweep because they are lined with high piles of debris. Nor could the strongest, most dedicated sweeper accomplish anything: Havana has so many army vehicles driving around that it looks like an army base, but a sanitation truck stands out in traffic like an emerald. Campos, however, had an objective on this street by the portico. He went to his cart, took out the broom, swept leaves away from a drain, and then pushed the puddles into the drain. He took out a shovel that had a broken handle and scooped up leaves and some sticks, placed them in his garbage drums, and went on to the rest of his route.

An open-air bar was at the first corner. An old woman in a yellow housedress stood at the bar and drank rum with her husband. The woman's legs were streaked with bright blue veins and the husband wore muddy rubber boots. The bartender, who wore a shirt that was several sizes too big for him, had one foot up on a ledge and smoked a cigarette and stared at the street. I went automatically to the bar, but Campos stood in the street and held up two fingers to show that he works until 2:00 P.M. and would not drink on his job.

Campos pushed on. He swept the gutter in front of a small store, a minimart, that had a long line of people waiting to buy things. Inside, the store had a couple of rows of empty shelves and a shelf lined with a single row of cans of condensed milk. Another shelf had several jars of mayonnaise and about a dozen cans of creamed chicken. Under the front counter were two old boxes filled with thick black cigars. On the floor behind the counter was an open wooden barrel of lard that had flies circling it. Another open barrel contained flour. A sign on the wall proclaimed that there had been a revolution.

Out in the street, Campos now had a hemp bag tied to the handle of his cart. Somewhere over the day, if he found a breadline that was not too long — breadlines seemed to be everywhere and they never seemed to move — he would buy a loaf to bring home. We agreed to meet later. I went to the bar and he strolled on.

Making an appointment such as this is at least difficult in Havana this week. Reporters are awarded escorts, who appear to be special agents and station themselves between the people and the reporter. I won a special agent who was tall and amiable, but always present, so I lost him right after breakfast, hooked up with an interpreter, and went looking for a working citizen of Havana. We started in a Catholic church, where a couple of women stood through Mass — there were no pews — and a dog wandered among them. It was the only Mass of the day; most of the priests in Cuba had been from Spain and they departed when Castro took over, leaving Havana with little Catholic religious guidance, and the countryside probably with none. Outside after Mass, we found that the women preferred not to talk, but then a few blocks away we came upon Campos, an aristocrat of his island.

When he finished work at 2:00 P.M., Campos took his sweeper's cart to a yard and, bread sticking out of his hemp bag, left for home. He took two buses, the entire ride costing only five cents, but for the second bus, Campos had to stand on a muddy corner for over an hour. The interpreter did not travel by bus with us. All the way home, Campos kept fumbling with his hands and laughing in embarrassment because he could not speak English to his visitor. The fact that the visitor was unable to speak Spanish went unnoticed by Campos.

The ride was long and in a crowded bus, whose shock absorbers were useless. The street outside was crowded with people who stood for no particular reason except to watch the traffic. At almost each group of stores, most of them empty, there was an office for the Committee for the Defense of the Revolution. Each of these offices has a mimeograph machine for propaganda leaflets and for the use of people who oversee delivery of municipal services and medical care. The committee offices also keep names of every resident in the vicinity and are the central desk for all spying on and denouncing of the man next door. A backyard fence that can be dangerous.

Campos got off the bus at a muddy corner with no stores and walked down a mud street to a railroad crossing. He turned onto the tracks, which ran between tin-roofed huts. The rain had left long puddles around the shacks, many of which had tar-paper roofs, with oilcloth spread over the tar paper. Old auto tires and rocks were atop the oilcloth to keep it from blowing away.

Campos's hut was three steps away from the tracks. It was cinderblock with a tin roof. He removed his boots before entering. When his visitors tried to remove their shoes, too, Campos stopped them. He went inside and came out with a machete, which he used to scrape the mud from the visitors' shoes before leading them inside.

The low ceiling had damp spots from the heavy rains. The hut is one room that is partitioned into three tiny bedrooms. In the front room, there is a bed, a television set, and four wooden chairs, the bed decorated with two bride dolls. Campos explained that his son and daughter-in-law sleep here. They have been married only five years, he said. In the next room there are two beds for other sons. Campos and his wife sleep in the last partition, which looks into the kitchen.

His wife, Deisy Rojas, a plump woman with long black hair,

squealed with delight when she saw that her husband had brought guests home. She motioned to her daughter-in-law, who immediately sat at the small Formica kitchen table and spread rice on a cloth and began to pick impurities out of the rice. Campos sent one of his sons out to get beer and he was embarrassed when his son came back and said he could find no beer in the neighborhood.

Campos showed pictures of his family. "See, there are eight children," he said. "So I told you the truth when I said to you today at work that I have eight children. Do you see that if one tells the truth, one has nothing to worry about? If I had told you a different number of children you would have been here and found out that Campos lies. But I told you the truth. See? Here are the pictures of the eight children."

The married son asked if a medicine he had written down on a piece of paper could somehow be sent to him from America. He said that he and his wife are attempting to have children, and the doctor prescribed this medicine for her, but there is none of it in Cuba. It is common in Havana for people to ask for medicine; there is not enough coming from Russia and America does not permit medical supplies to be traded to Cuba.

The other son, the one Campos wanted to play baseball, walked in. He cannot play until he finds a job, because a sports license in Cuba is given only after clearance with the employment authorities, a rule that hampered the career of Campos's son, for he was more afraid of work than of drowning.

The women put a clean tablecloth on the kitchen table and served a dinner of bean soup, rice, tomatoes, and meat patties that were the equivalent of Spam. The cooking was done on a two-burner kerosene stove. The kitchen had one spigot for water. The hut has a toilet, but no bath or shower.

The guests were nervous about eating the meat because Cubans are allowed only three-quarters of a pound of meat every nine days, but Campos, who would not sit until his guests ate, would have been outraged if the meat was left untouched. He made a speech about this: "In spite of us being poor, we have love and an open heart," he said. "We share whatever we have with people."

Campos's delivery had a little Castro to it, the chin rising in self-satisfaction, and he was asked if he had seen Fidel's speech on television the other night. Castro spoke on the twentieth anniversary of the revolution.

"I was the one in this house who paid attention," Campos said.

He was asked if the other people who lived in his area had watched. He thought they had. "They are all hoping to hear that they will increase the rationing, but this they did not hear."

Castro's speech had been concerned mostly with America. "Cuba will not be bought by the Yankee dollar," he said. He also said, "American cannot buy Cuba." After he said each of these statements for the fifth or sixth time, Fidel's head turned momentarily to the wings, as if in prayer and hope that somebody like Paul Austen of the Coca-Cola Company suddenly would run onto the stage and buy Cuba. On the stage as Fidel spoke was the Cuban Communist Central Committee, which was all white or damn near, except for one token black, a man so old as to be harmless. Meanwhile, in the audience drawn from Communist and Third World countries, Russian generals and their wives, all with chests jutting out equally, shifted in horror as their neighbors, Africans as black as Baldwin pianos and wearing dashikis, rubbed shoulders with them.

In his speech, Castro said little about Cuban troops fighting in Africa. Now, in this hut in Havana, Campos was asked about it.

"I lost my nephew there," Campos said. "He was nineteen. He was killed in Ethiopia five months ago."

The wife, Deisy Rojas, said, "They told us that once the boy finished combat, he died in an accident. They always say that it is an accident."

"The last time I saw him," Campos said, "he came to this house with his record player and his girlfriend and they danced and then they said good-bye and he went to Africa. That is the last time I see my nephew."

"How did they tell the family that he was dead?"

"A committee came to my brother's house and said that the boy had died in Ethiopia."

The wife said, "He is dead five months and the mother has not received the corpse and she is very upset."

"There was a symbolic burial," Campos said. "Five or six soldiers had a small coffin and they were standing guard over it at the place where the regiment has its headquarters."

"The mother is still very upset," Deisy Rojas said. "She has not received the corpse. The mother says that when you see the body you can be more relaxed. When you do not see the body you always wonder and worry."

At seven-thirty, everybody left the kitchen and sat on the bed and chairs in the front room to watch a television show called "The Adventurers." It is Cuba's most popular show, a nightly half hour of people rushing about and firing blank guns from behind stage scenery. The show concludes each night, as it did on this one, with a fuse burning to the top of a drum of dynamite. Tomorrow, you will see if the fuse reaches the explosive. Campos adored the burning fuse.

His face went blank, however, and his eyelids lowered when the national news came on at eight. The news opened with a report on a Latin American congress of students which will be held in Havana in March. The next story was about a province which leads in building cooperatives. Footage of a crack sugarcane cutting brigade followed. Then there was a story about a commemorative service for policemen who died defending the Bay of Pigs.

Now there was a long report on the opening of a newspaper in the city of Sancti-Spíritus. The film showed printers at Linotype machines made in Russia. Following this there was much footage of printers' hands placing type in galleys.

"The workers you see are the most important to a newspaper," the voice over the film said. "The workers on the paper are more important than the writers. The writers for the new newspaper were chosen from the different political organizations of the province."

Now the sports announcer came on. "Ah," Campos said. His eyes opened and he sat up. But his face immediately became sad as he heard the announcer say that the baseball game had been rained out.

The evening over, Campos insisted on leading his guests out along the railroad tracks. There was nobody standing in the darkness in the mud. One hut had a light on, and the light beamed through several openings in the tin roof.

The interpreter, who had driven out, had his car waiting where a mud street crossed the railroad tracks. Campos shook hands. We left for the hotel. He went back to his hut to sleep so he could rise at 5:00 A.M. and walk through the mud to the bus to another day of his job sweeping the streets of Havana.

(*January 1979*)

They Always Shoot the Young

JERUSALEM — A panel in the large wooden door opened and the face of a young man appeared. "What it is you want?" he said.

"To come in," he was told.

"Nobody is allowed to wait inside," the young man said. "This is the rule of the hospital. Today is very bad. Everyone must wait outside. Don't you see that the other people are doing this?" The women sat on the steps of the hospital at Ramallah, a Palestinian town on the West Bank, and the men were up on a wall at the end of the building.

"Do you have a person named El Huj in there?" the young man was asked. El Huj was one of four university students shot by Israeli troops during a Palestinian demonstration the day before.

"Oh. That is a different matter." He opened the door and told us to wait while he went upstairs and brought down a young doctor.

"You cannot see him, but he is all right, I think."

"The bullet came in from the back and came out the front."

"He was shot in the back?" a woman said.

"The entrance of the wound is from the back," the doctor said again. "He is sixteen. That is what helped him."

A few blocks away, truck tires had been thrown in the middle of Ramallah's main street and set afire, to both block traffic and announce, by the black smoke rising over the street, that anyone who wished to cause trouble and throw stones at the soldiers should hurry to the place where the smoke was coming from.

The ones throwing the burning tires into the street were in their late teens and early twenties. They were followed by packs of small children. There is a general strike of Palestinian people on the West Bank to protest the peace talks. The military commander then closed all the schools. The streets and alleys of Ramallah were crowded with children all day. If you stood on a street corner for more than a few moments, you became surrounded by children and had to walk in half steps.

Wherever there are Arabs, the numbers stun. In Cairo, after walking the streets and alleys for a couple of days, I fell asleep at night with waves of people coming at me. There are so many people there that the official census figure has to be picked from the sky. And it is similar in these Arab places outside of Jerusalem. There is no pill, and abortion is a word used by university women. And in the alleys there are only small children bumping into your legs as you walk, so many children bumping that you still feel them hours later. The figure is 3 million Palestinians in the Middle East. I hope nobody has to feed the numbers over 3 million.

One of the older boys in the street in Ramallah crouched down and peered through the black smoke and saw an Israeli armored personnel carrier turn the corner. The older boy began to run and everybody followed him, spilling down alleys and across lots where goats grazed.

The armored personnel carrier rolled down the street without stopping. The Israeli soldiers held up atomatic weapons and watched fiercely for any sudden motions. After the vehicle went by, the smallest boys rushed out of the alleys and jeered the Israelis.

This was on the day that Jimmy Carter trudged to his diplomatic success in getting Egypt and Israel to agree that their future is not in bleeding. It is a treaty that mentions the Palestinians with words such as linkage and autonomy. But no Israeli leader ever will allow the Palestinians to have a country of their own on Israel's border. And the Palestinian millions appear to be led by Arafat, a terrorist, and he demands land for a country, that vague word in a treaty. So peace is something that Israel probably still must scratch out of the years to come. The great danger, Egypt, has been removed. But the Palestinians remain. Yesterday, the West Bank was heavily patrolled by Israelis, and in the north, artillery fired at Palestine Liberation Organization rocket bases in Lebanon.

"We are only beginning to gather strength," Ramondo Tawhil was saying in the living room of her house in a comfortable residential part of Ramallah. Ramondo is considered the voice of the PLO in the district. She has all the prerequisites of a revolutionary: a banker husband, a daughter in medical school, a son in engineering school, and rhetoric for any occasion.

"There were four boys shot yesterday, not three," she said. "Someday the bullet of the oppression will melt to water in the face of the resistance."

She patted the midsection of a figure that many say causes as much trouble among Arabs as oil. "I must diet," she said. "The best diet is to be in jail. I lost eleven kilos [about twenty-four pounds] in jail last year. I am under house arrest now. If I go out of the house, they claim I am inciting. They will put me in jail. It might be good for my diet. No, I have been last year in jail. Once is enough."

"Have you spoken to Arafat about the peace treaty?" she was asked.

"Why me? It is Carter who should speak to Arafat. Carter should look at Iran and then he would know he should speak to Arafat. Your Mr. Carter, the prophet, should go directly to Arafat. He speaks for all Palestinians."

Which was not thoroughly accurate. Sometimes, the Palestinians do not talk to themselves. Later in the day, in Bethlehem, which was a grim town, with soldiers standing on rooftops in the rain and truckloads of troops at roadblocks, the home of the former mayor of the city was pointed out as an illustration of the troubles among Palestinians.

The Palestinian Christians who live in the town of Bethlehem do not speak to the Palestinian Muslims who live in the refugee camp at Bethlehem. The former mayor, Bandak, a Christian, went beyond this; his animosity toward the Muslims was extraordinary and the Muslims were always eager to return it. Bandak then stole much money as mayor and bought land directly across the street from the entrance to the refugee camp. He built an expensive stone house and atop the house placed a high television tower. Running down the tower, in the kind of letters used to advertise cigarettes, is the name "Bandak." Across the street in the refugee camp, every time a Muslim raises his head he must see Bandak's name. Then, when he left office, Bandak had the city council name the street in front of the refugee camp "Bandak Street." Each time a Muslim leaves the refugee camp, he spits at the sign that says he lives on Bandak Street.

The Bethlehem refugee camp is an old one. The Israelis have provided electricity and water, and most of the men in the camp work at jobs in Israel at Israeli pay. So the conditions of the camp are better than usual and Israel receives credit for the manner in which it handles the camp. But Israel cannot take care of the millions of other Palestinians, and at the same time the Palestinians don't want Israel around them, even if Israel is making sure they have light and can eat.

An old man sat at a table in a hut in the camp where he sells note pads and candy bars. He said his name was Muhammad Abdullah, and when asked for his age, he wrote the number thirty-seven. The number sixty-two was jotted down and shown to him. He shook his head and printed out forty-two. When the figure eighty-four was printed in retaliation, Abdullah became angry and wrote down the number fifty-eight. Finally, after fifteen minutes of bargaining, he admitted to being seventy-one.

When he was asked about the peace treaty, he shook his head. "We are no peace treaty. We are Palestinians. We must wait and we will get our peace."

(March 1978)

Nobody Bothered to Brush Away the Flies

CAIRO — Two little girls in rags and bare feet stood on the dusty embankment and held a water buffalo by a frayed rope. One was seven and the other four and they did not know what they were supposed to see as the train went by them and, as there were only a couple of other people standing on the embankment, neither Jimmy Carter nor Anwar Sadat came out to wave.

When the last car was gone, the brother, Hosam Aly Badawy, seventeen, came for his sisters. The little girls tugged on the rope and led the water buffalo across the road to the place where they live, a compound of low stone huts with thatched roofs and ground covered with animal droppings.

"Welcome to our village," Hosam said. "Welcome to Jimmy Carter. This is the village of Cuffer Megahed."

The children dropped the rope holding the water buffalo and sat down in the mud and animal droppings in front of the doorway to their hut. They sat with their legs drawn up and showed bare bottoms under their long rags. Their bottoms were as dirty as their feet.

Hosam took us into the hut. It has no door and there was no electricity or water inside. The floor was dirt. Two roosters and a goat were in the center room. The water buffalo also stays in this room, the brother said. He pushed open a wooden door to a small windowless room where the seven members of his family sleep on mats on the dirt floor. Another wooden door led to another windowless room that had a rough wooden table that is used for eating, the brother said.

They cook in a small fireplace in the room where the animals stay. There is an opening in this room that looks out on a mound of debris behind the hut.

"Jimmy Carter for peace," the brother said.

Outside, a woman cloaked in black climbed up a hill from a depression, at the bottom of which was a creek of water that did not seem to move. The woman carried a basin of water into one of the dark huts.

"It is good that Jimmy Carter came," Hosam said. His sisters sat on the ground, hands not bothering to brush the flies, and stared with great dark eyes at their brother.

Down along the railroad tracks, in the imperial train that moved slowly over the land, Anwar Sadat sat in a blue pin-striped suit, tailored to the stitch, and smoked a pipe and told Jimmy Carter and reporters that this country they were passing through, this place where Cuffer Megahed sits, was a beautiful place and that once he had been stationed here. "It was my Georgia," Sadat said.

He thought that this would please Carter, to mention Georgia, but it was not the place that Jimmy Carter thought of when he looked out from his train yesterday. Carter was riding across the Delta of the Nile, but he really was in New Hampshire.

The car driving me was able to leave Cuffer Megahed, pass the train, and arrive in Alexandria long before Carter and Sadat arrived. And, as you came into Alexandria, the first thing you saw was a banner hanging across the street saying, in English, "We Trust Carter." On the next block was another banner in English saying, "Man of Honor for an Honorable Peace," and, again, a few buildings down, another banner, the theme of the day and perhaps the theme from now until the primaries of 1980: "We Trust Carter."

There were so many banners praising Carter in English draped around the rest of the city that it was obvious that they were there for American television. Once, when Jimmy Carter went after voters he went retail, door-to-door, firehouse to legion hall, coffee party to bowling league, in the state of New Hampshire.

He can do this no more. Now he must get at the voters wholesale. He must do it with the television of days such as yesterday, from a place that seems exotic to people in New Hampshire and Iowa, a place that makes great television footage. A place like Egypt. Jimmy Carter is here to thwart war and change the lives of people who live in Egypt and Israel, and therefore remove danger for the United States. But even as he attempts to do something that could be historic, he still is a politician, and a politician is at his best when he has two reasons for an action: one for the good of all and the second for the good of himself. And yesterday, Jimmy Carter worked to save lives in the Middle East, and also his own job. No matter how magnificent the undertaking, the most sacred of political laws applies: "Where's mine?"

Back in Washington, before boarding the plane to Cairo, I asked Tip O'Neill, the Speaker of the House, what the chances were for the peace agreement, and O'Neill said, "It's done, don't worry about it. He has got the thing put together as sure as you're talking to me." And then yesterday on the train going to Alexandria, Sadat told reporters that he was ready to sign an agreement right now. Immediately, Jimmy Carter said that, oh, it was much tougher than this, that he had no agreement and that he still had to work very hard to get one. Interpreted properly, his statement said, "Stop messing with my suspense."

As Carter's train approached the station in Alexandria, the politicians from Alexandria stood in the square outside the station in suits and sunglasses. One of them, the director of civil defense for Alexandria, Mogazi Eldib, was asked about a banner that said, "We Trust Carter — Alexandria Spinning and Weaving Co."

"How did that banner get put up?" Eldib was asked.

"The people everywhere love Jimmy Carter," he said.

"Did any Americans ask you to get some banners up?" he was asked.

"The mayor of the city said that the people were to be allowed to put up banners," he said.

"Who did all the sign painting?" he was asked.

"Many painters did the signs. Painters from all over."

"Did they get paid for the work?" he was asked.

"Oh, no, they are preparing the signs themselves. It is like a present to Jimmy Carter. All the people like Jimmy Carter."

He walked out toward the street and looked at the crowds. "A million people here today to see Jimmy Carter," he said. "Well over a million people are here."

He took off his glasses. "I was to America once," he said. "The company that manufactures ambulances and fire engines flew me to Dallas to inspect things that I could buy for our city."

"Did you like it?" he was asked.

He closed his eyes and his jowls melted into a big smile.

"It was beautiful," he said.

Then Mogazi Eldib put his glasses back on and said something to a plainclothes cop, who immediately ran to the sidewalk and pushed a crowd of people away from a building and to the curb, to pack it tighter. Mogazi knew his business: make the American look good.

The train pulled in and Carter came out of the station with a smile that was about to become a full laugh. He raised his hand to the crowds and they roared and waved and white birds were let out of a cage and into the sky. Two trucks packed with American television network cameras were directly in front of Carter as he went through the city. Each time Carter smiled at a banner and waved to the crowd, with the cameras trained on him, he was telling Jerry Brown to go door-to-door in New Hampshire: he, Carter, was doing it differently this time.

On the car ride back to Cairo, it was dusk as you went by Cuffer Megahed again. The people were driving cows back from the fields and into their stone huts and the air was thick with dust and there were many children now, maybe over a hundred of them, coming barefoot back from the fields where they had worked on the day Jimmy Carter passed by on his campaign trail.

(March 1979)

Abdel Aaty's Legs

CAIRO — It was a large tricycle and the chain ran up the front to the handlebars, which served as pedals. He sat on a large wooden seat, his legs dangling, and cranked the tricycle with his hands, and cars skimmed by him and blew their horns in anger that he would be in their way.

I had heard that tricycles of this type are given by the government to those who lost legs in the wars against Israel, and I stepped out into the traffic in front of the railroad station and waved to him. He nodded and his hands pumped the tricycle in front of cars that seemed to be trying to hit him on his way to the curb.

The tricycle was old, and the tires were bald. He had an old cushion on his seat. He looked at me with a right eye that was a full inch off. His teeth were the color of cracked wheat. His green sweater was ripped at the shoulder.

When he was asked if he had lost a leg in the war, he bent over and pulled up his right pant leg and showed that the leg was plastic. He pulled up the other pant leg and showed that this, too, was plastic.

"A mine?" he was asked.

"The shooting," he said. "October 6 [1973] is the date that the shooting was. The Sinai was the place where there was the shooting."

He said his name was Abdel Aaty, and that he was thirty-two now. Two policemen left their traffic posts and came over to listen to the conversation. Immediately a car stopped short alongside us.

"What is the matter?" the driver called through the window. He was a handsome dark-haired man, in a plaid sports jacket and white shirt.

"Nothing. We're just talking about how he lost his legs in the war," I told the driver.

The driver looked at Abdel Aaty in distaste. "He did not lose his legs in the war; he is nothing but a beggar," the driver said.

Abdel Aaty became angry. "I was in the Sinai," he said.

"You are a beggar," the driver said to Aaty. The driver said to me, "Have nothing to do with this man, he is a beggar."

Aaty pulled up both pant legs to show his false legs.

The driver shifted about in great effort and opened the car door. He pulled up his right pant leg to show that his leg was plastic. "This is a leg that was lost in the war," he said. "I will prove it to you." He went into the dashboard and brought out a picture of President Sadat shaking his hand when he was in an army hospital.

"I was a captain," he said. He gave his name as Atef Badawi.

Abdel Aaty reached inside his sweater and brought out a small green book. "Now I will show you," he said. He handed the book, a veteran's identification, to Badawi, who inspected it, checked the photo against Aaty's face, and then read the page that said Aaty had lost both legs in battle.

Badawi returned the book. "He is right," Badawi said to me. "You now must write that this man should be given a car that a handicapped person can drive. He must have something more than a bike." Badawi waved and drove away.

"Why didn't he believe you at first?" I asked Aaty.

"He thinks he is the most important person to lose a leg," he said. "Many people have no legs from the war."

Aaty was right. In the 1973 war, Egypt suffered 150,000 casualties and the armless and legless could be seen anywhere you went in Cairo yesterday.

"When did you realize the legs were gone?" I asked him.

"It takes one week until you understand what has happened," he said. "Then I knew that I had given something for Egypt. My legs were a present to Egypt."

"Can you work all right?" he was asked.

"Oh, I have four children. They are since the war. I am fine. The shooting went only to the legs."

"I meant a job."

"Oh. I am a telephone operator at a hospital," he said. "The job is on the first floor. I live in an apartment on the first floor. I am all right."

"What do you think of the peace meetings?" he was asked.

"They are silly," he said. "If the Palestinians do not get their lands back, what does it matter what Egypt and Israel sign? In six months, a year, there will be trouble because the Palestinians have not their land. That is why I went to the war. Israel takes the shirt from you and you must go to get it back from them."

"Don't you think your country should try living under a peace treaty?" he was asked.

"What does it matter?" he said. "All the lands must be given back. We must get the Sinai back and the Palestinians must get their land, too. Who is Israel to keep land? Your country's land is something you give your legs for."

Aaty was asked, "Is there any way you can get a car?"

"The government is not rich enough to give us cars. We are too many. They give us bikes. There is no way I can make enough money to buy a car myself. But I would like one so I could run it into the people who honk their horns at me."

He had started pumping the tricycle. Without looking, he veered for the center of the street and so many horns started to honk and so many cars barely missed him that I closed my eyes. The two traffic policemen who had been standing with us started to laugh.

Abdel Aaty hand-pedaled his tricycle onto a dirt road that went alongside railroad tracks. At an underpass, there were deep puddles of water and his hands pumped furiously to get the tricycle through the water. The cuffs of his pants were sopping. He now had to pump his way over many blocks on a dirt road. Several times the tricycle seemed about to tip over when it hit a hole.

The street was lined with tenements. Entire families sat in the dirt in front of the buildings.

Goats and chickens picked at the litter in the dirt alley. Women in shawls sat against the walls and offered for sale piles of tomatoes and string beans that had a light coating of flies. At number eleven, Abdel rolled his tricycle to the doorstep and called into the darkness. A plump woman in a scarf emerged. Abdel reached up and placed his hands against the sides of the entrance. In rhythm, from six years of practice, his wife took the tricycle from under him. Abdel stood on his plastic legs and gripped the sides of the doorway with his hands. The wife tugged the tricycle up the single step and into the dark hallway. Abdel placed a hand into the hallway, measured the distance, and then swung himself into the hallway and back onto his tricycle. A door opened in the rear of the dark hallway and two young boys in pajamas stood in it. They smiled as their father, Abdel Aaty, home for the day, hand-pedaled his tricycle up to the door. His sons stepped out of the way as he rolled it into the rooms where he lives with his family and without his legs.

(*March 1979*)

With One Piece of Shrapnel

JERUSALEM — Nobody knew more about it yesterday than Youval Hamzany, who was not in the government building when the ministers gathered at 10:00 A.M. to vote for a peace treaty while the world waited.

There were fifteen ministers present, and a half dozen coat holders, and they walked up the staircase in groups of two and three, if that many were speaking to each other, and went into a cabinet room that had a picture of Herzl and the flag of Israel as the only things on the wall. They closed the door and started to argue. And, meanwhile, Youval Hamzany, whose vote could weigh more than any of them, sat in his wheelchair in the sun outside the Beit Holochem, or Soldiers Center, over in Tel Aviv.

The Beit Holochem is a large modern building, where the Israeli war veterans who are blind or paralyzed or have arms or legs off come to exercise in the special privacy that the damaged prefer. Hamzany, accompanied by a therapist and a man named Rafy Horowitz, had just been helped out of his car and was about to be wheeled inside for a swim.

"The peace treaty should be made," he said. His jaws worked to make the words come out. "But you must be suspicious. If the Arab says there is not peace, then you hold on to your gun. If the Arab says there is peace, then you still hold on to your gun."

He spoke in both English and Hebrew, each haltingly, and he also seemed to have trouble seeing through his thick glasses.

"Can you see me?" he was asked.

"Not with this one," he said. A trembling hand came up and pointed to the right eye, which was glass.

"How did it happen?" he was asked.

"In 1970 I was at the Suez in, how you say it, a bunker. I looked through the periscope at the Egyptian soldiers and this made a light that they saw."

"The sun caused it to glitter," Rafy Horowitz said.

"Yes, that was the light. The sun. The Egyptians see me and bomb this bunker I was in and one shrapnel went into here." He slowly turned his head and a trembling hand clapped the back of his hair. He said something in Hebrew.

"He says the shrapnel went into his head between the bottom of the helmet and the top of his flak jacket," Rafy Horowitz said.

"Perhaps this can happen no more now," Hamzany said. "There should be peace and I should be the last." He laughed. "One piece of shrapnel, he is responsible for all of this." The hand indicated the wheelchair.

"He had more shrapnel in the rest of his body," Rafy Horowitz said.

"But this one, he is the most expensive," Hamzany said. "In the Hadassah Hospital, I could not move. One day the doctor came in and said to me, what was I going to do? I would never be able to move very much. I said I had taken some of the matriculation test for the university before I was in the army. I said now I wanted to take the rest of the test and get to be a lawyer. The doctor said that I should not do that because I was injured in my mind."

"The doctor tried to kill him a second time," Rafy Horowitz said.

"The doctor told me that being a lawyer was not a good idea for me," Hamzany said.

"What did you do?" he was asked.

"I do what I want," he said. "I could see the doctor was crazy. The doctor was saying to me that I am injured in the mind and that I cannot think the right way. I am in bed and I remember my history book of Napoleon. I forgot nothing. I could recite from Hayyim Bialik. He is our national poet. The doctor says my mind is hurt and I recite in bed, 'I used to journey at the heat of summer's day ... To the kingdom of magnificent tranquillity ... To the forest's dense thickets.' So I decide that my trouble is technical. I cannot walk and it is hard to talk. I can't see exactly. But I knew exactly what it was. My will was strong."

"You got to college?"

"I listened to tapes," he said. "I knew everything."

"And you did the law?"

"One more year and I am a lawyer," he said.

"He is a law clerk now," Rafy Horowitz said. "Nothing the matter with that memory of his."

"I remember the doctor's name, too," Hamzany said.

The therapist wheeled him inside the building, helped him change, and then rolled him out to the indoor pool. Hamzany slid off the chair and into the water and then held on to the side of the pool and listened as somebody said that the news on the radio reported that the debate was still going on at the cabinet meeting.

"You must be careful of Sadat's position," he said. "The whole world is against Israel. Now Sadat has become this close to us. Now the whole world could gang up on Sadat, too. And how do we know that Sadat does not die tomorrow? What then? We must think of many things."

A handsome, dark-haired guy swam over and joined the conversation. He gave his name as Avi Adri. He tapped a scar at the base of his throat. "The peace is the final part of my wound," he said. "The peace could mean nobody is getting hurt anymore. I hope this is true." When he swam away, his legs trailed behind him. A therapist said the bullet had gone through his throat and damaged his spine.

Hamzany began to swim. His body was long and once must have been powerful. He moved torturously, using only a weak left arm, and his body dipped under the surface between strokes. As he swam, a light-haired guy holding a black Seeing Eye dog walked to the side of the pool. A therapist took the dog and the light-haired guy stood until he heard Hamzany swim past him and then jumped in. The Seeing Eye dog barked at the splashing water. Then a man with only the nubs of legs was wheeled up to the pool. The man bumped his way off the chair and onto the side of the pool and then into the water. He did this confidently. Nobody gives uncomfortable stares at anything at Beit Holochem. After thirty years of war, mangled bodies are common in Israel. On a Saturday, 5600 people can be found at Beit Holochem. When Hamzany came back up the pool, he stopped again and talked. This time, the man with nubs for legs breaststroked over and entered the conversation.

"Shouldn't we keep the Sinai?" he asked. Hamzany said no.

"But if we keep the Sinai and Egypt attacks, Egypt will only be attacking the Sinai," the man said. "But if we give the Sinai back to Egypt and then Egypt attacks, it will be attacking Israel directly."

"No, this way there will be no war," Hamzany said. "But if we keep the Sinai, Egypt will have to make war to get it back. It is better to give it to them."

"We can beat Egypt, poof, anytime," the man said.

"We have done that already," Hamzany said slowly. "We have destroyed them and look at where we are."

Hamzany reached up and offered a wet hand as I started to leave.

"If I get in trouble in a year, will you defend me?" I asked him.

"Yes," he said.

"I have to go back to Jerusalem to find out about the vote," I said.

"I will save you the trouble," he said. "They will vote yes today. You will see that. I would vote yes and so will they."

They did. At 5:00 P.M. the door of the cabinet room opened and Menachem Begin walked out into the second-floor hallway, looked around, and saw Schlomo, the man who carries the mail around for him.

"Okay, that's that," Begin said to Schlomo. "It's all over. I'm going to call Carter."

(*March 1979*)

"How Much of the Guy Is Going To Be Left?"

OREM, UTAH — Beautiful. Nobody is going to leave here friends.

All day yesterday, Gary Gilmore and the warden, mean old Smith, were mad at each other because Gilmore wants to be standing, not sitting down like the warden wants him to, when the firing squad bangs away tomorrow morning at the Utah State Prison. Gilmore thinks that when he is sitting down it makes his pituitary gland come too close to his heart. This is bad because if somebody on the execution squad delivers a little high, a thirty-caliber bullet could smash the pituitary, which Gary has willed to a nephew. Ask any doctor, Gilmore yelled at the warden yesterday, if a pituitary is in pieces, like a cracked walnut, what good is it?

Late in the day, the warden still said that Gilmore has to be sitting down tomorrow. And with a hood covering his head. The warden admitted to Gilmore that the hood was not for him. The hood is for the firing squad. They don't like to look at the face of the person they are killing.

"I won't move," Gilmore promised the warden.

The warden does not take Gary's promises. But as nightfall came out of the mountains, Gilmore still was looking to manipulate the warden. And many people on the outside were hoping that he would be successful, that he would persuade them to let him stand up and be killed tomorrow, because the less mess there is with this execution, the best chance to salvage a few loose organs.

Gilmore is scheduled to be shot at 7:49 A.M. tomorrow. His body will immediately be rushed to a hospital, where doctors will strip it down for parts, much as body and fender workers pounce on a car.

The prison, however, is twenty-five miles from the hospital. With Monday-morning traffic, the trip could take an hour. Who knows how much of Gary Gilmore will be usable by the time they slop him onto a chopping block tomorrow and let the doctors go to work?

Authorities have discussed rushing the body out by helicopter. This now is considered impossible. Reporters covering the execution would hang onto the helicopter skids, in a scene reminiscent of the last days of Vietnam.

So there was much debate and writing yesterday about this Monday-morning rush to the hospital. All agreed that the eyes are all right. Somebody merely has to pluck the eyeballs right out of the head and then get into the eyeballs for the corneas. That's fine. You've got plenty of time with an eye. The same with the bones. There's plenty of good cancellate bone around the hips, good spongy bone that lasts a while, and someday you can toss it in, like parsley, during a spinal operation.

The kidney is the problem. The bullets make tracks through the body, and introduce so much contamination that nearly all the doctors say they do not want Gary Gilmore's kidneys. Unless, a surgeon said last night, he could get at Gary Gilmore and take out a kidney *before* the execution. This opinion was relayed to Gary Gilmore yesterday and he said he was going to spring it on the warden right after church this morning.

The heart, of course, is considered a major problem.

There were a number of requests yesterday for toes. They were coming from diabetics who have had their toes amputated. Toes, of course, do not transplant so well. What surprised doctors was the number of diabetics in Utah. The state is firmly controlled by the Church of Jesus Christ of Latter-Day Saints and all church members are bound not to touch whisky. Yet people still get diabetes and lose toes.

The skin, however, is a much more hopeful story. Doctors regard it as a chance to get a big roll of wrapping paper. "The minute he gets here, we'll strip him down just like a calf," a doctor said yesterday. "Skin grafts, burn centers, we can find all sorts of places to put his skin. The only problem is, how much of it is there going to be? With four men shooting him, I can't speculate on how much of Gilmore's skin they're going to blow away."

This question was taken to Gallenson's Sporting Goods store in Salt Lake City. Everybody says this is the store that supplies the prison with guns for executions. The only sporting goods in the store appear to be guns. There is one counter with a sign saying, "Toys for Kids." The toys on display are starter's pistols.

The owner, Marv Gallenson, was asked about the guns he sold to the prison. "Sold them?" Gallenson said. He puffed on a pipe. "Loaned them," he said finally.

"What kind of guns are they?" he was asked.

"Model sixty-four, Winchester thirty-thirty."

"That's a real good one, isn't it?" he was asked.

He puffed on his pipe. After a long wait, he took the pipe out of his mouth. "It gets the job done, 'specially at fifteen feet."

"How much of the guy is going to be left?"

A woman behind the counter, her name is Debbie, began to giggle. "He won't feel no pain."

A book titled *A Study of Executions in Utah* was produced. The book said that in executions by firing squad, "sometimes the blood runs out the back quite strongly, other times it does not. They bleed internally."

The feeling was that there will be enough of Gary Gilmore's skin left for doctors to use as cold cuts.

"But you'll just have to see," a man named Kelb Ibholm said. He was behind the counter. In his hand was one of his favorites, a Colt Combat Commander.

"They're coming out in stainless steel now," Kelb said. "You know what this one's for, don't you?"

When nobody answered, he said, "For Alabama porch monkeys. You know what they are?"

"No."

Everybody in the store laughed.

(January 1977)

Beyond Politics

Know that the day belongs to Pamela Mayo, whose husband, an air force sergeant, died in the desert in Iran last April. In the recording of the 444 days of the hostages in Iran, in tales of spies and clerks, of political fakery and national will, of honor and dishonor, the purity of her husband's act places him above all. He died trying to rescue other human beings.

On morning television yesterday, each mention of the hostages would cause one of Pam Mayo's kids to call out and the others in the family of four boys and a mother to run through the house to the set.

"The reason that it's so important to us is that maybe it won't be over for us until it's over for them," Pam Mayo, who is thirty-one, was saying. Her husband, Joel Mayo, who was known as Buck, was an in-flight engineer on C-130 transports. In Iran, age thirty-four, he died in the darkness when a helicopter crashed into a C-130.

She lives as a stranger in the town where she was born, Harrisville, Michigan. In the morning, as she heard discussions on television about the difficulties the hostages could have in becoming used to having families around them again, she thought of the day in 1966 when she met her husband. She was eighteen and in high school and a girlfriend brought him into her mother's kitchen in Harrisville. He was an airman, assigned to the base fire department at Wurtsmith Air Force Base at Oscoda, Michigan. He was Irish and Indian from Florida and she was Yugoslavian from the forest land of upper Michigan. They were married and began thirteen and a half years of living on air bases.

And she remembered the last time she saw him. It was a spring night at Fort Walton Beach, Florida, and he was leaving for temporary duty that he would not talk about. Many weeks before that, FBI agents suddenly started interviewing his family and friends because, they said, Buck was being given a "top secret" security clearance. Once that happened, his wife never asked him about his military work.

Usually, when Buck was going away, he spent the last hours teasing his wife or working on something around the house. Varnish a table, fix a bike, tighten a doorknob. This time, last April, Buck Mayo was listless and said nothing. It was the first time, his wife said to herself, that he ever had seemed reluctant to go anyplace with his squadron.

They had his favorite dinner, pork chops. During it, he said nothing. After dinner, she had the young kids in the tub and he came in and said good-bye to them. She walked him out to the carport, and he stood by their 1969 station wagon.

"No sense you coming," he said. "I'll drive over to the squadron and leave the car locked in the parking lot. Get somebody to drive you over in the morning and pick it up."

"Well, I don't want to haul the kids out of the bathtub," she said.

"That's what I mean," he said.

There was no reason to ask him where he was going. She was a military wife and she knew that she was supposed to say nothing. At the same time, it was plain that it was Iran. The only way to snatch the hostages was by air.

Buck kissed her good-bye. During the kiss, the notion ran through her that he would die. The kiss in front of the 1969 car became one of the horrible moments of her life.

And then he was gone, and she changed her life. Television news was not allowed in the house. The kids put on cartoons, or old horror movies, but she wanted no news reports as she walked about her house.

On April 25, she and her children slept through the night while the ones who determined her life sat by phones in the White House.

That there were hostages in the first place was President Carter's fault. He had allowed people with personal interests — John McCloy, Henry Kissinger, and David Rockefeller — to cause him to place his caution aside and allow the shah of Iran to enter a hospital in New York. Tehran erupted, and the hostages were taken. At first, in his reelection campaign, Carter found that the country's willingness to support a president in time of trouble was an asset in Democratic primaries. But then Carter lost five of seven primaries and caucuses and the issue of the hostages became an ominous one.

At the same time, it was intolerable that they were being held, and people of the nation, particularly those who were older, increasingly called for America to stand up to these screaming Iranians they watched each night on television. ·

"This country needs a win," one of Carter's people said one day. And now, on April 25, cynical politics and patriotism were mingled, and as the Mayo family slept in Florida, the father landed in the desert in Iran on the raid that was designed to get back hostages, bring America to its feet, as if for a great football touchdown, and insure a president's reelection.

When Pam Mayo woke up in the morning, one of the kids called from the bedroom, "They tried to rescue the hostages last night. It didn't work."

Now, Pam Mayo told herself, we'll see if you know how to keep yourself under control. She said nothing and got the kids off for school and then went to her job as lunchroom cashier at the grammar school. When she came in, the woman in charge, Brunelle, said, "Have you heard the news?"

"Yes," Pam said.

"Are you going to be all right?" Brunelle asked.

"As long as the other girls can forget trying to be television news announcers and talk about the weather," Pam said.

Brunelle laughed and went to her office. Pam sat in the cafeteria kitchen and had coffee. Her husband, she told herself, was dead.

A few minutes later, Brunelle came into the cafeteria. "Pam, could you come with me for a minute?" she said.

Pam put down the coffee and followed the woman into the office. Inside were a doctor, a priest, the base commander, and a sergeant and his wife.

"You didn't have to come," Pam Mayo told the doctor.

Then they told her what she had known from the moment Buck Mayo kissed her good-bye.

And today, the nation celebrates its hostages; it examines them and pampers them and exults, and President Carter leaves office with his engineer's determination intact; he had taken this problem and finally solved it. And Pam Mayo and her children, who gave the most, sit in front of a television set in Michigan and cheer.

"When I came back here, people didn't know how to take me," she was saying. "I was alone. I wasn't divorced or embittered by my husband. And they had seen me on television. This is a small town up here. It's just like a Southern town without an accent. I've been away for over thirteen years. Everything is taking a lot of time. Now it might be a little different. It's over for the hostages and now it's over for me. I can begin the rest of my life."

She never understood the politics of Iran. Last fall in Michigan, she forgot to register and did not vote in the November election. She doesn't want anybody tormenting her with the idea that her husband might have died because of a political campaign. All she knows is that he died as a hero of his country and today, the day that belongs to her, we celebrate his heroism.

(February 1981)

The Catholics Will Not Sit This One Out

The president and Haig the General somehow might be able to get their small war going in El Salvador, but it won't be a real good one. This is because American Catholics, who used to erupt with joy at the notion of drawing blood, are against it.

Oh, perhaps the Washington administration can have a war without the full support of Catholics, but there just won't be as many people killed as there could be with traditional Catholic participation.

The Catholics are against American military action in El Salvador, all right. The murder of an archbishop as he said Mass in the city of San Salvador, and then the murder and rape of two Maryknoll nuns, another nun, and a lay Catholic worker, took care of the Catholics' position on El Salvador. Also, Catholics have started to complicate their faith so much that many now accept an unpopular cause as a part of patriotism.

The amount of spontaneous communicating about El Salvador among Catholics in this country is equaled only by their most highly organized, official campaigns against such as abortion. And their position on El Salvador could produce quicker success than the anti-abortion campaign. The peace movement of the eighties, if one is needed, will come out of the Catholic parishes. You can't drop very much napalm on children with this kind of opposition at home.

The Catholic stand has nothing to do with Senator Edward Kennedy's legislation calling for the halt of all military aid to El Salvador until there is an investigation of the political killing. Nor is Catholic opposition directed by the organization of American Catholic bishops, whose policy calls for the end of military aid to the El Salvador government. The outcry this time is unorganized and powerful.

Once, there was Francis Cardinal Spellman of New York taking his annual Christmas trip to Korea or South Vietnam, where he did everything but bless the bombs. Today, Catholics around the country are in receipt of such letters as this, written by Peter L. Gerety, archbishop of Newark.

"The administration's macho strutting and shrill efforts to give answers to what is going on down in El Salvador are not responding to the right questions. The blood of martyred Sisters, clergymen and lay people, the blood of God's poor cried out to heaven like Abel's. How can we shut our ears to it?"

Or from Sister Patricia Hartigan, chairperson, social sciences, Our Lady of Mercy Academy, Syosset.

"Many of us are struggling to bring the world's attention to the plight of the poor in this Latin American country."

Or from Terrence Breshnahan, Berkeley, California.

"I have been writing letters to everyone in the government I could think of, protesting our policy in El Salvador."

And from the Maryknoll Order, two of whose nuns were murdered by right-wing extremists in El Salvador. The Reverend Thomas Marti of Maryknoll writes:

"It is evident that those of us who are deeply concerned with regard to social justice and human rights in El Salvador, as well as throughout the world, are working in an entirely different framework than President Reagan and his administration. For myself, I am frightened with regard to the prospects that lie ahead for the poor struggling with justice in the Third World, as well as for the poor in America. The age of martyrs is not something from past history."

Another Maryknoll member, the Reverend Darryl L. Hunt, writes:

"The real issue in El Salvador is genocide, oppression and exploitation. If anything, that is a north-south, First–Third World type of issue, not the east-west cold war confrontation being hyped into the picture."

Forget the Berrigans, who are identified with the sixties. Catholics still don't like anybody who was in the streets in the sixties. Last Friday, the Berrigans were convicted in Pennsylvania of smashing nuclear missile cones at an electronics plant, and there were few expressions of outrage or even sympathy from Catholics. But the same Catholics who were against the Berrigans oppose American involvement in El Salvador.

All of which reveals something about the president's ability to make judgments.

To Ronald Reagan's mind, reared on the simplicity and shallowness of 1940s movie scripts, El Salvador is different from Vietnam because it is closer to home. In our front yard, as he said at a press conference. He sees El Salvador only as a difference of intensity. Why, gosh, sure there can be no Vietnams in this administration because Vietnam is eleven thousand miles away and we won't travel that far to have a war. It is, however, permissible to try to win a war in El Salvador because it is so close. Reagan then attempts to proceed as if he had the same support once given to our war in Vietnam.

And this leaves Haig the General in one of his good suits. He can stand all day, turning adjectives into verbs for a country that has lost its sentence structure to television, but he is not going to be able to raise the old-fashioned Catholic liking for war even when imprudent. If this were thirty years ago, with McCarthy at home and Korea abroad, Haig the General would have a nice shot at a dictatorship. However, his Catholicism also seems to be about thirty years behind the times. He sees only God against Communism, and meanwhile his religion has been struggling so much with tyranny from within that it now is beginning to recognize it from without.

This change in the church started with the day Pope John XXIII walked out of the Vatican and went into a prison in Rome. He also encouraged such as Teilhard de Chardin, whose book *The Divine Milieu* crashed into traditional Catholicism, and the challenge to thought began.

Therefore, as the president and Haig the General attempt to advance simplicity as a proper motive for life or death, the Catholics they need for a good small war refuse to follow. Haig the General can write all his memos about the need to teach Moscow a lesson by maiming people in El Salvador, but they will not make it with a Catholic society that reads John Courtney Murray and of murdered nuns. Any minute now, we might even hear a prominent Catholic say that we are backing the wrong side in El Salvador.

(January 1981)

On Supporting Murderers

Last December 3, three American Catholic nuns and a social worker were assassinated on a highway in El Salvador. One of the nuns, Ita Ford, left a brother, William Ford, who is a lawyer in Manhattan. Since the murder of his sister, William Ford has shown some interest in the investigation, which has been proceeding in El Salvador with less efficiency than is usually displayed in killings. Ford points out that his sister Ita was running a refugee camp that was filled with people who were running away from government helicopters which kept firing on their villages. Ford says that Ita then was murdered by government people. He feels if an investigation of his sister's death shows that the government of El Salvador was involved, then United States military involvement in El Salvador would be indictable.

"I think an investigation would show that our government contributes to the support of a group that murdered my sister, and that if we continue to support this group we will then be helping them to murder other people. I don't think the business of this country is supporting murderers."

The investigation has been going on for 106 days now. Yesterday Ford said, "I keep asking the State Department to tell me what El Salvador is doing about my sister's death, and also what the United States is doing to supervise the matter. El Salvador is uninterested in finding out who did it because the murderers obviously would be from the government. And the United States is only interested in pressing more guns into the hands of these murderers."

While Ford has been demanding that somebody tell him who murdered his sister, Washington has been busy informing the public about El Salvador in traditional government style. First, Haig the General announced that arms for left-wing guerrillas were pouring into El Salvador from Nicaragua and Cuba, and this was clearly a testing of our national will by Russia.

When Haig tried to get American Catholics to support this view, several bishops refused. William Ford said yesterday that he understands that Haig placed great pressure on New York's Cardinal Cooke and was turned down. Catholic periodicals became filled with items such as these, which appeared in *The Founder,* published by a Jesuit retreat house on Staten Island named Manresa: "Almost 75 percent of the Salvadoran children under five suffer from malnutrition. In the last two years alone, the number of landless peasants has doubled. Over 90 percent of the Salvadoran people earn less than $100 a year."

With policy now producing complaints rather than backing, Washington suddenly announced that the immense flow of arms from Nicaragua and Cuba has stopped. Government people were not asked if they had invented the huge shipment in the first place. American advisers and arms still go to El Salvador, but with much less excitement about the chances for a good small war. However, the investigation into the murder of the four dead American women still is treated as an annoying exercise. After all, if the case were solved, perhaps the American public would support no part of even a subdued adventure in El Salvador, although Haig the General flared up again yesterday in favor of a small war.

William Ford had on his desk yesterday a paper titled, "Chronology of the Investigation into the Deaths of the American Churchwomen." It was on paper that bore no letterhead or signature. "It came from the State Department," Ford said. "They won't even put their name on it. They act like they're ashamed of it."

A glance at the entries showed the level of intensity placed into the investigation by both Washington and El Salvador from the start, when a new government coming into power in Washington had made it plain that it considered any opposition in El Salvador to be Communist:

Dec. 6: Rogers/Bowdler Mission arrives in El Salvador for four days of meetings with Government of El Salvador officials and others knowledgeable about the case.

Dec. 8: Salvadoran Government establishes a Special Commission to investigate the murders.

Dec. 9: The Federal Bureau of Investigation sends a senior agent to El Salvador to furnish technical assistance to the Investigative Commission.

Dec. 12: FBI technicians arrive in El Salvador. Rogers/Bowdler Mission reports to President that the Salvadoran Government has pledged to investigate the murders and notes that evidence suggesting that Salvadoran security forces were involved either in the murders or afterward is circumstantial.

Dec. 19: The Commission reports that it has been unable to find shell casings or cartridges at the crime scene, hence they lack any ballistic evidence.

Dec. 20–Jan. 5: Christmas vacation in El Salvador delays work of the Commission.

Jan 6: The FBI representative returns to El Salvador, taking with him the results of FBI lab work and the autopsies, along with request for more comparative materials, such as fingerprints from the nuns buried in El Salvador.

Jan. 21: The Minister of Defense and the Commander of the National Guard advise us that they want the investigation carried to its conclusion and the guilty parties found and punished.

Feb. 10: The Attorney General asks the First Criminal Court of Zacatecoluca to prepare a diagram, with photos, and seek clues at the site where the four dead were found on Dec. 3.

Yesterday Ford said, "My sister was traveling in a van. There were fingerprints all over the van. I asked if they got a list of National Guard people on duty that day. I'm told they had. I wanted to know why they didn't take prints off the van and match them with the prints of the National Guard people on duty that day. I'm told they didn't do it. I asked why. The authorities in El Salvador said, 'We didn't know which prints on the van belonged to the women.'

"When I call our State Department, I usually can't get anybody in and it is difficult to get them to return calls. They seem to regard this investigation as an inconvenience that distracts them from their grand scheme in El Salvador. They keep talking about supporting the middle between the right wing and the left wing in El Salvador.

What they call the middle is the government security forces that murdered my sister and thousands of others."

Today, Ford and Michael Donovan, brother of Jean Donovan, the social worker who was murdered, go to Washington, where they have an appointment with James Cheek, the assistant undersecretary of state in charge of Central American affairs. Ford was skeptical yesterday of what good the meeting would do.

Which is normal. A couple of weeks ago, Cheek was in New York, at the Bar Association building on Forty-fourth Street, telling an audience that the United States had to stop the Communists from going into El Salvador and imposing a government that the people don't want.

Questioned about our support for the present El Salvador government, Cheek said, "We never claimed that the present government in El Salvador had popular support."

The noise that followed this ended the meeting. It will be marvelous to hear what he says, on behalf of his government, to Ford and Donovan in Washington today. After all, they only want to know about their sisters who were murdered, and such a thing could get in the way of government will.

(*March 1981*)

McEvoy's Catch

The first sea engagement of the war occurred on the afternoon of April 18, when the British submarine HMS *Porpoise,* said to be en route to the Falkland Islands, ran into the fishing nets of Raymond McEvoy in deep, cold water off Howth, Ireland. There are many, many Breslins on McEvoy's mother's side, thus causing great pride here.

McEvoy, with crew of four, was bottom fishing for prawns in 100 meters of water. He had out 30 fathoms of net on 200 fathoms of wire and was moving along, fishing away, and then his trawler, the *Sharelga,* stopped dead in the water. It began going backward. The *Sharelga,* 70 feet, had a 425 horsepower engine, which could do nothing as the trawler began to pick up speed backward.

"We hadn't a clue what was happening to us," McEvoy recalled yesterday. Mickey Kelly, a crew member, thought at first that they had run into a great fish. McEvoy's uncle, Noel Kirwan, suggested that they were being attacked by a monster. But then when McEvoy estimated that they were going backward at nearly 10 knots, his considerable powers of reasoning told him that he had a submarine in his nets.

He thought of casting his gear away and freeing his trawler of the submarine. Then he declared he would not do this. "I've got thousands of pounds' worth of gear there. Am I supposed to let some Brit submarine make off with it? Who'll pay me?" McEvoy, with admirable stubbornness, decided that he would keep his fishing gear until the submarine sent up enough pound notes to cover the surface of the sea for thousands of yards.

The submarine did no such thing. Somewhere in the water under the trawler, the submarine ran on, uncaring about anything above it. In order to get rid of whatever it was that was dragging along, the submarine dove. First, McEvoy's trawler listed to port. Then it tilted more, and suddenly it capsized.

The water was chill; a traditional Irish suicide is to dive into the sea and expire from shock; but McEvoy's fear was so great he never felt the water. He plunged in, bobbed up, and threw himself upon the capsized trawler, which now was motionless, the Brit submarine having ripped the nets off it.

McEvoy looked about anxiously, for the others, in the tradition of winter sea fishermen, could not swim: why should one learn how to prolong agony? Each of the crewmen, however, got a hand on the boat and pulled himself up. Shortly, another trawler picked them up.

When McEvoy returned to his fishing village of Clogher Head, up the coast from Dublin, he immediately reported to barside, Sail Inn, Gene McKenna, Prop., that he just lost an engagement to a submarine.

"Are we sure it wasn't a monster?" his uncle Noel Kirwan said again.

"It was a submarine," McEvoy said.

Everybody in the bar listened and said nothing. Gene McKenna, back home in Ireland after many years behind the stick at Clancy's Bar, Thirty-eighth and Third, Manhattan, was disturbed by the silence.

"I believe you," he said to McEvoy.

"I do, too," another fisherman at the bar said. He held up his glass to Noel Kirwan. "Congratulations on nearly catching the Loch Ness Monster."

The next day, when McEvoy went into the nearby town of Drogheda to report the loss of his trawler, people on the street called out to him, "Mind yourself, there's a submarine coming up behind you."

McEvoy insisted to layperson and government official alike that he was stating the truth, but of course modern life is so distorted that even the words of a reputable man whose life has been spent in one village are held out as lies. People seemed much more comfortable with the denials of the British ambassador, Sir Leonard Figg, a man who is as comfortable with untruth as he is with afternoon tea, as befits a leading member of, and I say again today, the foulest race on the face of the earth.

"No vessel of Her Majesty's fleet was anywhere near the fishing trawler on the day described," Sir Figg announced.

"That was a submarine," Raymond McEvoy said.

Sir Figg smirked and went to his tea. Raymond McEvoy ground his teeth and headed for a pint. In the bar, Gene McKenna, Prop., expertly kept the criticism down.

"Five men could've drowned," McEvoy said. "We were afraid for our lives. I don't see where there's any joke about this."

And then on the surface of the Irish Sea there were found a number of disposable bags, used on British submarines. Confronted with this evidence, Sir Figg coughed and excused himself. He returned several days later to announce that indeed it had been a British sub that had pulled the trawler and caused it to capsize. He made a public apology to McEvoy and then said, "The British have accepted full liability for the incident and have undertaken to pay all fair and reasonable claims arising."

At the Sail Inn, village of Clogher Head, McEvoy looked up from his pint and announced that it didn't matter what the Brits promised, for his trawler actually was irreplaceable.

"Eight hundred thousand pounds couldn't get me another vessel like it," he said on the phone yesterday. "No, I'd say that in your money I would have to spend close to two million dollars before I would have a boat that would even make me remember what my old boat was like."

He then said he would remain on call until Sir Figg arrives with hard currency for his vessel, which cannot be replaced.

McEvoy sat at the Sail Inn yesterday knowing that he also had caused great political changes. Because of the first sea engagement of the war, between Raymond McEvoy's *Sharelga* and HMS *Porpoise,* the Republic of Ireland dropped its support of Britain in the Falkland Islands crisis. Irish Defense Minister Paddy Power has labeled the British "the aggressor in the Falklands."

(*May 1982*)

Why the Falklands Leave Harry Cold

Across the street, in an hour or so, the United Nations was to begin meeting on the matter of murder by governments in the Falkland Islands. And here in a hotel lobby on First Avenue, yesterday, as you listened to Harry Dunleavy talk, it became even more obvious that any comments on the Falkland Islands should come from a higher order than a Foreign Service bureaucrat — from, at least, a poet with the view of W. H. Auden, who once wrote: "But when they speak of Principles, look out: perhaps their generals are already poring over maps."

Yesterday, Harry Dunleavy was saying, "When I lived in the Falkland Islands — I was there from 1964 until 1967 and I know things haven't changed since because I've kept in touch with people there — there were two thousand and one people. Five hundred of them were Chileans, who worked on farms and were paid pittances. The English-speaking people were British subjects, but they're allowed to go to Britain only on vacation. They couldn't move to Britain and work and get a job. They were third generation on the Falkland Islands and the British immigration policy wouldn't allow them to enter Britain permanently. Anybody who moved went to New Zealand.

"People who stayed didn't have anything to do but play darts and go after one another's wives. Everybody was married two or three times. There were remarriages that lasted two months. A lot of the people were totally illiterate, I can tell you that. I was the radio operator. When I finished that job, I went to school and came up here to the South Bronx and taught. There was no difference. A farmer on East Falkland and a boy from Puerto Rico in school in the Bronx. The same. In the Falklands, there was one elementary school in Port Stanley and a one-room schoolhouse out in Darwin. The mail boat from Montevideo used to come once a month; so nobody in the Falklands had to bother reading anything, not even a postcard. Play darts and chase somebody's wife, that was the life."

He was asked how people made their living. "The government jobs, like mine, were held down by people from London. I lived in London and got the job in the Falklands through regular civil service. When I got to Port Stanley, the men were angry. The first man who spoke to me said, 'How did you get the job?' Mainly, they farmed; I think sixty percent of the land was owned by the Falkland Island Company. The shareholders were in London.

"What else was there? Three churches — Church of England, Presbyterian, and Roman Catholic. Four pubs — the Rose, Ship Hotel, Vicary, and the Globe. One other place, the Monstar, had to be closed because that was the place they picked to have all the fights. What were the fights about? Wives, what else?"

Dunleavy gestured at the UN building across the street. "Whatever they do, they ought to stop it today. I wouldn't want to be fighting down there in June. It drops to zero. The water system freezes. When I was there, we went as long as three weeks without any water from the taps. There was loads of snow. Port Stanley is built on a hill and all the streets are good for in June is sleigh riding. Luckily, there are a lot of good peat bogs in the area, so the people can make turf fires to keep warm.

"I can tell you one thing: I never met many people on the Falklands who were happy. The people living there are the last ones on earth who would want to die for the place. I don't see why anybody else would, either."

Now, across the street, the limousines were going through the gates of the UN. Standing in the sullen afternoon at the entrance of the Security Council Building was Noel Dorr of Ireland, who first requested the session. Dorr expected the afternoon to produce theater, the ritualization of the real conflict.

"Anything that develops must come out of private conferences," he said. "I said in a speech the other day that seventy-five percent of the points at issue have been agreed. What we have to do now is to preserve the agreement that is there or otherwise it will melt like snow. It would become dead leaves. While youngsters die."

"Do you understand what they're fighting over?" he was asked.

"One side sees this as the last vestiges of colonialism. It is burned into them in school. The other side says dictators can't be allowed to grab, or dictators will begin to grab all over the world. What do we do? I hope we can find out how to say 'stop' and still allow them to save their principles."

Which is the word with which older generals in Buenos Aires, and an older woman in London, cause young men to die in a place called the Falkland Islands, which, as Harry Dunleavy was saying yesterday afternoon, aren't good for much else than stealing another man's wife.

(May 1982)

Just Like Old Times: A New Maine Event?

Pictures of the carrier *Nimitz* boiling through the water off Libya and sending its F-14 Grumman Tomcat fighters into the air produced a slight uneasiness yesterday. Which was the result of reading about the Exocet missile, which was used shockingly well by these unseasoned Argentineans against the British in the Falklands. As described in a Jane's book of weaponry, the Exocet can be fired from a plane twenty-five miles away, well out of sight and sound, and the missile then races across the water at a height of only six to ten feet. Whatever it hits, from whaleboat to great carrier, goes away fast.

The Exocet is made by the French, who probably gave it the drugstore name in order to sell it around the world like aspirin. And it stands for all those spooky computer-directed things that are out there in the world now, in places like Libya, and make it risky to let some big old aircraft carrier sit out there like a fat man in a bathtub.

You look at the pictures on the *Nimitz* again, and of course the phrase "Remember the *Nimitz!*" immediately slips into the ear. Slips in easily.

As a slogan, it is about as good as "Remember the *Maine!*" That one came out of another time when the government wanted to give the folks a thrill by dispatching a big ship to keep somebody small in line. I believe the *Maine* was sent to Cuba.

In my past in my business, I sat one night in the sports department of the old Hearst paper, the *Journal-American,* checking the horse-race charts. On the other side of the space there was an old man from the wire room who one night showed me ancient copies, or maybe they were facsimiles, I couldn't tell, of telegrams that were sent to and from the Hearst paper in 1898.

One was from Frederic Remington, the Western artist, who was at the Hotel Inglaterra in Havana. His wire was addressed to William Randolph Hearst, Sr., and it read:

EVERYTHING IS QUIET. THERE IS NO TROUBLE HERE. THERE WILL BE NO WAR. I WISH TO RETURN.

And the wire sent back to him from the New York *Journal,* as it was known then, read:

THE CHIEF SAYS: PLEASE REMAIN. YOU FURNISH THE PICTURES AND I'LL FURNISH THE WAR.
SIGNED WILLICOMBE, SECRETARY TO MR. HEARST.

About a year earlier, Hearst had entered a newspaper circulation war in New York with a paper owned by the publisher Pulitzer. Hearst hired Pulitzer's editor, Arthur Brisbane, at a salary of a hundred and fifty dollars a week, but with a guarantee of a dollar extra per week for each circulation gain of a thousand papers. Brisbane, who loved money, went to work.

First, there was an all-color supplement that, the *Journal* announced, "will be of iridescent polychromous effulgence that makes the rainbow look like a lead pipe."

Did well for the *Journal,* but not enough. The Chief and Brisbane then got on the movement for Cuban independence from Spain. Hearst sent Remington and reporter Richard Harding Davis, who always gave his editors what they needed for the front page that day, to Havana. Remington saw no danger. But when he was told that if he saw nothing then he should use his imagination, the word reached the rest of the Hearst team. And other papers in the circulation war copied.

The *Journal* demanded a show of muscle. Send in the fleet. Soon, the whole country wanted the fleet sent in to give Spain a scare. President McKinley ordered the battleship *Maine* to steam into Havana Harbor. McKinley was a lot of things, but he was not an imbecile and he finally gave in. Who was he to be against that greatest of aids to an incumbent, a rousing small war?

For sailors on the *Maine,* the Havana Harbor was a magnificent sight, with the water rolling in from the open sea, slapping the bulkheads, and sending spray high into the air and onto the streets of what could be the world's prettiest waterfront.

And then on the night of February 15, 1898, there was an explosion in the forward section of the *Maine* and it touched off other explosions and the *Maine* went to the bottom of Havana Harbor and 260 died. Just like old times. The Spanish did it, everybody said. And the newspapers, and now the country, had the nice small war they all wanted.

At the newspaper in New York, circulation shot up, and Brisbane, the editor, soon was making a thousand dollars a week. Around the country, the unemployed were swept off the streets and into uniform, and the voters rallied behind the president. It was terrific for business. The only losers were those unfortunates who were killed or maimed.

It happened. Started right here in New York. You could look it up.

And then you could take another look at the pictures today of the *Nimitz* sailing in the water off Libya at a time when we have a lot of restlessness and unemployment here in America. A good small war would fix it all.

Beautiful. Some ninety-five years ago after a nation said, "Remember the *Maine!"* it seems as if we're risking the same thing. We have a president, Reagan, whose head is at least two inches thicker than McKinley's, and who likes living in Washington better perhaps than anybody we've ever had there.

"Remember the *Nimitz!"* is just as easy and could be just as popular to say.

The *Nimitz* couldn't have any more than a mere sixty-three hundred aboard.

(February 1983)

7

"The Smallest Slight
Can Make a Feud"

What a super idea! Send Bess Myerson to Jerusalem to cover Anwar Sadat's historic peace mission to Israel. She would be a big hit with the *News's* Jewish readers, an exclusive promotion that would zoom circulation.

Myerson was not just a famous name. She was a leader in the Jewish community, a champion of Jewish causes, a member of committees and speaker at dinners, a super fund-raiser for Israel. She was a close friend of Teddy Kolek, the mayor of Jerusalem, and personally knew all of Israel's leaders. She would have contacts no mere reporter would have; she could provide special insights that our regular staffers could not.

Bess hugged the proposal. She had been writing a consumer affairs column for us ever since she first left her job as Mayor Lindsay's consumer affairs commissioner. She knew the editors and was used to working for the paper. Most of all, it would be a dream fulfilled for a Jewish girl from the Bronx to be present at so momentous an event in the life of Israel.

In the exhilaration of the hour, we had a second inspiration, which was to dispatch Breslin on the same story. But brilliant ideas, like chemicals, can sometimes explode when mixed. Breslin, as it happened, hated Bess almost more than anyone else in the world and was furious at the prospect of having to share a big story with her. He had been sniping at her in his column on a fairly regular basis, almost always including her in his annual list of "People I'm Not Talking To," even attacking some of her business connections as conflicts of interest, and ridiculing the advice she gave *News* readers. "Question to Bess," he once wrote. " 'What do I do about my insurance rates?' Answer by Bess, 'Ask your insurance agent.' "

We complained that it didn't help the paper a bit to have one colleague attacking another, in Bess's case undermining a valuable feature for which we were paying good money. We were already

contending with a number of other feuds — our star sports columnists Dick Young and Mike Lupica were also throwing grenades at
each other, for example — so we worried that readers might get the
impression the paper was a squabbling shambles. Breslin instantly
got the point and, ever the team player, offered a solution: fire
Myerson. He said we were stupid to sign her on in the first place and
if she were no longer working for the paper he could attack her
without embarrassing us.

We rejected his advice, only dropping her column later, when she
decided to run for the Senate, so at the time of the Sadat story in
November 1977, Breslin found himself thrown into Bess's arms, so
to speak, which most men would welcome but he did not. He was
forced to fly out of the city on the same plane, had to struggle to
avoid her for six hours during a layover at the Rome airport, and
then spent four days in Jerusalem refusing to cooperate or even
speak to her and using costly phone calls to denounce his editors in
New York. On top of everything else, our man in Israel was so busy
coping with his feuding visitors he didn't have enough time for his
own reporting. The copy got through somehow and, as hoped, provided a special New York perspective on the rituals of peace. But it
was a newsroom nightmare behind the scenes and, predictably,
Breslin returned to New York full of evil intent, determined to attack his fellow columnist as frequently as possible.

His conduct, of course, was based on his guiding principle that
revenge is a human necessity which, in Myerson's case, had to do
with *Slow Dancing in the Big City,* a movie scripted by her daughter
Barra Grant. In it Paul Sorvino played a dull slob of a newspaper
reporter who was supposed to be Breslin. The movie fell criminally
short of Breslin's image of himself, which resembles Pat O'Brien in
Front Page more than anyone else. He was also upset because "if I
get paid for working in the *Daily News,* then why don't I get paid for
working in the film?" He had, in fact, acted in another unmemor-
able movie, *If Ever I See You Again,* and believed he was so loaded
with talent he could easily play himself. All things considered,
therefore, he felt the need for vengeance and, because his lawyers
said he couldn't sue, he attacked Bess in his columns, without the
slightest concern for the discomfiture of his editors.

Breslin agrees with Hammurabi in the matter of an eye for an eye,
arguing that if you turn one cheek someone will take a shot at the
other one "as sure as you're here" so that the best policy is to assume

"no slight, no difference is so small that it cannot be converted into a feud." From the evidence of his columns, it would appear that Breslin has suffered a simply astronomical number of slights. His enemies list is a cast of thousands and ranges from governors and senators and mayors, police commissioners and judges, to writers on the *Village Voice* and former longtime friends like Governor Carey.

So stern is Breslin's rule about revenge that he even has turned against some of his own favorite characters, exemplary citizens like Fat Thomas, the bookie, who loyally supplied Breslin with hot tips on the horses and inspired scores of great columns. But when Thomas slipped one day and privately dropped a slur on top of his Boswell, he committed a feudal felony requiring punishment. Breslin admitted it was "the equivalent of a breakup inside the Warsaw Pact," but said the friendship had to go. Regretfully, he added Thomas to his "Not Talking To" list.

Like a medieval knight or Sicilian don, Breslin generally takes these matters seriously. To him, a feud is not just a health-giving cathartic for aroused emotions; it is the weapon of choice for righting wrongs and defending honors. But he also knows that feuds sell newspapers, in the same way they sell Shakespeare's plays. Can anyone imagine Romeo and Juliet without the Capulets and Montagues? So trace amounts of commercial motive have been found in some of Breslin's feuds, as for example in his ego clash with Garry Trudeau.

Trudeau, creator of the satiric comic strip "Doonesbury," started the proceedings in 1977 with a week-long sequence in which he charcoal-grilled Breslin for his flamboyant coverage of the famous Son of Sam murder case. In one episode, someone telephones the *Daily News* requesting coverage of a murder he is about to commit and is immediately referred to Breslin. Our hero was insulted by the criticism, and pretended to be doubly so when we later overlooked the offense and signed Trudeau to cover the 1980 political conventions for us.

Beginning with the Republican meetings in Detroit, Trudeau wrote daily pieces and accompanied them with spot cartoons. These gave Breslin the target he had been looking for. He waited until the Democrats arrived in New York, when he knew the entire national press corps would see and savor his columns. Then he opened fire, attacking Trudeau for using "Yale Quadrangle Bow Wow wow quips, nice and snotty" to show cleverness and impress the media but mystify ordinary readers. If Trudeau could sell lousy writing, he said, he could sell lousy cartoons, and promptly produced a terrible sample with the caption: "Officer, when did you first observe the woman was naked?" "When I saw she had no clothes on."

Breslin made it sound as if he were really steamed, which was good for circulation and got the paper a lot of attention at the convention. We worried briefly that Trudeau might quit covering for us but he was more interested in hitting back, which he did to the delight of all concerned, charging, among other things, that Breslin should at least have had the guts to admit he was just seeking revenge for the "Doonesbury" attack on his Son of Sam coverage.

Another Breslin feud, however, did absolutely nothing for our circulation and even less for our high blood pressure. This involved Clay Felker, the founder of *New York* magazine. Breslin was one of the magazine's original cast of star writers, getting a piece of the action in return, but he later broke with Felker, quit the magazine, and became Felker's blood enemy forevermore. So almost as soon as he began writing a column for the *News,* he started firing shots at his former editor.

This complicated our relations with *New York* magazine, which had been favorably disposed toward the *News,* but Felker understood Breslin's complaints and didn't hold us responsible. The problem was strictly small bore until 1980, when O'Neill had an idea which some people said was crazy but he thought was brilliant. This was to make Felker the editor of a new afternoon newspaper which the *News* had decided to launch. The theory was that Felker, who by this time had been forced out of his *New York* magazine, would do something no editor already at the newspaper could do: he would send a message that the newspaper, *New York Today,* would be completely different from the morning *Daily News,* which would remain targeted on its middle-class readers. It would be sophisticated like *New York* magazine, upscale, aimed at the same affluent readers who bought the *Times* and *Wall Street Journal* in the morning.

Just dandy! Except that Breslin had an apoplectic fit. Bringing Felker into the city room, into *his* city room, where he would see him, maybe even bump into him on the way to the coffee wagon, was an appalling development. He fumed to O'Neill and Brink. He became almost apoplectic in complaining to his city desk pals Richard Oliver and Sam Roberts. He figured the editors had lost their minds. He feared out loud for the future of the newspaper. He rumbled ominously in print. Some other staffers, believing the new project was a mistake and culturally at odds with the new editors and writers assembled under Felker, cheered Breslin on. And O'Neill and Brink found themselves spending almost as much time keeping peace inside the newsroom as they did combating outside competition.

When the afternoon edition was finally abandoned by the *News* management in 1981, for reasons having nothing to do with Felker, all the critics considered themselves vindicated. Breslin bubbled with self-congratulation when Felker departed and the city room returned again to its old chaotic but familiar condition, full of raucous tabloid noises, purged of chic talk and upscale ambition. He continued to include Felker in his "Not Talking To" list, but with the afternoon edition gone, he acted less in anger than in ritual unforgiveness.

On this one issue of never forgiving, Breslin and his victims are in complete accord. There is no record that anyone Breslin has attacked has ever given him absolution. And to walk through the corridors of power in New York is to walk through endless ranks of Breslin enemies. He may be popular with the punters in the bars along Queens Boulevard, but he is not popular with the high and mighty.

All of which starts a smile rolling slowly across Breslin's face. "Beautiful," he says.

— M.J.O.

Stander, as in Stand-Up

When they were after him, when he was young and he had everything to lose, Lionel Stander did exactly what everybody knew he would do. He curled his lip in disdain and he brought his voice up from its bed of gravel and let the sound fill the hearing room of the House Un-American Activities Committee. He was ordered to stop shouting, but he acted as if he never heard anybody. Lionel Stander was there to make a fight.

He is sixty-nine now. He is a great movie character actor who is known by too few. This is because twenty-five years of his career were stolen from him when a collection of stool pigeons said he was a Communist and a menace to the nation. Politicians wanted Stander to cower and inform. Instead, he gave them chaos. It was a display of citizenship which is on his record forever.

Lionel was in New York this week to celebrate his good part in United Artists' tremendous hit *New York, New York.* And you could sit and talk with him about anything: he comes off the newspaper rewrite desks and out of the artist's lofts of New York. But with Lionel Stander, everything always comes down to this day in 1953 when he came before the House Un-American Activities Committee at Foley Square in Manhattan.

He had been in Philadelphia the night before, appearing in the stage musical *Pal Joey.* In Stander's jacket in the dressing room was the subpoena saying he had to appear at Foley Square in Manhattan at 9:00 A.M. the next day. After the curtain, Lionel got dressed and drove to New York. He arrived in the white lights of midtown at 2:00 A.M.

"This is terrific," he said. "What a marvelous way to begin an evening."

He went into a joint and had a drink and met a girl named Ruthie. "You're sensational," he told her. "Let's go around to a few places."

In another place there was a girl named Rita. Lionel looked at her and said: "You're fantastic."

With Ruthie and Rita clinging to his arms, Lionel began to use up the night. The three of them closed the Stork Club. Then Lionel took the girls uptown to an after-hours place. And then Lionel and Ruthie and Rita all got lost together and they had a terrific time. In the morning, while they all got dressed in a small but wonderful hotel room, Lionel had to tell the girls to behave because he had to go downtown to testify in the big probe of Communists.

"Oh, are you a Communist?" Ruthie asked him.

"I've got no time for Communists," Stander said. "They're political morons and all they do is compromise. I want a real revolution."

"Oh, I'm glad you're not some crummy Communist," Rita said to him.

At nine o'clock on May 6, 1953, Lionel Stander stormed into the courtroom at Foley Square, striding down the middle aisle with Ruthie and Rita hanging on to him. He then took the witness chair.

A congressman named Clardy said that there had been earlier testimony about Stander's wife being a Communist. "We will not ask you any questions about your wife," Clardy said.

"Which one?" Lionel said. In the audience, Ruthie and Rita began to giggle.

Clardy, annoyed, said that the name of the wife was Lucy. "Do you remember her under that name?" the congressman asked.

"Yeah," Stander said. "I remember her. Vaguely."

Ruthie and Rita really liked that answer. They let out a howl. This made Lionel feel very good. Immediately he began to abuse the House Un-American Activities Committee. First Lionel made them turn off the television lights. Then Lionel began to talk. A river's tide has less stamina.

"I know a lot about subversion in the entertainment world," he began. "I know a group of fanatics that are trying to deprive individuals of their civil rights, livelihood, without due process of law. I was one of their first victims. They're former Bundists and America-Fighters and anti-Semites."

The chairman was banging his gavel. "No witness can insult this committee," he told Stander.

"Why, you just asked me to tell you about subversive activities," Lionel said. "I'm shocked. I'm not a dupe or a dope ..."

On he went, roaring and rambling in the witness stand. The committee could not handle him. Stander then went on to further shock all decent people. As the *News* observed, "And then, before anybody knew it, he hauled in the First Amendment again."

At the end, the committee, embarrassed, asked him to go away. They would fail to call many witnesses through fear of finding more Standers. The committee liked witnesses who broke into tears and named other people. Lionel walked out of the courtroom with Ruthie and Rita. The three went out for cocktails and lunch. He had been blacklisted from films in the late forties. Now, it would be twenty-five years before Lionel Stander would be allowed to work at his trade in this country. But all Lionel cared about on this day was that he stood up.

Now, the other night, over vodka, Stander was remembering some of this. His left eyelid droops a little. The once curly hair is becoming sparse on top. His face is paunchy. But the energy pours from him when he talks. "I'm not bitter about anything that happened to me," he said. "I just despised a whole lot of sons of bitches.

You know the worst of them all, don't you? The guys who always disappear when the chips are down are the effin' liberals. I like only radicals and conservatives.

"I was completely blacklisted and you couldn't get a person to say a word for me. America was so delicately balanced at the time that my face or figure on television or in a movie would tilt America to complete anarchy. So Preston Sturges finally used me. He was no liberal. He was an aristocrat. He liked a monarchy. But he was the first one to use me after all those years. Twenty-five years. Not one of the effin' liberals. The liberals. Dalton Trumbo is full of ——. Lillian Hellman's book is a rip-off at eight ninety-five. Liberals. When there is a real revolution I'm going to be first commissar and there'll be no liberals."

He got up to answer the door. He has, if you'll watch him in a movie, one of these great walking styles you find only in the most accomplished of actors. I first saw this stride up close on a day in 1970. There was a movie being made of a book called *The Gang That Couldn't Shoot Straight* and the director had asked me to stop into Johnny Joyce's restaurant on Second Avenue to meet a new actor they were putting in the picture, Robert De Niro. From Joyce's we went up to a rehearsal studio, where De Niro read lines with Lionel Stander, who had just come in from Rome. Stander worked with De Niro for a couple of hours. Then Lionel excused himself and I remember him walking down the hall toward a telephone, walking with this great, menacing stride. He was going to call his agent in Rome to tell him that De Niro, whoever he was, was going to be the greatest actor in the history of the business and the agent better grab him.

Now, at the door of his hotel suite, somebody handed him pipe tobacco. Stander took it and walked back to his seat. His wife, Stephanie, a blonde who appears to be a half century younger than Lionel, came into the room with Lionel's four-year-old daughter.

"That's my family planning," Stander said. "I have children from four to forty-three. Of course it took six wives to do it."

His wide mouth turned into a leer. "Say, if you write anything," he said softly, "don't say anything about that girl Rita. I think she got married."

(June 1977)

The Man in a $20 Hotel Room

He came into Manhattan by bus from Hackensack, which is the place in New Jersey where he lives and knows nobody, and nobody knows him, except the landlord and this little ten-year-old girl up the street who jumps up and down when she sees him and says, "You're a writer, somebody told me you're a writer."

He took a room at the Mansfield Hotel on West Forty-fourth Street. The room costs twenty dollars a day. The bathroom is down the hall and there is no television in the room, for which he is happy. He used to stay at the Iroquois Hotel across the street, but late one night, when he wanted to take a bath, he found that the tub had no stopper. He went down to the Iroquois lobby and complained. "Tell it to City Hall," a clerk said. He went upstairs and took a glass ashtray and put it upside down over the drain and then ran his bath. He got up in the morning and moved across the street to the Mansfield. Who knows how long ago it happened? The important thing is that he bad-mouths the Iroquois today, and he will bad-mouth the Iroquois until the day he dies or the hotel collapses.

His name is Nelson Algren and he wrote books called *The Man With the Golden Arm* and *The Neon Wilderness* and *A Walk on the Wild Side*. He is a poet who deals in realism. *The Man With the Golden Arm* in 1949 was the first book ever to mention the presence of heroin in the poor neighborhoods and moved Carl Sandburg to say that Algren's characters "can linger in your mind with a strange midnight dignity."

When you say today that Nelson Algren is a great American writer, there are not enough people, particularly young people, who have heard of the name. This is something that should not be. His books are in paperback and there can be no reason why they should not be read, for the rewards are so great. After the tenth car chase on television, after the eighty-fifth shooting, here is what awaits you if you pick up *The Man With the Golden Arm* and read how Nelson Algren started the first page of his book:

> The captain never drank. Yet, toward nightfall in that smoke-colored season between Indian summer and December's first true snow, he would sometimes feel half drunken. He would hang his coat neatly over the back of the chair in the leaden station house

twilight, say he was beat from lack of sleep and lay his head across his arms upon the query-room desk.

Yet it wasn't work that wearied him so and his sleep was harassed by more than smoke-colored rain. The city had filled him with the guilt of others; he was numbed by his charge sheet's accusations. For twenty years, upon the same scarred desk, he had been recording larceny and arson, sodomy and simony, boosting, hijacking and shootings in sudden affray; blackmail and terrorism, incest and pauperism, embezzlement and horse theft, tampering and procuring, abduction and quackery, adultery and mackery. Till the finger of guilt, pointing so sternly for so long across the query-room blotter, had grown bored with it all at last and turned, capriciously, to touch the fibers of the dark gray muscle behind the captain's light gray eyes. So that though by daylight he remained the pursuer, there had come nights, this windless first week of December, when he had dreamed he was being pursued.

"You owe us another one," Algren was told when he was found on Forty-fourth Street, yesterday morning.

"I don't owe anything," Algren said. It was 8:00 A.M. and he was walking across the street to a coffee shop. His blue eyes, set in an old social worker's face, were amused. He was dressed in a rumpled blue jacket and wine shirt, worn the night before and open at the neck to reveal the top of his T-shirt.

The table in the coffee shop had not been cleared yet, and Algren was pleased to see that the change still was alongside a plate.

"We made fifty cents already," he said.

"When was the last time you were in Chicago?" he was asked. Algren always was Chicago. You could imagine him nowhere else.

"A year ago," he said. "Got in a brawl there. I won it. Sonofabitch there ran into an accident. I was the accident. He was standing over by the wall with a green beer bottle and I had this glass of brandy. Now, I can't throw. But just as he was starting to throw the beer bottle, I threw the brandy glass. His beer bottle went wide. My brandy glass hit him right over the eye and he went down.

"Now, you don't knock a man down with an empty brandy glass. I think, I just wonder, did I throw it so fast that the ice and brandy were still in the glass when it hit him? I threw so fast that it didn't have a chance to spill out? I just wonder."

"How long have you been around here?" he was asked.

"I came at the end of 1974 to Paterson. I had trouble with the landlady. She was the only Puerto Rican woman with a pacemaker in the United States. It made her batty. The pacemaker really was in her head. I wanted to get a phone put in. The only place the company guys could put the wires was the basement. Landlady wouldn't let them in. The guys from the phone company were black and the Puerto Rican landlady was afraid of blacks. She was as afraid of them as the whites are, and the whites are terrified. I said to the guys from the phone company, "Fellas, you see what it is here." They laughed. They said, 'Oh, yeah, we know.'

"Then the landlady heard I was in Paterson to write a book about Rubin Carter. She came in and said, 'You move.' I said, 'I've got a lease.' She said, 'You got no lease.' That's how I got to Hackensack."

Algren left Chicago in 1974, when a magazine paid him $1250 to write about Rubin Carter, who was in the midst of winning a new murder trial. The fee was a big one for Algren. He should be a wealthy man. Fifty years from now, he will be studied in schools as perhaps one-two-three in his time, and a student will wonder how this man lived with all his riches.

But Algren's books came when Hollywood stole more casually than now, and when writers' agents were not much of a contest for publishers. The magazine article grew into a nonfiction book about Carter, who lost and went back to prison. Carter's name now produces fatigue to anybody seeing it in print.

"So why don't you sit down and start a fiction book, use Carter as a basis, use anybody. Why don't you start an Algren novel?" I asked him yesterday.

He shifted in his seat. He has been bothered with this before.

"People say to me, 'When are you going to give us the big one?' I say, 'When you start reading the little ones.' "

I said to him, repeating something several publishing people had told me the night before, "If you sit down and write one chapter of a novel, an Algren novel, and send it in, your agent could grab you so much money to finish it, nothing would matter anymore. There's millions around for a writer like you."

He shrugged. "I never chase a book," he said. "If it ain't there, it ain't there."

"What do you do with yourself?" he was asked.

"I'm up early, six, seven. Read a paper. Look at the race results. Then I don't know what I do. Always something in the type-writer. A book review for Chicago, probably. I look at it and wonder if it ever gets done. At noon I go to the Hackensack YMCA Executive Health Club. I exercise with all the other executives. I come back to bed at one and I start reading. Once a month, I go over to the racetrack."

"What do you read?" he was asked.

"I reread Dickens. You never can do that enough. Some of the other stuff. I had to review a book that has in it exactly what Fitzgerald was wearing and who was in the bar and what they had on the day Fitzgerald said to Hemingway, 'The rich are different than us.' And Hemingway said, 'Yes, they have more money.' Now what all that means some fifty years later is something I don't know. What it meant the day they said it is something I don't know, either.

"I read Gabriel García Marquéz. *Solitude* is a great book. Nothing around today to compare to it. He's in a different sense of time than anybody else. And *Autumn of the Patriarch* reads like one sentence. He can shift from first to third person and you don't even notice it."

"What about you giving us a novel?" I asked him.

He got up to leave. He was going back to his twenty-dollar hotel room until noon, when he'd walk down the street to pick up his friend Studs Terkel, in from Chicago for the opening of his Broadway musical, *Working*. Nelson Algren was going to take Studs over to Gleason's Gym, where Freddy Brown, the fight trainer, was going to show Algren a fighter he thought Nelson would like.

Nobody else saw Algren yesterday. Nobody was looking for him. In all of New York, only Freddy Brown seemed to understand that Nelson Algren is one of the great ones.

(May 1978)

Rooting for Skylab

Somewhere up there, 150 miles into the sky, the Skylab space station tripped over a shaft of hot air and began its fall. Scientists in Houston switched switches and even had the porter change all the fuses. Skylab kept falling. When the scientists launched Skylab on May 14, 1973, they were certain that it would not fall down for 1000 years; that theory now is about 945 years short of being correct.

So Skylab dives into our atmosphere sometime this week, becoming a couple of hundred pieces of fried metal, temperatures in the vicinity of two thousand degrees. One of the pieces is expected to be the terrific lead-lined safe that holds all the film taken by the Skylab space station. The three-thousand-pound safe is as big as a new Kelvinator, and it is my favorite part of Skylab.

Because the safe is used to hold film, I consider it part of the communications industry, which is purportedly my trade, and therefore if I am going to be hit by the Skylab space station when it rains down, sizzling like Canadian bacon, I want to be hit by the safe holding the film.

Oh, I should be hit all right, don't worry about that: I'm no good and I can prove it. And at the same time, I have a method of being hit by the Skylab space station that is going to do more for the populace than simply to have a hot old safe come whistling on top of Breslin alone.

When that fiery film safe comes down this week, I am going to be standing in the middle of the exciting dance floor at Studio 54. Skylab safe bombs Studio 54. Breslin, a memory. Studio 54, large faggots swirling in the breeze. Greatest public service ever!

Yet I can accomplish even more. I can throw a party at Studio 54, the kind of party you read about in all the papers so much, and when my Skylab space station film safe comes bursting down, I'll have my whole party right out with me on the terrific dance floor and this will do the entire country a favor.

For here are the people who most surely should be invited to my terrific Skylab space station party at Studio 54.

BIANCA JAGGER — I always ask what it is that she *does*, and of course nobody I ask knows, but this merely shows the truncated life I lead. Bianca Jagger is one of the world's foremost empty people, a pane of glass that pretends to frolic. It would be unjust to have Studio 54 disappear and not take Bianca with it.

MARGARET TRUDEAU — I don't think we ever have seen anybody cling to a last name with such tenacity. Oh, I think I shall be a great photographer, Margaret Trudeau announces one day. Oh, I think I shall be a great movie actress, Margaret Trudeau announces the next day. Oh, I think I shall save Nicaragua, Margaret Trudeau announces on the third day. And mostly she is at Studio 54, with the intellect of a cup of water, stalking a cameraman. The husband Trudeau is home with the kids.

TRUMAN CAPOTE — I watched him on a daytime television show one day recently, and he was vicious about nothing and was cruel to shadows and in love with the whole thing. I kept looking for a great second like Freddy Brown or Ray Arcel to climb through the ropes, a towel around the neck, wet sponge in one hand, cotton-tipped sticks behind the ears, and take Truman back to the corner. Once he was a person of great ability. Now he is a little guy prancing around Studio 54 and using his energies to do battle with Lee Radziwill. The handicapping says that there is no way for Truman to change, and at the same time it is intolerable for him to end up like this. So we'd best send a limousine for him so he can be at my party for the Skylab space station safe.

BESS MYERSON — Smile, phone call, push. She once had a job as consumer affairs commissioner for Mayor Lindsay and she worked at this job exclusively, as long as television cameras were around.

She is still known as a consumer advocate. She writes a column about it. (Question to Bess: "What do I do about my insurance rates?" Answer by Bess: "Ask your insurance agent.")

And in the business and political world, middle-aged men dissolve when she smiles, phones, pushes. Now the middle-aged men are getting together to run her for the United States Senate. Bess herself goes around saying that she is running. And the men with money cheer. That smile is a winner! Here comes our Bess. She stands for nothing except the placing of her name on a payroll. Rather than have all the money people run an empty smile for an office important to people without money, I think it is best that we ask Bess to the Skylab party at Studio 54.

JANN WENNER — The publisher of *Rolling Stone,* a tabloid solely for the rock music business. It sells only 450,000 copies and exists on big pictures of sacks of bones clinging to guitars and wearing tight silk pants. Wenner had the instinct to enter a void: publishing people thought rock music was merely loud noise. *Rolling Stone* became a tremendous financial success, as is rock music. Great Wenner win! However, Wenner then decided that he was a literary genius, and he told the world of this. The gossip columns and magazines began to say it was so. (See Clay Felker, who also was lucky enough to step into a void at *New York* magazine.) All the while, Wenner's newspaper was as important as a loudspeaker and he became a little swaggerer who thought a truly good editorial idea was to pay a writer in the dark. Wenner has the editorial ability found in a pair of shoes. Whenever he has left the mothering arms of the rock business, he has arrived home on a shutter. Recently, he took over *Look* magazine amidst claims that he would change the magazine and all of publishing with his genius. Wenner then put out an issue that caused paramedics to rush to the *Look* offices. (Again, see Felker and his move to *Esquire,* where he was able to display all that he knows, which is close to nothing.)

Yet all the gossip columnists and magazines and press section writers still refer, automatically, to Wenner as a genius. Rather than spend my valuable time educating these people . . . I only have a couple of days left around here . . . why don't I simply invite Wenner to the Skylab space station party and take another phony out of the picture with me?

THE WHOLE *VILLAGE VOICE* — Once, the *Voice* had Norman Mailer writing about J. Edgar Hoover. Now the paper consists of impenetrable sentences about the agonies of a gay in Elyria, Ohio, who is so proud that he is gay that he doesn't do another blessed thing in the whole world except be gay. Because of places like the *Village Voice,* a regular person doesn't dare order cheese in a restaurant in Manhattan. The gays have taken over cheese just as they take over bars and entire city blocks. There are so many gays typing out nonsense about eating cheese with their lovers that I now am afraid when I ask a waiter in Manhattan for a slice of Brie he's going to kiss me. Therefore, let me get the whole *Voice* into Studio 54, where they all belong, and many people in the city will forget how bad I was and they will erect statues to me. People also will be able to have Camembert again.

BILLY MARTIN — The manager of the New York baseball team. He has too much to say, and most always about nothing.

STEVE RUBELL — For the same reason. He runs Studio 54 and he believes he is so important, and tells this to so many people, that I am going to be certain that he is not at the door of his joint when I have my party. He is going to be right where he can do the most good for everybody, standing between Bianca and Margaret, and right behind me, when the Skylab space station comes steaming through the roof and does the whole world a favor.

(July 1979)

"Are You John Lennon?"

Writer's note for this book: I was home in bed in Forest Hills, Queens, at 11:20 P.M. when the phone and television at once said Lennon was shot. I was dressed and into Manhattan, to Roosevelt Hospital, the Dakota, up to the precinct, grabbed a cop inside, back to the Dakota, grabbed a cop outside, and to the Daily News. *I wrote this column and it made a 1:30 A.M. deadline. I don't think there is anybody else who can do this kind of work this quickly.*

I particularly like the mistake in it. Moran from Williams Avenue in the Bronx. It is Willis Avenue.

As I can't use a terminal — the keys don't make the noise I need and require too light a touch for me to make them work — a desk clerk put my typewritten copy into the terminal. He made the Williams Avenue error. I sure as hell know Willis Avenue, having had a drink in every bar there when it was Irish and having centered a whole novel on the street now that it is Puerto Rican. The mistake and the reasons for it are testimony to the speed with which it was done.

That summer in Breezy Point, when he was eighteen and out of Madison High in Brooklyn, there was the Beatles on the radio at the beach through the hot days and on the jukebox through the nights in the Sugar Bowl and Kennedys. He was young and he let his hair grow and there were girls and it was the important part of life.

Last year, Tony Palma even went to see *Beatlemania.*

And now, last night, a thirty-four-year-old man, he sat in a patrol car at Eighty-second Street and Columbus Avenue and the call came over the radio: "Man shot, One West Seventy-second Street."

Palma and his partner, Herb Frauenberger, rushed through the Manhattan streets to an address they knew as one of the most famous living places in the country, the Dakota apartments.

Another patrol car was there ahead of them, and as Palma got out he saw the officers had a man up against the building and were handcuffing him.

"Where's the guy shot?" Palma said.

"In the back," one of the cops said.

Palma went through the gates into the Dakota courtyard and up into the office, where a guy in a red shirt and jeans was on his face on the floor. Palma rolled the guy over. Blood was coming out of the mouth and covering the face. The chest was wet with blood.

Palma took the arms and Frauenberger took the legs. They carried the guy out to the street. Somebody told them to put the body in another patrol car.

Jim Moran's patrol car was waiting. Moran is from the South Bronx, from Williams Avenue, and he was brought up on Tony Bennett records in the jukeboxes. When he became a cop in 1964, he was put on patrol guarding the Beatles at their hotel. Girls screamed and pushed and Moran laughed. Once, it was all fun.

Now responding to the call, "Man shot, One West Seventy-second," Jim Moran, a forty-five-year-old policeman, pulled up in front of the Dakota and Tony Palma and Herb Frauenberger put this guy with blood all over him in the backseat.

As Moran started driving away, he heard people in the street shouting, "That's John Lennon!"

Moran was driving with Bill Gamble. As they went through the streets to Roosevelt Hospital, Moran looked in the backseat and said, "Are you John Lennon?" The guy in the back nodded and groaned.

Back on Seventy-second Street, somebody told Palma, "Take the woman." And a shaking woman, another victim's wife, crumpled into the backseat as Palma started for Roosevelt Hospital. She said nothing to the two cops and they said nothing to her. Homicide is not a talking matter.

Jim Moran, with John Lennon in the backseat, was on the radio as he drove to the hospital. "Have paramedics meet us at the emergency entrance," he called. When he pulled up to the hospital, they were waiting for him with a cart. As Lennon was being wheeled through the doors into the emergency room, the doctors were on him.

"John Lennon," somebody said.

"Yes, it is," Moran said.

Now Tony Palma pulled up to the emergency entrance. He let the woman out and she ran to the doors. Somebody called to Palma, "That's Yoko Ono."

"Yeah?" Palma said.

"They just took John Lennon in," the guy said.

Palma walked into the emergency room. Moran was there already. The doctors had John Lennon on a table in a trauma room, working on the chest, inserting tubes.

Tony Palma said to himself, I don't think so. Moran shook his head. He thought about his two kids, who know every one of the Beatles' big tunes. And Jim Moran and Tony Palma, older now, cops in a world with no fun, stood in the emergency room as John Lennon, whose music they knew, whose music was known everywhere on earth, became another person who died after being shot with a gun on the streets of New York.

(December 1980)

Growing Up with Sandra

The appointment of Sandra Day O'Connor to the United States Supreme Court speaks eloquently for the position that there are emotional and value changes going on in this country that we have been neither mature enough nor fair enough to allow in the past.

The first time most of us ever heard of these changes was in the sixties, years now generally thought of as having been so contaminated by sin and weakness that the nation nearly disintegrated.

It was in the sixties, during Vietnam, that it was decided that the country no longer could shoot its way into every triumph. And it was in the sixties that most of us began to learn about the cause of women as people.

Today, Sandra Day O'Connor's appointment shows just how many bogs women have traversed. Now, a United States senator who votes against her appointment is a man seeking to have a musical comedy written about him. However, research into the past shows how much we had to grow as a people to reach this point.

For a long time now, Karen Berger Morello, a lawyer with the Victims Services Agency, has been researching a book about women in the field of law. She started her work when she learned that Charlotte E. Ray, the first black woman to practice law in America, had died in frustration around the corner from Morello's home in the Woodside section of Queens.

In gathering material, Morello found this decision by the United States Supreme Court, which is reprinted here today to illustrate a nation's rise from cave thinking.

The Supreme Court decision was in December 1872 in the case of Mrs. Myra Bradwell, who had been denied the right to practice law in Illinois because "as a married woman she would be bound neither by her expressed contracts nor by those contracts which it is the policy of the law to create between attorney and client." Myra Bradwell took the case to the Supreme Court in Washington, and this was the decision, written by one Justice Miller, that the court handed down as the law of America:

> "We agree that there are privileges and immunities belonging to citizens ... and that it is these and these alone which a state is forbidden to abridge. But the right to admission to practice in the courts of a state is not one of them.
>
> It certainly cannot be affirmed as an historical fact that this has ever been established as one of the fundamental privileges and immunities of the sex. On the contrary, the civil law, as well as Nature herself, has always recognized a wide difference in the respective fears and destinies of man and woman. Man is, or should be, woman's protector and defender. The natural and proper timidity and delicacies which belong to the female sex evidently unfit it for many of the occupations of civil life. The constitution of the family organization, which is founded in the divine ordinance, as well as in the nature of things, indicates the domestic sphere as that which properly belongs to the domain and functions of womanhood. The harmony, not to say identity of interest and views which belong, or should belong, to the family institution is repugnant to the idea of a woman adopting a distinct and independent career from that of her husband ... It became a maxim of that system of jurisprudence that a woman had no legal existence separate from her husband, who was regarded as her head and representative in the social state; and, notwithstanding some recent modifications of this civil status, many of the special rules of law flowing from and dependent upon this cardinal principle still exist ... One of these is that a married woman is incapable without her husband's consent of making contracts which shall be binding on her or him ...
>
> It is true that many women are unmarried and not affected by any of the duties, complications, and incapacities arising out of the married state but these are exceptions to the general rule. The paramount destiny and mission of women are to fulfill the noble and benign offices of wife and mother. This is the law of the Creator. And the rules of civil society must be adopted to the general constitution of things ...
>
> The humane movements of modern society which have for their object the multiplication of avenues for women's advancement, and of occupations adapted to her condition and sex, have my heartiest

concurrence. But I am not prepared to say that it is one of her fundamental rights and privileges to be admitted into every office and position, including those which require highly special qualifications and demand special responsibilities . . . In view of the peculiar characteristics, destiny, and mission of women, it is within the province of the Legislature to ordain what offices, positions and callings shall be filled and discharged by men and shall receive the benefit of those energies and responsibilities and that decision and firmness which are presumed to predominate in the sterner sex.

After the Bradwell decision, apparently the Creator decided to change the brand of female. Before Bradwell, women had proper timidity. Now there are Sandra Day O'Connors, who run political campaigns and elbow through the Arizona legislature, and become the first woman to be appointed to the Supreme Court.

(July 1981)

The Irish Servant Girl

Chicago is the only city in the world where anyone would even consider the possibility that a cardinal is a crook.

It also is the only city in the world where a cardinal would have a lawyer with as much contempt for people as does the one representing John Patrick Cardinal Cody. The cardinal's lawyer announced, "He's answerable to Rome and to God, but not to the *Sun-Times*." The last being the newspaper that printed stories charging the cardinal with maneuvering $1 million of church funds to a friend, Helen Dolan Wilson.

In presenting a most arrogant defense, the cardinal of Chicago and those about him have taken a local controversy and turned it into a matter far more important than some grubby dispute over money, and one that now is too weighty to be solely in the hands of people in Chicago.

First, the cardinal chose to take the charges into the streets, wearing his red hat and announcing that an attack on him was an attack against his church. In doing this, he failed to take into consideration those who feel that the Catholic Church is somewhat larger than that.

Then Helen Dolan Wilson sat down for a newspaper interview while fingering "a delicate, silver rosary."

The question of money becomes of no concern when matched against the larger issue of Helen Dolan Wilson's presence: the role of women in the Catholic Church.

For long years, she apparently lived the routine of an Irish servant girl, which is the one the church likes best for the women who make up the bulk of its membership. In 1940, the cardinal took out a $100,000 insurance policy and gave it to the woman, who then borrowed sums of money on it and made investments. For more than forty years, Cody kept the matter hidden, and now somebody must search out the policy and find the insurable interest that was attested to in order to allow the woman to own a policy on a man who soon was to become a bishop.

As this goes on, Helen Wilson becomes only a symbol. Perhaps the entire church might begin to inspect itself and locate the suppressed knowledge that has caused so much inner turmoil and has ruined so many good lives over the centuries.

There is no reason for the Catholic Church to continue the policy of sexual disorder that it now pursues. There is no basis anywhere in its body of faith for priests to be celibate and women to be excluded from ordination as priests.

It is a church that insists it has faith in the hereafter and an intellect now, yet its official policy is to resent and deny the female. And it is a church that gazes steadily at a bare wall, rather than move the head a fraction and notice that too many of its members are reduced to carrying out a secret relationship with women, thus turning people with supposedly noble purposes into participants in some cheap backstairs drama.

Nowhere did the Lord ever suggest celibacy or any policy of indignity toward women. Denial of women by the church started with the Roman people and was over land; only those with family lineage could own property. As abbeys controlled great landscapes, the idea was to keep the head monk without children, for then if he died, the property would revert to the religious order and not to the monk's eldest son.

Out of this cold business grew a church with an official policy against women and also one with at least some members carrying on secret relationships with women. The aging males in Rome who control the church do so with a negative use of tradition. Why not married priests? Why not women as priests? "We never did it before, therefore we cannot."

Its leaders always saw sex as a threat. So women were the official danger; they could be held out as something holy — the Madonna complex — but never treated as people, for then all would be ruined.

And now today, the Cody story unfolds at a unique point. Surely the time dies on a policy of preserving an ignorant past as if it were the word of God. In places such as southern France, the Catholic Church is down to one priest for every four parishes, and quickly the choice must be made: either there are priests who are married men or priests who happen to be women, or great numbers of Catholics will have the chance to attend Mass and receive Communion only once a month at best. In the United States, Catholics will face the same situation within five years at most.

The answer must be to end the fear, to get everybody off the back staircases, and for the Catholic Church, for the first time in centuries, to admit that women too are people.

It was Brendan Behan, rolling down Dublin's Grafton Street, who was so much ahead of everybody. "Ah, Sister," he bellowed at a nun, "may all your children be bishops." The man meant no blasphemy; he was simply a delightful human being telling a woman he was rooting for her.

(September 1981)

Trickling Down

In preparing for Vicki's inauguration, I visited Harry Winston's jewelry shop on Fifth Avenue yesterday to ask if he would care to loan a couple of small items for Vicki to wear at the gala. Winston's is famous for doing things like this: it loaned Nancy Reagan a necklace and earrings worth more than $100,000 for the presidential inaugural a year and a half ago, and Nancy, treating it all as if it were a borrowed book, never gave the jewelry back. Vicki, who is to be inaugurated as "Bushwick Mother of the Year," would certainly return the jewels, as I will prove conclusively as we go along here.

Vicki herself noted yesterday, "When people borrow something in Bushwick, they either give it back or they move."

"What kind of diamonds do you want for your party?" I asked Vicki. It is going to be held at El Coqui on Knickerbocker Avenue.

"I'd rather get food stamps," she said.

"You can't. The Reagans are mad at food stamps. They don't mind free diamonds."

"Do the best you can," she said. "But I'd still rather have food stamps for a week than a ring for a night."

I arrived at Winston's in the morning and found the front door locked. Inside the small foyer, a man stirred from a chair and opened the door. His face was pleasant but also appeared to be the result of a few thousand nights in precinct squad rooms.

"I want to borrow some jewels from Harry Winston," I said.

The man made a face. Behind him, a woman at a small desk picked up a phone. I then was shown into a small office that had a table covered with black pool-table cloth. On the wall was a button labeled "Police Call Alarm." I don't know whether Winston installed it exclusively as protection against people from Washington, but it sure helps. Norma Smith, a trim, light-haired woman, walked in and sat down.

"Would you like some coffee?" she asked.

"No, just a few diamonds for an affair we're having."

The woman smiled. Please go home, the smile said.

"You loaned Nancy Reagan diamonds and she never gave them back. My people will return them. After the end of the night, they'll wrap them up in a handkerchief and a guy who works as a porter around here will return them in the morning."

"We didn't loan Mrs. Reagan the jewelry," Norma Smith said.

"You gave it to her?"

"You'll have to ask the White House."

She was firm, and also slightly uncomfortable. It seems that some weeks ago the Winston people, apparently disappointed that Nancy Reagan had not returned the jewels and yet not able to figure out exactly how to get them back, did some quiet complaining. The notion seemed to be that this would reach Nancy Reagan and she would return the jewels.

In fairness to Winston's, there is a bit of a problem in getting something returned from the White House. In New York, we have many ways of collecting from normal people, all the way from letters through collection agents and on to lions.

Once, the Gallos kept a lion in the basement of their headquarters on President Street in Brooklyn and debtors were hauled in, the lion growled, the debt was paid. There now is one group that keeps a lion on 117th Street in East Harlem. Winston's could have gotten the jewelry back by having the men of 117th Street parade the lion up to a Secret Service agent. The lion would snap at him and the Secret Service agent would run to Nancy Reagan and tell her to return the diamonds. The Winston people apparently, decided to stick with word of mouth.

It wound up in the news. Immediately, Nancy Reagan's office announced that the jewels were being sent back. A year and a half late, but the check truly is in the mail. But by now there was so much out in the open, and Winston's announced that everybody was wrong, that the jewels never were loaned to Nancy Reagan at all. They were donated to start a collection to be worn by the wives of future presidents.

"People give furniture as a gift to the White House," the woman at Winston's was saying yesterday. "A lot of times our First Ladies don't look correct. I think this country's First Lady should have diamonds, don't you?"

"How about loaning some for my 'Bushwick Mother of the Year'?" I asked.

The Winston woman stood up, smiled, and the meeting was over. On the way out I pointed to a necklace hanging in a cabinet on the wall.

"How much is that?" I asked.

"About twenty thousand dollars."

I started to say, "I'll take it," but I don't think she understood me. I was asking to borrow diamonds for Vicki, a mother of three in Bushwick, and the Winston woman was more comfortable dealing with things about Nancy Reagan, who seems to keep what she gets.

Every time somebody complains about Nancy Reagan hanging on to a dress she was supposed to return, there is a sigh from the White House and then an announcement that the dress has been donated by the designer to a museum. What effect this type of maneuvering has on the rest of the government can only be speculated on at this point.

Richard Allen, working as national security adviser, accepted $1000 and two watches to arrange a magazine interview with Nancy Reagan. Then on one road trip the White House staff had pizza delivered to the hotel and accepted it as a gift.

Somebody on the White House staff then was found double-billing for these trips. Small things, but enough to arouse the detective in some people. When it is loose at the top, gentlemen, the hands get busy all down the line.

Meanwhile, far away from any appearances of glamour, you have Vicki, our Bushwick Mother of the Year. In the midst of nothing she and her three children have a nobility that seems to be missing in most other places.

There was an Election Day when Vicki had a job as a poll watcher at the grammar school attended by her nine-year-old son. Vicki began work at 6:00 A.M. At noon, her son ran in from the school cafeteria with a hamburger bun, which he handed to his mother.

"That's nice of you," Vicki said proudly.

The boy stared at the bun. His head moved as he remembered something. He wheeled and went back to the lunchroom. He came running back to his mother, and in his hands was the hamburger meat.

(May 1982)

Even I'm Better than This

One of the lawyers moved about, causing the seat to squeak loudly.

"Settle down," I told him. "You're going to move like that when the movie starts and maybe it will cause us all to miss a couple of important words."

The lawyer grimaced. The other lawyer said, "We still have a few minutes. Perhaps one of us should go for popcorn."

"Nobody gets popcorn," I said. The two of them were being paid for every moment that they were spending in this theater, and I wasn't going to have them digging into boxes and pushing popcorn into their mouths while my chances disappeared through inattentiveness.

We were sitting in the last two rows of the Cinema II theater on Third Avenue, and we were waiting for the start of a movie called *Slow Dancing in the Big City.* It has been described by one television reviewer as "the movie where Jimmy Breslin falls in love with a ballet dancer." The male lead in the movie, Paul Sorvino, is a columnist for the *Daily News.* Everybody says that Sorvino is really me. If I get paid for working for the *Daily News* newspaper, I thought, then why don't I get paid for working for the *Daily News* in the film?

I had the two lawyers with me because we were going to sue the picture and everybody connected with it.

"How's that U.S. fifty and fifty-one?" I said to one of the laywers.

"Oh, it's still on the books," he said.

"Well, we'll see," the other lawyer said.

"What do you mean, we'll see?" I said to him. "You mean, they'll see."

My U.S. 50–51 has to do with the rights of privacy. Rights of privacy and the commercial use of a person's name or picture.

"Actually, the Spahn case is the landmark in the field," the other lawyer said.

"I know; he's my new hero," I said. Warren Spahn was a left-handed baseball pitcher who did something far greater with his life than strike out hitters. Once, when someone tried to appropriate his life and put it in a book, Spahn sued and won. Usually, I'm against somebody like Warren Spahn. That is when I am writing books about someone like Warren Spahn. Now I was the one they were writing about, making a movie about, and everything was different. "Sue!" I said to the lawyers as the lights went down and the movie started.

On the screen, in big letters, was the name "United Artists."

"I'm going to own you!" I said.

The screen said, "A Transamerica Company."

"What's that?" I said.

"A conglomerate for a holding company," one of the lawyers said.

"They don't know what they're holding right now," I said.

On the screen was a *Daily News* delivery truck moving through the night streets. A voice over the film, Sorvino's voice, seemed to be talking a story out loud as he was typing it. Sorvino's voice was saying, "The Eskimo had no last name . . ." As the voice went on, the truck moved and now we saw the big ad on the side of the *News* delivery truck, "New York Loves Friedlander, The Heart of the Apple."

In my hands was a copy of a review in the *New Yorker* magazine by Pauline Kael. She said, "Her neighbor in 3B, Lou Friedlander (Paul Sorvino), is a Jimmy Breslin-like columnist who works for the *News*." She says the casting of Sorvino is suicidal because he can't play a "rambunctious personality-kid" columnist who identifies himself with the big city. "There's no street-smart energy flow from Sorvino." I wonder what those bloodless people at *The New Yorker* think of as "street-smart." Their version of it was, during the blackout that caused looting throughout the city, to have a reporter detail the wisdom of Diana Vreeland as she dined by candlelight.

Anyway, if Sorvino did anything to me, or if the writer, Barra Grant, and I don't like her, had him do anything to me, these two lawyers, sitting in the row behind me, would grab it. And we all would go home with a piece of a movie company.

And now, on the screen, the *News* delivery truck was gone, and here was Sorvino typing away as he talked about the story he was writing. He had so many time changes, a "later" and then "that afternoon," and a "the next day," that you lost track of what he was trying to say.

"He doesn't live well," one of the lawyers said.

"If he keeps writing this badly, he won't deserve to live at all," I said.

Here he was, typing away on one sheet of paper. When I first worked on a newspaper, I went to see a movie called *The Harder They Fall,* and in the last scene Humphrey Bogart sat down to write a newspaper story with one sheet of paper in the typewriter. Someday they will let a movie reporter stuff in the two and three sheets of paper that everyone uses to protect the roller and keep a two-finger style from punching through the paper at every "o."

When he finished the column, Sorvino got up and walked over to his bed and went to sleep for the night.

"Now I can sue," I said.

"For what? Where's the libel?" one of the lawyers said behind me.

"He goes to bed without turning the column in to the paper," I said. "He's not going to get paid. The only reason you write is to get paid. This is a personal attack on me."

On the screen came the ballet dancer I am supposed to fall in love with. Her name is Anne Ditchburn and she is from the National Ballet of Canada. She was whirling unhappily about a large room, like an Iroquois with a problem. She grunted and sulked and then flopped down on the floor and went to sleep. I observed her carefully. Anne Ditchburn could stab fatally with her rib cage, which is almost entirely uncovered by usual anatomy. She also cannot even begin to act.

I concentrate, however, on Sorvino. He types with a pencil in his mouth and two beer cans on the desk. Beer. I know of no person who writes English even for a bare living who is able to work with as much as a mouthful of beer in him. The business of reaching into the air for words that are there as you begin to reach but are gone as you are about to touch them, dust tumbling away in the air, cannot be done with any stimulus. The novelist John Cheever says he can spot a glass of sherry in someone's writing. And if I have two beers in me before I start a column, a note in the newspaper the next day reads, "Jimmy Breslin is off today. He has diphtheria."

The language given to Sorvino is a steady, monotonous "I ain't got to next Thursday . . . he's da next Gene Krupa . . . Hi dere . . . should you be doin' that? I mean, ain't you supposed to be on some kinda wheat germ or somethin'?" And then the screenwriter turns a phrase for Sorvino, "One bit of dis and it's Smile City." Which is the kind of phrase I always turn. Beautiful.

"They make me sound dumb," I said.

"Well, that might be a rather difficult case for us to try," the lawyer said. He's so smart.

I was certain that I had a good case with the language they had me saying. I will bring in as a witness Alistair Cooke, who always compliments me when I talk with him.

As they had Sorvino speak on, I waited for the one mistake that would let me retire. I was waiting for them to have Sorvino say "between you and I." All my life, I have judged everybody by whether or not he uses "between you and I." It is the one most revealing mistake in the English language. If the person says "between you and I," then I know he is uneducated, no matter what kind of paper is framed on his wall, and I also know that he is essentially a fool.

But as I sat in the theater, certain that the people who put this movie out would have Sorvino say "between you and I," it didn't happen.

Nothing else happened, either. This was a movie with no plot, dialogue, or shame. Sorvino looks like a Breslin who has lived a life of cottage cheese. Which is not a bad idea when I get near a mirror. Sorvino also looks like he'd better get a script soon. I saw him on stage in *Championship Season,* and he was fine. But parroting the infantile script for *Slow Dancing in the Big City,* he is dreadful. And they tell me that to see him in *Blood Brothers* is a similar experience.

But I watched on, hoping that they would do something to libel me and fill my pockets. They had Sorvino go into a Puerto Rican bar. The Puerto Ricans were menacing and then they jumped Sorvino. Suddenly, I found it painful to watch any more.

There is one great danger for a newsman who walks into a Puerto Rican or a black bar. You stand an excellent chance of suffering permanent injury to the writing hand while taking down all the legitimate complaints against the government that the people voice to you. A newspaperman, to these people, has something to do with government, and they need help with housing, Medicaid, welfare, family court, and every other imaginable part of the bureaucracy. There is today no such thing as the old Damon Runyon tough-guy-with-the-heart-of-gold-journalism. Better a reporter today has a grasp of the city bureaucracy, the pressure points, and the personnel.

So, as the Puerto Ricans began to rough up Breslin on the screen, without one of them complaining about the validity of a seventy-two-hour dispossess notice, I stopped watching the picture altogether. I squirmed in the seat, causing it to squeak loudly.

I turned around to apologize to the lawyers. I didn't want to break their concentration. One had his head on his chest as if he had been mugged. The other had his hand propping up his chin. He gave a gentlemanly snore.

(November 1978)

People I'm Not Talking To This Year

Whenever somebody does something bad to me, I write an account of it on a piece of paper and then at night transcribe the notes into a copybook and thus into my life permanently, or at least for a full year. The copybook prevents me from forgetting any feud, which is important, as it would be the worst sin of all, the sin of omission, if I failed to hold up my end of the disagreement.

Perhaps some think that if you turn the other cheek you are displaying maturity. I believe that if you turn one cheek, then you only have one left.

I live therefore in the spirit and memory of my friend Eddie Borden, who was arrested for gambling back in the times when that was considered a crime and not a means for newspapers to raise circulation, and was told by a guard that bail had just been posted for him. He walked to the last set of bars, peered through them, and saw both freedom and his most hated enemy, Eddie Walker, on the other side.

"What's he doing here?" Borden asked the guard.

"He put up bail for you," the guard said.

"Give the bum his money back," Bordon said. He turned and walked back to the freight elevator that took people up to the cell blocks.

It is in this spirit that I go through my marvelous copybook and present my list of People I'm Not Talking To This Year:

WHISPERING MILLSTEIN — He is in a law company with GOOD-TIME CHARLIE GOLDSTEIN. Goldstein was part of the legal-government complex called Our Thing that runs this city and state just as the military-industrial complex runs the nation. Goldstein was paid more than $4 million in two years by the State Urban Development Corporation as a legal consultant. Goldstein called it a public service. When I wrote about this in my newspaper, the *Daily News* newspaper, Goldstein first had somebody from his company call my newspaper and try to put the muscle on, as would some cheap tough guy. The newspaper's lawyer, RETAINER TYLER, was careful to pass on the threats, for he is first a lawyer, and thus part of Our Thing. And now we come to Whispering Millstein. He stands at a cocktail party and says, so ominously, that he sure hopes that scruffy Breslin knows the law about slander. Of course, a lot of worried faces came up to me after the party and said, "Say, you could get hurt." At this point, I was supposed to quit. This is how Our Thing works in New York. It probably is the same in every state in the country. Great power. But let me tell you what I did. First, I said I was going to challenge Good-Time Charlie Goldstein and Whispering Millstein to a duel, with seconds, guns on the Palisades or swords on Park Avenue. I practiced shot and wonderful quick thrust. But then Cuomo, the incoming governor, who was not a member of Our Thing, told me to challenge them to a lawsuit. He wanted me to suck them in and then he would step out from behind me and put them all into a trash basket. I issued the challenge and stood on a street corner for days waiting for one of them to show up with lawsuit papers. They dogged it. Nobody showed and Good-Time Charlie Goldstein disappeared from "public service" and the public funds that go with it. His man Whispering Millstein uttered no more. Nobody came to me with cocktail-party stories anymore. But that doesn't mean I forget anything. He may have quit, but I do not.

LIEUTENANT ANDREW MURPHY of the 109th Precinct — With three prisoners in front of his desk, Murphy stopped everything so he could make some cheap remark about me to somebody. I received a phone call about it as soon as one of the prisoners was allowed his phone calls. Of all the remarks made about me by all the police in New York during the last year, my notes show that Murphy uttered the lowest.

MARTY STEADMAN — He sits up all night writing ads or letters to the editor attacking me personally. Then he runs around all day with his hands in the air and crying that he never did it. Just another stool pigeon.

FAT THOMAS — He slows as he steps into the twilight of the twentieth century; perhaps he is as slow as the horses he bets on. But he still thinks that he can snarl at people as if he were some Tartar conqueror. I also was told about all the bad things he said about me on Metropolitan Avenue the other night.

STEVE BERGER — I just found a notation in my book about how Berger, a man who genuflects in front of politicians, used to sneak into the *Daily News* newspaper on behalf of Ed Koch and spread a lot of bad stories about me to the bosses. I have studied my notes on this for some time. I now emerge from the dugout to take my turn at bat.

MARK and ZEV of the Pastrami King — Shelley Chevlowe went to get sandwiches for Abe Deutscher and me and Mark and Zev treated Shelley very bad and now it is a major feud on Queens Boulevard that cannot be handled.

BELLA ABZUG — For what she said to Ronnie Eldridge about me.

SOCIETY CAREY — Greatest of tragedies! Society Carey's helicopter gets a cough and has to be grounded. They find a smaller helicopter, which has only one pilot. Society Carey grouses. He wants two pilots. No one is available. So a state trooper puts on a baseball hat and earphones and slips in and poses as the co-pilot. Society Carey is happy. He has two pilots. The state trooper in the baseball hat is happy. He is flying in a helicopter for the first time in his life.

This is what the public pays for, and what those who know Society Carey best think of him.

Society Carey circles his desk with his new red hair and old red face and he says my name and then he says "mongrel" and "cur." Of course somebody goes to the phone and calls me; Society Carey can't go into the next room without somebody calling me up. Forget about a restaurant, the waiters and customers line up at the phone booth. So I know what he thinks about me, but it's not half as bad as what I think about him. Even at the end of the world, at any Last Judgment, where everybody has to stand around and say hello like they love each other, I am going to raise my hand and say, "If it's all the same, the one person in the whole history of the world I don't want to talk to is Society Carey."

KOCH THE MAYOR — He made a big thing about not being able to support Mario Cuomo because of Breslin and Newfield. The first insult is that he mentioned me in the same breath with Newfield, about which I will tell you later.

Koch has done this before, too. One day in City Hall he said that Breslin and Newfield are part of the Elaine's crowd that doesn't like him. I don't know about Newfield, but I have been in Elaine's maybe three times in my life, even though Elaine and I have only the greatest memories of each other from another life, when we were young and vibrant in the weeds in the empty lot at Sutphin Boulevard and 101st Avenue in Jamaica.

I think that using Breslin's name was a way for Koch to keep himself from facing the cold, uncomfortable fact that Cuomo was here, was not going away, and was ready for one of those reasonable public discussions in front of a lot of people, the idea of which causes Koch to freeze; in the small of the night he sees Mario Cuomo answering a question.

Koch has made it harder to walk around this city. He throws his arms in the air and screams how great he is, while taxpapers step into potholes and do flips. He says the crime is going down, but the people with their heads opened believe it is still rising. I am beginning to think that if, by mouth or mannerism, you help impress on the poor of this city the idea that they have no future, then each year a few more of the young poor will go out and act as if they have no future.

I truly loved Koch at the antihandgun rally after John Lennon was shot. Because Koch's fund-raising dinner was run by his great friend David Margolis, chairman of Colt Industries. This is the company that makes the great Colt handguns that go off all over the city. Koch also took Margolis to Rome, where they visited the pope, who had been shot by a handgun. This is known as great taste.

Most people will come to realize soon that Koch is the loudest mirage we've ever had. See the next election.

MONTALVO from St. Anne's Avenue — He yelled at me in the street one day. Maybe he doesn't remember it, but I do.

JAMES J. COMERFORD — The Joseph McCarthy of the Saint Patrick's Day Parade Committee. Among the thousands of charges he hurls about, never has anybody heard him utter the great truth, that the only thing he ever did for anybody Irish was to get his own name on a city payroll.

CHRISTOPHER LEHMANN-HAUPT — He gets permanent listing. Once, in his book reviews, he proclaimed that a book I wrote should not have been written. Marvelous idea! Ban books. Every time you let a German near a typewriter to do anything except repair it, he goes straight to authoritarianism. Ban books. Meanwhile in New Jersey, a local politician who became a federal judge, Lacey, took up the same cause. A reporter named Farber, who works on the paper where Lehmann-Haupt works, *The New York Times* newspaper, was writing a book on a case in Lacey's court and Lacey screamed and put Farber in jail. Immediately, I thought it would be a terrific idea for Lehmann-Haupt and the judge to hang out together, seeing as they have the same views. Then someday Lacey the Judge could put Lehmann-Haupt in jail.

DAVID GARTH — There is nothing that pleases him more than the sight of a turned back.

AL NEWMAN — He is the big bail bondsman. Once in the last year, I made a terrible mistake. I went to Sidney Krautt's party in Atlantic Beach and I forgot my copybook. When Al Newman came up to me, I knew I shouldn't have been talking to him, but I couldn't remember why. So I spoke to him. When I got home, I looked him up in my book and memorized what Al Newman once did to me and now, by rote, I know what to do if I see Al Newman on the street: cut him off with a glare.

JACK NEWFIELD — And the whole *Village Voice* newspaper with him. Each year, with these people, it is a different game. Once, Newfield put my picture in his newspaper and said I was one of the greediest people in New York. Because I wrote a book for money. Let him try to do the book, never mind get the money for it. Another time, I don't know exactly what the point was, but they put in my picture and said I was selling out the whole industry. Now this year, all of a sudden, Newfield decides to change. So here is this picture in the *Village Voice* the other day and it said underneath, "Jimmy Breslin, real good guy this time." No, thank you. I felt better about

Newfield and his place when they were saying that I was greedy and bad. I don't believe in correcting the past by suddenly putting down five or six good words. Maybe Newfield likes me this year. But I didn't like him the year before last and last year and now for sure I'm not going to talk to him for all of this year.

DOUG IRELAND — Standing broke on the sidewalk outside a magazine. Runs inside and types them out a personal attack on me. Grabs ninety-five dollars and runs back onto the street. I'm not Frankie McPhillip, but Doug Ireland sure as hell is Gypo Nolan. Ireland edges out Marty Steadman as stool pigeon of the year.

WILLIAM SHAWN — The one worst weeper I ever came across. He is the editor of the *New Yorker* magazine. When he's not in freaking tears. In his magazine, he ran a long editorial that attacked people on newspapers who had to write about Son of Sam because he was real. One of the reasons why the killer was caught was that he had in his car window an envelope with printing familiar to police because they had received samples of his printing from me. When I called Shawn up and told him this, his immediate reaction was to weep: "Oh, I knew something like this would happen."

CIRCULATION WEIGHART — He was the editor of my newspaper, the *Daily News,* at a time when policewoman Cibella Borges was fired by middle-aged Irish Roman Catholics because she had posed for dirty naked pictures about a year before being sworn. Stories about Cibella infuriated cops and their friends and papers were sold. Then the police commissioner, Dead Body McGuire, snuck around to the *Daily News* newspaper with the pictures of Cibella Borges. Greatest filth! Oh, look at this dirty naked little slut! Circulation Weighart then sabotaged his own paper in order to receive a pat on the head from the police chief. Dead Body McGuire now has a job as a plant guard. Circulation Weighart is somewhere right now, but he sure isn't the editor of the *Daily News* anymore. How can these children pester Breslin?

THE ALSO RANS — Whitey Lewis; Morgenthau the Tireless — the man for whom the phrase "No Heavy Lifting" was coined; Arthur Lonschein, who likes to write nasty letters and then smile sweetly and say he doesn't remember doing it; Joe Cannon; John O'Mara, Cusamano; Nick from the Forge Diner; Kay O'Hare; Sy Rotker; Weinstein the Judge; John Keenan — the Keenan who was a bookmaker with a loose mouth and they made him a federal judge; Superior Cohn; John Neckland; Tony from Tutto Bene — he is on this list not for a year, but forever; Fel — soon, he'll be what he is worth mentioning, one letter; Suzanne White; Darnell Price; Joey Beglane; Podhoretz's wife; Gael Greene — the secret about her is that she has absolutely no taste; Rughead Hauptman; Bill Flanagan — one of the troubles in this country is that they sell typewriters to anyone; and, as always, Kleinstuber.

(1976-1983)

"You're Cheaper Off"

The corner where Atlantic Avenue meets Ashford Street in the East New York section of Brooklyn is not exactly the most inviting place in the world on a sultry evening in July. The south side of the avenue is a hazy, brooding wasteland of burned-out houses and empty lots, block after block of them with only an occasional place of business like a butcher shop holding out bravely against the tide. The north side of Atlantic is still crowded with weathered frame houses, but now the fires of arson are beginning to lick at them, too.

There is, however, an oasis of sorts nestled amidst all the squalor, plunked down right next to a garment factory on Atlantic Avenue and directly across from a Consolidated Edison truck terminal. This is Charlie's Restaurant, an establishment that does not appear in any of the numerous guides to New York eating places. Charlie's, logically enough, is owned by a man named Charlie, who lives upstairs, does all the cooking himself, and opens his place of business only for people he knows.

And so it was that on a warm evening in July 1982, Charlie opened his doors to a good friend, Jimmy Breslin, columnist of the New York *Daily News,* who brought along his two eldest sons, the twins Kevin and James, his daughters Rosemary and Kelly, and the youngest of the Breslin brood, sons Patrick and Christopher. Also in the party were a widow named Ronnie Eldridge and her three children, Lucy, Emily, and Danny.

For the Eldridge children, coming from swank Central Park West in Manhattan, Charlie's place was a revelation, a bit unsettling in the seediness of its location, perhaps, but delightful in its privacy and the superb quality of its food. The Breslin kids had been there before, but now, as they gathered around a long table in a back room (appropriately for Breslin, the horse player, under pictures of two handicap horses of the 1950s, Vertex and Bardstown), Charlie's food was not the subject uppermost in everybody's mind.

For this was the Big Night, the night when Jimmy and Ronnie broke the news to their collective children that they were going to get married. This was for Breslin a very large step, and the truth was that neither he nor Ronnie Eldridge knew quite what to expect.

What actually happened was a pleasant surprise, for the time being anyway.

Breslin and Ronnie instantly found out what almost all parents eventually learn: that their kids are always miles ahead of them. "Everybody knew what the dinner was about," Breslin recalls ruefully, "that a marriage was going to take place and this was the start of a thing called getting along."

Charlie's linguine, his chicken and sausage and cheesecake disappeared, washed down with wine and accompanied by a good deal of talk and laughter.

"I sat back and thought," Jimmy says now, "well, they know it is inevitable and the marriage is not based on hatred out of divorce. We're doing all right.

"The next morning, Ronnie reported over the phone that everything had gone well. I said the same. Terrific, two reasonably intelligent people with kids who could accept things."

Ah, little did Breslin know that the winds of rebellion were already beginning to blow.

That same night, Lucy Eldridge, then twenty and a student at Hamilton College, said to her mother, "Are you sure you've given this enough thought? I don't think you have."

And in Forest Hills, Queens, where dwelt the Breslins, Kelly Breslin, age seventeen and a student at the High School for the Performing Arts, sniffed to the woman next door, "My father isn't going to marry *her*."

Thus was the start of a family feud that endures to this day. "It is," says Breslin with the air of a man on whom the wisdom of the ages has finally dawned, "a total disaster."

Painful as it has turned out to be, the whole episode of Breslin's remarriage is instructive because it points up the very large role that his family has played in his professional life. Breslin is a man ridden with guilt about his role as the father of six children. He never spent enough time with them, he will tell you, his face a picture of despair, not only in his earlier saloon-hopping days when he was growing in prestige as a writer, but even later when, a solid success in his field, he might have spared them more of himself but was obliged to devote his attentions to the ailing Rosemary.

Indifferent father though he may have been, Breslin throughout his career has always turned to members of his family — even his in-laws — for some of his most penetrating, poignant, and funny columns.

During the late 1970s and early 1980s, when business-page writers were bending their bar graphs and flexing their economic maxims trying to explain inflation, Breslin found a simple way to do it through the street-wise words of his mother-in-law, the mother of the former Rosemary Dattolico. "You're cheaper off," she used to say time after time, if you just followed her advice and shopped around, plodding from store to store until you found the pineapple juice that was fifty-nine cents a can instead of seventy-three.

By all accounts, it was the birth of his twins, Kevin and James, that motivated Breslin to soft-pedal the fun life of a newspaperman-about-town and at least begin to think about the serious business of making a living. All those mouths to feed, et cetera ...

Sterling Lord, who has been Breslin's literary agent for nearly twenty-five years, recalls that when he first took Jimmy on, about this time, he was in debt to a lot of people, mostly merchants with whom the family did business.

"He got a kick out of being dunned by them," Lord says. "It was part of his combative nature. But I thought it was my job to clean up those debts, and I did it in about a year and a half.

"But then Breslin came in with his hangdog look and told me the kick had gone out of life. He asked me, couldn't I just keep one little bill going? So we let one go just so he could be dunned by somebody. It was the B and B clothing store of Jamaica. I don't know whether it is still there or not." (It is).

If the birth of the twins convinced Breslin that filling mouths with food was serious business, it was his first wife, Rosemary, who was the real driving force behind him. She was his companion-in-arms, his gentle prodder, and sometimes his comforter. When Breslin thought that perhaps he should learn to drive, Rosemary told him, no. "It's better for you to take the subway, read the paper, and talk to people," she told him. Breslin wrote of her: "She thought that the word duty meant that each day there should be a word or a gesture that would cause someone to smile over the life about them." Michael Daly says that some people were fonder of Rosemary than of Breslin. "When they went to Northern Ireland," he recalls, "people there loved Rosemary, but wondered, 'Who is that weird little fat man she's married to?' "

Breslin's attention to his wife in her declining years, when they would slip away on the *QE2* as often as they could, was, he concedes now, hardest on their three youngest children. "We should have taken a lot more of a hand with them," he says. "What we did was spend money on them to keep them quiet."

Rosemary died in June of 1981, and Breslin sat down at the one place where he could express his grief best: his typewriter. The eulogy he composed and read at services at Our Lady of Mercy Catholic Church in Forest Hills was (and is) one of the most moving ever written by a husband to his wife.

"We of the family who remain have a special burden," one passage said. "We have lived with nobility."

For months Breslin was a stricken man. "It was," says Michael Daly, "the worst thing that ever happened to him." Yet he carried on his column, and, paradoxically, his fumbling efforts to fill the void left by Rosemary, to somehow hold his little family together, yielded some of his most hilarious columns.

Actually, Breslin had already gotten a taste of family responsibility in Rosemary's final years of cancer, when she was sometimes confined to her bed and the lord and master found himself coping with such alien and incomprehensible things as broken oven doors and balky children who couldn't seem to do a simple book report. It was at this juncture that Breslin fell to musing in print about the perilous state of marriage. And in so doing he summed up in a few simple words what philosophers fill whole books to tell us about the relative roles of husband and wife. "No male member of a family," wrote Breslin, "truly goes out by himself to make a living; he has behind him each day a wall, as strong as anything thrown up by a bricklayer, that prevents anything from home spilling onto him and making his task impossible."

After Rosemary's death, Breslin's problems with his kids grew deeper, yet his sense of humor was equal to the challenge.

In column after column he wrung his hands over their lack of respect for authority, their poor report cards, their tendency to disappear at night when he thoughtfully stayed home in order to spend time with his family. Finally, he had had enough. There came a time when Mayor Edward Koch of New York, a bachelor, and Carol

Bellamy, the unmarried president of the New York City Council, found it prudent to assure parental voters, just before elections, that there was absolutely nothing in this world they would like more than children of their own. Okay, said Breslin, he had the answer: they could have his miserable kids, and welcome to them. "You're going to Koch," he informed Kelly Breslin, while consigning Patrick and Christopher to Bellamy. "I felt tremendous," he wrote in his column. "I not only had removed a problem from my life, one that was about to kill me, but I had done the city a tremendous favor, I had helped the political careers of our great leaders . . ."

Ah, if only life's problems could be solved so simply.

The truth, of course, is that Breslin's woes simply became manifold when he chose to remarry. The decision he and Ronnie Eldridge made that the families should reside in her West Side apartment was an early source of trouble, because it meant that the Breslin home in Forest Hills was now expendable. It had been a comfortable place, where the master was always on the phone, the kids came and went, and the television blared nonstop — although Jimmy himself scarcely ever watched it. Getting rid of the house wasn't going to be easy.

"The young kids wanted to keep it," Breslin says, because of the good times associated with it, "but yet they didn't want to" because of the sad memories of their mother. The house was sold.

Thus was the die cast and the two families were joined in Manhattan, a fusion only slightly less volatile than the joining of hydrogen and oxygen. Breslin has never made any secret of the bruised feelings between his Irish Catholic kids and the Jewish children of Ronnie Eldridge; he has written about them frankly and openly in his column. Some may wonder why he would choose to air his private life in public — but that has always been Breslin's way, to write about what is bothering him most at any given time. If that happens to be his family, well, so be it. And if his troubles reverberate through the lives of *Daily News* readers and sell thousands of newspapers, amen to that, too.

— W.B.

Grape-Nuts Pays

There was, yesterday, an offer for me to do a television commercial for a coffee company. The matter was debated at great length with my wife, the former Rosemary Dattolico.

"How much?" she said.

"Pretty good," I said. I showed her the figures.

She looked at them. "I better take your suit to the cleaners," she said.

"I don't know how it will look," I said. "I'm supposed to be a newsman now and here I'm out plugging a coffee. It was different when I wasn't in daily news work."

"What time do you have to be there to make the commercial?" she said.

Once, the former Rosemary Dattolico listened to great arguments, delivered in the rhythm of purity, about how much harm television newsmen did to themselves by pitching products on such as the "Today" show. The former Rosemary Dattolico agreed. Then she read a story about how the owner of the television station, RCA, makes guidance systems for missiles. The next morning, the former Rosemary Dattolico waved a finger at Tom Brokaw on the television and said, "You could sell a little dogfood and nobody gets hurt."

Now, yesterday, she looked at me and waited for me to call up and say, yes, I'll do a commercial. I said I had one other problem before I did this: I drink decaffeinated coffee. I love real coffee but I always drink coffee in such amounts, twenty and thirty cups a day while writing, that the real coffee used to make triphammers go off inside my chest at 3:00 A.M. I'd wake up and start praying.

"If I make the commercial, I'll have to drink real coffee," I said.

"So?" the former Rosemary Dattolico said.

"Well, you know what it can do to me."

She looked at the figures again. She shrugged. "So you could have a few little chest pains."

I picked up the phone and called the person handling the business and said, yes, I'll do the commercial. The woman said to me, "Now, you understand what it's going to be like to do one of these commercials. You'll have to do all these retakes and things like that."

I said to her, "What, are you kidding? I can tell you stories about them."

Which I can:

Two years ago, when I was not a daily newsman, a man named Paul McDonough from Benton and Bowles advertising called me up and asked if I wanted to do a thirty-second commercial for Grape-Nuts. I happened to like the cereal and I happened to love the money he mentioned. I said yes so loud that he had to hold the phone away.

A day or so later, I was in his office on Third Avenue. McDonough looked me over. The man who would direct the commercial stared at me. Finally, McDonough told a young woman in the office, "Go to Brooks Brothers and buy Jimmy a sweater."

The young woman nodded. "What size are you?" she asked.

"I don't tell that in Confession," I said. "I'll go out and buy the sweater."

"But you can't," she said.

"Yes, I can."

I could see the young woman was becoming upset. "You don't understand, I get paid for doing this," she said. "I'm in charge of the clothes." As I learned, she was one of the approximately one hundred people who work on a single commercial. Work for good money, too.

Some days later, at seven-thirty of a brisk March morning, I arrived at a building on the West Side that houses one of the fifty or so television production facilities that can be found stuck between the taxicab garages and storage warehouses. I counted forty-five people walking around when I came in. All their motion was directed at a table, bathed in hot light, on which sat a box of Grape-Nuts, a bowl, a milk pitcher, and a sugar bowl.

First, a woman took me into a room and made me up. The young woman from the agency then handed me my Brooks Brothers sweater. I was then trotted out to the table.

I sat on a stool behind it and went over the lines, which I'd memorized the night before. A guy named George, one of the crew, was next to me. He put some Grape-Nuts onto a spoon. Then he poured milk over it. I was to hold up the spoon, say my lines brightly, then stick the spoon into my mouth.

As George handed me the spoon, a scream came from out beyond the lights.

"You've drowned the Grape-Nuts!"

"I'm sorry!" George said. He then got a new spoon and put in more Grape-Nuts and less milk. I held this spoon up to the hot lights.

"Good," a voice said. "I want the Grape-Nuts to be able to hold their heads up high."

My job at this point was to hold up the spoon, tell the camera lens that Grape-Nuts were solid — that was the key word, solid; a solid guy telling you about solid food — and, after this, jam the spoonful of Grape-Nuts into my mouth.

As I was about to start, George put a big plastic bucket at my feet. On a low table next to it was a large glass of water.

"What's that?" I said.

"Your spit bucket," he said.

"What for?"

George seemed surprised. "You got to spit them out after every mouthful," he said. "Wash out your mouth with water and spit into the bucket. You can't swallow them every time. You'll be doing this scene so many times you'll make yourself sick. Besides, it takes you too long to chew up Grape-Nuts. We'll be here two days waiting for you to finish chewing. Just say your line to the camera, put the Grape-Nuts into your mouth, hold it, and then the camera will cut. Then you spit out and we go on to the next line."

I held up the spoon. Somebody behind the lights shouted, "Rolling!" and I said into the camera lens, with great early-morning cheer, "Grape-Nuts, the solid food."

I opened my mouth and shoveled in the Grape-Nuts. My jawbone went crazy. It couldn't start chomping on those Grape-Nuts. But I held it steady.

"All right, cut," somebody said.

I leaned over, took a great gulp of the water, threw my head back and swilled it around, then bent over, like a prizefighter between rounds, and spit everything into the bucket.

I looked up, ready to go on to the next line.

"We'll do that one over," a voice said.

"Don't drown the Grape-Nuts!" a voice called to George.

I did it again. I gave it a "solid" and then cleaned the spoon. When I heard the word "cut," I went right to the water. As I was leaning over and spitting, I heard a voice say, "We'll try that again.

Hit the 'solid' a little harder, Jimmy." Somebody else said, "Grape-Nuts, take three."

I came up and did it again. And again. I remember that at about eleven-thirty that morning, after doing take twenty-one, I leaned over to spit. When I looked into the plastic bucket, by now nearly full, with all that stuff sloshing around, I became sick to my stomach and I spit out for real.

George told me not to worry about it. He told me that the last time they had made a Grape-Nuts commercial, they used a ten-year-old kid who insisted on eating the Grape-Nuts each time. His name was Mitchell and he said he loved Grape-Nuts. The crew had to wait through each take until Mitchell got the last Grape-Nut out of his teeth. When they came to the final parts of the shooting, late in the afternoon, Mitchell looked up woozily and the director clapped his hands and said, "All right, Mitchell, here we go."

"I can't eat any more," Mitchell said.

"Mitchell. Once more, all right, fella?"

Mitchell put down the spoon. "Makin' me sick."

Mitchell's mother asked if her son couldn't finish the job the next morning. The agency people shuddered. It would cost $15,000 if they had to reassemble the camera crew for another day. The agency man said to Mitchell, "If you eat your cereal, I'll buy a bike." Mitchell shook his head.

The director turned to Mitchell's mother, "If you get him to eat, I'll buy you a car."

The mother advanced on Mitchell. She coaxed him. He shook his head. She pinched him. He still shook his head. Then through the studio there came this great infant yelp as Mitchell's mother stuck him with a pin.

The last take of the commercial was made with Mitchell, afraid of the pin, chomping away on his third box of Grape-Nuts.

And now, here on my Grape-Nuts commercial, they waited until I stopped retching. Then somebody washed out the spit bucket and gave me a new glass of water and here we went, saying "solid" and then spitting away until late in the afternoon.

Yesterday, after remembering this and talking about it, I began to think about the great new commercial, my coffee commercial. Right away, the former Rosemary Dattolico said: "You'll need a lot of extra shirts for the commercial. The coffee is liable to be hot and you'll burn yourself and spit it all over like a slob. Just don't complain to anybody about the hot coffee. I'll give you plenty of shirts. Just change your shirt and go back to work. Bring home the moneys."

(*October 1977*)

The Imagination Hurts

ABOARD THE QE2 — Rather than go home when I left the building, I headed for the Chinese restaurant around the corner. It was closed and I slipped down the side street to Costello's, where one thing led to another and by midnight I was so taken with the profundity of my thoughts that I wanted to stay forever.

I arrived home in time to catch the staples of end-of-the-night television: an aggressive Lutheran minister, the "Star-Spangled Banner," and a man with diseased kidneys who was pleading for one of mine. When the kidney commercial dissolved I was up at the head of the bed, and thus badly outpositioned when there suddenly appeared on the screen the commercial of the fat man running for the train, gasping and strangling for air, the briefcase so heavy it nearly causes him to trip. He sweats and sucks in air and the announcer's voice says, "This man is about to have a heart attack."

I tumbled down the bed and felt my ankle twist as I dived for the television dial. I was too late, however. On the screen the man's eyes widened in horror and his tongue flopped out and he made the sound of a man being garroted. He pitched onto his face on the train platform. I turned the dial to the aggressive Lutheran on Channel 4, but it was too late: already I felt twinges in my chest.

I looked up at the ceiling and said, "If I get through the night I'll never take another drink or smoke another cigar."

The twinges only increased. It has long been my contention that the heart-attack commercial has caused more deaths than an epidemic. I sat up for the next two hours counting my heartbeats. I once read someplace that this old catcher for the Brooklyn Dodgers, Babe Phelps, used to remain awake all night counting his heartbeats. Phelps said that you can miss three heartbeats in a row, but if you miss a fourth you die on the spot. Phelps, who did not want to die without knowing it, lost his job in the big leagues because he

usually was too exhausted from counting his heartbeat all night to
be able to play baseball. However, I was taken with his theory, and I
think of it whenever I get nervous. So on this night I counted heartbeats and stopped only when I betrayed myself and fell asleep.

Sometime around 7:00 A.M. the phone rang. A man who did not
identify himself said, "I just want you to know that Sam DiFalco
dropped dead last night. He just keeled over and dropped dead. He
fell right into the arms of his best friend. Bang, just like that."

As the caller told me this, I cradled the phone with my shoulder. I
had to do this because both hands were clutching my chest. When
the man hung up, I did two things: I said a prayer for Sam DiFalco,
the former Manhattan surrogate, whose life had been full, and then
I said a second prayer for myself. I figured I had only minutes to go.

I kept the phone next to me on the bed and had a hand on the dial
so that I could reach the emergency number — 911. For the next
couple of hours I counted heartbeats and stared at the television and
then at about ten-thirty, during a morning movie called *The Group,* I
decided that I ought to get up, that this too had passed, and that a
day's work would cause any lingering symptoms to disappear.

When I tried to get going, I was held almost motionless by what
seemed like the worst hangover I had had in perhaps years. I sat at
the typewriter like a zombie. I made one capital letter on the paper,
threw it away, and went back to bed and dozed through most of the
middle of the day. When I woke up I felt worse. Then at a little after
5:00 P.M., I was propped up in bed and here came Dr. Frank Field
on the Channel 4 television station. Field began talking about a new
way to help heart-attack victims stay alive. Behind him there appeared this plastic replica of a human heart, a thing as big as your
front door, and I began to pulsate as Dr. Frank Field talked about
heart attacks.

Fadoom-fadoom-fadoom-fadoom. The next fadoom I heard was
in my chest. My chest began to go faster than Frank Field's plastic
heart.

I also was very warm, burning up, I admitted to myself. I could
feel the sweat on my forehead. That made it official: whenever
they're sweating, they're in trouble.

I called a cab and dressed quickly. I could try to get to Dr. Kevin
Cahill's office in Manhattan, but the chances were that I would die
en route. Also if I did get there, Cahill would yell at me because I
didn't lose the weight he told me to.

I decided that I was giving myself a better chance if I stayed in Queens. I had the cab take me to the offices of Dr. Benjamin Stein, on Ninety-ninth Street, right off Queens Boulevard.

At Dr. Stein's office, I cut past the receptionist and walked in to the doctor as an emergency patient.

"How are you?" he said.

"I'm almost gone," I said.

"How's everybody else at home?" he asked.

"All right, I guess. But I'm almost gone."

He took my pulse. "Going to beat the band," he said.

"I told you," I said.

Some blood-pressure machine showed nothing, but I knew more than the machine. Then Dr. Stein picked up a tongue depressor and said, "Open your mouth." I never knew that you can look down a person's throat and see his heart. I told myself that in the future I'd buy a thousand tongue depressors and stand in front of a mirror all night, looking down my throat at my heart, rather than sit upright in bed all night counting missed heartbeats.

"Throat sore?" he asked me. I shook my head. No. He pulled out the tongue depressor and next poked in my ears with a small flashlight. Then he stuck a thermometer in my mouth. When he took it out, he shrugged.

"You have a hundred and two," he said. "You've got an infection, that's your trouble. That's why your chest is beating so fast. When you have a fever, the heart has to pump more blood to cool the body."

I insisted that there was more than that. He made a face and had the nurse take me inside and fix wires to me and take an electrocardiogram. When it was finished, Stein stretched the long strips of what seemed to be celluloid paper onto his desk and he began to study the lines on the paper. He went to a file and took out another electrocardiogram I had at his office. Stein calls it the George McGovern electrocardiogram. It was taken on the Thursday before the election of 1972.

On the day, there was a meeting on Queens Boulevard of everybody involved in a decision, a full year earlier, that Matty Troy, then the county leader, should become the first one in the country to endorse Senator George McGovern. There is no question that Troy's move helped get McGovern the Democratic nomination. And on this particular day, there was no question that it was not going to work out in the general election. A figure man looked up from computer readouts and said, "Nixon could carry the county by two hundred thousand votes."

Lou Wallach turned pale. "That means local candidates could lose their jobs, too."

The figure man said, "Bus drivers could get thrown out."

"This thing is your fault too," Lou Wallach said to me. About four of us felt sick and wound up in Ben Stein's office. He checked everything and said we were fine, although every time I see McGovern's picture my chest acts up. And now, nearly six years later, Ben Stein had my McGovern tapes out on his desk and he was comparing them with the test I just had.

"Nothing," he said. "I told you. You have a simple infection in your chest someplace and you're building it into a cemetery plot."

I tapped the strips of paper on his desk. "I remember the McGovern one," I said. "I really was sick that day. Something happened, and I don't care what the record shows."

Stein sent me home with a prescription for an antibiotic. I stayed in bed a couple of days and then said, the hell with it, I'm going away. And so the other night, I walked onto the *QE2* to sail for England. After I had been to the stateroom and got the luggage arranged, I went for a walk about the ship and upstairs, in a lounge, I heard a low, sweet voice say hello to me. I turned around to see George McGovern.

"Are you traveling, too?" he asked.

I nodded. I did not speak to him because I was busy counting my heartbeats, which had become irregular the moment I saw him. Skip four beats and you die. Die right there, die, die, dead.

McGovern said something else. I mumbled to him and then left for the stateroom right away. I had a great decision to make: Do I call the captain and ask him to let me get off the ship on a tugboat, or do I stay where I am and risk dying at sea?

(July 1978)

I'm Not Making Some South American Rich

"You're cheaper off if you do it my way," the former Rosemary Dattolico's mother was saying. "I shop store-to-store. I can wait. I can watch. I'm not spoiled like everybody else. I saved two dollars one day last week going store-to-store and I said, well, that's two dollars for my bingo game. You see? You're cheaper off."

She looked at a pot that had about two tablespoons of spinach left in it, not a strand more, and she took the spinach and put it into a small bowl, covered it with a saucer, and jammed it into a refrigerator that contained rows of similarly covered bowls. All these bowls together wouldn't be enough to serve a cat, but she nodded happily after closing the refrigerator door. "Waste not, want not," she said.

She sat down and poured a cup of coffee from a pot she had just made. She had used about two thirds of the coffee necessary, and the result tasted like hot water that may or may not have something added. Her daughter, the former Rosemary Dattolico, made a face.

"I'm not making some South American rich," her mother said. "Besides, you were raised on it this way. You never noticed the difference."

"I do now," the former Rosemary Dattolico said.

The mother sniffed. "Give a beggar a horse and he'll ride to hell."

"You sound like you're getting ready for the Depression," she was told.

"Ready? You bet I am. Besides, what do you think we got now? I go out to buy food and the price is too high for me to buy it. What's the difference if I'm trying to buy with a dime or a dollar? I still can't buy the food. To me, it's the Depression. Believe me, I know what to do. I know how to buy. I'm not going to lose my home this time."

She said, "In one place on the avenue I found pineapple juice for fifty-nine cents. It's seventy-three cents everyplace else. I went in another store and bought ten pounds of potatoes for seventy-nine cents. In the next place it was a dollar twenty-nine. But you've got to keep walking. You can't stay in the store where you get a buy. They give you a break on one thing, they look to make it up on other things. Take advantage of the break and then run to the next place.

"I only eat in season, too. You ate lettuce all summer long. You don't need lettuce in the winter. Eat turnips instead. I wouldn't buy turnips like when they were twenty-five cents a pound in the summer. I buy when turnips come down to fifteen cents a pound in the winter. Turnips, what's the matter with turnips, a pound for fifteen cents. Buy rice. A ten-pound bag of rice doesn't cost. You can use rice for a hundred things. These Chinese are not so dumb."

She lit a cigarette.

"When I shop, I'm out on the sidewalk and remind myself the day the Globe Bank failed," she said. "Then when I go inside shopping, I use my wits."

The Depression arranged all of her life. Since the Depression, she always has regarded any other problem as a bothersome dwarf. When the last Depression ended, she immediately began to prepare, financially and mentally, for the next. Once, she only suspected it would come. Now, reading the headlines, seeing the prices, she is certain that everything will snap.

"Huh. Will I ever forget the day the Globe Bank failed? During the week I put in the last few dollars I had around the house. I think I put a couple into a fifty-dollar Christmas Club we had and a couple of more into a savings account. Frieda's daughter worked in the bank. She's dead now, poor thing, but I can remember talking to her in the bank that day. When I went home, I didn't have more than a dollar or two in the house. We tried to save everything in those days.

"The next day was a Saturday, and I was cleaning windows when I heard this man yelling out in the street, "The bank's closed." I went outside and the woman next door came out and said somebody had told her that the bank had closed. I walked up to Myrtle Avenue and, sure enough, here's everybody walking to the Globe Bank. When we got there, here's Frieda's daughter, she's dead now, poor thing, out on the sidewalk crying. The bank was locked. They didn't put a sign in the window or anything. They just shut the door and went home.

"That ended any holidays we were gonna have that year. Forget holidays. We worried about food. Oh, the big shots that had money in the bank, they got their money out, all right. Frieda's daughter, the poor thing, told me that. The man that had a department store on the avenue came around and they gave him all his money. The slobs like us never saw a cent. Well, that's not exactly right. A couple of years later, I got a check for three dollars. That was my settlement. You mark my words, that's the way it's gonna be this time, too. You won't be able to heat your house, but you'll see limousines riding all over the place.

"They made a saloon out of the bank, you know. They called it the Red Parrot. My girlfriend's daughter had her wedding reception there. I was invited to it, but I couldn't go. I went to the church, but I couldn't go to the reception. I couldn't walk into that saloon with all the misery that place caused me."

She shook her head. "I don't know what these people are going to do today. I'm used to doing without. People today aren't. Well, I'll tell them one thing. They better go to church. Churches gave out food during the Depression."

She put out her cigarette, finished the weak coffee and washed out the cup and saucer, turned out the kitchen light, and went in to watch television for the night.

(December 1977)

Give a Beggar a Horse . . .

"You're cheaper off," the former Rosemary Dattolico's mother said. "You're cheaper off if you plan ahead." She dodged in and out of the crowd in a King Kullen supermarket, the third store of her day. She says that to survive at this time, people no longer can do their shopping in one store.

"See this?" she said. Her hand tapped a bag of Diamond Walnuts that were priced at ninety-nine cents.

Her youngest daughter, accompanying her, on this last day of shopping for Christmas dinner, said, "Ma, you've got a cabinet full of walnuts home."

"You bet I have. A month ago, I got them for seventy-nine cents. I wanted to have walnuts for after dinner Christmas so I went and bought all my walnuts at Pathmark for seventy-nine cents. Coffee in the same store was selling for five seventy-nine. I needed coffee, but that was too much. What I did was buy my walnuts for seventy-nine cents and then go to the Key Food that was selling walnuts for ninety-nine cents and coffee for four sixty-nine. So I bought my coffee in the place that was selling the walnuts for ninety-nine cents and I bought my walnuts in the place that was selling coffee for five seventy-nine. See? You just have to plan ahead and go to more than one store. You're cheaper off."

"Ma, who could run around five weeks before Christmas buying walnuts?" her daughter asked.

The mother glared at her. "And you'd come the last day and spend forty cents more for everything. Give a beggar a horse and she'll ride it to hell, that's what I always say."

She looked at the string beans. "Can you imagine? You have to pay seventy-nine cents for string beans. What are they? You need a bunch of them to make up something as big as your finger and they want seventy-nine cents for them. Then people are supposed to think they're not getting gypped. Boy, I'm telling you, somebody's getting rich off us."

Her youngest daughter, standing at the bin of string beans, said to her, "How much of these do you want, Ma?"

"Oh, I don't want none of them. I told you, I wouldn't pay seventy-nine cents for string beans that you need to make up a thing as big as your finger."

The daughter shrugged and they walked on. The former Rosemary Dattolico's mother waved in triumph at shelves of canned cranberry. "A month ago, I got four cans for a dollar. Now look at it. Three cans for a dollar. That's why you've got to think ahead. Things get so dear so fast that the help in these stores get tired from changing prices every hour. There. Look. Crispy saltines eighty-nine cents. You know what they were when I bought them a month ago? They were fifty-nine cents."

"Who could walk around making plans to buy saltines?" her youngest daughter said.

"Who could ride a horse to hell," the mother said.

The daughter started taking something from a shelf. "What's that you're getting?" the mother said.

"Asparagus," the daughter said.

"Well, you can just put it back, asparagus. You might as well be swallowing gold. Look at that, one fifty-nine a can. Not in my house.

"What does it matter what you call it, inflation or recession. If the food is too dear for you to buy, by me that's a Depression.

"You see, there'll be bunco parties soon. Ahahah! Do I remember them! The man next door was a plumber with four kids. He could work all the time, but nobody could pay him. The man actually had no food in the house. So what we did for Christmas, we ran a bunco party down my cellar.

"You don't know bunco. You play it with dice. Anna Heyer used to come with her lucky dice. They were black with white dots. One day I looked at them and I saw that all the edges were rounded. Can you imagine? She seemed like a simple woman on the block and she was a cheat at bunco. I used to drop the dice right in front of me on the table and put my hand over them so fast that nobody knew what I had shot. I made them take my word for it. But Anna Heyer cheated.

"What we did, we charged everybody a quarter to come down in my basement and play bunco. We sold little things. We crocheted pot holders and sold them for extra. Some people gave more than a quarter to play. I had a cousin who was a butcher who left a dollar. My sister helped, too. My sister worked for the phone company, made nice money in them days. When my sister played bunco she used to go like this when she rolled the dice."

The former Rosemary Dattolico's mother made a sweeping motion with her arm. "Then my sister would say, 'Baby needs nothing; mommy needs the shoes.'

"We gave them coffee and homemade cake at the bunco party. The coffee cost twenty-nine cents a pound for the Eight O'Clock brand and thirty-four cents for Red Circle, which is what we used mostly. The other brand, Bokar, cost thirty-nine cents and I wasn't using that for a bunco party. Anyway, we got forty dollars for the plumber for Christmas with the bunco party. Never mind, you'll see some of them yourself pretty soon."

She stopped and began scolding a young woman from the neighborhood who came along with boxes of eighty-nine-cent paper napkins atop her shopping cart. The former Rosemary Dattolico's mother tapped the paper napkins.

"You can just go right over there and put these back and get Hudson napkins for forty-nine cents," she said to the young woman. "Somebody on an income of twelve thousand dollars can't afford paper napkins that cost eighty-nine cents."

The young woman said, "You're broke, a little fancy you need."

"Nonsense," the former Rosemary Dattolico's mother said. She sent the young woman back to the shelves to change the paper napkins and her ultimate advice followed the young woman: "You're cheaper off."

(*December 1979*)

Don't Tell Me You're Working Late

When I came into the kitchen, I nearly shattered my leg on a chair that was tilted against the oven. I was told that if I moved the chair, there wouldn't be any dinner; the oven door was falling off, had been this way for days and, as there was nobody in the house to take care of such things, a chair would have to serve as a crutch for the wounded oven.

I promptly took over and called the oven place and was told that it would all take a little time, for I also needed a carpenter and electrician. Heart surgery can be scheduled on shorter notice. When I hung up, I reminded myself to walk around the chair; I would be repeating the maneuver many times.

In the next room, the youngest kid sat with his book report. This is the holiday week, and he thought that he shouldn't be doing schoolwork, but I wanted him to keep at it, and I tried to explain to him that it wasn't punishment, that there should be no negative feelings about advancement. I did not get through to him. He sat with his book report as if he were in a cell in Attica.

"Relax, this is going to be fun," I said. When he didn't answer, I shouted: "Did you hear me? I said this was going to be great!"

In the third paragraph of the book report he had a sentence that said: "He had went to Saratoga."

"Atrocious!" I said. "How can you do that? 'Had went.' It's 'had gone.' You're dealing with the past of 'go.' "

" 'Went' is past," the kid said.

"You're supposed to use 'had gone,' " I said.

"Why not 'had went'?" he asked.

"Because I said so!" I shouted.

We both were a little tense. Women always manage things without the use of force, but I can't get anything done that way and so I decided to go off by myself in the house and think about things.

My wife is indisposed and I'm taking care of the family administration for a while. And here, late of the afternoon during which I discovered the damaged oven, among other things, I sat and began to realize what it must be like for a woman to be doing this full time . . .

At this exact hour, the end of a day's work, the man of the house would be sauntering off the job and into a bar to start throwing money around and telling everybody how great he was.

"Chatting up the girls!" I said aloud.

How, I asked myself, would you like to be sitting here, or in any of a few hundred thousand other houses, with a broken stove, with all these kids, and with a washing machine that probably will bust down tonight; to be sitting here broke and all the while the man of the house is out throwing a drink down and smiling at some girl? And, upon arriving home three or four hours late, says nothing beyond the term "Working late."

This started me to thinking, perhaps for the first time in my small life, of the role of men and women in a marriage.

In my upbringing, the term "wife" meant exactly what it had meant for seven thousand years or so: a woman available to do anything.

The term "husband" was best expressed one day by my friend Johnny Crash, International Union of Operating Engineers, who, over big beers at the end of the day, said proudly, "I give my wife everything she needs or *asts* for."

This is probably the official proclamation of males who live in a world where the value system is the gross annual income of the person you're talking to. The man focuses singly on his job, reaching for as much glory as possible in the way of money and titles. If the job does not produce sufficient glory, then a few drinks after work allow the guy to start talking about himself in terms so flattering that even he finds himself unrecognizable.

The woman is simply somebody waiting at home who does pieces of work, who is handed money, much as a bartender is handed a tip, and who also allows the man to live without having to face too many relationships. The wife fends off relatives and children and friends and school guidance counselors. She handles the flood of tears, a broken stove, and the identities and desires of children under one roof.

For this, she receives a great deal of repression and "everything she needs and anything she *asts* for."

I'm beginning to think, as I step around a chair in the kitchen this week, that it is at this point, the passing of money from man to woman, where things could change, where an enormous impact could be made in the manner in which we all live. As I am allowed a glimpse of what it takes to manage the living of a family, I see that no male member of a family truly goes out by himself to make a living; he has behind him each day a wall, as strong as anything thrown up by a bricklayer, that prevents anything from home spilling onto him and making his task impossible.

Therefore, as I see things from the kitchen, it perhaps would be very good if wives at home received some direct compensation for their part in assisting the man at his job. Rather than sit and depend upon handouts — *ast* for something — they should get by right, by check in the mail, direct from the husband's place of business each week, something like one third of his salary. It would come in the woman's name and be hers to spend or hide. Of course, she would probably use it as she always has used anything handed to her; I don't think women would blow the house money as readily as a man does. I do think the idea of the check arriving in her name would ease the rage that must mount in women when, at the end of the day, no husband appears because he is out spending money and glorifying himself, most often with women.

Most certainly any marital relationship worth talking about must come down to something more than a person getting paid. But until humans perfect the art of living with each other, I think the wife should somehow get a good piece of the husband's check, and in her own name.

(December 1979)

I Never Could Drive

I am one of a half dozen or so in New York who is over the age of fourteen and does not drive a car. There is nothing particularly unusual about this in my case; it is just another part of a life of noisy desperation.

When I first went to work for a living, it was for the publisher Newhouse, who felt that the best reporters were those suffering from malnutrition. Nobody I knew was raising any down payments for cars on a Newhouse salary.

By the time I went somewhere else, and earned more money, I had living patterns that appeared to be in opposition to saving for a car. The main one being spending time in barrooms. I loved them, and left them only when I had to. As the barrooms cost me more money than I earned, I never was able to figure out how to buy a car. Oh, I wanted a car. If I had a car, I could get from one bar to another much faster than I could by subway or bus. And I sure liked going into a lot of different bars. If I was in one place and my tab caused the owner to glare, I swallowed up and headed for a place where credit was easier. Furthermore, I don't think I ever was in a bar I didn't love, and some days I wanted to be in all of them at the same time.

A friend once advised me that if I would stay out of bars for about four months in a row, I would have enough money saved to place on a car.

"I could die too," I said.

Time went by and I was married and I bought a car, but my wife, the former Rosemary Dattolico, took it over. One day I said to her, "I think I'll learn how to drive." She said, "It's way better for you to take the subway, read the paper and talk to people. I'm only thinking of your career."

Once, I thought about two cars in the family, but decided that wouldn't be right, with all the thirsty people in the world.

So I wound up depending almost entirely on the Union Turnpike stop of the IND line, on Queens Boulevard three blocks from my house. Yesterday, this was no good to me because of the transit strike. On a bright morning, then, I got out onto a traffic island on Queens Boulevard, waited for a red light, walked up to a car, and said to the man in it, "I'll ride to the city with you."

"Not with me you won't," he said.

At another red light, a car with two men in it pulled up. The driver looked at me, then turned to the guy in the seat with him, a man whose face was as pleasant as a wire fence. They muttered to each other. Then the driver looked out at me and said, "Want a lift? We need a third." Many people say the rule allowing cars with three or more people into midtown Manhattan is something that should remain after the strike.

I looked at the driver and the sour-faced man with him. "Did you two have a tie vote on me?" I asked. They didn't answer. "I'll ride with you if you give me ten dollars," I said. They pulled away.

Rather than wait anymore for a ride, I went down the hill to where a cluster of TWU pickets stood at the entrance to the subway trainyards. The pickets had just received paychecks and a couple of them showed me the stubs. The pickets worked in the yards as car inspectors, which, they said, meant they had to inspect the cars and make repairs on them. Sal Congemi's stub showed a gross of $344.80 for a forty-hour week and a take-home of $213.33. He said he was married and had two kids. Another, Carmine Cavallaro, showed a take-home of $240.47 for a forty-hour week. Out of a number of checks I found one that had twelve hours of overtime, bringing the gross to $455.14. As the guy was single, and was repaying a pension loan at $20.03 and had a deduction of $37.53 for savings bonds, his net was $221.19.

These figures are well above amounts earned by most subway riders, the factory women and shipping clerks and dishwashers who come from Hunts Point and Bushwick and Coney Island. To the subway rider, a pension is unheard of. Many of the transit workers are not even required to pay anything into their pension fund. A transit worker's four-week vacation sounds to a rider like some great notion out of a poem, a song of hope. The only four weeks a subway rider gets off is because of a layoff.

At the same time, the strikers yesterday said that on their take-home pay they simply cannot raise a family and pay bills. It is something that is heard everywhere in the country. People taking home $250 a week or less aren't making it. The most effective political commercial perhaps I've ever seen was on television Sunday night. A guy in a cap stood by his yellow pickup truck and announced what bills he couldn't pay and that his wife couldn't keep up with food prices. He said the family couldn't have a vacation this year. Then he got in the truck and growled, "This year I'm voting Republican."

The management in the transit strike is the Metropolitan Transportation Authority, which already has lost $250 million. It now says it can't afford to pay the workers any more than an offered 6 percent. But if it can't afford this, then somebody can argue that it can't afford the lost $250 million, either. In a time of budget problems people on the top naturally and easily try to even things up by standing on the backs of people working for a living. The governor gets a new helicopter and a car cleaner cannot get a raise that will give him half the rate of inflation. The mayor screams about productivity and his own productivity shows that in the last week he hasn't been able to do his job and settle the strike.

Along with their checks yesterday, the strikers received a letter from the Transportation Authority reminding them that they are in violation of the state civil service law, the Taylor Law, and that "an amount equal to twice the daily rate of pay will be deducted from your wages for each day or part thereof that you have been engaged in the strike." This is a problem of law and cannot be waived aside in the final hours of negotiations to end the strike. Under the law, as of yesterday morning the strikers owed at least ten days' pay and they were in a union that has no money to pay for them. The case is in the hands of Justice John A. Monteleone in Brooklyn. He is a man whose general philosophy now is "It's a terrible thing to make an error."

You can expect Monteleone to proceed with such caution that both sides, strikers and Transportation Authority, will be begging for a settlement. Justice Monteleone will be contemplating the matters on his desk and then allow that both sides will hear from him when he finally decides on a course for which there can be no criticism. Yesterday, the strikers waved their Taylor Law letters and said angrily that they would be out for a long time. Longer than anybody thinks, when you add Monteleone's position into this strike.

I left the group of pickets and walked back up the hill to Queens Boulevard. Alongside the empty subway entrance was the Allen and Loftus Bar. I went inside. The place was as dark as a movie house and had a great view of the bright street outside. One man at the bar had handicapped the daily double. Another commented on the surprisingly large house on Sunday night. The bartender, Jack Stevens, announced that everybody's friend Pete Reardon was ill.

Soon it was between the bar and trying to get to Manhattan somehow without a car. Therefore, I stayed where I belonged.

(*April 1980*)

She Said Good-bye with Charm

Jimmy Breslin's wife, the former Rosemary Dattolico, was buried yesterday. She died Tuesday morning after a long illness. Breslin wrote the following eulogy and read it at the funeral services at Our Lady of Mercy Catholic Church in Forest Hills, Queens. We wanted to share it with our readers.

About a year ago, when she was unwell to the point where even she became unsure, she offered during prayer to her God a suggestion that she thought was quite good.

Her youngest had experienced difficulty through the start of his schooling. Then suddenly, he had expressed great interest in attending one school.

His mother developed great faith in the situation.

And so, she proposed, give me this year while my son goes to this school. Let me try to help him as best I can. Then that should do it. He will be on his way.

And I will be perfectly happy to be on my way.

Providing the school works out.

The year went by and the youngest attended school and she lived despite the gloomy signs given by her body. For a period, she simply willed herself to improve. The mind over a blood count.

And her youngest suddenly grew. A plant nourished.

Whatever she had asked for, she appeared to be receiving.

And now, the other day, from the depths of a hospital bed, with her body in revolt, she looked up and said, "The report card was pretty good. But now I don't feel like keeping my part of the deal."

Which was her notion of fairness. For all of her life, she believed that true evenhandedness meant that those in need always were allowed more.

And now, at the end, she desired to follow her own counsel.

So as she left us, she did so with that most elusive of qualities, a little bit of charm.

We of her family who remain have a special burden. We have lived with nobility.

She was a person who regarded life as one long attempt to provide a happy moment or so for another person.

Always, she was outraged by those who rushed about, shouldering past others, their sides lathered with effort, horses in some cheap race, as they pawed for material success.

She knew that life belonged to those who seek out the weary, sit with the defeated, understand the clumsy.

And do this not as some duty. But do it with the cheerful realization that we are a part of it all.

She thought the word "duty" meant that each day there should be a word or a gesture that would cause someone else to smile over the life about them. Her contempt was reserved for those who would not attempt this. Who are you, she would rail, to go through a day, knowing that another day is to follow, and another after that, and knowing that it is all ceaseless, and still you refuse to join with us and help soften the path of those about you?

She was a woman utterly unspoiled. I thank God for the high privilege of having known her so well.

She ran my life and those of her children almost totally. She leaves us with a tradition of decency that we must attempt to carry on. Her strength was such that even if those of us here today stumble now and then, I think the Rosemary Dattolico line of decency will reveal itself time after time in whatever generations there are to come.

As was said of another aristocrat such as this one:

Earth, receive an honored guest.

(*June 1981*)

Take My Kids, Please

There was a television interview in which Koch the Mayor, a bachelor, was quoted as saying that he would like to have children. Somebody put his head out of the mayor's office and said, yes, that was right, the mayor had said that he wanted children.

"Children?" somebody asked.

"You bet. He hears they're terrific."

The word went about City Hall. Everybody began saying, "Yeah, children!"

Immediately, there came the sound of feet running out of the offices of City Council President Carol Bellamy, who also has never married. Here was a young woman assistant to Bellamy calling out to all in City Hall:

"Put down that Carol wants children too."

"Carol wants children?" somebody said.

"Sure Carol wants children, Carol says children are fantastic. Make sure you put it in the story that Carol Bellamy wants children. Don't just put down that Koch is the only one in City Hall who wants children. Remember Carol Bellamy wants children too."   When these stories reached my house at night, I read them with the eye of a criminal. Certainly, there was great political maneuvering on the part of Koch and Bellamy, for it is becoming clear that the long period of admiration by newspeople for those living isolated, insulated lives is about over. How, people are wondering, can anybody be so effective in high office in a place like New York when the person appears to be a product of an estranged, alienated culture? Apparently, Koch and Bellamy have decided, after reading a poll perhaps, that it would look great with the electorate if they had children. But in order for them to have children at this point, right now, today, in time for elections, somebody would have to give them the children.

I was in the kitchen of the house I now run and one corner of the room was blocked by garbage cans.

"Why aren't they outside?" I asked.

"Because there is no room in the big garbage cans," a son, P. Breslin, said.

"Why isn't there room?"

"Because I didn't put them out this morning. The truck came too early."

"What's too early?"

"The truck came before I woke up."

"Bellamy," I said.

"What?" P. Breslin asked.

"I said you go to Bellamy," I said.

I went to the stairs and called up, "How are you doing up there?" For the last hour, son C. Breslin had been in his room, supposedly doing a history report for school.

There was no answer. I called up again. Still no answer. I went up the stairs and found that the reason he didn't answer was that the music was on so loud in his room that he would have been unable to hear a dynamite explosion. C. Breslin was jiggling to the music, and on the desk in front of him was a sheet of paper as blank as his stare.

"Two for Bellamy," I said.

"What?" C. Bellamy shouted.

I screamed, "I said Bellamy now has two kids!"

I asked downstairs for the whereabouts of K. Breslin. She did her homework and went out, I was told. "She said, don't worry, she'd call."

"What time did she go out?"

"About eight."

At seven-thirty, on my way home, I had called daughter K. Breslin and she said she had two hours of schoolwork to do and was just getting to it. Daughter K. Breslin is the one who does so well in school that the teachers no longer send me home failure forms; the teachers now take out large sheets of blank paper and fill them with the accounts of her scholastic career.

As promised, she did call me that night. I had been sitting up waiting for her, and at 1:00 A.M. she called me from a phone booth on Queens Boulevard and said she had been trying for hours to get into the house, but nobody heard her ringing the bell. I had been sitting approximately four and one half feet inside the front door for the entire night. She arrived home on roller skates, and I immediately took a deep breath and tried to scream in order to alleviate chest pains. She held up her hand and said, "You're making a nervous wreck out of me." She skated through the living room and went upstairs to bed.

"Koch!" I shouted.

"What?" she called.

"You're going to Koch."

And now yesterday I sat in the house with three children of mine, each of whom I can well do without, and with a daughter from another family, L. Oliver, a daughter whose family wishes she would run away for good. Oh, yes, there are people who wish their children would disappear on them. Many people. The children are generally over the age of twelve. For of course anybody can take care of children up to the age of twelve. In those years before twelve, children are dazzling and humorous and can be cared for with a large amount of work, but at the same time the work is uncomplicated. At age twelve, however, all children reach into the air and from somewhere grasp a lance and from then on they hold the lance at the chest of the parent. If the parent tries to back away from the lance, the child simply extends the arm so the lance remains, still digging into the chest of the parent. There is no escaping the lance, and of course one day, the child over twelve simply pushes the lance and it pierces the parent and kills him.

So here I was with these four kids over the age of twelve, four kids who are unwanted for a good reason, and on the table in front of me was this great fresh news that Koch the Mayor and Carol Bellamy need sudden children to save their political careers.

"They have them," I announced.

"Have what?" one of the kids said.

"They have two children. You two go to Bellamy on Monday morning," I said to C. and P. Breslin. "She lives in Brooklyn." I turned to K. Breslin and L. Oliver. "You two go down to City Hall on Monday morning and sit on a bench and if anybody asks you who you are just say, 'We're the Koch children.' When he comes out to go home, you go with him. Good-bye and good luck."

I felt tremendous. I not only had removed a problem from my life, one that was about to kill me, but I had done the city a tremendous favor — I had helped the political careers of our great leaders who suddenly found themselves in need of children. In one day, I had done a service for the city in which I live and in which I once attempted to raise children, which I announce today is impossible for me to do, so I am giving them away to a couple of needy people.

(February 1982)

Sure, and They'll Kill You

The police department personnel files have a section titled "Social Condition" in which the officer's personal life is detailed in the fewest number of words possible: "married, two children." Or, "divorced says he is living with mother." There is a coldness to this that I like very much, and I always describe my personal situation in those same terms: "head of household and in charge of household." Behind this wooden label the turmoil of life can be hidden, which is fine with me.

The other morning, for example, the phone woke me up, and the voice of daughter K. Breslin's high school principal began speaking harshly.

"You better come up here and we'll have a talk," he said.

"I can't," I said.

"Well, if you can't make it today, then let's set a date right now," he said.

"I can't do it anytime," I said. "I went to high school for five years. I'm not going back for anybody else."

When I hung up, I had to arise, and didn't feel like it, and thought immediately of a man I knew, Jock Whitney, who had just died. Whitney once told me that he never had been awakened in the morning in his life. He simply slept until incentive arose from his unconscious and caused him to stir, or a bright morning sun remained on his eyes until they opened. But no human hand or a mechanical device ever was allowed to force him awake. This happens only to the very rich or the very poor. As I am stuck between these two categories, I found myself pushed out of bed to start a day of working in the regular world, and also trying to oversee things that happen under my roof. The two do not go together.

The next day, for example, there arrived in the mail a note from the high school that listed, in the form of an indictment, the things that my daughter K. Breslin was doing wrong in school. I immediately had a focal seizure in my stomach. I get these, instead of the generalized convulsion that such things as a note from school warrant. While I fussed with the note, I had on my desk high piles of paper that were attempts at a title for a marvelous novel I have just finished. The editor, Michael Korda of Simon and Schuster, had given me until late that afternoon to find a ringing title or he would take command and title the book himself. As I regard somebody's else's hand on my work as an attack on my person, I sat down with my attempted titles and scrolled away through the day. Each time I tried to make a decision, the focal seizure in my stomach caused my mind to wander to the note from high school. I found myself writing down as a book title "Inattentive in Class." I called editor Korda and received an extension.

At three o'clock, the phone rang. "I'm going to Lauren's house for dinner," daughter K. Breslin said.

"You get right home after it, because we have something to talk about," I said.

"Sure. We're eating early. I'll be home by seven."

At seven I was restless. At eight, I was angry. Seething at nine. I was sitting alone in the house and waiting for one of three kids. The other two are stories by themselves. When things like this happen, I always imagine a housewife who sits waiting for a husband to come home from work. "I've got to attend a meeting, so I'll be a little late tonight," the husband says. "Fine," the woman says. Maybe they are dumb, I say to myself. For in New York in these times, there is no such thing as a business meeting after working hours. At five o'clock, everybody flees because they are afraid of getting beaten over the head after dark.

Therefore, if a husband calls home with this kind of story, it means that he is out in a bar someplace trying his best to lure a considerably younger woman into a room someplace with him. And all these wives sit in their kitchens and say over the phone, "Fine, you go to your meeting, I'll have dinner waiting."

Fools. Not until there is a system under which the housewife receives one half of the man's salary, mailed to her at home, will marriages be on a truly even footing. For then men without enough money to buy drinks for these younger women will have to go home on time for dinner.

While I was contemplating this, daughter K. Breslin called. "I'm staying at Lauren's. Her mother says it's all right." Without another word, Lauren's mother got on the phone. She said it was fine. Then she hung up. I was left looking at walls.

Yesterday morning, daughter K. Breslin arrived home.

"Hi," she said cheerfully.

Her eyes caught the high school note in my hands. Immediately, she was in tears.

"I told you about that last week," she wailed.

"The note just came," I said.

"But I told you I've never worked harder in my life than in the last weeks. He had no right to send that note today."

She was crying so loudly that my words couldn't be heard. Finally, I waved my hand to indicate that everything was all right.

"Can I go to the movies with Lauren?" she said. Her voice was low and her eyes were dry as paper.

"I guess so," I said.

"Great. Give me five dollars."

With one motion she was gone. I looked around the house, picked up my coat, and went to the racetrack. There, in the cold wind blowing from Jamaica Bay, my friends Eddie Day and Bubba Flynn stood alone at the end of the grandstand.

"Do you need money?" Eddie Kay said.

"I need a victory," I said.

"There it is," Eddie Kay said. He pointed to his "must" horse, Born Great, prancing on the cold dirt before the first race. I rushed to the window and went for whatever I had in my pocket. The horse was seventeen to one. Standing with Eddie Kay and Bubba Flynn, I watched Born Great shoot out of the gate and take a fine lead, maybe six lengths, going into the backstretch.

"This is marvelous. I feel better," I said.

"If the horse don't stop," Eddie Kay said.

Born Great ran on, but now other horses appeared to be running faster.

"He just stopped," Eddie Kay said.

Out on the track, they were passing Born Great on both sides, much as both the E and F trains pass the GG local in the morning rush hour.

·

"At least it's only the first race," Eddie Kay said.

"It's the last for me," I said.

I walked out of the track and went out to Rockaway Boulevard and got a cab home. I sat down with the note from high school, the program from the racetrack, and the titles for the book. Somewhere out of the three pieces of paper, a thought might arise. If not, I'll simply run to where I belong — a bar.

(*February 1982*)

Get Mad at Somebody

Mind aflame, attempting to pursue my living, and here from the kitchen came angry footfalls and people screeching. I left my typing machine and walked to the noise.

On the kitchen floor were boxes from a supermarket, and standing over them, quarreling, were two of the children I once announced I would put up for adoption, and today I renew that vow: daughter K. Breslin and son C. Breslin. For some time, both have been in charge of purchasing food for the house.

The boxes from the supermarket seemed to be filled entirely with crackers and cake.

"She spent a hundred and fifty dollars and didn't buy anything to eat," son C. Breslin said.

"Yes, I did," daughter K. Breslin said. She went into one of the boxes and brought out a can of coffee. "This cost five dollars. How can you buy much food if one can costs five dollars?"

"The rest is all cake and crackers," C. Breslin said.

"The store was crowded, and everybody pushed me," she said. "So I just bought from one aisle."

"Why didn't you help?" I asked the brother.

"I was at the park."

I shrugged. Nothing you can do. So I said to them, "Put whatever it is you bought away and go in and do some homework."

"I don't have any homework today." Two voices, never stronger, said it as one.

And drove me out of the place. Hands in the air in surrender, I announced that the flame was gone, that there was no way I could continue to work in the house and that I was leaving immediately for a trip in hopes of clearing my head, which has been totally clogged by family.

With dispatch, I was on the phone and made arrangements with Cunard Line to book me on the *QE2*. I have sailed on this ship many times before and always found it refreshing. I deliver spellbinding lectures to audiences and then retire to the bar and toast myself while looking at the sparkling ocean.

This time, I was to reach the *QE2* by flying from Kennedy to London, taking the marvelous boat train to Southampton, dashing into the Horse and Groom at the foot of Oxford Street for a quick drink — Cheerio! — and then go across to the docks and board the *QE2* for a cruise to Palma, Barcelona, Cannes, Naples, Messina, Málaga, Lisbon, return to Southampton, thence plow out into the North Atlantic for the run to New York Harbor. Absolutely marvelous trip!

Yesterday, while packing for my journey, passport and tickets on the dresser, cab waiting to take me to the airport, there was a phone call for me which I took in great agitation, for I was quite busy assembling my wardrobe.

"Cunard here," a man said. "Awfully sorry to disturb you, sir. Unfortunately, very sorry to trouble you, but due to the incident in the Falkland Islands, by orders of Her Majesty's government the *QE2* has been requisitioned. Terribly sorry to bother you, but it seems you can't possibly sail on her at this time."

"What are they requisitioning her for?" I asked.

"Troops, dear boy. You see, we have this incident in the Falklands, and it does require certain troops."

My first thought was that this was Cunard getting back at me for the statement I made a few columns back that the British were the foulest people on the face of the earth. How could they be so small? I asked myself.

Just because I said a thing like that, now they won't let me on their ship. Tragic loss of humor.

But the news reports in a few minutes stated that, indeed, the *QE2* had been called up to carry troops to the Falklands. And I stood in Queens and thought about the back bar of the *QE2*, the one that goes late.

Now, rather than have me in top style at the bar, my stories utterly charming, the place would be shuttered and there would be British territorials clumping around the room. A place of song and story and drink suddenly turned into a waiting room for young men on their way to kill strangers.

(April 1981)

Unhinged

LOS ANGELES — Outside El Huachito, a small restaurant that sits in a crowded, dusty part of Los Angeles, the pickup trucks went by slowly, their backs filled with Mexican children whose black hair was lustrous in the morning sun. Instantly I hated the children because of what they were, children. In the restaurant, I had just put my hand in my pants pocket and discovered that among old papers were the report cards of my two youngest children. The report cards were deplorable, and as I scanned them, I banged my hand on the table.

The heavy woman in the kitchen called out to me in Spanish. When she saw that I didn't understand, she called to a young guy who was drinking soda at a table by the window.

"She says that she will take care of you, but you don't have to get so mad," he said to me. "What do you want?"

"Tell her I'm sorry and that I want coffee."

He told that to the woman, and she said something else. The young guy said to me, "She says that if you don't order food, it means you don't like her cooking."

"Tell her to give me something that will make me sick," I said.

The young guy looked at me.

"No, I mean it. Feed me a dish of fever."

He thought I was acting strangely, but I most certainly was not, it was a reasonable reaction, caused by the life I live. In Queens, in New York, I am at this time solely in charge of a household that includes more children than I care to have at this time. This is because I have learned that the number one characteristic of children is not an ability to eat, but rather an ability to betray.

It was some days ago, when the calendar indicated the month still was June, when I looked at the two youngest, daughter K. Breslin and son C. Breslin, and asked, "Hey, they've had me running around working. I didn't have a chance to see your report cards."

K. Breslin shrugged. "It comes in the mail."

I said, "I didn't ask you how it gets here. I asked you where it is."

"If you didn't get it yet, then it didn't come in the mail yet," she said. Her voice was harsh, the face wounded. I was, she indicated, just another cheap accuser.

"All right. I'll wait." I then addressed son C. Breslin. "So how about yours?"

"In the mail," he said.

"You're lying to me," I shouted.

C. Breslin went out of the room like a windstorm; his sister followed. The front door slammed behind them. Alone in the house, I decided that I had made another terrible error as a parent and I would rectify it with a highly original maneuver: I would leave the two of them extra money for the night.

Several days later, I had breakfast with the two of them and then stood up to leave for work. "Hey," I said, offhand, brightly, handling my role perfectly, "when is that mailman getting here?"

"We're going to the beach today," K. Breslin said.

"We need money," C. Breslin said.

Of course, I lost that skirmish. And somewhere here, June became July, and I found myself walking around the house one afternoon, and I didn't exactly have report cards on my mind, but I did take a look in daughter K. Breslin's room. A lively but completely disorganized teenage girl. I saw there was no place to step because the floor was entirely covered with dirty clothes, wet towels, tape decks, posters, tennis racquets, and a skateboard. To prevent a broken bone, I put my toe under the skateboard and slipped it out of the way. Now on the floor there appeared, at shoetip, a couple of crumpled envelopes. I stooped over and picked them up. One contained the final report card for K. Breslin, and the other, the final report card for C. Breslin.

Both report cards had been issued during the heart of June. Both were horrendous. I walked to my bedroom, found the door closed, pulled back my right foot and kicked. The door flew off the hinges, as if I were charging in on terrorists.

At dusk, when the two arrived home from the beach, I stood in the open door to my bedroom and waved the report cards and screamed, "How could you do this to me?"

Daughter K. Breslin thought for a small part of a moment. Then she wailed, "Look what you're doing to our house!"

I stuffed the report cards in my pocket and went out for a walk. And as these things happen, the kids duck, I get busy, and the passage of a few days allows a new coating on the nerves, and with it, new hope.

And now, on Friday, I had to go to Los Angeles, whether I wanted to or not. I stood in the bedroom with my bag packed and called through the still-open doorway to the kids, "Can you get along while I'm gone?"

"No worry," C. Breslin said.

"We'll be fine," K. Breslin said.

"I'm three thousand miles away. I don't want to get a phone call that will give me a seizure."

They laughed.

"All right, I'm going," I said. "What are you going to do tonight?"

"Not much," C. Breslin said.

"I'll decide what we do, and you don't have to worry about a thing," daughter K. Breslin said.

Good kids, really, I told myself on the way to the airport. And so I flew out to Los Angeles, and now yesterday morning here I sat in this restaurant in the middle of this depressing, dusty neighborhood, and as I pointed out, I put my hand in my pocket, and here were these report cards, and I sat here and looked at them again, and the look produced such anger again that I banged the table and annoyed the woman in the kitchen. Now with a cup of coffee in front of me, I took the report cards out and examined them calmly.

Son C. Breslin's mark in math was the tough one. The reason for the mark was inattention in class. I guess I shouldn't have looked at it at all, because this brought me to another boil.

Then I looked at daughter K. Breslin's card. For her biology mark, the number was fifty-five. I looked at it for a while. Biology, fifty-five. Now I looked out at the street, a street in a strange town a couple of thousand miles away from Queens. My heart and breath froze. I have a daughter of about seventeen who is home without a great parent in the house in the summertime and the best she could do in school was to get a fifty-five in biology.

"I have to be crazy," I said to the guy in the restaurant.

"Yes," he said. He laughed at this, but I did not. I grabbed the pay phone and called Queens. K. Breslin answered.

"What are you doing?" I accused.

"I'm beat," she said. "We were up late last night putting your door back on the hinges. Somebody has to have a little common sense in this house."

(July 1982)

Mix Me a Family

Some months ago, I married a woman named Mrs. Eldridge, who has three children; I have six. Therefore, we placed nine children from two marriages under one roof and asked them to get along famously.

Both first marriages had ended with somebody unfortunately passing away. So the nine children had no other parents outside the house to run to with complaints. Similarly, Mrs. Eldridge and Breslin had only themselves to be mad at.

Also, I am the only one in the marriage, and certainly one of the few in Western civilization, who has two mothers-in-law.

Because of this, I today turn from temporal subjects that usually fill this space — politics, urban mayhem, and essays on daily incompetents — and write of a matter that will be here as long as the earth persists: the attempted mixing under one roof of human beings not of the same parentage. Oh, yes, *attempted* is the proper word.

The entire matter started in the face of a culture gap: Mrs. Eldridge of the West Side, on a spring day, standing on the sidewalk outside Costello's on Forty-fourth Street, which is near my place of business, and, not seeing me because the inside of Costello's is as black as a basement, calling through the door: "How can you *stay* there?"

"It tastes good. C'mon in."

"You told me we were going for a nice walk."

"Well, I lied."

And at the outset of the marriage, when we put all the kids together for the first time, daughter K. Breslin whispered to me, "This is making me very unhappy."

"What's the matter?" I asked.

"Them." She was pointing at the three Eldridge children.

"You'll just have to try," I said.

"Oh, yes. Yes, there's one other thing," K. Breslin said.

"What's that?"

"Her." She pointed at Mrs. Eldridge.

I provide dialogue by K. Breslin because at that time I could not hear what the three Eldridge children were saying. They were in a huddle with their mother that resembled a basketball team at a timeout. Once in a while, a head would pop up and glare at K. Breslin. So it was obvious that the Eldridge family huddle was not about the *Essays* of Charles Lamb. Immediately, daughter L. Eldridge went up to her college at 116th Street and Broadway and enrolled in a special study program in France. The program lasts a year.

"The courses they're giving you in France aren't the ones you're supposed to be taking," her mother said.

"I'll take whatever they give. The best thing is that the course takes all year," L. Eldridge said, packing as she spoke.

We have this week religious holidays of great significance to at least a couple of faiths. As Eldridge is Jewish and Breslin is Catholic, this is an excellent time to observe what actually happens when different people are asked to live with each other.

Passover is today and Easter is on Sunday. These are the first holidays we have attempted. We dogged it last Christmas. We had workmen pull the kitchen out and told the nine kids that it was too bad, but there could be no joyous gatherings for Christmas or New Year's because the workmen wouldn't be finished with the new kitchen until at least February and therefore they had best try an aunt's house.

This week, with kitchen installed and holidays here, we took it on.

For Passover arrangements, my wife's mother, which makes the woman one of my two mothers-in-law, arrived at the house and looked at the crowd of Queens Irish Catholics surrounding her daughter. Mrs. Eldridge's mother dropped her head as if suffering from a severe neck injury and stared at the floor.

"What's the matter?" I asked her.

"I came here to see my daughter."

"Well, here she is."

She stared at the Irish about her daughter.

"That's not my daughter."

Meanwhile, in Queens, on Seventy-fourth Street, in Glendale, my other mother-in-law was busy in the kitchen.

"I'd like to invite you to a Passover seder with the Eldridges," I said.

"Is that what you want?" she said.

"Yes."

"Why don't they come here for Easter dinner?" she answered.

As for the children involved at this time of religious holidays, I give this report — Son D. Eldridge, student: "I love big, new families. But I'm pretty busy in school." Daughter E. Eldridge, student: "I won't be able to get home from school in time for the seder." School being two and a half hours outside of New York. What about Easter Sunday? "I don't think you'll see me on Easter." Daughter L. Eldridge, student abroad (by postcard): "Feel terrible that I can't be home for the holidays with all of you."

On the other side — Daughter K. Breslin, student: "A seder? I'm going to my friend's house." Which friend? "My friend." Son C. Breslin, student: "I like everybody a lot but I'm not feeling too good today." What about Sunday? "We'll see what happens then." Son P. Breslin, student: "Is it all right if I go with my friends tonight and spend the weekend?" Daughter R. Breslin, worker: "I'm going to New Jersey." Sons J. and K. Breslin, workers, have not been heard from except a note stating: "Don't count on us."

This, then, is a report on the lengths the parents and children go to to accommodate each other, to work toward achieving the great sense of "we" that stepfamilies are said to love. So far the only "we" that can be found under our roof is: "We don't want to go with them."

The Eldridge-Breslin Passover-Easter will consist of two persons.

(March 1983)